Social Geography

Critical Introductions to Geography

Critical Introductions to Geography is a series of textbooks for undergraduate courses covering the key geographical subdisciplines and providing broad and introductory treatment with a critical edge. They are designed for the North American and international market and take a lively and engaging approach with a distinct geographical voice that distinguishes them from more traditional and out-dated texts.

Prospective authors interested in the series should contact the series editor:
John Paul Jones III
Department of Geography and Regional Development
University of Arizona
jpjones@email.arizona.edu

Published

Cultural Geography
Don Mitchell

Political Ecology
Paul Robbins

Geographies of Globalization
Andrew Herod

Geographies of Media and Communication
Paul Adams

Social Geography
Vincent J. Del Casino Jr

Forthcoming

Research Methods in Geography
John Paul Jones III and Basil Gomez

Mapping
Jeremy Crampton

Environment and Society
Paul Robbins, John Hintz and Sarah Moore

Geographic Thought
Tim Cresswell

Cultural Landscape
Donald Mitchell and Carolyn Breitbach

Social Geography

A Critical Introduction

Vincent J. Del Casino Jr

WILEY-BLACKWELL

A John Wiley & Sons, Ltd., Publication

Blackwell Publishing was acquired by John Wiley & Sons in February 2007. Blackwell's
publishing program has been merged with Wiley's global Scientific, Technical, and Medical
business to form Wiley-Blackwell.

Registered Office
John Wiley & Sons Ltd, The Atrium, Southern Gate, Chichester, West Sussex, PO19 8SQ,
United Kingdom

Editorial Offices
350 Main Street, Malden, MA 02148-5020, USA
9600 Garsington Road, Oxford, OX4 2DQ, UK
The Atrium, Southern Gate, Chichester, West Sussex, PO19 8SQ, UK

For details of our global editorial offices, for customer services, and for information
about how to apply for permission to reuse the copyright material in this book please
see our website at www.wiley.com/wiley-blackwell.

The right of Vincent J Del Casino Jr to be identified as the author of this work has been
asserted in accordance with the Copyright, Designs and Patents Act 1988.

Library of Congress Cataloging-in-Publication Data

Del Casino, Vincent J.
   Social geography : a critical introduction / Vincent J. Del Casino Jr.
     p. cm. — (Critical introductions to geography)
   Includes bibliographical references and index.
   ISBN 978-1-4051-5499-4 (hardcover : alk. paper) — ISBN 978-1-4051-5500-7
(pbk. : alk. paper)   1. Human geography.   I. Title.
   GF41.D427 2009
   304.2—dc22

2008032201

A catalogue record for this book is available from the British Library.

Set in 10.5/13pt Minion by Graphicraft Limited, Hong Kong
Printed in Singapore by Utopia Press Pte Ltd

01   2009

Contents

Figures

Tables

Boxes

Abbreviations

AAG	Association of American Geographers
ADC	adult day center
AIDS	acquired immune deficiency syndrome
ALR	assisted living residence
ANT	actor-network theory
BDSM	bondage, discipline/domination, submission/sadism, masochism
BSE	bovine spongiform encephalopathy
CAM	complementary and alternative medicine
DTM	Demographic Transition Model
ED	erectile dysfunction
FTAA	Free Trade of the Americas
GHB	gamma-hydroxy butyrate
GIS	geographic information system
GPS	geographic positioning system
GSci	geographic information science
HIV	human immunodeficiency virus
HRC	Human Rights Commission
LCP	Live-in Caregiver Program
LGBs	lesbians, gay men, and bisexual individuals
LGBTQI	lesbian, gay, bisexual, transgendered, queer, or intersexed
NGLTF	National Gay and Lesbian Task Force
NGO	nongovernmental (development) organization
NIMBY	not in my backyard
PAR	participant action research
PPGIS	public participatory geographic information science
RCF	residential care facility
ROC	"Reclaiming Our Children" campaign
SARS	severe acute respiratory syndrome

STI	sexually transmitted infection
TRIPS	Trade-Related aspects of Intellectual Property Rights
UNICEF	United Nations Children's Fund
WWW	World Wide Web

Acknowledgements

The author and publishers gratefully acknowledge the following for permission to reproduce copyright material.

Figure 3.1 A model of social space or "spatiality." Adapted from Gregory, D. (2000) Spatiality, in R. J. Johnston, D. Gregory, G. Pratt and M. Watts (Eds.) *The Dictionary of Human Geography, Fourth Edition.* Oxford, UK and Cambridge, USA: Blackwell, pp. 780–782.

Figure 4.3 The triangle of human ecology. M. Meade and J. Erickson (2000) The Human Ecology of Disease, in *Medical Geography, Second Edition.* Guildford Press, p25 figure 2-2.

Figure 5.1 (a) A model of the Indo-Fijian transnational community. (b) A model of the Punjabi transnational community. Adapted from Voigt-Graf, C. (2004) Towards a geography of transnational spaces: Indian transnational communities in Australia. *Global Networks*, 4 (1): 25–49.

Figure 5.2 (a) Appalshop in the Appalachian Regional Commission Area. (b) Appalshop's major government and corporate funding sources, 1996–7. Del Casino, V., Grimes, A., Jones, J. P., Hanna, S. (2000) Methodological Frameworks for the Geography of Organizations. *Geoforum*, 31: p531–532 figures 1 and 2. © Elsevier 2005.

Table 9.1 Selected demographic and housing characteristics: three retirement communities and the Phoenix Metro Area overall, 2000. McHugh, K., and Larson-Keagy, E. (2005) These White Walls: the dialectic of retirement communities. *Journal of Aging Studies*, 19: p245 table 2. © Elsevier 2005.

Figure 9.5 Gay Retirement Guide, Retire with Pride website. (Downloaded May 1, 2008 from http://www.gayretirementguide.com/, reprinted with permission.)

Elsevier Limited for permission to reproduce extracts from Del Casino, V. (2007) Flaccid theory and the geographies of sexual health in the age of Viagra™. *Health & Place*, 13 (4): 904–911. © Elsevier 2007.

Sage Publications Inc. for permission to reproduce extracts from Del Casino, V. (2007) Disease, in P. Robbins (Ed.) *Encyclopedia of Environment and Society*. Thousand Oaks, Sage Publications, Inc., pp. 467–471.

Every effort has been made to trace copyright holders and to obtain their permission for the use of copyright material. The publisher apologizes for any errors or omissions and would be grateful if notified of any corrections that should be incorporated in future reprints or editions of this book.

Cover Image

Michael Cataldi uses installation art as a way to challenge the complacency of those in power to alleviate the problems of modern urban life. In this photo, he places potting soil and impatients to illustrate the growing concern over potholes in Baltimore, Maryland. More than this, though, this art project highlights the mundane ways in which we can challenge authority and power and temporary fills the gaps left behind by societies marked by growing inequality.

Introduction

Everywhere I look these days I am confronted with the realities of a world shaped by massive inequality and increasing intolerance. Since I began this writing project almost three years ago, HIV cases have risen dramatically in some of the poorest parts of the world. Human trafficking of women and children is being expanded across international borders. Global climate change is intensifying hurricanes and cyclones, directly impacting people who live on land that has been deforested. The current government in Burma refuses to help its citizens, who are starving in the aftermath of the most recent cyclone to sweep through that country. Asthma rates among children living in cities as different as Los Angeles and Nairobi continue to climb, differentially affecting people of color and ethnic minorities. Class differences are being exacerbated by a global economic system that is focused on the generation of wealth instead of the provision of needed resources. Wars are being fought (and planned) by so-called global superpowers, such as the US, based on a narrow and naive reading of ethnic, religious, and political systems and practices. While globalization theorists may think we are living in a world that is becoming more spatially interconnected, the data show just the opposite. The world is becoming more divided, increasingly segregated and differentiated across the lines of race, ethnicity, class, gender, sexuality, age, and ability. More people may be "plugged in" to a global telecommunications network than ever before but others remain completely outside this "revolution."

I am inspired, at the same time, by people who struggle against structural and social violences. Anti-globalization movements challenge the presumptions of a global economic system that is trying to dismantle local economic differences in favor of a singular and monolithic capitalist system. Activists fight to advance the rights of ethnic minorities, working class folk, people with disabilities, as well as gay, lesbian, and bisexual youth. Students in high schools are creating clubs that celebrate sexual difference and holding rallies calling for a cessation of violence against women. Indigenous leaders from poor, farming backgrounds, such as Evo Morales in Bolivia, are being elected national leaders and taking the world stage. New social networks are spreading across the globe, informing local activist movements to fight for the rights of the world's most disenfranchised. That 500 people living with HIV and AIDS in Thailand led a 2006 protest against a US–Thailand Free Trade Agreement is testament to the powerful coalitions that can be built. People in community organizations and nongovernmental agencies are working tirelessly to create alternative development paths for some of the world's poorest people, while groups fight for the rights of minorities to gain formal citizenship within countries in which they have lived their whole lives. The latest US presidential primary featured, for the first time, an African-American candidate and a female candidate, both of whom were serious contenders for the Democratic Party nomination. That the US electorate is even considering electing a president of mixed-raced background is a staggering achievement. Couple these accomplishments with the mundane and everyday actions of people who work tirelessly against inequality and for more open and tolerant communities, and there is a lot about which we can be hopeful.

Social geographers are interested in these issues because all of them are about the organization, regulation, control, and contestation of space. Put simply, social practices happen somewhere, and the spatial organization of the world impacts how those social practices unfold. As an example, imagine South Africa under the system of apartheid. Under that particular social system, racist ideologies were reinforced through strict spatial segregation. If you were black or colored in South Africa, signs told you where you were and were not to go. Even when no signs appeared, an underlying spatial logic became part of everyone's personal geography in South Africa. Black Africans didn't need to be told not to enter white suburbs without permission. Perhaps less obviously, but no less powerfully, is the spatial practice of a five star hotel in Bangkok, Thailand. In the lobby are two people. One is a western tourist wearing shorts, a t-shirt, and flip-flops. Another is a Thai person, also wearing shorts, a t-shirt, and flip-flops. The western tourist is asked if she would like a seat in the lobby, while the Thai person is asked to leave. It doesn't take a staunch political system to enforce and encode racism in this hotel. Not surprisingly, though, you would rarely find a Thai person who comes from a certain working class background in the lobby of such a hotel. The geography of belonging is part of their everyday worlds. In different ways, then, both spaces, the apartheid state of South Africa and the hotel of Bangkok, impose a distinct geography of inequality and difference.

On the flip side, a struggle for adequate resources must be accompanied by a struggle for equitable access to agricultural spaces, health care spaces, or educational spaces. The Americans with Disabilities Act is an act based in geography. It is about creating equitable access to all public spaces and the resources those spaces control. In a different way, gay pride parades and civil rights marches are struggles to control public space and make what is often geographically hidden – heterosexism and racism – visible. In making such an outward geographic gesture, the goal is both to make people aware of the social issues surrounding heterosexism and racism and to change how people use public (and private) space. No less powerful, but equally important, might be the flying of a gay pride flag in front of one's house, signaling that not all households are centered in a normative heterosexuality. For social geographers, then, studying how people use space to construct more tolerant and plural societies is centrally important to their work.

In this book, I want to argue that social geography is centrally placed to examine all these issues. I make this slightly bold assertion for several reasons. First, social geography has a long history of studying inequality and difference. Social geography's traditions include the study of environmental justice, racial segregation, gender and sexual diversity, and mental and physical disabilities, for example. Second, social geography is a field of study that has a strong relationship to sociology and social theory. This provides social geography with one of the most theoretically and methodologically diverse "toolkits" for investigating social inequalities and differences from a wide range of perspectives and approaches. Third, social geographers are interested in affecting change with their scholarship and activism. This includes their activism within the discipline of geography as well as in the communities – both "near" and "far" – in which their work and lives are situated. This is not to argue that social geography exists in a "black box" distinct from the other areas of geography. In fact, I will be at pains to argue that social geography is a richer field of inquiry today because of its relationships with (and occasional antagonisms toward) environmental geography, political and economic geography, and cultural geography. With this in mind, let me briefly trace out the "remainder" of this text.

This Book's Modest Goals

Although my assertions about social geography's value as a field of study are somewhat bold, my goals for this book are rather modest. This book's main aim is as an "introduction" to the very complex and diverse sets of perspectives, approaches, and topics that are of interest to social geographers. As an "introduction," I cannot and will not claim that this book is comprehensive. Nor will I insist that this book's organizational framework is the only way to conceptualize social geography. To do so would be patently absurd. There are dozens of ways that one could interpret and organize the field of social geography. The one I provide here, then, is based on my reading of the field as its stands today. In providing a framework for understanding social geography, my reading of the history of the discipline is also strategic, setting out an argument about how social geographers may benefit from understanding a certain set of "past" social geographies. Over the course of researching, writing, and editing this book, I have become even more convinced of the importance of social geography. I hope that over the course of this book, students will also become as engaged and enlivened by the diversity of social geographic research and inquiry as I have become. I have a tremendous amount of respect for the social geographers outlined in this book. That I couldn't do more to showcase their diversity is the downside of such a volume. That students might take what social geographers have taught us and apply it, expand it, and rework it is, at the same time, an exciting prospect.

In Part I of this book, I introduce students to the history of social geography. This history is, as I mentioned, a selective one. The three chapters, taken together, however, give students a sense of the range, depth, and breadth of social geographic research and inquiry. Chapter 1 introduces some of the basic concepts and ideas governing this book. It provides students with a brief overview of the relationship, as well, between social geography and social theory. Chapter 2 is dedicated to the history of the discipline. This history illustrates social geography's tension-filled but productive relationship with other geographic subdisciplines over the twentieth and nascent twenty-first centuries. In particular, it examines social geography in relation to environmental and ecological geographies, urban geographies, political-economic geographies, cultural geographies, as well as post-social and post-human geographies. That social geography has maintained its integrity in relation to these different areas of inquiry is a testament to its value. Chapter 3 concludes this section with an overview of social geography's variegated methodological approaches. This chapter is focused on methodology as a meso-level process and not on the nuts and bolts of methods and techniques. As such, chapter 3 introduces students to the types of questions, data, and approaches one might use in social geography. It does so by tracing quantitative, qualitative, and mixed methods, and participatory action research approaches. Overall, this section presents an argument that current social geographic research is theoretically, methodologically, and substantively diverse, while also being integrated by its interest in the study of inequality and difference.

Part II delves deeper into a substantive discussion of social geographic research, focusing on what I am calling "Social Geographies Across the Life Course." The chapters in this section follow on the arguments made in Part I, where I lay out a framework for a social geography of inequality and difference. This section expands on that framework, delving deeper into some of social geography's core concepts. Chapter 4 starts off this section, then, asking "when is social geography not about health?" In this chapter, I examine how inequalities and differences have been studied from the perspectives of medical and health geography. While not all social geographers would call what they do medical or health geography, the questions that social geographers ask are often related to questions of how people maintain a healthy life. Throughout this chapter, students are also introduced to social theorists whose research informs medical and health geography today. Chapter 5 examines two more of social geography's central conceptual objects – communities and organizations. Social geographers are interested in communities and organizations because it is through these diverse spaces that inequalities and differences are often "worked out." Relying on the work of scholars such as Benedict Anderson and Michel Foucault, this chapter challenges students to conceptualize communities and organizations as both material and social spaces. Put simply, this chapter examines "the community" as real and imagined, while organizations are discussed as both material objects (prisons) and ways of socially organizing the world (through the practice of surveillance). Chapter 6 concludes this section with a discussion of social activism, movements, and justice. Guiding social geographic inquiry is an interest in "doing" something to affect change. At the level of activism, social geographers challenge the practices of inequality within the field of geography, while through social movements social geographers study and participate in organizational efforts to open up spaces of difference.

Part III, titled "Social Geographies through the Life Course," examines the geographies of children and young people (chapter 7), the geographies of the "mid-life" (chapter 8), and the geographies of age and ageing (chapter 9). In recent years, social geographers have called into question the field's adultcentrism, which has marginalized studies of children and older people in favor of an underexamined adult subject. While these chapters are also thoroughly committed to tracing important intergenerational relationships between children and young people as well as young adults and older adults, they are focused on issues and concerns that are central to certain stages of the life course. Chapter 7 examines how social geographers have studied the spaces of childhood and youthood, focusing on issues such as play, schooling, sex and sexuality, and teenage violence. Chapter 8 treads on ground that has been less directly explored, offering a conceptual examination of what is being called "mid-life" geographies. In this chapter, I argue that social geographers need to examine the taken-for-granted mid-life adult subject who has, until recently, been undertheorized and underinvestigated in social geography. In chapter 9, I examine the geographies of age and ageing. Through a discussion of global demographics, this chapter introduces students to the changing dynamics of age. The chapter then moves into a discussion of geographical gerontology and the study of ageing as a process. Working across four "spaces" of ageing, this chapter concludes with a discussion of the dynamic social geographies of ageing and older people.

Part IV is the concluding section. This section is organized around two shorter chapters. Chapter 10 re-engages with a discussion that began in chapter 2 regarding post-social and post-human geographies. In this chapter, I ask how the "post-social" turn in human geography is providing new challenges to social geography. I argue that social geographers can learn a lot from the post-social turn by rethinking their own research questions, data, and analytic frameworks. Chapter 11 returns to where we began, asking how social geographers can (and do) engage in debates about and problems related to questions of inequality and difference. I conclude with an argument for a hopeful social geography, one in which social geographers remained engaged with the mundane and extraordinary struggles that have been the centerpiece of social geography.

Thanks and Appreciations

The content found in this book is no one else's fault but my own; although its completion is the result of the tremendous intellectual and personal support I have received over the years. That support began early in my undergraduate career at

Bucknell University, where I first learned from Paul Susman and Richard Peterec that geography was not a "thing" but a "process." Both guided my early endeavors in geography and supported me as I moved forward. That I am still interested in geography and the "teaching of" this variegated discipline is completely a result of their inspirations. From there, I took a turn as a rather naive but hopeful master's student at the University of Wisconsin, Madison, where I had the great fortune to work with Dan Doeppers and Gerry Kearns among others. Gerry remains an important influence, and continues to push me to think about the politics of my own work and research. During my time in Madison I met two of my dearest friends – Karen Till and Josh Hane – both of whom provided rigorous and thorough intellectual encouragement (and debate). While Josh's life was cut short, his powerful and indelible mark on my life remains. I have never thought about "a map" or "cartography" without also thinking about him. If Madison was the place where I started to ask the hard "whys" and "hows" of geography, the University of Kentucky was were I began to "pull it all (some of it?) together." Kentucky was a tremendously exciting place to "be" a geographer. It was where I was first introduced to social theory and the relationship between that disparate body of knowledge and geography. While you should never "blame" them for my interpretations of the field, some of what you find in parts of these pages I first learned in the research and writing collaborations I developed with faculty, such as John Paul Jones, Richard Ulack, and Tom Leinbach, and in the classrooms of Sue Roberts, Wolfgang Natter, and John Pickles. While the faculty at Kentucky played an important role in my development as a "social geographer," it was my peers who made the experience so dynamic. Stephen Hanna and I first developed our friendship, and our side life as co-authors, in the offices of Miller Hall. Stephen's incredible intellect has affected me tremendously, and his influence is felt throughout this volume. In addition, I had the great privilege to spend an inordinate number of hours "hanging" with Mary Gilmartin, Susan Mains, and Carolyn Gallaher. Their research and political commitments continue to be an inspiration for my own work, and their ongoing friendship a source of delight. I would also be remiss if I did not recognize that many of my ideas for this project were first encouraged during my time working with Kathie Gibso – at the Australian National University.

The most immediate inspiration for this book, though, has come out of my recent experience as a faculty member at California State University, Long Beach, where I have worked for the past eight years. I wrote this book because I wanted to teach a course on "social geography" and I needed the material. Along the way, I have had support from my university and colleagues. Parts of this book were written during my sabbatical in 2006 and with support from my university's Scholarly and Creative Activity Fund in 2007 and 2008. My colleague, Chrys Rodrigue – probably the most widely trained and intellectually "liberal" thinker I know – has been an outstanding mentor. I also received feedback on this text from a group of great colleagues and students in the department's Human Geography Reading Group. Paul Laris, Christy Jocoy, Deborah Thien, Unna Lassiter, and Kevin Flaherty all provided comment. Deborah and Unna, particularly, took extra time to read parts of this book and make extended suggestions. Many of my graduate students, including Keith Miller, Bridget Cooney, Maribel Enriquez, Julienne Gard, Wanjiru Njuguna, Ryan Good, Nazie Naraghi, Cyd Schantz, John Anisko, Simon Wright, and Sarah Goggin, have also provided inspiration along the way with their own great research. Friends and colleagues, including Amy Bentley-Smith, Houri Berberian, Patricia Cleary, Kathleen Divito, Tim Keirn, Claire Martin, Brett Mizelle, Sean Smith, Sarah Schrant, Kim Trimble, and Hugh Wilford, have provided additional encouragement along the way. In addition, I have had the distinct pleasure of working on joint research projects with Christy Jocoy as well as Dennis Fisher and Lee Kochems. Lee, in particular, has challenged, prodded, and pushed me to think very critically about my own subject. I have to thank Justin Vaughn and Ben Thatcher at Blackwell for their ongoing support and kind, but firm, nudges, to get this book completed. I also have to thank Ally Dunnett and Tom Bates, who worked on the production side of things at Blackwell. They were great at answering all my silly little questions. John Paul Jones, the editor of the Critical Introduction series, also spent a lot of time with this manuscript, pushing me to clarify key concepts and ideas. Sallie Marston provided feedback as well, and helped me "think through" the history of social geography in a co-authored piece we recently wrote together.

My parents and my sister, Joan, Vincent, and Christina, have also been absolutely wonderful over the years, and their support essential. Finally, this book owes a huge debt of gratitude and thanks to Catherine Brooks. She has been supportive in so many ways during this process. She has read and reflected on pages in this book, she has offered comfort and encouragement throughout, and worked extra hard to make sure that I remained sane while I tried to balance life between "home" and "work." She is an absolute inspiration as both a person and an intellectual. And, finally, I would like to thank Salvatore. The newest addition to our expanding social world, your smile is absolutely energetic, and your passion and excitement infectious. You make the most amazing invisible tea I have ever had at a "tea party." So, thanks.

Part I

Historicizing Social Geography: From Theory to Methodology

This part introduces students to the variety of theoretical and methodological approaches social geographers employ in their research and analysis. Social geographers share a common interest in examining inequalities and difference but do so in a number of unique ways. From a rather open position toward "best practices," it is suggested that different approaches answer different questions and that social geographers have to begin by asking what theory works best with what methodological approach. It is possible that social geographers can (and should) work through a number of different approaches while trying to answer questions of importance to the field, in particular, and society, more generally.

Chapter 1

Social Geography? What's That?

- The Demise of the Social and the Rise of an "Ownership Society"
- What Is Social Geography?
  - Social theory and social geography
  - A primer on "society" and "space"
  - Sociospatial difference and inequality examined
- On a "Critical" Social Geography
- Where Do We Go from Here?

The Demise of the Social and Rise of an "Ownership Society"

In 2003, former US President George W. Bush declared the creation of an "ownership society." His bold social agenda, to improve the lives of US citizens by empowering them to take control of their own selves, is, in fact, a framework for a post-society world, where governments and the collective whole are no longer responsible for individuals. Thus, while individual rights and freedoms are vigorously defended in an ownership society, social programs and protections, such as affirmative action and anti-discrimination laws, are dismantled. In Bush's post-society world, every individual has the same opportunities and chances to buy a home, choose a job, and raise a family. As such, society and social relations of class, gender, race, ethnicity, and sexuality are largely irrelevant to modern-day discussions of political organization or economic development. Yet, as we know, social categories, such as African-American, Gay, Sunni Muslim, Migrant Worker,

American Citizen, continue to be powerful markers of difference, and in some cases inequality, in the world today. This is true even as globalization has intensified networked relations and rapidly increased flows of knowledge, communication, people, and ideas in the post-Second World War period.

Despite Bush's declarations that society should no longer be the default level of support for the individual, the social remains an incredibly important organizing framework across the world. Social identities and groupings – organized through nation-states, neighborhoods, or social networks – are continually used to distinguish both physical and social differences in numerous ways. One need only consider the emergence of Al Qaeda as a loosely configured social network based in an Islamist ideology or the Christian Conservative movement as a political force in the United States (and beyond). Both are social organizations/networks determined to maintain the boundaries of differences between an "us" and a "them." More generally, as Hurricane Katrina, which hit the Gulf Coast of the United States in 2005, clearly shows, social differences mean that certain groups and peoples are disadvantaged and disenfranchised by political and economic systems that choose to ignore the needs of some people while paying attention to others. Thus, while so-called natural disasters are sometimes "great equalizers" because they can kill and maim indiscriminately, they often expose social differences and inequalities. The deaths of thousands of poorer coastal dwellers in Sri Lanka and Indonesia during the Indian Ocean tsunami of 2004 attests to how certain social groups are much more likely to be exposed to danger because of their level of impoverishment.

At the same time, social organizations, groups, and identities can come together to support a broader collective set of needs or desires. Queer social movements reorganize difference around a positive center instead of a negative margin. By claiming the social identity "queer," peoples of various ethnic, racial, national, or gendered groups create social networks and connections that affirm the rights of individuals to be publicly and privately gay, lesbian, bisexual, transgendered, transsexual, or intersexed without discrimination. In being actively queer, it is clear that difference is not inherently negative. In fact, difference is positively asserted through the conscious and active development of multicultural or pluralistic societies and institutions, where differences are cultivated within a framework of acceptance, tolerance, and mutual support. This applies not only to what are considered the "traditional" areas of social difference based in race, class, ethnicity, gender, and sexuality, but also to other sites of difference. As an example, homeless and migrant labor advocates assert the rights of these particular social groups, who are socially, politically, and economically marginalized, by reidentifying them as productive, contributing members of society. New social networks, organized around anti-globalization movements, also provide challenges to the intensification of capitalist development in places across the globe. While loosely connected, these social networks of activists share a common interest in minimizing the destructive impacts of unfettered capitalism, constructing a common identity that works across other social boundaries, such as race, class, ethnicity, nationality, gender, age, or sexuality.

While studying the social involves analyzing groups and broader categories, it is also possible to focus on the everyday practices of individuals and their negotiations of the broader social milieu. Everyday practices operate in the context of social rules and orders, which are not always overtly displayed. In fact, social order is often maintained because individuals consciously and unconsciously reinforce those orders through their own practices. Take the very mundane act of using a public restroom. In many societies, the public restroom is clearly marked with a gendered identity, either male or female. Using the public restroom "properly" reaffirms the difference between men and women as it is inscribed on the door of this public space. Interestingly, despite the social difference between men and women being thought of as fixed and permanent – as it is written on the bathroom door after all – gender as a social category is quite unstable. Remaining with our bathroom example for a moment we can see how, in certain places, gender categories are organized much differently. In Thailand, some college campuses have established bathrooms for *kathoey*, transgendered men. At the University of California at Berkeley and Vassar College in the US some bathrooms are unisex and men and women use them simultaneously. These new social and spatial frameworks are always situated within a broader context, as individuals and groups struggle to live in a world defined by their complicated interrelationship to "others." In this case, people negotiate how bathroom spaces are being defined for and by the loosely defined categories "men" and "women."

Tracing social differences and inequalities across the globe, it is clear that networks, relations, groups, and identities are organized not just socially but geographically as well. It is possible to examine where certain social groups are concentrated and how those concentrations are related to other social groups and concentrations. National censuses often provide geographers with a wealth of data that can be mapped and analyzed for spatial relationships, investigating the location of African-American populations in the United States, the distributions of birthrates in Italy, or the dynamic change in HIV cases in Zimbabwe over time. These patterns can be compared to other data patterns to see if poverty and race/ethnicity or poverty and health are related spatially: asking are they proximate, overlapping, or identical? Of course, there are always potential problems in defining who belongs to one social group or another. In fact, this is a problem that social scientists struggle with everyday. Yet we know that these groupings are at work in the world around us; they become part of how we see ourselves not just as members of societies but also as members of certain places and communities.

However we choose to define and in some cases demarcate social groupings, we can investigate how certain spaces and places are distinguished by their relationship to various social identities and categories. Take, for example, Kurdistan, a non-existent nation-state that remains an important geographic framework for the assertion of Kurdish ethnic self-determination in Southwest Asia (see Figure 1.1). Despite the fact that the Kurds are spread across five different states – Turkey, Syria, Iraq, Iran, and Armenia – there remains a strong ethnic interest linking that identity to an independent national space. At a more microlevel, there are ethnic enclaves

Figure 1.1   A map of "Kurdistan." (Cartography by James Woods, CSU, Long Beach, Department of Geography.)

in urban centers, such as Algerian neighborhoods in Paris, which are complicated by the politics of inclusion and exclusion that mark such spaces. We can see how social relations constitute the lived spaces of everyday interaction, and how spaces are material markers of certain social experiences.

It is clear, then, that there are a lot of concepts relevant to social geographic analysis, not the least of which is what is meant by the terms social, geography, and social geography. As you can already tell from this limited introduction, the "social" is a complicated term, often linked to a number of other terms, such as identity, category, relation, system, network, or group. When the term "social" is used with the term "geography" it becomes even more complex because now we must consider what we mean by how the social is also always geographic. We also have to tease out the spatial dynamics of everyday social life in order to investigate the complicated relationships between society and space. Fortunately, this is not a new endeavor for geographers. Geographers before us have traced out the diverse ways to study the social and society. It is to this history of ideas that we must turn to ground what social geographers are doing today in a longer trajectory of thoughts, approaches, and practices. In so doing, we can begin to enjoy social geography not as a singular way of knowing and seeing the world, but as it really is, a varied and contested set of theoretical and methodological concerns.

What Is Social Geography?

As part of my doctoral program in the 1990s, I spent eighteen months living and researching nongovernmental health care programs for people living with HIV and AIDS in Chiang Mai, Thailand. During that time, I was asked over and over again: What do you do? What are you studying? At first, I offered a complicated, and to be honest a rather convoluted, description of myself as a geographer: "I study how spaces are organized for the purposes of health and health care" or " I am interested in how people experience different places differently." As is the case in many other places, people were perplexed by my interest in geography and HIV/AIDS. What could a geographer possibly be studying about AIDS? "Are you mapping AIDS?" someone might ask. Over time, as my Thai language skills improved, I nuanced my response to these questions; I began to identify not as a geographer (*nakphumisat*) but as a social geographer (*nakphumisat thang sangkhom*). This qualification seemed to work, as people began to identify me as someone who was interested in social issues related to the practices of social institutions, such as the health care and educational sectors, governmental and political organizations, and nongovernmental and community-based networks and associations. At the time, I didn't think much of this switch. To be honest, like most of my colleagues in graduate school, I wasn't a big fan of subdsicplinary labels. But, upon reflection, I see this qualification, as someone who is a *social geographer* and not just a geographer, as an important one. It is important because it signals that my interests lie in questions related to the social, to the dynamic geographies of difference and inequality that are central to the everyday lives of so many people, not the least of whom were people at the center of my research, those living with HIV and AIDS in northern Thailand.

Even though I codified my identity as a social geographer, and, as a result, created a rather simple definition of my work, I believe that social geography is much more complex than its singular status initially belies. It is better thought of as a constellation of theoretical and methodological approaches that converge and diverge in an attempt to understand and explain the spatial organization of what we could think of broadly as difference and inequality. Interestingly, tracing the histories of these various social geographic theories and approaches is complicated by the fact that, at least in the context of the United States from where I am writing, social geography as a subdisciplinary identity has ebbed and flowed over the past 100 years of academic geography.[1] At the same time, many social geographic questions are being investigated under the guise of political, economic, urban, and, more commonly, cultural geography. Many of these geographies are, for me at least, informed by various social theories: they trace out the ways in which social life and interaction is constructed and produced through political institutions, economic organizations, urban spatial arrangements, or cultural practices. It is to this intersection between social theory and social geography that I now turn. Although theory is something that is often constructed as "scary" or "abstract," I want to suggest that social theories inform all of our social geographies. No one should be afraid to be theoretical. Instead, we need to understand, no matter what question interests us, how that question is informed by our theories about the social world.

Social theory and social geography

In the simplest sense, theory is a set of assumptions used to explain a subject of study. Theories can never perfectly represent the world "as it is." If they could, cartographers would be able to create a one-to-one representation of the world, where everything that exists in every place could be located on their map. But they don't. Instead, cartographers, like all social scientists, make choices about what should be included on the map. These choices are informed by the question they are trying to answer or address (MacEachren 2004) and by the social context in which they are making that map (Pickles 2004). Like cartographers, social geographers, from those who claim to work in the scientific method to those who classify themselves as social constructionists, understand today – to differing degrees — that theories are representations, sometimes striving toward although never completely explaining the "real world." More generally, people think theoretically all the time; theory is, in fact, part of our own everyday lives. You have certainly heard someone quip, "That was a Freudian slip." Well, who was this Freud person anyway, and why did his theorizations about the human conscious and subconscious slip anyway? If you start to really think about it, while we don't always discuss our theoretical assumptions overtly in every context, theories permeate thinking not only about social geography but also cultural geography (Mitchell 2000), economic geography (Wood and Roberts 2008), and, even, physical geography (Inkpen 2004).

Social theory, more specifically, is the set of assumptions utilized to explain social life, be that the distribution of social groups across space, the social construction of nature and culture, or the social regulation of political and economic development and institutions. In recent years, geographers have become much more interested in being explicit about these social theoretical assumptions. They are critically reflecting on the past work of geographers, which might not have explicitly articulated their theoretical positions. This critical historical work suggests that social geography is informed by a number of theoretical approaches, often identified by an overarching (political) theoretical perspective, e.g. anarchism (Kropotkin 1971), environmental determinism (Semple 1910), possibilism (Vidal del la Blache 1903), positivism (Schaefer 1953), marxism (Peet 1977), feminism (Rose 1993), queer theory (Browne et al. 2007), postmodernism (Soja 1989), or poststructuralism (Doel 1999). Each of these theoretical perspectives presents a unique definition of the relationships between society and space, terms informed by each theory's own set of assumptions.

These assumptions are based in a social theorist's ontology (their understanding of how the world is structured to produce knowledge) and epistemology (their understanding of how we know the world). Ontologically speaking, social theorists employ different understandings of how the world *is*, conceptually presupposing the context in which societies develop and individuals interact. As an example, some social theorists – certain Marxists, for example – believe that the world is organized through deep social structures based in capitalism, through which a set of historically constituted social categories – capitalist and worker – regulate all social interaction. These thinkers believe that societies based in capitalism structure individual social experiences relationally through the struggle between the working class and the elite. For them, there is an ontological order in the world structured by capitalism even if they can't see it clearly. This order mediates everything people do. Epistemologically, social theorists ask how it might be possible to understand that same social world. Again, social theorists who believe that deep structures organize the world into categories of being, such as capitalist or laborer, might also suggest that they study capitalism through the study of subjective experiences of capitalist development. Put simply, it is possible to study the effects of capitalism through the subjective experiences of production and reproduction. In all cases, social theorists build upon an accepted vocabulary of understanding used to describe societal forms of existence (their ontology) as well as "how we can get to know these different possibilities of existence" (their epistemology) (Kuhkle 2006: 146). It is these social theoretical vocabularies and their ontological and epistemological assumptions with which we will be interested throughout the first part of this book (see Box 1.1). Importantly, we will also ask how these various vocabularies and assumptions inform social geographic methodologies – the process by which theorists translate their ontologies and epistemologies, defining what the research data will be, what approaches or procedures will be followed, and what core principles and objects/subjects will be examined.

Box 1.1   Social Theory and Social Geography

Environmental determinism. A philosophy positing that social development is determined by the environmental conditions in which societies develop. This philosophical position generally fell out of favor in geography in the early twentieth century.

Possibilism. This theory, which is attached to the French school of cultural geography in the early twentieth century, suggests that while the physical environment offers certain constraints on the social world, humans can modify the environment to meet their needs.

Anarchism. This is both a philosophy and a political position. It suggests that society is owned collectively, while arguing that societies should eliminate (or minimize) government influence to maximize individual freedoms through voluntarism. This philosophical approach held limited appeal in geography at the turn of the twentieth century. It was resurrected in the 1970s as part of the social relevance movement in the discipline, and still holds sway with certain thinkers in social geography today.

Positivism. A philosophical position arguing that research must be based on empirical observations, which can be tested, repeated, and developed into scientific laws. Positivist geographers create models of and laws pertaining to the social and spatial organization of societies through the use of the scientific method. Positivism informed a significant amount of social geography for the better part of the 1960s and 1970s, although the development of critical rationalism modified this scientific method in the 1970s.

Critical rationalism. Karl Popper proposed in the 1960s that theory does not reflect the real world. It is not possible to determine a truth; it is only possible to assess whether or not a hypothesis is false. In the process of building theory, critical rationalists develop a number of hypotheses to analyze whether or not an initial premise is false. Many quantitative social geographers rely on a critical rationalist approach today, testing hypotheses to determine their "truthfulness."

Structuralism. A theoretical framework that developed in the study of linguistics and cultural anthropology, which suggests that individual linguistic practices (signifiers) represent underlying sociocultural and political-economic processes (signified) in which they are produced. Broadly speaking, structuralist thinking began to be used by Marxists, feminists, and other radical geographers in the 1970s and 1980s.

Marxism. Marxists argue that capitalism is productive of an uneven geography that privileges exploitation of the working classes' limited access to resources in and across space. Led by a number of key "radical geographers" in the 1970s, Marxist geography began with the basic assumption that capitalism structures all social and spatial relations. Marxist geography is still represented in the work of social (and cultural) geographers today, and remains an important political position for many in the field, who seek to challenge systems of inequality based in class (race, gender, and sexual) politics.

Feminism. Feminism is both a theoretical position – informing a critique of patriarchy – and a political position – focusing on the politics of equity and equality for women. Feminism entered geography in the 1970s and was first seen as a corrective to the discipline's masculinist narratives. While first wave feminists sought to increase the visibility of women in the discipline, second and third wave feminists now theorize the relationship between gender, difference, and inequality from a variety of perspectives.

Postcolonialism. This set of theoretical approaches developed in the 1970s and entered geography in the 1980s and 1990s. Based in a specific critique of colonialism and neocolonialism, postcolonial theory is diverse and encompasses approaches that refocus intellectual narratives away from the "center" (i.e. former colonial powers) and toward the "margins" (i.e. former colonial spaces). It is also informed by subaltern studies and, confusingly, the term also refers to a period: the postcolonial.

Queer theory. Queer theory is both a theoretical position – informing critiques of heternormativity – and a political position – opening up space for various sexualities and sexual differences. Queer theorists work against the presumption that all space is heterosexual. Queer theory also suggests that spaces of difference must be central to social geography. Like feminist geographies, queer geographies argue that questions related to social justice, particularly, although not exclusively, around decentering normative notions of sexuality, be of direct concern to the discipline.

Postmodernism. This term refers to a variegated set of philosophical approaches. In geography, postmodern philosophies developed in the 1980s as a challenge to structuralism as well as the other philosophies positing that deep structures, such as capitalism or patriarchy, determine social and spatial relations. As a philosophy, postmodernism has informed a number of theorizations of urban space and the relationship between social and spatial identities. Postmodern philosophy underpins social geography's expanded interest in understanding and examining difference(s).

Poststructuralism. A theoretical framework that developed out of a critique of structuralism, suggesting that linguistic practices, discourses, and texts have no essential characteristic but are constructed temporarily through the deployment of power. In geography, poststructuralist theory informs the study of representations and representational politics as well as the politics of identity and subjectivity. Poststructuralism is better conceptualized as a broad set of theories informed by a number of different philosophies, such as deconstruction and psychoanalysis, rather than a singular theoretical approach or methodology.

Quick Exercise

Identify an article of interest in social geography. Using the definitions set out above try to determine what social theoretical approach the author of that article is using in her or his analysis.

In its own ways, each social theory provides a language defining what the social means, articulates unique questions about social life, and conceives of social data in particular ways. As we delve further into the history of social geographic ideas and practices we will tease out the differing ways in which social geographers frame some of their key terms, including society, the social, and geography, as well as terms associated with social geographic inquiry, including social space, group, identity, justice, network, relation, and production and reproduction, to name a few. Moreover, we will investigate the social contexts in which this work is being conducted: we will treat social geographers and their work as part of societies – e.g. US society – and social networks and organizations – e.g. the Association of American Geographers (AAG) – as we examine how they construct their social theories in relation to those contexts.

By suggesting that social theories are always situated, it is important to also understand that social theories are not ideas floating around "out there" beyond us. They are constructed, realized, and utilized in various places to explain both particular experiences and general processes. What I mean to suggest is that social theory is always engaged in what Derek Gregory (1994: 79, his emphasis) calls "an *intervention in* social life." It is an "intervention" because social theory does not take place "in some isolated laboratory, [is] not 'applied' from outside, but *worked with*" to make "social life intelligible" (ibid., his emphasis). Gregory argues that researchers have to consciously consider how their theorizations of social life are part of the processes of reorganizing (or complicating) the world in which we live. This is a concern that is echoed by numerous other scholars, including those working in the areas of feminist geography (Moss and Falconer Al-Hindi 2007), cultural geography (Mitchell 2000), and critical cartography and GIS (Pickles 1995), to name just a few. Like Freud's "slip," then, social theories about geographic process, form, and practice overtly and covertly inform urban planning projects or social development programs. Even when researchers take objectivity seriously, believing themselves to be good scientists who are distanced and impartial, they might employ that objectivity in ways that validate their claims to change how the social world is spatially organized – creating residential and commercial zoning patterns that seem to "make sense" to them. As Gregory's understanding of social theory suggests, social geographers cannot pretend that they somehow exist completely outside the world about which they are researching or writing (Katz 1994). Moreover, it suggests that there is nothing wrong with intervening and critically addressing questions of how social differences are spatially organized, how and why spatial inequalities emerge, or what social geographers can do to address how differences and inequalities might be rearticulated to create new spatial formations that appreciate difference or mediate inequality.

This does not mean that social geographers have always worked with this particular reading of what is often called "critical social theory" (Agger 2006). In fact, geographers have been complicit in exacerbating differences through their use of theories that have suggested in the past that certain societies, races, and ethnic groups were inferior to others (Huntington 1915). Social geographers have also deployed their trade in various colonial and imperial projects (see Godlewska and Smith 1994); they have also been criticized for being blind to gender and sexualized differences (Rose 1993; Bell and Valentine 1995). From a situated position today, though, it is possible to employ critical social theories to explain how and why some geographers have taken up these particular perspectives. Throughout the remainder of this text, then, we will consider the relationships between social theories, broadly conceived, and social geographies, in all their complexity. This text will do so, as well, by sign-posting where social geography "touches down" with broader social theoretical concerns, introducing along the way social theorists who are not typically identified as social geographers but whose work can help to explain the complex relationships between the social and the spatial, society and space (Hubbard et al. 2004).

A primer on "society" and "space"

Before we move any further, it is necessary to delve a bit deeper into some basic concepts and terms in social geography. First of all, social geography is focused on an analysis of societies. Yet society is, itself, a highly contested term. In its simplest sense, society refers to the collective sense of connectivity between various individuals, the social relationships they develop. One can, for example, think of societies as spatially diffuse, constructed through various social networks across space (e.g. a cyberspace society, such as a society of gamers or MySpace bloggers, or a diasporic society, such as the Jews or the Palestinians). Society also has a politically material (or regional) definition, constituted by the bounding of various spaces into discrete political units (e.g. towns, cities, counties, provinces, countries, or nations). In this political case, one could think of the society of the United States of America or Papua New Guinea, with all the potential nationalist undertones that such a definition might bring to a discussion in social geography. Importantly, society is not simply "out there"; it is a term and concept that social scientists, activists, and politicians use to describe, identify, and sometimes validate the identities of those they seek to study, the processes that they hope to explain, and the broader connections and relationships between one set of societal networks or regions and another.

Confusing matters is the fact that the "social" is a term that applies to both the mundane sets of everyday relations in which people engage (e.g. our "social" circle) *and* the sets of social groups, identities, or communities to which people might "belong" (queer, feminist, black nationalist, etc). This means, of course, that social geographers might define the "social" in a number of different ways. First, they might think of the "social" as the relationships between people and the communities to which they belong. We can think about our own communities, both the communities to which we consciously subscribe, such as our friends, and the networks that we are part of because of our particular location, such as our schools or neighborhoods. Second, the social can be conceptualized as a set of categories or identities. These are often constituted through descriptive adjectives based in definition of age, gender, race, ethnicity, class, or sexuality. Social geographers must therefore be aware of the complicated ways in which social scientists have thought about and applied these adjectives.

Of course, the breadth of possible social categories explodes when we examine how social categories are used in everyday practice (e.g. African-American, conservative Christian, or gay Latino), further complicating any definition of "society." As John Urry (2000: 2) argues, "the material transformations that are remaking the 'social', especially those diverse mobilities that, through multiple senses, imaginative travel, movements of images and information, virtuality and physical movement, are materially constructing the 'social as society' into the 'social as mobility'" in ways that belie any straightforward definition of the terms "society" or the "social." Social geographers have also concerned themselves with a "mobile social" in their studies of nomadism (Dorn 1997; May 2000) and hybridity (MacLeod 1998; Whatmore 2002), focusing attention on the fluid and contested nature of social categories and spaces. This is a challenge to the historical focus on a fixed and discrete notion of space, and it also highlights the importance of studying social networks and interactions.

If the terms "society" and the "social" are not confusing enough, geographers expand the meanings of these terms by examining the relationship between society and space, the social and the spatial. This means, of course, that we need to have a broad understanding of what geographers mean by the terms space and the spatial. Naturally, of course, nothing is ever as easy or straightforward as we would hope; the definitions of these terms vary depending on the theoretical and methodological assumptions you use as a geographer. First, spatial scientists utilize an absolute or discrete view of space. In this view, space is seen as a "backdrop" to social relations, a plane across which one can plot various locations, points, and nodes. Social geographers also place boundaries around space, examining differences and similarities across and between discrete spatial units. And, they investigate the development of spatial networks across space and analyze how certain social attributes "decay" over distance from a particular point in space. Furthermore, they can expand their spatial analysis temporally, by examining how objects in and across space change over time, or investigate how the relationships between objects in space-time change in relation to each other. So, a spatial scientist might map the spatial organization of various ethnic groups in a city, examining that representation in relation to another map of income distributions. Using the census tract as a basis for such a map, they might be able to identify areas with high concentrations of poverty that are correlated to certain distributions of one or more ethnic groups. Or they might trace the diffusion of a culture group by tracking certain characteristics as they are placed upon what Carl Sauer (1925) called the cultural landscape, investigating the artifacts of human practice through an analysis of various physical material objects, such as houses, street signs, or other mundane objects.

Second, humanistic geographers believe that space is not simply a backdrop to social relations, but that spaces are repositories of human meaning. Put simply, people construct social spaces, or places, through their interactions with the cultural landscape, which is both material and symbolic. Through human action, people create unique place meanings and each place is invested with its own *sense* or *feeling*. This means that social spaces or places develop over time to both include and exclude individuals, creating feelings of being "in place" and "out of place." Humanistically inspired geographers are particularly interested in how various representations of place and immaterial social processes, tied to religion, language, or ethnicity, are used by individuals to construct their own lifeworlds. And, very often, humanistic geographers use the term "space" to refer to "a realm without meaning," although more and more humanistic geographers use the term "social space" synonymously with the term "place," where both are juxtaposed to an "abstract" or "empty" space (Cresswell 2004: 10). Furthermore, humanistic geographers contrast their vision of place as "lived experience" with landscape, which "focus[es] on the material topography of a portion of land (that which can be seen) with the notion of vision (the way it is seen)" (ibid.).

Third, radical geographers argue that spaces are both produced by *and* productive of various social relations of, for example, economic production and reproduction. This is what Ed Soja (1980) has defined as the "socio-spatial dialectic," where social relations are said to construct certain spaces and those spaces act upon social relations or processes. Unlike the subjectively inspired humanistic perspective of social space, whereby individuals construct their own meanings of the world and their places, a radical view suggests that the spatial organization of society mediates, and in certain ways controls, experiences of places. For example, the processes of capitalism regulate the spatial organization of the city. As a result, poverty and crime are contained in specific underprivileged spaces, which effectively maintain economic- and racist-based inequalities. The spaces of poverty are necessary because capitalism is reliant on what Marx called an "industrial reserve army" of labor, a ready-made unskilled pool or workers that can be pulled out of poor areas temporarily for work when the market is doing well. Spaces are structured to sustain social differences and inequalities, producing what Neil Smith (1984) calls "uneven development" at the local and global scales. In similar ways, feminist Marxist scholars have suggested that the spatial organization of society not only favors free market capitalism and certain privileges for elites but does so in ways that disenfranchise women and the spaces and practices of reproduction (Mitchell et al. 2004). Put simply, space is not a backdrop or a site of meaning, it is an actor helping to construct and regulate social relations between individuals, groups, and societies.

Fourth, poststructuralist geographers argue that space is a social construction constituted through the use of language. Space is made "real" through the use of certain discourses – or ways of defining and marking it. Of particular interest to poststructuralist geographers has been the "representational turn" in geography, whereby key geographic concepts – region, periphery, and network – are thought of as texts, which can be read like other representations, such as the map. Put this way, landscapes are more than the material relics that we, as humans, leave on them; they are texts that are organized through relations of power to produce certain effects and affects. There is nothing "essential" to the landscape, though, as these spaces are organized through the dominant social narratives situated in a particular point in time and space. As Susan Mains (2006: 112) suggests, the use of various spatial discourses about "certain people, social practices, or places" helps to create a "normal" or "naturalized" image of what is supposed to happen in any given space. Importantly, poststructuralist geographers do not believe that only those in dominant, or what are called hegemonic, positions are capable of constructing spatial discourses. Resistant spaces – in the form of territorial markers like graffiti, for example – contest dominant narratives of what is "appropriate" or "inappropriate" spatially. Poststructuralist space is thus a performed space of both power and resistance. As such, social identities are tied to how people perform where and who they are as individuals, community members, and social beings.

What all this complexity means, really, is that social geographers have developed a large vocabulary of terms and concepts related to their views of space. Each view of space is tied to a number of key concepts within the discipline more generally. These concepts underwrite different methodological approaches and frameworks, an issue with which we will deal more extensively in Chapter 3. In the meantime, though, we want to begin to reflect on this complexity and relish in it. While it can be confusing and daunting, it also illustrates that social geographers have created a wide array of analytic tools for asking questions about the spatial organization, distribution, and relationship of and between its twin concerns of social difference and inequality.

Sociospatial difference and inequality examined

Before we go any further, it is important to briefly outline what have historically been the two main conceptual centerpieces of social geographic inquiry and analysis: difference and inequality. While social geographers have treated these concepts quite differently over time, the basic notion that the social world is spatially organized through the use and understanding of social difference has been fairly consistent. In fact, social geographers have long based their analyses in the study of the spatial differences that emerge across and through social categories of ability, age, class, ethnicity, gender, race, and, in recent years, sexuality, focusing, for example, on the spatial distribution of certain ethnic groups as they cluster in and across the city. Many social geographers have also been concerned with how the spatial organization of the social world impacts on experiences of these various categories of difference. Put simply, social geographers not only want to study the distribution and diffusion of social differences across space, they also want to study how humans understand their "place in the world" through their experiences of spaces that are, themselves, invested with social meanings attached to various categories of difference. Thus, they are interested in examining the spatial organization of social differences and the development of ethnic neighborhoods and how those same neighborhoods are experienced, understood, and interpreted by those who live in and travel through them.

At the same time, social geographers are concerned not only for how social differences are sociospatially organized and experienced, but how these organizational and experiential dynamics impact on individual and group access to key resources, be those economic, political, or social. Social geographers are therefore deeply concerned with the embedded inequalities found in everyday spaces; they want to not only understand who lives where but why they live where they do and what that might mean for their life on a day-to-day basis. This concern for the study of social inequality is most notable in social geography's longtime study of the relationship between the spatial organization of race, ethnicity, and poverty (e.g. Morrill 1973). Moreover, social geographers have taken their concerns regarding the inequality of resource allocation to the study of gender, analyzing how the spatial organization of resources might disenfranchise women more than men (Jones and Kodras 1990; Kodras et al. 1994). In sum, social geography is committed to an analysis of how the spatial organization of society differentially enfranchises certain social groups and peoples while disenfranchising others. Social geography, then, is most concerned with the inequities that may be constituted through the embodied and material experiences of, for example, being "abled" or "disabled" (Gleeson 1999), "young" or "old" (Aitken 2001; Andrews and Phillips 2005). And social geographers continually recognize that the very basis of these social categories of difference are based in historical and spatial context: the meaning of disability changes in time and space and, therefore, the spatial organization of spaces for people who may be physically disabled changes as well (Parr and Butler 1999).

The twin concern for the geography of difference and inequality informs social geography's larger empirical questions, which tend to focus on issues such as homelessness, poverty, race and racism, production and reproduction, sexism and heterosexism, ableism, mental and physical health, crime, children's spaces, and community and social activism, to name just a few. Social geographers are motivated by these issues because they are concerned with how spaces are organized to reflect the differences that exist across social categories as well as how some spaces reinforce certain differences (both positively and negatively) and accessibility (in terms of both inequality and equality). This is why social geography has a "global imagination" and remains concerned with *both* how differences and inequalities are experienced by individuals and communities *and* how those differences and inequalities are organized in and across broader global (world) regions. Social geographic research thus overlaps with the work of development and postcolonial geographers interested in understanding how the world is organized across a global north (e.g. "developed" countries) and global south (e.g. "developing" countries) divide (see Box 1.2). Further breaking down questions of scale, though, social geographers are committed to investigating the experiences of those people from the so-called global south who live, work, and try to survive in the global north, illustrating the world's growing social interconnectivity (Merrill 2006).

Over the course of social geography's development, social geographers have grown more concerned with how people "experience" social difference and inequality. In so doing, social geographers are motivated to challenge and complicate social

Box 1.2   Defining the "Global North" and the "Global South"

There is no easy way to discuss "difference" at a global scale, and the terms used to explain global differences are informed by the historical and geographical situations in which they are being used. The terms "global north" and "global south" are an attempt to correct the use of other economically based terms, such as First World and Third World and developed world and developing world, as well as core and periphery. Global north and global south are terms that provide a more open definition of global difference, one based in social relations and cultural differences *and* political and economic disparity. In mapping the global north and global south, it is possible to discern a broad trend line that divides the world, roughly, between a wealthier north and a poorer south. This is approximate to the famous Brandt Line, which was proposed by German Chancellor William Brandt, to distinguish global difference. There are immediate exceptions to this line and to a global north/global south distinction, including the fact that Australia, New Zealand, and sometimes South Africa are considered part of the global north.

This language is by no means perfect, and other geographers have suggested an alternative language, including the use of the terms "minority" and "majority" worlds. Samantha Punch (2000: 60) argues: the "Minority World refers to the 'First World' and Majority World refers to the 'Third World'. This is because the Majority World has the greatest proportion of the world's population and the largest land mass compared to the smaller size of the Minority World . . . present terms used to differentiate the economically richer and poorer regions of the world are either incorrect (East–West, North–South) or have negative connotations for the poorer countries." It is also essential to remember that any global definition will generalize away the complexity found within the global north and global south. It is important to be cognizant of the very complicated politics of difference and inequality found within these two regional constructs. For purposes of consistency with the broader literature, including a growing scholarship on the "global south," this text will continue to use these terms. As you read, though, you should also make your own decisions about terminology and how best to describe difference at a global scale.

Quick Exercise

Go to the library and do a journal-based literature search on the terms "global north" and "geography" and "global south" and "geography." Then, narrow the search to "social geography" from "geography." What topics of study are typically associated with these terms?

models that ignore differences. There is, after all, not just a single geography of gender, race, ethnicity, or sexuality, which are further complicated by the intersections between these categories as well as others, such as age, ability, and nationality. The study of differences and inequalities is thus motivated by social geography's general concern with issues related to equity and justice. And, while social geographers sometimes disagree about how to go about enacting change or constructing equality and access, they are all interested in understanding how differences and inequalities are produced and constructed as well as experienced and challenged.

On a "Critical" Social Geography

As this is a book in a series titled *Critical Introductions*, I thought it important to reflect on the term critical social geography. I do so because scholars often use the term "critical" differently. For some, to be critical simply means to be analytical, while for others, critical geography is a political practice, tied to an interest in realigning the relations of power that construct inequalities. For some others still, to be critical means to relish in difference, celebrating the diversity of possibilities and social identities they might embody and spaces they might inhabit. For me, criticality is all these things at once. A critical social geographer is not interested in the status quo because it is understood that the world has developed in ways that are inequitable and unjust. To be critical is to also understand that the world is marked by social and spatial practices that constitute certain social identities and spaces as different in both negative and positive ways. We live in a world, unfortunately, marked by ableism, ethnocentrism, racism, sexism, ageism, and classism, and these practices are intimately tied to our spatial world in ways that mean we are not always allowed to celebrate our differences positively.

As for a "critical" view of space, there is value in being open and pluralistic. First and foremost, critical social geographers must understand that their views of space inform their geographic questions (Del Casino et al. 2000; Del Casino and Jones 2007). Those questions cannot and will not answer (or resolve) every geographic concern regarding inequality and difference. So, it is both possible and necessary to utilize different conceptualizations of space while trying to answer important social geographic questions. Being critical means being engaged in a project of understanding inequality and difference, however, in the hope of producing knowledge that will, in some small way, create positive change. To do this, many radical and even some poststructuralist geographers are rethinking the relationship between their own research and the tools of spatial science, particularly mapping technologies related to geographic information systems (GIS) or remote sensing (Elwood and Leitner 2003; Ghose and Elwood 2003). Other geographers are working across conceptual frameworks to develop research that utilizes humanistic and radical (Kearns and Joseph 1997) or spatial scientific and radical views of space (Lobao et al. 1999). It is therefore possible to utilize a number of different concepts of space and society in one study, and ask questions from a variety of different viewpoints that might let social geographers triangulate how and why inequalities remain or how differences are performed in and through space.

Where Do We Go from Here?

This brief discussion has just scratched the surface of social geography as a field of knowledge and way of knowing and understanding the world. It is now necessary to flush out the longer historical trajectory of social geography as a set of academic practices. To do this, it is important to step back and take a historical look at how social geography has developed over time, while considering the different ways in which social geographers have practiced their "science" in the recent past. Taking this historical perspective, this text will try to untangle the different ways that social geographers have conceptualized the relationship between society and space, the social and the spatial. It will also tease out the different concepts social geographers have used to examine these relationships. This brief march through disciplinary history is not simply an exercise in gazing at our own navels; it has analytic purpose. We want to understand how and why social geography developed the way it did and what this means for the questions and concerns social geographers have today. In the next chapter, then, we briefly trace the history of social geography's plurality.

To complete the first part of this text, Chapter 3 outlines the methodological approaches of social geographers. In this chapter, methodology is theorized as a mesolevel theoretical process through which social geographers translate their epistemological and ontological assumptions into their understanding of what their data might be and how they might go about asking questions of those data. This chapter also examines what methods and techniques might best be applied to a particular methodology. Each theoretical set of assumptions presupposes a particular view of space. Each view of space, in turn, also presupposes what the data will be and how one might go about collecting and analyzing them. As we move through this discussion of epistemology, ontology, and methodology, we will develop a sophisticated and complex reading of what social geography is and how we might develop our own skills as social geographers.

Note

1   There are other contexts, particularly the United Kingdom, Australia, Canada, France, Germany, and New Zealand, to name just a few, where social geographic traditions have flourished (see extended discussion in Kitchin 2007). Social geography has also been debated in these contexts (see, in the UK context, Philo 1991; Gregson 1993, 2003; Peach 1999; Valentine 2001).

Chapter 2

Social Geography in Three Acts and an Epilogue

- On the Histories of Social Geographic Thought
- Act I: Social or Environmental/Ecological Geographies?
  - Scene 1: Anarchy
  - Scene 2: Urban ecologies
  - Scene 3: Against the environmental grain
- Act II: Social or (Political) Economic Geographies?
  - Scene 1: Toward a socially relevant spatial science of class, race, and ability
  - Scene 2: On the political economy of "the social"
  - Scene 3: Humanizing the social and the dynamic study of space and place
  - Scene 4: Emerging alterities through feminism and sexuality studies in geography
- Act III: Social or Cultural Geographies?
  - Scene 1: The "cultural turn" and the "social category"
  - Scene 2: Complicating space, identity, body, and subjectivity
  - Scene 3: Rematerializing social geography?
- Epilogue: Post-Human Social Geographies?

On the Histories of Social Geographic Thought

There are an infinite number of ways to write the history of any subdiscipline. Believe me, I know, I have recently tried. Traditionally, one might trace the developments of social geography in relation to the various theoretical approaches taken in the discipline, from environmental determinism through regionalism and quantitative theory to Marxism, feminism, and poststructuralism. To be honest, I also began this project that way, hoping to sketch the variegated theoretical frameworks in geography and how they have conceptualized the social and the spatial, society and space. I became unsatisfied, however, with the narrative that was developing; it parodied what we already knew about the development of the discipline. And, to be honest, I have been more interested in thinking across theoretical and conceptual categories instead of simply through them. Importantly, as well, when working through the various approaches there is a tendency to privilege what comes at the end instead of seeing that many of these approaches remain at work today. What I also discovered as I tried to trace the history of social geography, at least as it has appeared in twentieth-century Anglophone geography, is that analyses of "the social" in geography have almost always worked in and through other subdisciplinary identities even as a nascent social geography developed in the post-Second World War period. Put simply, social relations as they have been examined in geography are always already informed by environmental, economic, political, cultural, and feminist narratives, to name just a few.

So why trace the history of social geography at all? First, in understanding how geographers have conceptualized what is meant by "the social" and "society" we can begin to understand the larger relationship between the social and the spatial as well as the relationship between society and nature, society and economy, or society and culture. Second, in comparing social geography in relation to a number of other subdisciplinary frameworks, we can investigate the alternative narratives (sometimes called subaltern or counterhegemonic) that distinguish the import-ance of a social geographic analysis versus other ways of seeing the world. Third, despite the fact that social geography has "ebbed" and "flowed" as a subdisciplinary identity, social geographic theory and inquiry remains central to the broader dis-cipline of geography. Fourth, geography is intimately engaged with sociology and sociological (or social) theory, which means that the relationships between various sociologies and geographies continue to hold import in our discipline's inter-disciplinary dialogues. Finally, despite the fact that social geography has found itself somewhat "submerged" under other disciplinary narratives, there is an advantage to taking as our starting point social geography's conceptual focus on questions of difference and inequality, questions that are not always of central concern to other ways of framing geographic questions.

In building this narrative across a number of "acts," I want to suggest that past ways of thinking remain important to how we understand social geography today. As we will see, certain themes continue to appear again and again as geographers struggle with the construction of their social geographies. For the purpose of brevity, the story begins in the late nineteenth and early twentieth centuries. At this time, geographers, many of whom were trained in physical geography, borrowed extensively from theoretical developments in the natural sciences, including Darwin's theories of evolution, to explain the spatial organization of society. Social geography emerged out of this moment with a variety of alternative ways of conceptualizing the spatial organization of society, from anarchism to urban ecology to non-environmental based models. In the post-Second World War period, geography as a discipline struggled with its own identity as a social science. The influence of positivism and quantitative methodologies across the social sciences was brought to bear on geography in this period, which looked to economic theories of *Homo economicus* (economic man) to increase its so-called rigor. Social geography, borrowing from economic theories, privileged the economic in its study of society: social relations are economic relations. Although working from a different theoretical lens, Marxist geographies developing at this time also privileged the economy in the study of social relations of production. Questions raised regarding social justice and equality were based, largely, in assumptions that capitalism structures social and spatial relations. At this time, however, geographers began to blur the boundaries between the social and the spatial in ways that complicated theories of a "social space." Moreover, humanist and feminist geographers, along with queer and critical race scholars in the field, began working against and through (political) economic approaches, offering alternative theorizations of social space as well as social production and reproduction. Out of these struggles, social questions related to human experiences of place and the gendering of space rethought how social geographers conceptualized the sociality of space and spatial relations and the spatiality of the social and social relations.

The post-Second World War period through the 1980s was thus a robust time for the theorizations of sociospatial relations in geography, despite the contested nature of the terms society and space. In the late 1980s, the "cultural turn" in geography further challenged the privileging of social analysis in geography, as representations and representational politics took centerstage in the discipline. The 1990s through the nascent twenty-first century has been a period of intense theoretical debate about the "state of social geography" and its place in the discipline. New ways of imagining sociospatial relations are now informed by various strains of poststructuralism as well as psychoanalysis, cultural studies, queer theory, and critical race theory. Geographers have also struggled in the wake of the cultural turn to "rematerialize" geographic analyses by once again privileging social relations of inequality. The theoretical ferment continues, with new calls from both sociology and geography to engage "post-society" and "post-human" studies. Sociologists have questioned the efficacy of taking "the society" as their starting point. Instead, the focus is now on networked relations and the complication of society as a presumed unified whole. Geographers have complicated the relationships between society and nature or human and animal by suggesting that narratives of human control over nature are too simple to explain our current (and past) global conditions. In some ways we come full circle, once again entertaining the question of the relationship between "social space" and "natural space" or "society" and "environment."

This chapter is not a complete history of social geography, but it does trace a set of "moments" when "the social" and social relations have found themselves centered in the discipline. What this chapter suggests is that social geography can be imagined in a number of different ways, and that these imaginings are tied to the historical and geographical contexts in which ideas are fermented. What we will also see as we trace these social geographic theorizations is that there are any number of ways to think about the social in geography and even more ways to consider how society and space inform each other. In this chapter, we will stay at the level of theory, examining the various epistemological and ontological assumptions that have been privileged in social geography at different points in time. In Chapter 3, we will trace the methodological approaches that parallel the various theoretical trajectories that social geography has taken. We begin our story by examining the relationship between social geography and environmental and ecological models for investigating social relations.

Act I: Social or Environmental/Ecological Geographies?

To set the scene for this first act, we have to imagine ourselves in the late nineteenth and early twentieth centuries, as many scholars were struggling with the theoretical relationships between society and physical environment. These struggles were situated within a broader intellectual framework contextualized by the emergence of Darwinian evolutionary thinking. Put simply, many scholars thought to apply Darwin's and other evolutionary theories (Livingstone 1992) about the biological world, including his notions of "natural selection," "survival of the fittest," and "mutation," to their explanations of the social world. Geographers, many of whom were working in a physical geography tradition during this time, were attracted, to varying degrees, to social models informed by theories emanating from the environmental and natural sciences. Many of these theories appear most explicitly in the work of the environmental determinist school of geography, whose proponents included Ellen Churchill Semple (1911) and Ellsworth Huntington (1915) in the United States. Put rather crudely, as environmental determinists these scholars believed that the physical environment (climate, landforms, vegetation patterns) determined development in the social world – including social characteristics, such as race and ethnicity.

These theories, in some of the worst instances, led geographers to propose deep-seated racist theorists of social development, suggesting tha certain climates bred societies (and peoples) that were less capable than others. Huntington argued that "the native races within the tropics are dull in thought and slow in action" (Huntington 1915: 56; cited in Cloke et al. 1991: 5). In another instance, Huntington theorized that the US South's economic development was retarded by the fact that so much of its working population was, in fact, of African origin – as the tropics bred sloth, laziness, and lower levels of intelligence. Not all geographers went to these extremes. Some actually sought to rethink, challenge, and/or abandon environmentally determinist theories for other theories to explain the development, distribution, and spatial organization of the social world. It is to these "somewhat" alternative theories of "the social" in geography that we now turn. This act's three scenes trace the four moments of difference in which social geographers sought out alternative explanations for why (and how) the social world was spatially differentiated. In some cases, these nascent social geographers suggested how to "intervene" into the spatial organizations of societies to address inequalities, particularly class-, race-, and gender-based economic differences. In tracing these early social geographies, we will begin to consider what these scholars have to say to us in the "now" as we struggle to construct our own social geographies.

Scene 1: Anarchy

We begin our journey in France where a geographer named Elisée Reclus might have been the first to employ the term "social geography" over 120 years ago (Eyles 1986). Looking at his work today, we might not recognize it as social geography per se. Reclus was, after all, particularly interested in the relationships between humans and the natural world, an area of research often characterized as nature–society studies, not social geography. But at the time, Reclus, like others around him, had to contend with the profound impact that Darwin's evolutionary theory brought to the world and to the discipline of geography. Unlike other geographers at the time, Reclus was not simply an academic, he was also an activist. His political philosophy was informed by anarchism, a social theory that suggests a "state of being without rule or government. Although some people might dream of building a society that has no governmental structure whatsoever, as a practical matter most anarchists would settle for a highly decentralized society in which there are no repressive controls" (Dunbar 1979: 157). In general, however, Reclus was known as a political pluralist and quite "tolerant," such that "he could embrace nearly everyone on the far left side of the political spectrum" (ibid.).

His own views of the society–space relationship are interesting and deserve attention, particularly because Reclus believed that "knowledge of peoples and places is necessary for improving understanding" (Dunbar 1978: 91). He saw geography, and the study of society–environment relations, as a lens through which he could engage his anarchist political philosophy. "Geography and anarchism are closely related, because the more one understands the world and its inhabitants, the more his prejudices and antagonisms decline, until at last he becomes a true world citizen" (ibid.). Because he was an anarchist, Reclus's discussion of "the social" was directly concerned with "social ills and their solutions . . . [as well as with] the importance of the study of geography in making an inventory of the world's resources and suggesting a plan for their equitable spread" (Dunbar 1981: 161). In particular, "Reclus stressed the mystical bond between man and nature" (Dunbar 1978: 44), suggesting that "Man [*sic*] is nature becoming self-conscious." Reclus thus argued that humans are not separate from but part of the natural world, arguing that "The action of man gives the greatest diversity of aspect to the earth's surface. On one hand it destroys, on the other it improves; according to the social state and the progress of each society, it contributes something to degrade nature, sometimes to embellish it" (Reclus 1864: 763; cited in Dunbar 1978: 44). Reclus equated "social progress" not with damage to the natural world but with the possibility of "giv[ing] the landscapes which surround him more charm, grace, and majesty" (ibid.). Reclus's geography was replete with examples of human modifications within the natural world that created positive change to the use of it. And, because of his own political philosophy, he argued that human change to the natural world was best when it benefited the larger whole and not the elite few. At the same time, he also sought to balance the anthropocentric (human-centered) narrative of much social theory, and instead theorized "humanity as emerging *within* nature rather than *out of* it" (Clark and Martin 2004: 24, their emphasis). His almost romantic view of human society as "natural" meant he was keenly aware of our use (and abuse) of the world's resources. Reclus's view was thus globally conscious; he was staunchly anti-racist and anti-imperialist. As Dunbar suggests, Reclus's witnessing of US slave culture repulsed him, as did the inequities inherent in the distributions of the world resources (also see Fleming 1988). Peter Kropotkin further suggested that Reclus's "work is free from absurd national conceit, or of national or racial prejudice; he has succeeded in indicating . . . what all men [*sic*] have in common – what unites them not divides them" (Kropotkin 1905: 341; cited in Stoddart 1975: 188). Reclus thus set out to both explain the spatial inequalities in and of societies and directly intervene in the social and spatial organization of the world.

Despite Reclus's prolific career and his advocacy for asking socially relevant questions, his work has only been selectively introduced into the history of geographic thought, and even more rarely into social geography (Clark and Martin 2004). Anne Buttimer (1971), who traces the extensive French school of geography and its contributions to geographic thought, does not engage with Reclus's work or theories. Dunbar believes that Reclus's contributions are there but that his own unique geography, as a French scholar working not in France but in Belgium and Switzerland, mitigated his impact. Despite his relative obscurity in the history of geographic thought, some geographers resurrected Reclus's research and political ideals in the 1970s and 1980s as part of a foundation for "radical" social and economic geographies (see Box 2.1).

Scene 2: Urban ecologies

In a different national context, at a slightly later historical moment, a group of scholars emerged with strong interests in social theoretical models of human society. Also influenced by environmental models, particularly models from plant ecology, a group of Chicago School sociologists had a significant impact on geography's development and its urban social school in particular. In fact, one could argue, at least in the context of the US, that social geography became significantly urban in the post-Chicago School years. In particular, the work of Robert Park, Ernest Burgess, and Robert McKenzie and their pathbreaking text, *The City* (1967 [1925]), outlined a theory of urban social organization based in a reading of "ecology theory

Box 2.1   Anarchist Geographies and "the Radical Turn"

Although the work of French geographer Elisée Reclus has remained marginal to the history of social geography, his anarchist philosophy inspired a number of social geographers in the 1970s. The reason why can be seen in earlier descriptions of Reclus and his work. In his obituary, published in *The Geographical Journal* in 1905, Peter Kropotkin, another anarchist geographer, wrote of Reclus:

> It must also be said that the human inhabitants of the globe are what interested Reclus most, much more than the animals or plants, or the flora and fauna of past ages. The Earth was the abode of man [*sic*], and what man has done and is doing to his abode, this is what absorbed his main attention (Kropotkin 1905).

It was this commitment to human society along with his global outlook that appealed to radical geographers, who saw in Reclus a challenge to the individualism found in behavioral geography and the localism (place-centrism) of humanistic geography. Reclus, and other anarchist geographers, were thus employed in the debates about "social relevance" in geography in the 1970s by radical geographers who argued that social justice studies in geography were not new but part of a longer tradition of geographic practice and inquiry. Stoddart wrote that "The discussion on relevance in geography which has taken place in *Area* [a journal of geography] since 1971 gives the impression that this a movement of recent development, replacing the 'New Geography' of the 1960s as a focus of activity. Just as there were earlier New Geographies, however, so a tradition of social relevance can be traced back to the beginnings of academic geography in this country [the United Kingdom]" (Stoddart 1975: 188). Stoddart goes on to describe the influence that Reclus and others had on human geographic thought and practice throughout the twentieth century, suggesting that it is important to examine disciplinary history when considering questions of relevance and concerns related to social justice and equality.

Quick Exercise

Go to your favorite web- or library-based search engine and type in the words "anarchy" and "geography." What do you find? Is anarchy being discussed in geography today? If so, how so? If not, why do you think it may be marginal?

[that] was Darwin's concept of the web of life. . . . Since man is an organic creature, Park argued that he [*sic*] is subject to the general laws of the organic world" (Robson 1969: 9–10; cited in Hamnett 1996, p. 8). Following on this theoretical innovation, "Burgess asked, 'In what way are individuals incorporated into the life of a city?'" (Fyfe and Kenny 2005: 19). In sum:

> Park, Burgess and McKenzie's inductive model, produced in 1925 and based on the city of Chicago, explained urban form as the result of a complex social ecology, where members of different migrant and immigrant groups competed for residential space in the city through the process of invasion and succession, such that one group was able to displace another through superior command over resources. The result of this rippling process of change was an urban social geography that reflected a pattern of distinctive neighborhoods as ecological niches within the larger metropolis (Del Casino and Marston 2006: 997).

As an inductively derived model and working from the ground up, observations were used to create a generic ecological model of the city. Armed with social Darwinian thinking, and theories of natural selection mediated by the struggle for a finite amount of resources, these sociologists tried to explain the spatial organization of the city's ethnic distinctions. First wave immigrants occupy inner city areas, known as "the loop," while second wave immigrant communities establish themselves over time in a second belt of housing settlements. Working further out of the city, successive waves of immigrants work their way out to the belt of the "residential" and "commuter" zones, moving from inner city apartments to single-family owner occupied housing. As each generation enters their newest zone, they bring their social and cultural practices with them, modifying those urban spaces based, in part, on economic upward mobility.

This model, Burgess argued, demonstrates that ethnic segregation is a key aspect of urban development:

> This differentiation into natural economic and cultural groupings gives form and character to the city. For segregation offers the group, and thereby the individuals who compose the group, a place and a role in the total organization of the city. Segregation limits development in certain directions, but it releases it in others. These areas tend to accentuate traits, to attract and develop their kind of individuals, and so to become further differentiated (Burgess 2005: 25).

Focusing on issues of "disorganization" (Hamnett 1996), such as crime, deviance, and promiscuity (key areas of social geographic analysis, particularly in the post-Second World War period), for example, Burgess and other Chicago School sociologists tried to explain the violence of the inner city.

For his part, Burgess believed that this ecological model only partially represented the day-to-day experiences of the city. He thus chose to focus his own energies on microstudies of particular ethnic neighborhoods as a microcosm of the successionist model of urban transition and ecology. Such empirically grounded work subsequently inspired researchers to use qualitative approaches, including ethnography and participant observation, in social geography (Ley 1977; S. Smith 1981, 1984; Jackson 1983).

Scene 3: Against the environmental grain

As some scholars sought to apply ecological and environmental approaches to the study of their social geographies, other scholars were trying to rethink the deep-seated tensions produced within these environment narratives. Some did this in very apolitical ways, while others directly addressed social inequities and inequalities. In 1907, G. W. Hoke published "The Study of Social Geography," trying to carve out a distinct subdisciplinary identity for examining social patterns. As Philo (1991) suggests, Hoke's piece is one of the first to explicitly discuss, at least in the English-speaking world, the nature and purpose of social geography. Hoke's (1907: 64–5) rendition of social geography is an interesting one:

> social geography deals with the distribution in space of social phenomena . . . its working programme may be stated as the "description of the sequence and relative significance" of those factors, the resultant of whose influences is the localization in space of a series of social phenomena chosen for investigation. Ultimately, by comparison with similar situations, and the elimination of the accidental, generalizations may be derived which will be of value in predicting the future distribution of similar phenomena. The subject deals, therefore, with the facts and products of human association as represented by group characteristics, industries, institutions, technology, customs, beliefs, and related phenomena; and estimates the significance of the various factors which have influenced their distributions.

In many ways, Hoke argued that the study of spatial patterns and relationships of social phenomena – be they ethnic group distributions or technological innovations – can be mapped, described, and compared across different spaces and through the "localization" of various social phenomena. On the surface, this is not much different from what someone might do in an introductory cartography or geographic information systems (GIS) course, where they might focus on the spatial organization and distribution of various social variables.

Guiding this reading of social geography was a belief that social phenomena are material, represented by objects such as technologies, industries, or institutions (Philo 1991: cited in Phillips 1998: 124). And, more simply, by studying these distributions it is possible to spatially articulate where one society begins and another ends (Gilbert and Steel 1945). Hoke's social geography is interesting because he was struggling against the strong influence of environmental determinism and evolutionary thinking in geography (Campbell and Livingstone 1983). Commenting on this theoretical moment, Hoke (1907: 65) suggested that "It is trite to note that the response, in terms of distribution, of a social group to any given environment is determined, not only by its 'physical circumstances,' but by the status, both technical and psychical, of that group as well." He further argued that "the same prairie land furnished a home, first for wandering tribes of Indian hunters, later for the agricultural and commercial white. In this case, the potent differentiating elements must be sought, not in the land, but in the character and attainment of the people" (ibid.). Hoke thus acknowledged environmental factors, but set out a distinction between society and nature, the social and the environmental, by privileging the power of societies to determine how they organize themselves into localities and how they can "write space" to mimic their own societal conventions and needs.

It is easy to locate Hoke's, Reclus's, Park's, or Burgess's research in the context of social geography because they participated in the academic spaces of the discipline. Other social geographies were being written that have been neglected in histories of the discipline. David Sibley's (1995) incredibly important volume, *Geographies of Exclusion*, points out that black scholars, such as W. E. B. DuBois, and early feminists, such as Jane Addams, were actively engaged in re-evaluating the dynamic social geographies of the city at the same time as the Chicago School sociologists. Their work, however, has been marginalized from a canonical reading of urban social geography. As Sibley notes, this is fairly ironic, at least in the case of DuBois, since Park was interested in the urban sociology of blacks in Chicago. Yet Park never mentions DuBois or his work. Sibley's fairly recent evaluation of the urban social geographic history is thus important because there remains a relative lack of discussion about DuBois and Addams in the urban social geographic literature (at least within the major texts on the subject: see, for example, Hamnett 1996; Fyfe and Kenny 2005).

Not unlike Park, though, DuBois believed that his work had real application. While Park's application influenced generations of urban planners and policy makers, DuBois "passionately believed that research could supply the basis for achieving a racially equalitarian [*sic*] society" (Rudwick 1974: 25; cited in Sibley 1995: 138). As Sibley explains, DuBois's research, empirically based in a door-to-door survey of the Seventh Ward of Philadelphia, employed then current sociological principles for studying economic and social difference not just across racial or ethnic groups but also within the black community itself, all in an attempt to explain spatial segregation driven by racism. Through his intensely detailed look at the daily geographies of blacks and whites in Philadelphia's Seventh Ward, DuBois traced the dynamic migratory patterns of blacks into the city, examined the ways in which housing markets were socially and spatially regulated through "discriminatory practices," and investigated the "connection between the job market and racial segregation" (Sibley 1995: 144–5). DuBois found that "the mass of the Negroes have been so often refused openings and discouraged in efforts to better their conditions that many of them say, as one said, 'I never apply – I know it is useless'" (DuBois 1967: 333; cited in Sibley 1995: 145).

DuBois's analysis employed a very complicated understanding of the relationship between society and space. Space and spatial relations as well as the spatial organization of the city no longer acted as a benign backdrop to social relations but reproduced discrimination and segregation that impoverished urban Black-Americans. His "observations are based on the actual experience of black people;

they give an idea of what it is like to be black in a predominantly white society and indicate how social geography is shaped both by white prejudice and social bonds within black culture" (Sibley 1995: 147). Working through more subjective geographies and employing a variety of qualitative methodologies, DuBois articulated the lived experience of the city for blacks in Philadelphia at the turn of the twentieth century. Yet "DuBois probably failed to make an impact, first, because of his methods" (Sibley 1995: 153), which did not follow the path taken by Park, Burgess, and other Chicago School sociologists. Furthermore, "DuBois eschewed Social Darwinism, recognizing that it provided a justification for the oppression of black people, and what he termed 'the colored races'" (Sibley 1995: 154). This, combined with the fact that he was largely shut out of the academic job market, meant that his theories and approaches to studying the social geographies of the city remained marginal to the discipline.

Not dissimilarly, but as Sibley explains for very different reasons, Jane Addams's research on urban social geography was also marginalized by the Chicago School sociologists. As a contemporary of both Park and Burgess, Addams had to contend with a number of discriminatory practices tied to both her politics and her gender that kept her work (and the work of her compatriots) out of the canon of social geographic theory. Addams helped found, in the late 1800s, the Hull House Settlement "to bring together the local working-class population and middle-class academics and social workers" (Sibley 1995: 163). Located in a working class ethnic neighborhood in Chicago, the Hull House Settlement was a conscious attempt to reorganize space to create a new and dynamic set of social relationships between academics and non-academics. Not only was the Hull House Settlement intentionally situated in a particular locale, it was networked to a broader global set of politics that linked Chicago to social movements throughout Europe and across the United States. Like DuBois, Addams and her Hull House colleagues, whose academic work was located in the University of Chicago School of Social Service and Administration, focused on the everyday lived experiences of working class individuals in Chicago.

Following on the traditions established by Addams and others, Edith Abbott helped write and publish a substantial long-term study titled *The Tenements of Chicago, 1908–1935*. Working from an ethnographic base, the authors of this particular volume were pained to describe the experiences and conditions of urban living in inner city Chicago. Through an examination of housing stock and rent prices, as well as the social composition of households, families, and neighborhoods, these scholars examined the lived experiences of urban economic development that ignored the needs of immigrant communities, the race and racial politics that marginalized certain populations from the profits of urban development, and offered suggestions of how to directly intervene to stem the problems associated with urban poverty, including poor health, sanitation, and housing conditions.

The marginalization of Addams and Abbott by Park and other urban sociologists is partially explained by the conflicting epistemological assumptions they held. Park operated under the assumptions that "human ecology was an abstract science, making use of facts of geography – a concrete science – to develop a theory through the application of the scientific method." This "scientific sociology" was intensely "apolitical" (Sibley 1995: 169). Addams and Abbott worked, however, from "concrete" experience. They were, at least according to Park and Burgess, incapable of producing abstract knowledge.[1] As Sibley suggests, this distinction between "sociology" and "social service" was highly gendered, with sociology representing the dominant masculine, scientific approach and social service the feminine, subaltern one.

However, the work of the Hull House scholars as well as those working in the School of Social Service and Administration resonates with the work of geographers, including David Harvey, whose *Social Justice and the City* (1973) makes somewhat parallel arguments about rent structures and discrimination (Sibley 1995). The grounded "ethnographic" work of the Hull House thus serves as a model of current social geographic work that engages in the subjective experiences of difference and inequality. It is time that such work is regularly articulated as part of a longer trajectory of social geographic inquiry and influence. Social geographers have a lot to learn from the depth and power of these subjective studies of poverty, race, class, and housing in the city.

Act II: Social or (Political) Economic Geographies?

Intellectual and political shifts in the post-Second World War period of geography would change the relationship between social geography and the rest of the field, as geographers began to rethink their discipline, its purpose, and its main theoretical inspirations. In particular, a new "spatial scientific" geography was enlivened through a more active engagement with quantitative social theory, while other geographers developed affinities for Marxist, humanist, and feminist social theories. Importantly, these advances were not always mutually exclusive: some scholars developed a Marxist spatial science or a feminist political economy perspective for studying spatial difference and inequality. All in all, in the post-Second World War period, particularly the period of the 1960s through the 1980s, an explosion of social geographic research sought to become more "relevant" to the societies within which this work was embedded.

In a broader context, the emergence of a geography concerned explicitly with "the social" and the relationships between society and space was informed by the broader theoretical and intellectual ferment of the time. This included the major shifts in social life, which witnessed an expanding urban and suburban experience in the developing worlds of North America and Europe as well as a massive and rapid decolonization of much of Africa, Asia, and the Pacific. Moreover, in the 1960s and 1970s, new social movements, such as the civil rights, feminist, and gay liberation movements, suggested that the categories of class, race, gender, and sexuality needed to be more critically examined and understood. In short, societies needed to be interrogated for how they created systems of economic and political authority and social and cultural power to privilege certain social groups over others.

Moreover, this period witnessed the Cold War politics of US-Soviet relations and the development of alternatives to the dominance of these two "superpowers," including the nonaligned movement of countries claiming autonomy from either side of this "war." It was also witness to the rethinking of sociocultural systems, such as religious practices, through the merging of economic concerns (socialism) with religious ones (Catholicism), e.g. the emergence of liberation theology in Latin America. In this period, questions of *social difference* – and the practices of discrimination and/or liberation – and *inequality* – at the microscales of cities and towns and at the global scales of developing and developed nation-states – informed the changing geographies of this time. Not all social geographers in the post-Second World War period took on all (or any) of these issues directly. Nonetheless, what we will see is that social geographers would, to varying degrees, start to investigate new nodes of difference and inequality and do so in ways that would largely evacuate the underlying environmental and ecological determinism of the previous period.

We begin by looking at what is often dubbed "the quantitative revolution," an era in geography ushered in by concerns with creating a more "rigorous" scientific geography. Next, we turn to the development of "radical geographies," which sought to reconcile geographic theories with sociological theories developing out of Marxist schools of thought. Taking a different tactic, we next examine the emergence of a "humanistic geography," a social theoretical geography strongly influenced by philosophies concerned with subjective experiences and interpretions about the world in which we live. Finally, we examine the growing importance of feminist geography and sexuality studies as critical correctives to masculinist-inspired Marxist and humanist geographies as well as valued new perspectives on our study of social geography. Throughout this act, we will interrogate how the study of difference and inequality has become a concern across a broader array of geographic concerns and subdisciplinary positions.

Scene 1: Toward a socially relevant spatial science of class, race, and ability

The post-Second World War period brought much intellectual ferment to the field of geography, which was struggling with its identity as a social science. As other disciplines, particularly economics and political science, advanced new, mathematic-ally driven models of human society, many geographers became concerned about their position within the academy and society more broadly. This moment of intellectual malaise presented geographers with a unique opportunity to rethink their field. In 1953, Schaefer explicitly argued that geography had become mired in a deeply descriptive science of places. The discipline offered little explanation of spatial patterns and why they looked the way they did, or spatial behavior and why people did what they did. Turning his attention to other social sciences, which he saw as more "scientifically rigorous," such as economics, Schaefer (1953: 227) suggested that "science is not so much interested in individual facts as in the patterns they exhibit." Schaefer's call for a "scientific geography" suggested that geography should be reorganized as a "spatial science," although Schaefer himself gave no real tools for developing that science (Johnston and Sidaway 2004). It was in the hands of other scholars that a new quantitative scientific geography began to emerge. For geographers interested in social questions, the development of a spatial scientific geography provided a new opportunity to develop their social geographies. This is particularly true because the emergence of quantitative geographies further legitimated the development of distinct "systematic schools" of geographic inquiry, such as economic geography, political geography, and social geography. Moreover, the emergence of systematic subfields further differentiated physical from human geographies, studies of the environment from studies of society (Johnston and Sidaway 2004).

In this context, social geography began to gain momentum as a fairly autonomous field of inquiry. As a systematic subdiscipline of geography, Pahl (1970: 81) argued, social geography should be the study of "the processes and patterns involved in an understanding of socially defined populations in their spatial settings." As he went on to suggest, "Just as economic geography is now more concerned with the theories of the location of economic activity, so social geography has become concerned with the theoretical location of social groups and social characteristics" (ibid.: 82). Unlike Hoke, whose social geography was defined solely by its study of distribution, Pahl further averred that studies of "distributions, however well presented, are not enough. Description does not necessarily imply comprehension and understanding" (ibid.).

In this period, there was a break from the earlier traditions, which were concerned with human–environment relations. As Pahl once again argued, "the field of social geography is concerned less with the relationships of social groups to the physical environment than with the patterns and processes involved in the segregation of social groups and settlements in space" (ibid.: 95). As geographers turned their attention to the social, they simultaneously sought to identify how a geographer might study that social world. In this way, geographers sought out their own "primitives" (Nystuen 1968), such as distance, location, and connectivity, which could be the core variables in a newly emerging spatial science. Richard Morrill (1970: 15; cited in Johnston and Sidaway 2004: 114) further suggested that geography should be concerned with the study of "space, space relations, and change in space – how physical space is structured, how men [*sic*] relate through space, how man has organized his society in space, and how our conception and use of space change." Within this theoretical framework of space, Morrill identified "five qualities relevant to the understanding of human behavior – (1) distance, the spatial dimension of separation; (2) accessibility; (3) agglomeration; (4) size; and (5) relative location" (ibid.). While we will deal more extensively with the methodological implications of this "turn" in Chapter 3, it is important to note that geographers began to more consistently employ methods that were quantitative, mathematical, and statistical. In many ways, then, these geographers sought to examine, to varying degrees, geography as geometry (Bunge 1962), a set of spatial patterns operating in and across the landscape that explained various spatial behaviors, such as where one group might locate relative to another or how mobility, and thus access to urban institutions such as hospitals or economic opportunities, was impacted by the spatial structure of the city.

For many social geographers working in this nascent spatial scientific tradition the study of spatial difference was not enough. They wanted to make a social difference and be "relevant," arguing that geography needed to contribute to both local and global society. "Geography does not belong to geographers alone," argued Bunge (1973a: 482), "any more than medicine to doctors . . . geography departments in the end must be accountable to the people among whom they lie." In this broad mindset, social geographers sought to apply their new found knowledge of spatial science to questions of social change, hoping to address the inequalities in access to social benefits, health care, and economic prosperity between the "haves" and the "have nots." Geographers, who witnessed social changes and challenges, began to question the spatialities of racism and poverty, for example. They also questioned the efficacy of an objective science that refused to engage with or intervene in societal problems. In fact, some of the early developments in a "race studies" in geography can be traced to the social analyses of geographers interested in problematizing the relationships between economic inequality, access to resources (including social services), the racial and ethnic makeup of certain neighborhood spaces, and the maintenance of ghetto spaces in the city (e.g. Morrill 1965; Bunge 1973b; Blaut 1983; *Economic Geography* 1972 (Vol. 48, No. 1) on "Black America").

This powerful pull toward applied social geographies was no more evidenced than in the area of welfare geography, an emergent field of inquiry that developed in the 1970s. Smith, in arguing for a renewed focus on inequality in the discipline, suggested:

> The question of who gets what *where* and how provides a framework for the restructuring of human geography in more "socially relevant" terms, without necessarily abandoning the rigour and sophistication of the quantitative era. It requires us to identify the desirable or undesirable aspects of human existence, to find out and measure how these are allocated between individuals or groups distinguished by place or area, and to examine and if possible model the processes which lead things to be as they are. In addition, the resurgence of applied geography requires that this knowledge be put to the service of society, in the design of predictably "better" spatial allocation of the benefits and penalties of modern life (Smith 1974: 289–90, original emphasis).

Smith went on to argue that indices of "quality of life" are "incapable of value-free scientific analysis" (ibid.: 290). As such, social geographers cannot operate in a black box of valueless science whose sole purpose is to refine theory, technique, and instrumentation. In constructing welfare geographies, social geographers must begin with the assumption that societies construct a certain degree of spatial inequality that can be mapped, illustrating the correlations between "physical needs (nutrition, shelter and health); cultural needs (education, leisure and recreation, and security); and higher needs (to be purchased with surplus income)" (Johnston and Sidaway 2004: 336).

In applying spatial science to everyday social problems, geographers also turned to some of its primitives: location, distance, and connectivity (Nystuen 1968). In terms of location, geographers asked questions about how society was spatially organized to reinforce spatial inequalities. Pushing even further, they began to suggest ways to reorganize society spatially to benefit the "have nots." Wolpert et al. (1975) examined how mental health facilities were spatially isolated in poor, inner city neighborhoods. The spatial fix of mental health care facilities limits the mobility of people with mental illnesses through their ongoing spatially marginalization. The social stigma attached to mental illness thus functions to produce a particular geography that is mitigated by a number of social actors, including service providers and local community members that determine where facilities are located (Takahashi 1998a, 1998b). With little regard for the individual geographies of people with mental illnesses, the system of health care and social services designed to help them instead constrains them. Worse yet, the resulting geographies continually create stigmatized people and places.

As these geographies of inequality moved to the fore in the field, social geographers began to emphasize questions related to poverty, racism, and health care, for example. Giggs's (1973: 72) study of schizophrenia sought to explain the relationship between mental health status and other sociogeographic variables as well as the development of "preventive policies" and the "planning of future hospitals" to serve those most in need (see also Shannon and Dever 1974). The location of facilities and services for those most in need thus became a critical site of social geographic analysis, as spatial scientists sought to explain social inequalities and how to best address those by changing the spatial organization of needed social service and health care organizations. They did so, mostly, by mapping these locations. Then, through the use of statistical analyses they assessed the relationships between individual/group location and social and economic status. Importantly, the arrival of a "socially relevant" spatial scientific approach to studying social difference and inequality remains pressing today, as geographers continue to struggle with how to best organize our social world spatially to meet the needs of various populations (Del Casino and Jones 2007).

Scene 2: On a political economy of the social

By the late 1960s, geographers were clearly engaging in broader social debates about inequality, justice, and politics. In the United States, this was marked by the emergence of *Antipode: A Journal of Radical Geography* in 1969, whose "goal is radical change" and the "replacement of institutions and institutional arrangements in our society that can no longer respond to changing societal needs" (Stea 1969: 1; cited in Hague 2002: 656). This idea of change was informed by the broader ongoing debate in the field about geography's "social relevance," which "was conceived not in a vague way, as 'feeling sorry for one's fellow human beings,' but as taking the side of the oppressed, advocating their causes, pressing for fundamental social change" (Peet 1998: 68).

For some geographers that change would take place through a much more thorough and consistent engagement with Marx and Marxist theory (Peet 1998). While *Antipode* provided one outlet for some of these discussions and debates about whether or not Marxism was the right approach for addressing social problems, the published work of some geographers, such as David Harvey, Doreen Massey, and Ed Soja, focused attention on the mutual constitution of the social and the spatial, society and space, through a deeper analysis of the processes of what Lefebvre called "the production of space." Put simply, spaces are organized to sustain inequalities and difference, while benefiting capitalist modes of production by generating certain uneven social geographies (N. Smith 1984). Within this emerging Marxist turn in geography, David Harvey's (1973) *Social Justice and the City* became a key text marking a watershed in how geographers theorized the relationship between social processes and the spatial organization of society. "Harvey's radical contribution to social geography through *Social Justice and the City* was to merge the social and the geographical and to lay out a framework for understanding how space is produced by social practice and how those spaces then shape the social groups who produced them" (Del Casino and Marston 2006: 997–8). In more consciously linking regional economic development to the distribution of "income," Harvey suggested that for there to be social and class-based justice there must be a system of distribution that addresses a broadly conceived "common good" across social groups and spaces. In the end, capitalists were not interested in that common good, for "capitalist means invariably serve their own capitalist ends" (Huberman and Sweezy 1969; cited in Harvey 1973: 113). So, it was necessary to construct new forms of justice that took as their primary concern the restructuring of the spatial distributions of resources so that all social groups benefited. Fundamentally, this meant transforming the means of production such that society itself could be transformed.

Resting at the heart of these theorizations were new conceptions of what geographers called social space or "spatiality." In this new conceptualization "human practice and space are integrated" (N. Smith 1984; cited in Peet 1998: 100). Space is given meaning and structure and those meanings and structures then act to constrain movements and mobilities. Social spaces help to maintain difference and inequality or similarity and equality, or some combination of these binary pairs. What this all means is that space is not a backdrop to social relations, a blank slate upon which social institutions or patterns can be mapped. "Rather, [space] is a structure created *by* society" (Soja 1980: 210, original emphasis). As Soja further argues:

> Whether it be form or content, and distributional pattern of the built environment, the relative location of centers of production and consumption, the political organization of space into territorial jurisdictions, the uneven geographical distribution of income and employment, or the ideological attachments to location symbols and spatial images, all organized space will be seen as rooted in a social origin and filled with social meaning.

Box 2.2   On Harvey's *Social Justice and the City*

David Harvey's research is central to the "radical" turn in social geography. *Social Justice and the City* is the first in a series of books that introduces Harvey's Marxist perspective and challenges the notion that geography can remain neutral when it comes to combating injustice, poverty, and inequality. It marked a turn from Harvey's first book, *Explanations in Geography* (1969), where he outlined an approach to a hypothetical-deductive spatial science, and signaled a broader trend toward the study of inequality in social geography. Harvey also nuanced his theory of space, arguing that space is absolute – a "thing in itself" – relative – "understood as a relationship between objects which exists only because objects exist and relate to each other" – and relational – "an object can be said to exist only insofar as it contains and represents within itself relationships to other objects." This move from an absolute to a relative and/or relational notion of space, inspired largely by the French social theorist Henri Lefebvre, demonstrated that urban stratification was produced through the social relations of capitalism. In Harvey's own words:

> space is neither absolute, relative or relational *in itself*, but it can become one or all simultaneously depending on the circumstances. The problem of proper conceptualization of space is resolved through human practice with respect to it. . . . The question "what is space?" is therefore replaced by the question "how is it that different human practices can create and make use of distinctive conceptualizations of space?" The property relationship, for example, creates absolute spaces within which monopoly control can operate. The movement of people, goods, services and information takes place in a relative space because it takes money, time, energy, and the like, to overcome the friction of distance. Parcels of land also capture benefits because they contain relationships with other parcels; the forces of demographic, market and retail potential are real enough within an urban system and in form of rent relational space comes into its own as an important aspect of human social practice. An understanding of urbanism and of the social-process-spatial-form theme requires that we understand how human activity creates the need for specific spatial concepts and how daily social practice solves with consummate ease seemingly deep philosophical mysteries concerning the nature of space and the relationship between social processes and spatial forms (Harvey 1973: 13–14, original emphasis).

Not all social geographers agreed with Harvey's conceptualization of the society–space relationship or his take on justice. That said, Harvey's attention to theories of space, social justice, and equity in urban spaces remains pressing today, particularly because cities are still sites of social and economic contestation and conflict. Geographers continue to reflect back on *Social Justice* and other works by Harvey when studying the complex society–space relationship.

Quick Exercise

Using a citation index – Web of Science, Google Scholar, Social Science Citation Index – locate recent articles or books that cite *Social Justice and the City*. Pick one and evaluate how Harvey's work is discussed.

For Marxist geographers the societies they studied were based in capitalism, the spaces that were produced by capitalism were clearly beneficial to those who controlled the means of production. Spatial power is social power and economic control is equivalent to social control. As Peet (1998: 107) stresses, "Once it is recognized that space is socially organized there is no longer a question of it being a separate structure with rules of transformation independent of the wider social framework." In this social theoretical framework, there is not one social space but many overlapping social spaces (e.g. the home, the market, the city), all defined by social practices tied to capitalist modes of production. At the same time, within these evolving Marxist geographies was a consideration of the subjective experience of uneven capitalist relations of social production and reproduction at the scale of the local. In short, what we discern from Marxist inspired social geography is that "social inequalities . . . can be investigated for the ways in which social and spatial relations work together, by facilitating flows of capital across spaces and creating new social structures of difference in distinct locations and at particular scales" (Del Casino and Jones 2007: 241).[2]

Scene 3: Humanizing the social and the dynamic study of space and place

Marxist geographers were not the only ones to theorize the relationship between society and space in geography. A second emergent set of geographies was born out of an engagement with humanist philosophies, which eschewed purely economic explanations of social difference and privileged subjective experiences of place and a theoretical framework informed by phenomenology. As Relph (1970: 195) explains, "Phenomenology is a philosophy in which it is assumed that knowledge does not exist independently of man [*sic*], but has to be gained from man's experience of the world." These new "humanistic geographers" turned their attention away from either an abstract space found in spatial science or a social space as theorized by Marxist geographers. Place as lived experience became an important site for the study of embodied experience, and the conceptual focus shifted to the human subject as an agent for the construction of places: individuals understood themselves as social beings through their experiences of and interactions with place, they gave place meaning and gained their own social meanings through their practices of place (referred to by some as social space as well: e.g. Buttimer 1969).

In Tuan's (1975) terms, humanistic geography focuses on how humans "made the earth into a home." While the human actor in spatial science was a rational one who responded to external stimuli in abstract space (i.e. moved according to the spatial patterns of economic production and consumption in the city set before him or her), the humanist actor internalized place and acted on and through it. So, as Buttimer (1969: 423) argues, "when spatially juxtaposed groups held widely contrasting ideas about [social] space [or place], tensions arose, which influenced spatial movements, thus affecting the geography of that sector [of the city]."

Humanistic geographers drew attention to subjective modes of knowing the world, while at the same time not losing sight of its order. Focusing on the intentionality of individuals and their "potential range of experiences" (Buttimer 1976: 290), humanistic geographers saw "man [*sic*]" as the "creative center of [his or her] world" (ibid.: 279). Starting at the point of rather idiosyncratic experience, humanistic geographers began to explore, in collective terms, "what it means to be human." Despite the focus on subjective experience of place, however, humanistic geographers also strove to understand core human "essence" – a broader social subconsciousness – something that "does not come . . . from location . . . [but comes from] the largely unselfconscious intentionality that defines places as profound centers of human existence" (Relph 1976: 43; cited in Cresswell 2004: 20). As Cresswell (2004: 20) suggests, "place [in humanistic geography] was seen as a universal and transhistorical part of the human condition. It was not so much places (in the world) that interested the humanists but 'place' as an idea, concept and way of being-in-the-world." For Tuan (1974) there was an "affective [and emotional] bond between people and places" (cited in Cresswell 2004: 20).

There are, of course, implications for the study of social relations when one moves from a spatial scientific reading of space and spatial relations to a humanistic one (Buttimer 1976; Entrikin 1976; Tuan 1976). Concerned with subjective experience, humanistic geographers turned their attention to how places are permeated by various social meanings and informed by people's understandings of being in place and being placeless (Relph 1976; Cresswell 1996). The proliferation of social inequalities, to paraphrase Cresswell (1996), means that certain people are "in place" and some are "out of place," pushed to the margins of society by the oppressive structures of race, gender, and class relations. Humanistic geographers are thus concerned with how places, as they come into being, shape and are shaped by social relations and inequalities. At the same time, they remain less concerned with "structures" per se, and more focused on everyday experiences and the emotional connections people have with their place in the world.

Scene 4: Emerging alterities through feminism and sexuality studies in geography

While Marxist geographers turned their attention to the concerns of capitalist class relations and humanists suggested a more sustained focus on the subjective experiences of place, feminist geographers called attention to the gendering of the society–space relationship. Monk and Hanson (1982: 12), even though not the first geographers to raise questions about the relationship between gender and geography, did suggest that "Geographers have . . . been more concerned with studying the spatial dimensions of social class than of social roles, such as gender roles. Yet for many individuals and groups, especially women, social roles are likely to have a greater impact than social class on spatial behavior." In shifting the discussion from one of class to one of role, Monk and Hanson, like other feminist geographers, moved the discussion from the realm of social *production* to the realm of social *reproduction* and the relationship between these two sets of geographic processes.[3] "Thus [while] geographers address the political economy of the international division of labor . . . [they] ignore the theoretical implications of the sexual division of labor" (ibid.: 15). Feminist geographers "translated [this new focus] first into a project to 'add women' to the field, both as producers of knowledge and as subjects of analysis . . . [by offering] ground-breaking research on the material realities of women's lives" (Nelson and Seager 2005: 3).

The development of feminist (social) geography was profound in that it marked a direct challenge to the basic assumptions that human experiences were centered on/in men's experiences of place and space. The new focus on the social category of gender and the ways in which gendered roles and experiences mediated our experience of place and space provided an opportunity to nuance older social geographies. Some sought to map gendered differences across space (Seager 2003; Nelson and Seager 2005). Others began to turn their attention to new empirical foci, such as the home (Blunt and Dowling 2006), and to rethink urban social geographies from the lens of feminist inquiry (Gilbert 1997). And feminist geographers, such as Gillian Rose (1993), offered a systematic critique of how geographic theories privileged men's gaze. According to Rose (1993: 60), for example, "Humanistic geography assumes masculinity as its implicit norm, and does so with all the authority of masculine claims to really know."

Importantly, this critique did more than simply "add women" to the mix. It suggested that geographers investigate how their theoretical lens informs their understanding of the world around them. As Bondi and Davidson (2005: 15) suggest:

> One of the most important effects of feminist geography has been to unsettle taken-for-granted assumptions about women's and men's "places" in the societies, communities, organizations, and relationships within which we live and work. Thus, feminist geography has opened up questions about ways in which spaces and places – from bathrooms to call centres, from urban parks to teaching spaces – are experienced differently by different people, and come to be associated with the presence or absence of different groups of people. . . . It has also prompted much reflection on what the categories "women" and "men" mean, and on the concept of gender, in the context of social identities and social relations more generally. One expression of this has been growing interest in a diversity of "masculinities" and "femininities"; that is, in different ways of being men and women.

Feminist geographers have thus worked through and across any number of theoretical approaches in developing their analyses of how various gendered differences and inequalities constitute the spaces of social production and, importantly, reproduction. This has included critiques of how "feminism has been consistently marginalized by mainstream geography" (Rose 1993). Just as importantly, feminist geographers have remained skeptical of purely economic explanations of social difference and inequality, encouraging geographers to investigate the interrelationship between class and gender as well as gender and other social categories based in race, ethnicity, and, eventually, sexuality.

> **Box 2.3**   "Beyond" Gillian Rose's *Feminism and Geography*
>
> In 1993, Gillian Rose published *Feminism and Geography*, a critique of the discipline's inherent masculinist perspective. Rose's analysis evaluates the problematic assumptions of geography's core philosophies and approaches. In her criticism, she argues that the default object/perspective in human geographic research has been not only men but also masculinist ways of knowing and seeing. In her interrogation of humanistic geography, Rose argues that "sense of place as a universal human trait" (p. 51) serves to erase the complex gendered – as well as raced, sexed, and classed – differences between men and women. In examining cultural geography's critical turn in landscape studies, Rose notes that "landscape painting [a central object for many critical cultural geographers] then involves not only class relations, but also gender relations" (p. 93). Importantly, Rose also outlines how "Feminist explorations of the different spaces of the contemporary city often reject the search for totality from a position of complete knowledge" (p. 133). In conclusion, Rose argues that:
>
> > The subject of feminism insists that spaces are extraordinarily complex. . . . Its multidimensionality refers to complicated and never self-evident matrix of historical, social, sexual, racial and class positions which women occupy, and its geometry is one strung out between paradoxical sites. These feminist maps are multiple and intersecting, provisional and shifting, and they require "ever more intricate skills in cartography" (Rose 1993: 155; citing Hirsch and Keller 1990: 370).
>
> While this was certainly not the first feminist critique or analysis offered in geography, this controversial text suggests that feminist geographers do not need to work with humanistic, Marxist, or cultural geography perspectives. It also encourages geographers to be critical at the level of epistemology, i.e. how we know what we know.
>
> At the same time, other feminist geographers pushed against the grain of other masculinist geographies. J. K. Gibson-Graham penned *The End of*

Capitalism (as We Knew It): A Feminist Critique of Political Economy in 1996, and Doreen Massey authored *Space, Place, and Gender* in 1994. Both of these volumes, which draw from different epistemological approaches to "doing geography," highlight the longer trajectory and tradition of feminist scholarship within the discipline.

Quick Exercise

1   Find a work of feminist geography that predates Rose's *Feminism and Geography*. What are some of the questions important to feminist geographers in the 1980s and early 1990s?
2   Find a work that postdates *Feminism and Geography*. How has Rose's controversial analysis been discussed by other feminist geographers?

So, as feminist geographies began to develop so to did a nascent sexuality studies in geography make present the unequal conditions associated with a variety of non-heterosexual categories, including lesbian women and gay men. Geographers such as Lauria and Knopp (1985) worked through a political economic approach to "understand the role of gay communities in urban redevelopment" (Brown and Knopp 2003: 314). The pioneering work of McNee (1984, 1985; cited in Brown and Knopp 2003: 314), for example,

> focused on where, how and why gays and lesbians are not able to express our *embodied difference* from heterosexuals, particularly our same-sex desire and practice but also other forms of gender non-conformity (for example, drag) and affiliations (for example, prostitution) that tend to make middle-class professionals (like geographers) "squeamish."

The 1980s, then, brought about the recognition that experiences of space were different depending on one's understandings and practices of certain sexual identities. Moreover, geographers interested in sexuality studies promoted research on inequalities that oppressed certain peoples and constructed spaces through a hegemonic heterosexuality (Brown 2000). Importantly, though, early attempts to investigate sexual geographies incorporated political-economic theories of urban design and development (Knopp 1990a, 1990b). Lauria and Knopp (1985), for example, investigated the sociospatial organization of the city through a "combination of Marxian-inspired theories of organizations and urban land use, feminist approaches to gender and sexuality, and some early lesbian/gay social theory to understand the role of gay communities in urban redevelopment" (Brown and Knopp 2003: 314). Extending Lauria's and Knopp's work on "gay men and the city," Rothenberg (1995: 180) suggests that lesbian women in Park Slope, New York have also "created a recognizable social space – recognizable most importantly to each other, but increasingly to the 'straight' population as well. The concentration can be attributed in large part to lesbian social networking, the success of which has contributed to the neighborhood's continuing gentrification, and consequently, to lesbian displacement." The initial work in the geographies of sexuality thus relied heavily on socioeconomic models, particularly those developed by Marxist geographers.

It is hard to underestimate the importance of feminist geography and later sexuality and space studies to the discipline of geography and to social geography more specifically. They challenged the broader assumptions of the discipline, expanding how social geographers theorize both difference and inequality. This challenge informed a number of important changes in how geographers "do" social geography, and also presented new possibilities and concerns. Social geography thus entered a new phase as feminist geography became more important to human geography more generally. At the same time, the expansion of sexuality studies in geography, and the emergence of an explicitly queer geography (Browne et al. 2007), began to push the boundaries of what might be "appropriate" topics for social geography, making space for the broadening of geographic study of sexualities (Bell and Valentine 1995). As a more recognized "queer geography" developed, however, new social theories entered the field and queer geographers, like others in the field of social geography, began to think "beyond" the economy. In this new phase, however, just as new sites of inquiry and difference became more important, social geography would be challenged by the re-emergence of a "new" cultural geography. Fortunately, as we will see, the focus of social geography will continue to evolve as new approaches and concepts enter the field.

Act III: Social or Cultural Geographies?

Critiques of both spatial scientific and Marxist geographies prompted many geographers to question the explicit and implicit assumptions that economic relations of capitalist production exclusively underpinned social geographic processes. These challenges prompted new openings and possibilities for a social geography that was concerned not only with issues of class but also with differences and inequalities based in categories of race, gender, ethnicity, sexuality, and even nationality. In some cases, this meant modifying economic approaches, developing a radical feminist geography, for example, that investigated the twin processes of class and gender relations simultaneously. In other cases, social geographers had to contend with the growing importance of new theories of social identity and subjectivity, which were emerging out of a revitalized "new" cultural geography. Led, in part, by prominent social geographers, such as Peter Jackson (1989), cultural geography turned its attention away from a theory of culture that presumed culture "was . . . an entity above man, not reducible to actions by individuals who are associated with it, mysteriously . . . [Culture responds] to laws of its own" (Duncan 1980: 182). Instead, culture was reconceptualized as a process, and a contested one at that, often constructed by those in positions of authority and power to maintain their positions over an oppressed majority. In this, cultural geographers called for greater attention to "the social construction of categories of social differentiation . . . [which] leads, of course . . . to challenging the supposed naturalness of the categories of social differentiation (gender, race, age, etc.) and to examinations and explorations of the ways in which (and means through which) such categories are (re)produced and interpreted/negotiated" (Gregson 1993: 527).

For Gregson, and others (e.g. Peach 1999), this "turn" toward the deconstruction of social processes and categories marginalized social geography's key concerns with the material experiences of inequality and difference. Nonetheless, the importance of interrogating the categories that underpinned understandings of inequality and difference suggested that social geographers needed to question some of their basic assumptions about how they viewed the theoretical relationship between key concepts, such as self and other, inside and outside, old and young, white and black, and north and south. Moreover, social geographers began to consider not only their historical objects of analysis, those in so-called marginal positions in society, but the normative assumptions about relatively uncontested hegemonic and privileged categories, such as whiteness, heterosexuality, and masculinity, which were underexamined in the field. The result of this robust period of theoretical ferment is a social geography that has both complicated its historical object of study – difference and inequality – and legitimated topics of inquiry that were once considered taboo in a discipline that has a historically conservative edge (Smith 2000b), such as sexuality studies and children's geographies.

This act traces the relationship between social geographic and cultural geographic thoughts and ideas. Importantly, both subfields have learned from each other and social geography has "emerged" from this engagement with a number of new and important lines of inquiry. We begin by examining the turn toward postmodern and poststructuralist theories of difference, developing a better understanding of how the "cultural turn" and its focus on representations and representational politics challenged the core of a self-identified "materialist" and "empirically grounded" social geography. Next, we trace the development of a number of alternative theoretical positions that call into question the ways in which social geographers investigate difference and inequality. This includes paying particular attention to the growing importance of theories of identity, subjectivity, and body politics. These new theoretical and methodological sites of inquiry suggest that it is important to work in the realm of both representation and experience simultaneously. Finally, we briefly examine the "backlash" to the "turn" and the implications for a social geography that would become, itself, differentiated across a number of modes of analysis and inquiry. Through a brief discussion of this challenge, it is suggested that social geographers can learn how to move toward a more open view of their own theoretical differences and disentangle certain methodological practices from particular theoretical positions.

Scene 1: The "cultural turn" and the "social category"

The "cultural turn" in geography enabled a new set of critiques of how social geographers think about the underlying assumptions of their theories about space and society. It was informed by the broader engagement of geographers with both postmodern and poststructural social theories. These theoretical positions challenged the basic assumptions of spatial science, Marxism, and humanism. In particular, they eschewed reductionist philosophies, which presumed that researchers could explain all experience by reducing its elements to the workings of capitalism, humanity, or patriarchy, for example. Also, they challenged essentialism, a philosophical position that suggests there is some innate and essential quality to all social categories. In challenging reductionist philosophy and essentialist thinking, the cultural turn in geography called into question a number of central assumptions that had, until fairly recently, structured social geographic thought. First, social geographers could no longer assume that the social categories of age, race, gender, class, ethnicity, sexuality, or nationality were natural. Instead, the social category became, itself, a social construction, a process whereby certain assumptions of what it meant to be a "woman" or "black" or "queer" or "working class" were constituted through various discourses and linguistic conventions. Second, by evacuating the category of its essential character, the cultural turn forced social geographers to historicize how and in what ways categories of analysis have been historically and geographically produced. This turned social geography's attention "inward," forcing a period of critical self-reflection. Social geographers could no longer simply assume that the categories of the census, and the social groups it distinguished and demarcated, were "true" representations of collective experience. They had to think about their own implicit, and perhaps explicit, role in the reproduction of essentialist thinking, which assumed that oppression or segregation was experienced equally by all those who somehow fit into certain marginalized categories.

Third, the cultural turn called into question the bounding of social categories, insisting that social geographers focus on concepts such as hybridity, identity, and subjectivity. This challenged some of the long-held assumptions of social geography, which suggested that spatial segregation could be neatly displayed across a grid of absolute space. This challenge called into question the concept of the boundary itself, as both a physical and social artifact, and forced social geography to reconsider how certain identities and subjective experiences of age, race, class, gender, age, sexuality, or nationality were constructed through various spatial representations. Fourth, over time, the cultural turn forced social geographers to consider how power and authority, as well as subversion and resistance, constructed our social categories. Following the work of social theorists such as Michel Foucault, social geographers investigated how social categories were naturalized, temporarily defined with certain meanings, through the effects of power: what it has meant to be white or black, gay or straight, masculine or feminine, is situated in a historical set of social relationships and practices. In very important ways this has meant that social geographers could no longer fix their "gaze" on so-called marginal populations.

They must also consider how categories of power – whiteness, heterosexuality, capitalism – were also partial and incomplete processes. Finally, and perhaps most importantly, the cultural turn forced social geographers to think about the constitutive nature of their social categories. Put simply, there is no "heterosexuality" without an "other," such as "homosexuality." In this way, then, the spaces that are tied to particular social categories through various cultural representations can never completely erase the "other" upon which they are based: there is no ghetto without neighborhoods of affluence.

From a political perspective, this move appeared to dismantle the very core of social geography, shifting its focus from one that investigated "real world" differences and inequalities to the realm of representational politics and the processes through which social categories were defined by "essentialized" and "naturalized" characteristics. It is not surprising, then, that some social and cultural geographers, particularly feminists, were concerned by how this "turn" appeared to shift attention away from "the oppression of women" (Domosh 2005: 38) and toward representational practices, such as art, film, landscape painting, and architecture. At the same time, the "cultural turn" opened social geography up to a new array of critical voices, ones that had been largely submerged under the weight of essentialist thinking. This included, for example, postcolonial scholars, whose work challenged the Eurocentric and Anglo-centered nature of human geography (Blunt and McEwan 2002; Gregory 2004). Subaltern voices began to "seep into" social geography as social geographers called into question the complex relationships between a global north and global south (Pratt 1992). Instead of "speaking for others," social geographers also reflected on how best to represent social difference and inequality themselves. As we will see in Chapter 3, this has helped to promote more explicit connections between research and politics through the development of "action research" projects.

The next scene explores some of the varied and contested theoretical possibilities that have resulted from the "turn." These possibilities have developed in concert with and in juxtapostion as well as opposition to the "cultural turn." There is no doubt, though, that as social geographers began to question the basis of the social category, they were forced to develop much more complex theories of how difference and inequality emerge in the day-to-day practices of individuals and social groups in and across differing sociospatial contexts.

Scene 2: Complicating space, identity, body, and subjectivity

It has been suggested that social geography, beginning particularly in the 1990s, became a bit more "open," concerned with a variety of subjects that had been quite marginal to the discipline as a whole. Historically, studying racial segregation was perfectly appropriate but studying the social construction of race and racism was treated more skeptically in the discipline. The "cultural turn" and the investment in theories concerned with challenging hegemonic assumptions about what constituted difference and inequality established a foothold, albeit a relatively small one at the beginning, for social geographers to take on topics that had long been marginal to the discipline as a whole. Various social processes and categories were now being called into question, and social geographers (along with many other geographers) took up the study of new axes of difference that were situated in discussions of sexuality, age, race, and nationalism. Social geography was becoming, among other things, more queer, a theoretical and political position that suggested social geographers challenge the underlying heteronormative assumptions of their research and practice as well as consider various identities and practices that were not typically investigated – such as lesbian, gay, bisexual, and transgendered subjectivities. As the theoretical breadth of social geographers was enhanced by their conscious engagement with new social theories, so too did the subjects of their research expand. Social geographers rethought a number of areas of social geographic research, including geographies of race (Pulido 2006), rural geographies (Cloke 2003a), urban social movements (Miller 2000), and geographies of ageing (Andrews and Phillips 2005), in new and innovative ways.

Of growing interest within this expanded social geography was the relationship between space and identity (Natter and Jones 1997). In particular, through a study of spatial representations, social geographers have suggested that social identities are constituted in and through the organization of spaces and representations. Put simply, space and identity are relationally constructed: identities are geographic in that they are constructed in and through particular spaces. As an example, our identities as students and teachers are constituted in relation to the spaces of universities and classrooms. Feminist geographers thus analyzed how spaces and identities are gendered, suggesting that there was nothing essential to the identities "women" and "men." More than this, though, social geographers have also suggested that space and identity are performances (Del Casino and Hanna 2000). As a performance, there is no inherent or essential characteristic to either space or identity. Instead, spatial identities are constructed through the varying ways of knowing the world (i.e. through one's epistemological lens). Individuals thus perform their identities in ways that reinforce certain spaces as "straight" or "gay," "colonial" or "postcolonial," for example. These performances of identity and space are translated through the social production of various spatial representations of the city and the country, the rural and the urban, the developed and the developing, for example. In fact, this line of argument suggests that performances of social identities can only be understood through interpretations of the relationships between space and representation (Del Casino and Hanna 2005).

As social geographers became more concerned with questions of the relationships between space and identity, they also turned their focus toward the study of identity politics. In particular, social geographers, with a concern for challenging the presumptions of various social norms – heterosexuality (Valentine 1993; Hubbard 2000), whiteness (Bonnett 1997; Dwyer and Jones 2000; Gallaher 2003), cultural practices, and globalization (Herod et al. 1998; Blunt and McEwan 2002; Binnie 2004) – engaged the highly problematic ways in which certain forms of power sutured certain spaces and identities together. Thus, while there is nothing essential to certain spaces that are deemed appropriate for white western tourists, in the non-western world certain spaces are structured as natural sites for the practices of tourism for particular peoples who occupy specific social identity positions. In the context of this new theorization of the hegemonic construction of spatialized identities, social geographers also conceptualized counterhegemonic and resistant geographies (Nelson 2006). At one level, this resistance exists in the constitution of "alternative" spaces, such as gay neighborhoods, collective and cooperative local economic organ-izations, or African-American or Native-American community organizations. At another level, spaces, and their apparently reified identities, are constantly being challenged through mundane acts and practices as individuals and groups trans-gress the so-called boundaries of, for example, capitalist space. As Gibson-Graham (2006) has suggested, social relations developed through gift economies and other forms of noncapitalist social production and reproduction subvert an apparently ubiquitous capitalist space economy.

Some geographers, however, have become concerned that a social geography based purely in the realm of identity fails to capture the complexity of human experiences: it focuses too much on the area of representation and difference, while relinquishing concerns for inequality (Gregson 2003). As a corrective, some feminist, health, queer, psychoanalytic, and postcolonial geographers have turned their atten-tion toward the study of subjectivity and the "body" (Longhurst 2001; Moss and Dyck 2002). Subjectivities are defined by the intimate relationship among the social and material body, other subjects, and broader ideological processes (Probyn 2003). Subject positions or subjectivities are "formed" through these relationships, which are themselves deeply engrained in the spaces in which and through which people live. In the words of Pile and Thrift (1997: 4), "the body or the self becomes a location within various power-riddled discursive positions, but where the body or the self is not a passive medium on which cultural meanings are merely inscribed." Subjectivities thus form in relation to the spaces people inhabit, including their own bodies. Again, as Pile and Thrift suggest, "Institutional practices such as the madhouse, prisons, schools and universities, rather than containing particular sub-ject positions create them: prisons create prisoners, universities create students. Prisoners and students are inconceivable outside the institutions that give them mean-ing" (ibid.). The move from identity to subjectivity suggests that social geographers investigate the materialities of individuals' everyday geographies. Perhaps over-simplistic in its interpretation, identity theory has been, to date, dominated by a concern for the field of representation and identity politics, whereas questions of subjectivity remain concerned with the realm of bodily, or corporeal, experience. It is not uncommon to find scholars who use identity and subjectivity in quite inter-changeable ways. But as social geographers have recently argued, it is important to further investigate how the formation of "the subject" is a process made real through the embodied practices of day-to-day activities, such as cooking, cleaning, eating, working, etc. (see Probyn 2003). Turning their attention toward questions of sub-jectivity, social geographers want to investigate not a singular and coherent subject but a subject that is constantly changing. After all, people draw from and work through so many different subject positions – class, race, gender, sexuality, ability – and spaces – schools, hospitals, neighborhoods, nations – in their everyday lives.

Scene 3: Rematerializing and reclaiming social geography

The turn toward more "embodied" social geographies has raised questions about the potentially problematic relationship between cultural geography, as the study of cultural representations and representational practices, and social geography, as the study of social inequalities and differences. As Gregson (2003: 54) has argued, it is necessary to have a "transparent debate within social and cultural geography." For Gregson, and others, the focus on individual bodily experiences has meant that social geographers have given less attention to broader social differences and inequalities. In light of these challenges, Gregson suggests social geographers need to examine "three issues":

> (1) what we mean by "the social", and – perhaps even more importantly – how this connects with and to society and societal reproduction and, therefore with economy and polity as well as culture; (2) what vision/s of society we have – for example, whether this is (still) about commitments to ameliorate and/or eradicate inequalities through redistribution, or is based on equality of opportunity – and whether these (still) construe themselves as broadly left; and (3) the role we attach to "the academic" – simply commentator or critic.

Extending this further, Gregson has also suggested that social geographers have become intensely focused on individual experience while leaving behind the core tenets of the subdiscipline's concern for social injustice and inequality. "This bodily (social) is predominantly represented as located within the 'scales' inhabited by individual bodies, notably homes and neighborhoods. This is very different from definitions of 'the social' that privilege other geographical scales, for instance nation-states or (western) cities, or indeed from readings of the body that connect to governance, regulation and citizenship" (ibid.: 43). As she also suggests, "there is a clear case to be made for reclaiming a 'social' that relates directly to the materiality of social life, specifically to the conditions of its organization and reproduction" (ibid.: 43). In shifting the debate away from bodies and experiences toward other "scales" of analysis, such as the nation-state, Gregson is concerned that social geography's ongoing focus on inequalities continues to be marginalized from the larger agenda of an "engaged" social geography.

More than this, even, is the fact that social geography provides an important entry point into questions of how social exclusion, inclusion, and marginalization operate spatially (Sibley 1995) and how spaces can be both "enabling" and "disabling" (Jackson 2003). Social geography is thus a subdiscipline that has dedicated itself over time to examining "inequality and its regulation" (Gregson 2003: 48), while also "revealing and challenging injustice" (Pain 2003: 650). That said, there is no doubt that cultural geographic theorizing has challenged the "integrity" of social geography. But the robust theorization that has developed over the past twenty years or so has enabled a more dynamic social geography, one that is capable of transgressing theoretical and methodological boundaries within subdisciplines and between geography and other social sciences and humanities-based scholarship.

Not to oversimplify a very complex story with a much longer historical trajectory, but social geography – despite warnings of its demise (Gregson 1993; Valentine 2001) – is now practiced across the discipline of geography (Del Casino and Marston 2006). In some cases, social geographers work in close theoretical connection to cultural geographers, investigating how the social is culturally constructed through languages, discourses, and representations, while others continue to consider how to examine difference and inequality as material constructs. Many do both simultaneously. Some scholars complicate traditional subdisciplinary boundaries further by focusing on empirical subjects, such as ability/disability, which work across any number of intellectual axes – feminist, political, social, and cultural, for example (Gleeson 1999). And social geographers have begun to challenge the efficacy of working with one particular theoretical or methodological approach, becoming much more serious about "mixing" approaches to answer complicated social geographic questions (Brown et al. 2005). A core of social geographers simply "remained behind," working through what social geography could and should be as it evolved in relation to this emergent cultural geographic dominance (see discussion by Peach 2000, 2002). While some social geographers continue to invest themselves, therefore, in spatial scientific approaches and practices, they continue to reconsider the use of new technological advances in geography as they work through their research interests related to the geographies of difference and inequality. Over the course of the past twenty years, many new social geographic analyses were developed, focusing on the body and embodied experience of social differences and inequalities, for example (Parr and Butler 1999; Moss and Dyck 2002). Others rearticulated social geography's commitment to questions of justice and equality, and invested their energies in the importance of social action research (Pain 2003, 2004, 2006). For these latter researchers, a growing concern emerged that cultural geography was becoming so focused on discourse and language that it had lost sight of the materialities of difference and inequality that constitute so many daily geographies (England 2006; cited in Del Casino and Marston 2006).

The debates about the relationship between cultural and social geography are not likely to be completely resolved any time soon. It is thus in the best interest of social geographers to continue to move forward, creatively constructing their own social geographies. They must do this, however, with the strict caveat in mind that social geography and its story is never complete. This text and project is therefore about opening up possibilities and not about closing down difference by fixing the boundaries of what is considered social geography. In this way, this text follows the tradition that cultural geographers have established to complicate the very partial nature of any category, be it social geography or cultural geography.

Epilogue: Post-Human Social Geographies?

As we have witnessed, the central questions of social geography have evolved and changed, with some theories holding a more dominant position than others in different times and spaces. At this point, however, it is clear that there is no one social geographic perspective. In fact, social geographers continue to trace their social geographies in and through any number of questions that intersect with other critical objects of analysis in geography more generally, including "nature," "economy," "politics," and "culture." In some ways, the "core" of social geography has remained focused on "the social" and how that social is constructed in and through societies. In recent years, though, questions about the integrity and naturalness of the concept of society have also been called into question (Urry 2000). In place of a fixed notion of society comes a new conceptual toolkit and vocabulary, including concepts such as networks and networked relations as well as globalization and globalizing processes (e.g. following Castells 2000), as well as concepts such as mobility (Cresswell 1996), nomads (Deleuze and Guattari 1987), and hybridity (Whatmore 2002). These new theoretical languages enable geographers to conceptualize societies not as singular points in time and space but, instead, as intertwined through larger processes and practices that exceed their boundaries. In some cases, people have argued that a rather monotonous global society through the process of McDonaldization is emerging. In other cases, scholars argue that the rapidity of these global processes has created "dystopias" and exacerbated differences, increasing tension across and through human boundaries.

Despite all the contestation and complexity, for the most part social geographers have remained interested in the "human" and the organization and construction of inequality and difference within and across human societies. Recently, however, the integrity of "the human" and thus "the social" has come under increasing pressure within the confines of sociological theory. As John Urry explains:

> it is *inhuman* objects that reconstitute social relations. Such relations are made and remade through machines, technologies, objects, texts, images, physical environments and so on. Human powers increasingly derive from the complex *interconnections* of human with material objects, including signs, machines, technologies, texts, physical environments, animals, plants, and waste products. People possess few powers which are uniquely human, while most can only be realized because of their connections with these inhuman components. The following inhuman developments are novel in their ontological depth and transformative powers: the miniaturization of electronic technologies into which humans are in various ways "plugged in" and which will inhabit most work and domestic environments; the transformation of biology into genetically coded information; the increasing scale and range of intensely mobile waste products and viruses; the hugely enhanced capacities to stimulate nature and culture; changing technologies which facilitate instantaneously rapid corporeal mobility; and informational and communicational flows which dramatically compress distances of time and space between people, corporations, and states (Urry 2000: 14, original emphasis).

Social geographers have seized on this moment of uncertainty, pushing the boundaries of what have typically been seen as the dichotomies of, for example, "the social" and "the natural," "society" and "nature." In some cases, social geographers are drawing from a very broad field called actor-network theory (ANT), which suggests that the so-called immaterial or nonhuman "are [identical to human] actors who bundle multiple intentions and act in ways that complement and extend humans" (Harvey 2001: 30; cited in Del Casino and Hanna 2005: 41). In this way, the "social" is not bound up in the "human," for human societies have never been and can never be distinctively "set off from" the various nonhuman actors present in our worlds (Braun 2004a). This concern has prompted a number of ethical questions pertaining to the relationships humans have with the so-called nonhuman. With this in mind, social geographers have engaged in debate and discussion about the relationship between animals and humans as well as "animals' role in the social construction of culture and individual human subjects" (Wolch et al. 2003: 188). This work suggests that the distinctions between animals and humans are at best artificial and are at most partial (also see the extended discussion in Wolch and Emel 1998).

The turn toward studies that break down the "human" in human geography thus questions the integrity of social geography. Moreover, these concerns have opened up new possibilities and horizons, or "lines of flight" (Deleuze and Guattari 1987), through which to explore "the social" and "the spatial." Importantly, though, it suggests that social geographers must continue to think outside the boundaries of what has historically constituted their social geographies if they are to even begin to scratch the surface of what mediates the society–space relationship. As George Henderson (cited in Del Casino and Marston 2006: 1004) suggested when asked what he thought constituted social geography:

> A little while ago, I might have been tempted to say: everything. That is, if we take notions of social constructionism, situated knowledges, and so on, seriously. But I am intrigued by work in the posthuman vein of late. I think it's becoming harder to sustain the very idea of "social geography." The notion of human–non-human assemblages exerts a powerful pull and I'm keen to see what becomes of it. At any rate, it does pose a huge challenge to the notion of the social that ought be taken seriously.

While the question of human–nonhuman assemblages will not monopolize this entire text, these new theories can help to address some of the other questions asked throughout this volume. In particular, we have to be sensitive to the fact that social geography tends to be human-centric. There is much value, then, in thinking through the possibilities that new theories of so-called human–nonhuman relations may articulate new ways of doing social geography. At the same time, social geography's general commitment to questions of difference and inequality reflect a larger set of concerns that already suggest that social geographers consider the nonhuman – the built environment, economic resources, health care products, and other consumptive goods – in their study of the everyday sociospatial organization of the world in and through which they all live, even if they do not always theorize nonhuman subjectivities in the same way in their social geographic studies.

Notes

1   Entrikin (1980) also discusses the difference between ecology and geography prior to geography's own "scientific revolution."
2   Scholarly debate about "working class studies" remains important today (e.g. Stenning 2008).
3   This work also challenged the notion that biological sex was a natural category for the basis of gender. The turn toward a social constructionist approach to the geographies of roles suggests that gender is a contested and historical category, which has no basis in an essential male/female sexual distinction (i.e. biological sex does not equate to a specific set of roles).

Chapter 3

Thinking Methodologically

■ A Social Geographer Walks into a Bar . . .
■ Theory–Methodology–Method
■ Asking Social Geographic Questions and Answering Them
   ■ Quantitative methodologies: induction/deduction
   ■ Qualitative methodologies: inside/outside
   ■ Across the divide: the challenge of mixed methodologies
   ■ From research to action through participation
■ Ready, Set, Go! "Doing" Social Geography

A Social Geographer Walks into a Bar . . .

One says, "Ouch!"[1] Another says, "Who built this bar in a low income neighborhood!" Another still says, "Who decided it was a bar in the first place? And, why do only straight people go in it?" It should be no surprise to any of us that depending on your theoretical and methodological assumptions, a space, such as a bar, might elicit different questions. A radical feminist geographer might want to investigate the subjective experience of patriarchy developed through the social relationships of the bar. Through observations and informal and formal interviews, a story of how the broader structures of patriarchy impinge on the social interactions that take place in this space may begin to develop. A spatial scientist might be interested in quantifying the bar's population by ethnicity, tracking from where in the city patrons had traveled to come to this particular place. Emerging from this approach could be a model of the spatial behavior of bar patrons, which might lead to a theory about the relationship between a bar's appeal and its distance from certain parts (and people) of the city. A poststructuralist social geographer might see the bar as a representational space through which certain spatialized rules and regulations about how one might perform his or her identity temporarily structure social interactions. In so doing, a qualitative study of the bar might demonstrate how people perform their identities (e.g. masculine/feminine/transgendered, straight/gay/bisexual, old/young) as they move through this space and interact with others.

In all three cases, these social geographers are interested in questions about how this particular space is organized, albeit in very different ways. Despite these differences, these scholars are going to have to make decisions critical to their research project if they are going to move forward. They are going to have to frame their research questions or hypotheses, determine what they consider as data, and articulate how they will go about collecting the data. This decision-making process is what is meant by the term methodology (Harding 1987). Put simply, methodology is a moment of translation, when the researcher *applies* his or her epistemological and ontological assumptions to the research question, concern, or problem. It is a mesolevel theoretical process that informs the choice of technique or method; these methodological decisions happen before the collection, categorization, description, or analysis of any data. It is thus necessary to investigate further the relationship between theory and method, asking how this relationship is translated through social geography's various methodological frameworks.

Theory–Methodology–Method

Theory does little good if someone cannot figure out how it helps them to frame their questions about the geographies of inequality and difference. It is also not very useful to simply develop skills in particular research techniques without understanding why and how to ask research questions. It is here, then, that researchers must turn to a discussion of methodology because:

> Methodology requires the translation of epistemological and ontological precepts and assumptions into "data" that can be analyzed. Stages in methodology include the definition and selection of objects of analysis, the conceptualization of appropriate data, and the formulation of research questions. It also involves assessments of reliability, validity, reflexivity, and research ethics (Del Casino et al. 2000: 253).

I want to suggest that there are at least four broad theories of space that social geographers commonly use when constructing their research questions, their understanding of geographic data, and how they conceptualize the relationship between themselves and those they claim to be "studying" or "working with." These four theories of space are further complicated by a social geographer's theoretical-political position, which can vary today from *post-positivist* to *critical race theorist* to *feminist* to *Marxist* to *queer* to *postcolonial theorist*. In reality, as social geographers practice their craft they tend to draw differently and differentially from these various theoretical positions, giving more weight to certain positions over others. And, these choices may or may not be related to their own personal experiences or their experiences in the field. In tracing these differences in methodology, it is healthy to be wary of privileging certain approaches over others. Each approach has both advantages and limitations, and as we will see below, many social geographers are becoming increasingly interested in using different theories of space as they mix methodologies, choosing to combine various theories and approaches to address complicated issues related to sociospatial inequalities or differences.

In Table 3.1, I briefly trace out these different approaches to space, highlighting the key concepts that each framework utilizes as well as the questions that relate to the varying concerns of social geographers. As we can see, a spatial scientific view of space frames social geographic questions around the notion of how social variables – related to categories of race, ethnicity, gender, sexuality, class – vary across space, creating patterns of inequality and difference. Spatial scientists also investigate social interactions across space, often quantifying interactions as well as social exchange and diffusion, while also tracing how social networks evolve over time and space. These distributional and diffusion-based analyses shed light on the spatial extensiveness and intensity of social activity, on the relationship between a society and its external environments, and on the spatial aspects of inter- and intrasociety exchanges. The methods employed by these geographers are often quantitative and cartographic, and they use statistical and geospatial techniques, such as geographic information systems (GIS), to analyze how and why certain social patterns have developed as well as the relationship between those patterns and other economic, political, or, even, cultural processes. Critical to the assumptions of spatial scientists is the notion that the world can be evaluated through an objective and distanced approach, and they have historically maintained a distinct boundary between the researcher and the researched. In fact, for spatial scientists their objectivity is a "tool" that can be wielded powerfully in their attempts to both trace inequalities and challenge what they believe are the underlying causes of that inequality.

When utilizing a humanistic view of space, social geography is concerned with how social spaces or places are invested with social meaning. Humanistic geographers focus their attention on the spatial meanings that circulate in and through places, asking how these circulations of meaning inform understandings of "the self" as a social being. Importantly, then, a humanistic view sees space as a result of human agency. Such analyses examine how social actors interpret and generate meanings of their place in the world, and how they might further "implant" these interpretations and meanings into the diverse settings of their social action. Typical of such analyses are empirically grounded studies of some "fundamental" geographical concepts, such as nature-culture, lived-space, place embeddedness, and conceived, perceived, and sensory space. Historically, humanistic geographers used historical archival techniques, interpretive methods, or other qualitative approaches, including ethnography and interviews, to "tease out" how social meanings of place emerge and develop in and across space. Methodologically, the key to humanistic research

Table 3.1 Social geography's methodological approaches

Theories of space	Methodological assumptions	Exemplary methodological questions	Researcher/researched relationship	Exemplary data, methods, and analytic approach
Spatial scientific ("mapping spatial relations")	■ Space is viewed as an objective container in which places (areas) exist as independent units with distinct and measurable attributes ■ Places (*i*) are specific sites that can be measured as nodes in space with spatial (*X*, *Y*), temporal (*T*) coordinates, as well as place-specific organizational characteristics ($Z_1, Z_2, Z_3 \ldots$) ■ Interactions (*U*) between places are measurable and quantifiable ■ Agents' (*j*) behaviors can be explained in terms of place-specific attributes ($X, Y, T, U, Z_1, Z_2, Z_3 \ldots$)	■ What are the distributions and interactions over space of social groups, resources, and activities? ■ How are societies spatially arranged in relation to different scales, from the local and regional levels to the international? ■ How do the above geographies affect the behaviors of, and resources available to, different social actors within the different places? ■ How do individual social actors cognitively map the internal and external dynamics of the spatial world around them?	■ Subjective impulses are controlled in favor of objective forms of research analysis and presentation ■ Researcher maintains a "distance" between subject and object	*Data* ■ Census (race, income, ethnicity, etc.) ■ Regional social indicator data (e.g. Human Development Index) ■ Likert scale questions *Method* ■ Hypothesis testing ■ Data mining ■ Structured survey/interview analysis *Analytic approach* ■ Factorial ecology/social area analysis ■ Mutlivariate statistics ■ Cartography and GIS
Humanistic ("interpreting spaces of meaning")	■ Space is constructed into particular places that are constituted by their own unique characteristics and "senses" ■ Place, not space, is the site for the production of the "life world" ■ Place is understood through the production of representations that mediate between an individual's "feelings" and "experiences" of "landscapes" and "cultures" ■ A "sense of place" changes over time and historical markers are left on the landscape representing specific feelings and experiences about place	■ How do different "senses of place" emerge in societies? ■ How do social actors differently interpret these "senses of place," and how do they affect their daily activities and the society's longer-term evolution? ■ How have places evolved over time and what mark has this left on the landscape? ■ How can we reconstruct past sociospatial dynamics through a rigorous examination of their relic landscapes? ■ In what ways have changing societal politics inhibited or promoted a sense of "placelessness" among particular peoples in the world?	Researcher rejects notion of "objectivity" and focuses on the subjective experiences of individual actors and the ways in which those experiences are constructed in relation to particular "senses of place"	*Data* ■ Archival material (e.g. diaries, government documents, local histories) ■ Landscapes/places ■ Place histories ■ Individual life stories and experiences *Method* ■ Ethnography ■ Participant observation ■ Historical textual analysis ■ Structured and unstructured interviews *Analytic approach* ■ Evaluate representations and meaning ■ Interpretation and thick description of social difference

	Conceptualization of space	Research questions	Role of researcher	Data / Method / Analytic approach
Radical ("analyzing the sociospatial dialectic")	■ Space is produced by and productive of social relations through the interactions of mediating structures ■ Space and society are dialectically related ■ Particular places are contextually mediated by broader spatial relations and social structures ■ Spatial and social structures and the production of places as well as the social actors existing in place are embedded in sociohistorical contexts ■ Spatial structures mediate the actions of social actors, creating distinct categories of social actors existing "in" and "out" of place	■ How are different spaces linked, mediated, and transformed through the macrolevel social organizations and in relation to superstructural social relations of capital? ■ How does the locally varying spatial organization of society differentially affect the internal structure and external relations of the social spaces (and how does this process differ for similar social groups and communities in different places)? ■ How is space both a resource and a constraint to actors embedded in various social settings, and how do local spaces, in turn, structure sociospatial relations through the production of different objects and events? ■ How does the social and spatial structuring of society relations mediate gender relations?	■ Researcher and research subject are both embedded in larger social and spatial structures, and thus the research findings are contingent on these structures and must be taken into account ■ Researcher and research subject can both challenge and reproduce structures of social relations	*Data* ■ Archival material ■ Regional and national socioeconomic indicators ■ Ethnographic material ■ Interactive problem assessment *Method* ■ Ethnography ■ Participant observation ■ Structured and unstructured interviews ■ Descriptive statistics ■ Participatory action research *Analytic approach* ■ Historical analysis of social change and inequality ■ Deep reading of structural dynamics and impact on place ■ Unpacking mechanisms of sociospatial inequality
Poststructural ("deconstructing space")	■ Space is conceptualized as constituted through flows of social relations that create temporary meanings in particular places ■ The social construction of space through discourses of power is considered key in understanding the production of identities and the performances of subjects ■ Spaces are intertextually and contextually linked to the wider operation of social power flowing through places ■ Politics temporarily produce "place-based" identities	■ What are the spatial imaginaries at work in social communities and groups, and how are these propagated beyond their "borders"? ■ What are the contestations over meanings produced in societies, and to what extent do they influence its spatial activism? ■ How are spatial knowledges and their conformative practices reproduced through the society's discursive regulation of rights, rules, and responsibilities? ■ How, in turn, do these spatial epistemologies within societies themselves become imposed upon and enacted in social space more generally? ■ How do societies spatially mark socially constructed identities?	■ Researcher eschews total knowledge, understanding that her/his interpretations are "views from somewhere" and, therefore, not whole, definitive, or final ■ Reflexivity includes a monitoring of the researcher's positions with respect to other organizations, such as the university, of which she/he is a part	*Data* ■ Visual representations of space ■ Textual data ■ Spatial practices and performances *Method* ■ Textual and visual interpretation and deconstruction ■ Discourse analysis ■ Ethnography ■ Participant observation ■ Unstructured/open-ended interviews *Analytic approach* ■ Archaeology/genealogy ■ Deconstruction ■ Discourse analysis ■ Critical theory

is the interpretation of subjective experience; it is much less interested in maintaining the distinction between researcher and researched. At the same time, while they are interested in tracing broader human connections and "senses of place," humanistic geographers also want to interrogate how social spaces are organized to create the effects of being "in place" and "out of place." Tracing, historically, how certain "senses of place" create exclusionary practices allows humanistic geographers to ask questions about the history of geographic meanings, which are used differently across space and in various places.

In some ways, the development of radical views of space in social geography "split the difference" between spatial scientific and humanistic approaches. Radical geographers begin with the assumption that the world is organized through larger processes that link places together in broader webs of sociospatial relations; they are concerned with the view that space and society cannot be arbitrarily pulled apart. As such, radical geographers are particularly concerned with how social relations produce and are produced by spatial structures. In this dialectical view of space, human agency is, to various degrees, regulated through social spaces or spatialities (see Figure 3.1). Radical geographers, then, tend to investigate how the broader structural processes of capitalism, patriarchy, racism, or heterosexism, for example, structure space to reinforce differences and inequalities, including access to needed resources. Like the spatial scientist, radical geographers are interested in the interconnections between places. In contrast, though, radical geographers see these interconnections as woven into everyday life: space is both a constraint and a resource as individuals, communities, and social groups struggle for access to societal services. These methodological concerns are translated into studies that focus more specifically on data that can be "unpacked," demonstrating the connections between, say, the flows of international capital and uneven development on the ground. Radical geographers might employ descriptive statistics, providing context for their larger argument about how resources are spatially distributed, while also involving themselves in action projects that overtly try to subvert and change systems of unequal relations of power. In similar ways to humanistic geographers, radical geographers tend to favor subjective research approaches over objective ones, although they are much more likely to draw from so-called objective descriptive statistics as they seek to explain the spatial organization of inequality in difference. In a different way from both humanistic and spatial scientific geographies, though, radical geographers focus on social change and therefore engage in projects that are overtly intended to reorganize the relations of space to advantage certain marginal peoples and groups over others.

A poststructuralist view of space tends to eschew theories of deep societal structures, focusing attention, instead, on the realm of spatial representations. Put simply, space is a social construction. As such, poststructuralists methodologically shift their questions and concerns toward how spaces are socially constructed to maintain relations of power and difference, while also examining how spaces serve as sites of resistance to authority and inequality. Social geographers that take a poststructuralist view of space will tend to methodologically focus on questions related

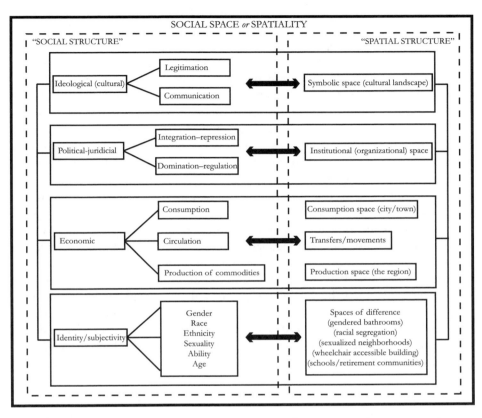

SOCIAL SPACE *or* SPATIALITY

"SOCIAL STRUCTURE"   "SPATIAL STRUCTURE"

Ideological (cultural) — Legitimation / Communication ⟷ Symbolic space (cultural landscape)

Political-juridicial — Integration–repression / Domination–regulation ⟷ Institutional (organizational) space

Economic — Consumption / Circulation / Production of commodities ⟷ Consumption space (city/town) / Transfers/movements / Production space (the region)

Identity/subjectivity — Gender / Race / Ethnicity / Sexuality / Ability / Age ⟷ Spaces of difference (gendered bathrooms) (racial segregation) (sexualized neighborhoods) (wheelchair accessible building) (schools/retirement communities)

Figure 3.1   A model of social space or "spatiality." This figure expands on the original, adding a "box" on identity/subjectivity. It also expands on the original by adding arrows that illustrate the dialectical nature of the social structure–spatial structure relationship. Spatiality, a term used to represent the entangled notion of social structure and spatial structure, is a way for social geographers to "escape" the society–space binary, illustrating a fully social space and spatial society. (Adapted from Gregory 2000: 781, reprinted with permission.)

to the construction of spatial identities and subjectivities. Like other geographers, poststructuralists are interested in sociospatial networks and flows of power but they investigate those flows through the study of representations. Because poststructuralist space is also thought of as produced through differences, poststructuralists are interested in the hybridity of space and identity as well as how spaces are always "more than" what they are claimed to be by various spatial representations.[2] A social constructionist view suggests that knowledge of the world is, at best, partial and that "the subject" is always situated somewhere. In constructing studies of space and spatial relations poststructuralists must always reflexively consider their own position and its impact on the research context.

Each view of space in Table 3.1 can be interpreted, modified, and/or challenged depending on the theoretical position – e.g. positivist, feminist, psychoanalytic, or postcolonial – of the social geographer. In fact, these "views of space" are not antecedents to the theoretical positions of social geographers but are actually wrapped up in them. As we traced out in Chapter 2, what is considered post-structuralist space would not likely have developed had social geographers not begun to engage with feminist, queer, or psychoanalytic theories of the relationships between society and space. Importantly, certain positions tend to favor certain views of space more than others. So social geographers whose primary influence is post-colonialism or critical race theory tend to favor radical or poststructuralist views of space. That said, this does not mean that feminist, Marxist, or queer social geo-graphers cannot and do not also use spatial scientific views of space. We can find numerous examples of how feminists have employed cartographic or other spatial analytic tools to illustrate how the organization of resources disadvantages women, while finding Marxist studies of inequality that rely heavily on both descriptive and inferential statistical approaches, showing relationships through the use of quanti-tative data about social areas. I think this marks an important moment for critical social geography: it may be possible to "go beyond" the original intent of one view of space or another and see how space is a multifaceted and complex process best examined through a number of different geographic questions about social difference and inequality. In the next section, we trace the differences in how social geogra-phers employ their methodological approaches and ask social geographic questions.

Asking Social Geographic Questions and Answering Them

Table 3.1 includes a sketch of a number of "exemplary methodological questions" based in the differing views of space in social geography. The questions asked, which are themselves tied to different views of space, inform what types of data will be collected, what methods or techniques will be used, and how to go about analyzing what has been collected. In the remainder of this chapter, I want to focus on the last column in the table and discuss how social geographers conceptualize data, methods, and analyses. There is no way to trace the diversity of methods and techniques social geographers use on a day-to-day basis. But we can begin to "scratch the surface" and understand what social geographers can and cannot accomplish when they choose one set of methodologies over another. In particular, this chapter examines how theoretical assumptions inform what a social geographer under-stands as data, method, and analysis when using one of four broad methodological approaches. These include: (a) quantitative methodologies; (b) qualitative methodo-logies; (c) mixed methodologies; and (d) participatory action research methodologies. Importantly, we must keep in mind that there is overlap in any categorical set of designations and this can be confusing. For example, quantitative researchers can collect and use qualitative data, while participatory action research scholars can use mixed methodologies. And many of these methodological approaches cut across the theories of space and theoretical positions of social geographers. Again, it is not outside the realm of possibility to have a feminist quantitative methodology or a Marxist participatory action research project. In the end, in "doing" social geography, any researcher is going to have to make choices. These choices will involve what questions they want to answer and what data and approach will best help them answer that question. In this way, the very process of methodology is a critical one, where social geographers begin to invest and commit themselves to a set of theoretical assumptions that help inform how they will analyze geographies of difference and inequality.

Quantitative methodologies: induction/deduction

For many of us, when we first enter university we think of "science" and the "scientific method." In this method, we often begin with a hypothesis that we then test to see if we can either prove or disprove our initial assumptions. On the surface, the scientific method is simple enough, with a number of key presumptions about how to "go about" doing science. First, this model of research assumes that we can explain certain aspects of the world and build models that generalize how the world "works." Second, it suggests that the world is ordered and operates under these laws. Third, the scientist, as an objective observer, can provide a distanced analysis of the generalizable characteristics of the world. And, fourth, for a model to be "true," it must be repeatable and thus verifiable under similar conditions. In seeking laws about the social world, social geographers began by borrowing theories from other disciplines, such as economics, and started to apply them to this new spatial science. Initially, many of these approaches were "deductive," organized from the top down using an empirical method to test if a hypothesis was true or false (Harvey 1969). Deductive geographies are based in the notion that there are spatial models and laws that are testable and verifiable through empirical investigation. Other geographers have argued that it is better to work from an inductive research position (Berry 1971): we start from the position of experience (i.e. the study of social phenomena), working from the ground up to discover trends and processes.

In the context of geography, numerous scholars have considered the value of both deductive and inductive scientific inquiry (see Figure 3.2). David Harvey (1969) in his often-cited *Explanation in Geography* argued that geographic analysis is best framed within a hypothetical-deductive model where the geographer posits a model and through a process of experimental tests and verifications determines the validity of the model. Other geographers, including Brian Berry (1964), proposed an inductive approach to geographic inquiry (see Figure 3.3). Berry developed "a geographic matrix, a conceptual device that carved up absolute space enabling researchers to theorize variations across any conceivable spatial unit. Berry's conceptualization helped underwrite countless studies of spatial variation, wherein

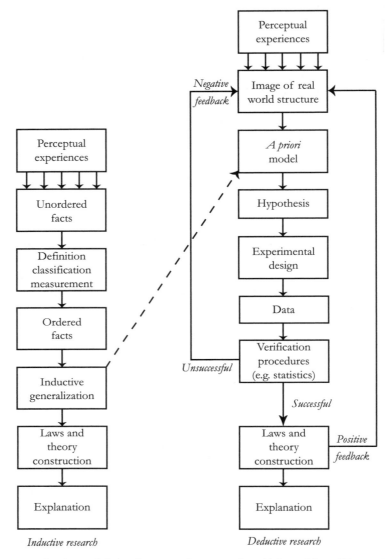

Figure 3.2 Inductive and deductive research approaches. (Adapted from Harvey 1969: 34.)

researchers measured, described, and (usually statistically) explained magnitudes or proportions of natural or social variables by reference to measures of other variables taken on the same spatial units" (Del Casino and Jones 2007: 236).

Social geographers have worked both deductively and inductively in examining questions of social geographic inequalities and differences. At the core, there are certain basic key objects that are investigated within a quantitative social geography. Although written in the 1970s, Ray Pahl's outline of the core tenets of a spatial scientific social geography still holds today. To begin:

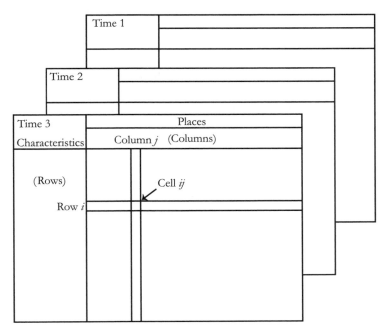

Figure 3.3 Berry's geographic matrix with an added "third dimension" (time). In the matrix each place "*j*" is assigned a geographic fact or attribute "*i*." The "geographic fact" is defined by some type of indicator, such as ethnicity or race, housing stock, or economic status. (Adapted from Berry 1964: 26–7.)

> The prime geographical factor is *distance*, whether actual physical distance or economic distance measured in time-cost terms. One might also add that "social distance" is also of interest to a social geographer. It appears that there is some indication that social mobility and geographical mobility are related and thus, in a society in which certain sections are able to move up a promotional ladder with differential economic rewards, there are strong pressures for these economic differences to be reflected in social differences (Pahl 1970: 95–6, original emphasis).

Relying on one of the core concepts in social geography, that of spatial difference, Pahl suggests that the economic and the social – i.e. the economic organization of class and the social implications of class – are related. He also grounds social geography in the study of distance, although that distance is quite differential; it is physical (measured in miles or kilometers), it is economic (measured in terms of cost), and it is social (measured in the immaterial limits imposed by, for example, class). Pahl continues:

> The social geographer is thus interested in the broad changes of *population structure and distribution* as the very necessary first stage in his [*sic*] analysis. From the basic demographic aspect, the analysis might proceed to such aspects as the geography of

mortality rates, religion or occupational groups. The binding framework of settlement pattern, whether of villages, towns, cities or metropolitan regions, can be analyzed within a particular socio-cultural background (ibid., emphasis added).

Second, then, social geographers concentrate their attention on the distributions of social groupings in and across space, and their relationships to the built environment. This view of what is "social" evacuates other objects, such as nature, from the picture of social geography; Pahl works within a growing systematic scientific geography that cleaves apart different geographic aspects for study. In his case, the focus is the social aspects of life. In concluding, Pahl argues:

> The mobility of socially defined groups is of fundamental interest, as is the changing function and nature of communities as their physical and social space relationship change. Naturally the social geographer is concerned with the *social* aspects of changing space use and is thus likely to have some training in and understanding of sociology (ibid., original emphasis).

Turning their attention to the "mobility of socially defined groups," social geographers can and should also study the "social aspects of changing space." Pahl recognizes the dangers of creating a "science" of social geography embedded in an approach that seeks generalizability, however. "Clearly if the study of one local community is taken as the means of gaining an imaginative insight into social geography," he suggests, "there is a danger of assuming that the patterns and processes which emerge and operate in one particular society will necessarily hold true for another" (ibid.: 98). The significance of local context becomes even more important for social geographers, such as Pahl, because of the contingencies that are always part of any place. In taking those contingencies into account, however, social geographers may be able to engage in important policy debates at the local level and construct methodologies, if not general spatial laws, that may be transferable across space.

In sum, Pahl argues that social geography is concerned with some broad conceptual language and tools, such as distance, distribution, and mobility, whose study can be taken to any context and tested for how they apply to a particular social situation. And he introduces (although he is certainly not the first) the notion of a social (immaterial) space as distinct from a physical (material) space. The argument that a social space of ideas, feelings, and meanings exists, and that geographers might study it, suggests that social geographers could (and should) study cognition, behavior, and spatial perception as well (following the work of, for example, Brown et al. 1972). Social spaces might be mutually constituted through social relations, but they are also perceived and experienced, suggesting that models of the social world might have to account for this complex variation; these social geographies could and should study how people mentally map society and their place in it (Gould and White 1974), as well as the patterns of social behavior tied those maps (Golledge and Stimson 1997).

The applications of scientific geographies to social questions and concerns are numerous. In fact, social geographers focus on both broad social patterns and processes at the regional and national scales (Kodras 1997; Finney and Simpson 2008) and the geographies of urban (e.g. Forrest et al. 2006; Goldhaber 2007) and rural environments (Wood 2005). Basing their studies in the examination of location, distribution, and difference, social geographers have employed spatial scientific approaches to the study of both the city and the countryside, mapping social difference and inequality often identified in national census data (Johnston et al. 2003), while also trying to identify general spatial laws and/or relationships that govern the organization of those differences. More than Hoke (1907), these geographers are interested in offering explanations for the patterns they study. And many of these new social geographies have been "tested" in the urban labs of modern cities.

In fact, the work of the Chicago School set the stage for much of this early spatial scientific work, as geographers sought to quantify, measure, and provide explanation for how and why cities were socially and economically differentiated. They did this mainly through the use of what has become known as social-area analysis and factorial ecology. Put simply, social-area analysis focuses

> on the social structure of the city as it is portrayed by different measures of population characteristics (for example, age structure, sex ratios, ethnic backgrounds, mobility rates, and educational levels), economic characteristics (for example, levels and occupations), health and welfare levels and housing quality (for example, proportions of houses in need of repair or age of housing), to mention only the major measures that are usually considered. These measures are obtained for different sub-areas of the city, which are usually census tracts in the case of United States cities, and the aim is to identify those key combinations of the different measures that provide an adequate basis upon which to differentiate the different sub-areas from one another (King and Golledge 1978: 238–9).

Working through the assumption that "urban aggregations are viewed not as unique phenomena, with their own organizing principles, but as components of a wider society" (Timms 1970: 253), social-area analysis in geography "is based on *a priori* reasoning from certain broad postulates concerning the nature of modern urban society" (ibid.: 255). Put simply, as urban economies become more complex and differentiated – moving from primary to secondary and tertiary economic activities, for example – the organization of the population also becomes differentiated. Timms (1970) adapts this model to the changes in the social organization of the city. This model, based in three postulates (or assumptions), leads to the use of certain variables for investigating one's postulates (see Figure 3.4). As Johnston (2000) suggests, however, deductive social-area analysis remained marginal in urban social geography because of the limits of the theory available from which to develop hypotheses.

To that end, urban social geographers have borrowed the methods of factorial ecology, a "purely" inductive approach to scientific inquiry developed in psychology (Timms 1971). When applying this method, one starts from the assumption that

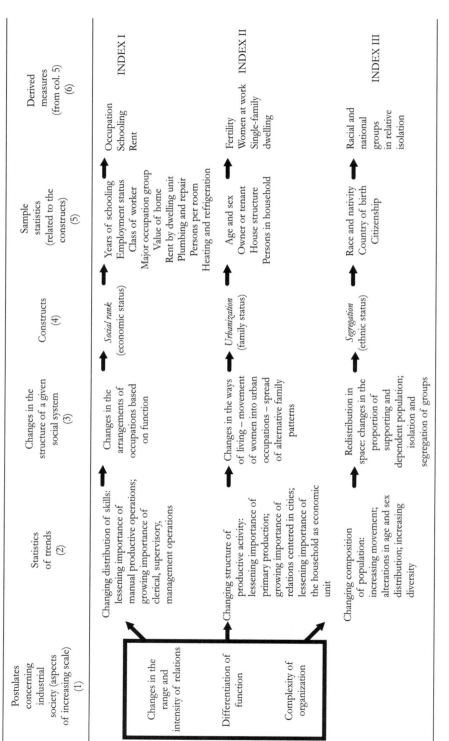

Figure 3.4 Timm's exemplary model for a social area analysis. (Adapted from Timms 1970: 254.)

"meaning in any situation has to be learned rather than posited by aprioristic theory" (Berry 1971: 214). Factorial analysis thus takes "the philosophical stance . . . that all social science concepts are ultimately rooted in the life-world of our social experience, which itself is organized into typical modes by the everyday language we and the social actors we study use, and the perceptual habits we and they have learned" (ibid.: 214–15). The basic assumption underpinning factorial ecology is that while these may be multiple variables (social measures, economic measures, crime statistics, etc.) there are strong relationships between many of these. It is possible to reduce a larger data set – often derived from the census – to two of three common factors, which can then be mapped to illustrate socioeconomic or ethnocultural homogeneity within various areas of the city (King and Golledge 1978).

Johnston (1976), for example, outlines how factorial designs can be employed to explain voting patterns or criminal behavior. Individual behavior in this case is *both* individual and social. Various patterns of voting might be explained by the "neighborhood effects" that include a "bombardment of information" (ibid.: 120) that might influence how one votes. Ecological models, Johnston suggests, might identify causality, helping to determine why and how certain patterns of behavior might emerge in different spaces. Giggs (1973) explores the relationships between the distribution of schizophrenia (a mental health illness) and socioenvironmental and socioeconomic factors in Nottingham, UK. He concludes that this particular mental illness is highly concentrated in poor, inner city "slum" areas. Although he cannot assert any direct causality, his study suggests that there exists a relationship between individual welfare and social structure and mental health, an area of strong interest for social geographers today. This work has given way to a plethora of work on the location of facilities using quantitative analyses (DeVerteuil 2000 gives an excellent summary of this work).

Social geographers also draw from a wide array of other statistical methods to study variations across space. This is particularly the case in the study of the spatial variation in poverty, housing, and disease. Kodras (1984) uses a regression analysis to examine the variability of use in Food Stamp welfare programs in the US (see also Kodras 1986). Starting with a national map of welfare participation, Kodras asks why participation varies spatially from state to state, suggesting that "Because the US welfare systems operates within a spatially complex environment . . . it is conceivable that the political, economic, and social forces affecting welfare participation may demonstrate variable effects from place to place" (Kodras 1986: 67). She uses a regression analysis to test, therefore, "the estimation of the causal relationships between two [or more] variables" (Kitchin and Tate 2000: 129). In Kodras's case, she tests the relationship between Food Stamp variability and economic, political, or social and cultural differences across the national map of the US at the state level. Put simply, is Food Stamp variability impacted by the relationship between "economic need" on the one hand and a "social stigma" to take welfare on the another, for example (Kodras 1986: 130). Ladusingh and Singh (2006) use a similar methodological framework to examine the relationship between child mortality and sociocultural and environmental variables in northeast India. Using a variety of statistics, these researchers demonstrate that local variation in child mortality is related to different sociocultural and educational practices in local communities. Community practice, they argue, "has too frequently been ignored by demographers, social statisticians and population geographers . . . we have shown the importance of community education and community hygiene in reducing the risk of child deaths under 5 years of age, in isolated tribal communities in Northeast India" (ibid.: 74). In this case, then, the local organization of knowledge at the community level directly affects child and infant mortality (death) rates.

Importantly, in all these approaches, the basic unit of analysis is some particular space or ecological unit. This space is conceptualized as discrete, meaning the internal dynamics of any one particular space is largely homogeneous, defined by the dominant factor present in that space. In many cases, particularly in places with detailed census mechanisms such as the US, the ecological unit in question is the census tract. The goal, then, is to build a methodological model that provides a localized but generalizable picture of how space is organized in and through social similarity and difference. Underpinning this methodological approach is a focus on the "the geographical study of social space" (Murdie 1969: 11; cited in Johnston 1986: 41). This space consists of "three ingredients: 1. Formal characteristics, summarised spatially as areas and obtained by mapping socio-economic criteria. 2. Functional characteristics, summarised spatially as points which serve as major foci of social activity. 3. Circulatory characteristics, summarised spatially as lines representing the flows of goods, services, people and ideas and including space perceived by individuals and social groups" (Johnston 1986: 41). In addition, this research tends to work through the concept of aggregation, whereby areas are assumed to be occupied by a relatively homogeneous social group. Thus, in the study of racial segregation it is assumed that all those identified as "Black" on the census have a relatively uniform, similar self-definition of their racial characteristics, although some quantitative social geographers are trying to disaggregate certain racial and ethnic categories to illustrate the social complexity of these terms as they apply to the spatial division of the city (Peach 1999).

Nowhere has the spatial scientific use of quantitative methods perhaps been more pronounced than in the social geographic study of segregation, inequality, and access to services. Beginning with Morrill's (1965, 1973) research on the ghetto and continuing to today (see various summaries of this work by Peach 1999, 2000, 2002), social geographers apply quantitative techniques to investigate the complex patterns of segregation that work across categories of, for example, race and ethnicity (Peach 2000).

In a modern-day context, new geographical technologies, such as geographic information systems (GIS), are being applied by social geographers to the study of the spatial distribution of inequalities and differences (see, for example, select chapters in Goodchild and Janelle 2004). More importantly, it is possible to systematically utilize these approaches to mathematically investigate urban patterns of segregation or a lack of access to certain key resources (e.g. Downey 2003). New technologies give social geographers the ability to do this at a much larger scale, but nonetheless the basic assumptions remain the same: the study of difference and inequality from the perspective of spatial science is to offer description of and explanation for how and why certain sociospatial patterns exist and, perhaps, persist over time (see Box 3.1).

Box 3.1   Social Geography and GIS

Social geographers use geographic information systems (GIS) as a way to organize, analyze, and represent spatial data, patterns, and relationships. Advances in geographic information sciences (GSci) continue to change how social geographers do research based in two key methodological traditions, quantitative spatial analysis and cartographic mapping (Schuurman 2004). For social geographers studying spatial patterns of inequality and difference, GIS tools are valuable for investigating the spatial relationships between social indicators and variables. The census, which includes massive quantities of social data, can be brought into a GIS and analyzed for the spatial relationships between, for example, poverty and race, ethnicity and education, or class and access to transportation. As Schuurman stresses in *GIS: A Short Introduction*, spatial data sets and GIS technologies are used across societies by "government agencies, businesses, community groups, universities, and hospitals" (p. 16) to address a myriad of social geographic concerns.

Social geographers are also interested in the democratic potential of GIS. The development of "public participation geographic information science" (PPGIS) crosses the boundaries of the university/community divide, as geographers, community groups, and activists collect and analyze spatial data using GIS technologies. Social geographers remain acutely aware that these struggles are always mediated by access to information, technological knowhow and capacity, and local political networks and relations (Ghose and Elwood 2003). At a more distanced level, social geographers use GIS technologies to "make contributions to risk assessment, primarily by supporting better modeling of geographical distributions of hazards, susceptible populations, exposures, and health outcomes" (Cromley and McLafferty 2002: 185).

The development of GIS and its application to social geographic questions has not been without its critics. These critiques examine the problematic nature in which GIS has been applied. This includes its history as a military-based technology and its application in the surveillance of populations. John Pickles's (1995) edited collection *Ground Truth: The Social Implications of Geographic Information Systems* highlights some of these concerns, urging geographers to interrogate the social context for the development of GIS and its use. In the ensuing years, many geographers have weighed in on this debate. Out of these debates, new GIS practices have developed, including PPGIS.

Social geographers continue to cross the boundaries between spatial science and other social geographic frameworks, including feminist geographies, in attempts to use GIS in analyses of gender relationships and politics (e.g. McLafferty 2002).

Quick Exercise

Draw up a list of possible social geographic questions that might involve the use of GIS. What variables do you need to collect/find to answer these questions? Where would you get these data? How might these data be applied to answer an immediate social geographic problem related to inequality in your own locale?

Qualitative methodologies: inside/outside

If quantitative social geographers seek to investigate broad spatial patterns and relationships, qualitative social geographers tend to focus on the everyday, situated experiences of individuals and groups in and through various spaces. This model of research is based in a broad set of presumptions about society and space, the social and the spatial. First, qualitative researchers are interested in engaging the situated and subjective experience of individuals and groups. As Jackson (1983: 43–4) suggests, "Participant observation [for example] holds an attraction for the social geographer . . . in providing a method with which an attempt to transcend the epistemological gulf between 'insider' and 'outside' can be made." It is this epistemological shift – from the researcher as distanced and objective observer to the researcher as situated and invested in subjective experience – that defines qualitative research, even if much qualitative research in geography is not based in participant observation specifically. Qualitative researchers also tend to work back and forth between grounded experience and broader theoretical insight (Burawoy et al. 1991); they are not analytically testing hypotheses or constructing mathematical models. Instead, they are interested in thick descriptions of social experiences and theoretically informed interpretations of social differences and inequalities (Geertz 1973). Second, qualitative methodologies focus on the subjective experiences of individuals and groups through ongoing and relatively open-ended interactions. Both quantitative and qualitative researchers use survey methods but quantitative researchers tend to use closed-ended questioning techniques seeking to elicit a set number of theoretically informed responses, while qualitative researchers tend to use open-ended and semi-structured techniques to allow for a conversation to develop over time. This means that qualitative researchers tend to privilege the voices of those people and experiences they are trying to represent. And, while qualitative researchers might try to aggregate the experiences of different people by explaining an overall "sense of place" or group experience of a particular space, they also want to allow for a multiplicity of voices and perspectives.

Third, working through subjective experience, qualitative researchers do not construct laws about the operation of society and/or space. Instead, they believe the world is messy and that their representations of that world can be, at best, partial and incomplete. Knowledge, following the work of Haraway (2004), is situated in experiences. To understand those situated experiences the focus should be on the mundane and everyday. Indeed, "All qualitative methodologies recognize the relevance and importance of 'lay' or 'folk' perspectives on the practicalities of everyday life. We choose these methods, then, as a way to challenge the way the world is structured, the way that knowledge is made, from the top down. . . . We are, then, adopting a *strategy that aims to place non-dominant, neglected, knowledges at the heart of the research agenda*" (Limb and Dwyer 2001: 25, original emphasis). In emphasizing a "bottom-up" view of the world, qualitative geographers tend to privilege locally situated experiences and complexity over broad grand theories, although this does not exclude studies of global processes, practices, and discourses through various textually or visually based approaches and methodologies (see extended discussion in Blunt et al. 2003).

Fourth, because qualitative research is intentionally and explicitly interested in experience, social geographers who use qualitative methodologies tend not to struggle with the same questions regarding reliability and repeatability with which quantitative social geographers struggle (Hay 2000). In fact, the idea that any two contexts can produce the same exact result, or even that any two researchers might produce the same exact narrative of experience in any given place, is generally rejected in a purely qualitative study. Despite the fact that qualitative research works against the notions of reliability and repeatability, qualitative researchers do, to varying degrees, address questions of validity in the research process. In some cases, qualitative researchers argue that validity comes in the use of methods that are consistent with the "norms" of their field (Lincoln and Guba 2000). Other qualitative researchers suggest that validity comes through the process of developing "community consent and a form a rigor – defensible reasoning, plausible along some other reality that is known to the author and reader – in ascribing salience to one interpretation over another and for framing and bounding an interpretive study itself" (ibid.: 178). For Baxter and Eyles (1997) that means developing "credible" methods of both data collection and analysis. Therefore, qualitative researchers tend to situate their research in the larger social context in which their study is embedded. So, rather than bracketing off the field into discrete, measurable, and quantifiable units, qualitative researchers try to broaden their studies through the ongoing "back and forth" engagement between individual and group experiences *and* local and global contexts.

Fifth, qualitative validity is marked by a deep and abiding concern for questions related to research ethics and reflexivity, or critical self-reflection (Winchester 1996; McDowell 1997; Crang 2002), although qualitative researchers also realize that identifying one's social and spatial position in the research process is highly problematic and contested (Rose 1997). As such, qualitative researchers, because they do not position themselves on the outside looking in, understand that they have an impact on what is going on in the field. Fine et al. (2000: 126–7) outline some key questions that qualitative researchers may ask when regarding their research responsibilities and position. These include:

1   Have I connected the "voices" and "stories" of individuals back to the set of historical, structural, and economic relations in which they are situated?
2   Have I deployed multiple methods so that very different kinds of analyses can be constructed?
3   Have I described the mundane?
4   Have some informants, constituencies, and/or participants reviewed the material with me and interpreted, dissented from, challenged my interpretations? And then how do I report these departures or disagreements in perspective?
5   How far do I want to go with respect to theorizing the words of informants?
6   Have I considered how these data could be used for progressive, conservative, or repressive social policies?
7   Where have I backed into the passive voice and decoupled my responsibility from my interpretation?
8   Who am I afraid will see these analyses? Who is rendered vulnerable, responsible, or exposed by these analyses? Am I willing to show him, her, or them the text before publication? If not, why not? Could I publish his, her, or their comments as an epilogue? What is the fear?
9   What dreams am I having about the material presented?
10 To what extent has my analysis offered an alternative to the "commonsense" or dominant discourse? What challenges might very different audiences pose to the analysis presented?

In considering these questions, researchers cannot allow themselves to be paralyzed; they have to accept that their work is a partial representation of what they see and do. This means they must begin by "recognizing the articificiality of the distinctions between research and politics, the operations of research and the research, the field and the 'not field,' the researcher and the participant; and the need to live by these distinctions in order to accomplish something, however partial and incomplete, to avoid paralysis, cynicism, the 'waste' of our training, skills, and talent" (Katz 1994: 67). All of this, of course, complicates the research process, making it sometimes hard to distinguish between research and action (see further discussion below).

  Sixth, qualitative researchers rely on data that is more-than-verbal, examining visual, haptic (touch), emotional, and affective data from a variety of sources (Crang 2003; Thien 2005; G. Rose 2007). Qualitative experience is not simply produced through the mundane act of speech and language; social experiences and spaces are always contextualized through a myriad number of interconnections to other spaces, peoples, and objects. Making these more-than-verbal data available for geographic analysis demands that researchers think about data as emerging from multiple sources – mundane daily actions, visual representations, musical compositions, built environments, nature–society relations. A qualitative methodological lens focuses attention on those objects and subjective experiences that are often "beyond" quantification (Thrift 1996).

Box 3.2   Qualitative Geography's Methodological Pluralism

When using the terms quantitative and qualitative, social geographers sometimes fail to fully appreciate the complex practices that these labels belie. At the most basic level, qualitative data have no magnitude, no measurable base from which to start. Gender – male, female, transgendered – is a qualitative variable. A Likert scale is a qualitative instrument measuring a relative difference in opinion (e.g. strongly agree verses strongly disagree). These qualitative data might be collected using **structured survey instruments** (a survey with a fixed set of answers/choices). These data can be analyzed to statistically describe a sample or correlate a relative measure of "strongly agree" with a particular gendered identity. Social geographers also collect **semi-structured interviews** (interviews where a set number of questions are given to all research participants) and then analyze those data with multiple coders, wherein each researcher analyzes the data for themes and then there is a quantitative test for intercoder reliability. These qualitative data may be calibrated and analyzed through key aspects of the scientific method.

   More often, qualitative data are conceptualized as partial and incomplete representations of the world. Qualitative researchers use semi-structured or **open-ended or non-structured interview** techniques to tell a subjective "story" about individual or collective experiences. These data are also coded, but the codes are developed out of the theoretical context or from the field experience (i.e. they are not "tested" in the same way that scientific geographers might test them). Social geographers also utilize **focus group** methodologies to collect data on the experiences of predefined social or community groups. The conversational style has both advantages and disadvantages, as sometimes there are issues of trust and privacy, particularly if members of a focus group do not know each other. That is why some social geographers engage in **participant observation** to collect qualitative, experiential data. These data are representations of experiences, practices, and spatial patterns found in the field and recorded in notebooks. They are transcribed at a later point to include "fieldnotes" (basic observations) and "headnotes" (on-the-spot analytic comments or assessments). The process of participant observation blurs the line between data collection and analysis (Plath 1990).

Qualitative methodologies also encompass more than verbal-based methodologies, and social geographers use other techniques to collect visual or haptic (tactile) data and experiences. **Visual methodologies** have become quite popular, including the use of **visual ethnography**. **Cognitive methodologies** are now also used to examine the importance of tactile and haptic understandings of space (e.g. in the study of blind or deaf individuals' experiences of certain geographies). Social geographers also examine visual and other representations to **deconstruct** the social and spatial power relations that might be found in representational forms, such as documentary films, advertising, popular media, or even maps.

Quick Exercise

In a group of two or three people, go to a public place – a restaurant, park, etc. – where people congregate. Each person should take detailed fieldnotes for one hour, focusing on how people interact and use this particular space. Once completed, each member of the group should transcribe these notes, making them readable and adding "headnotes" where appropriate. As a final step, compare the transcriptions within the group members. What are the similarities and differences? If there are differences, why do you think those differences exist?

The tradition of qualitative data collection, going out into the "field" and interacting with people and groups, is a long one in geography (Cloke et al. 2004), and many social geographers have had an interest in subjective experiences (Limb and Dwyer 2001). The Chicago School, and its intellectual descendents, used ethnographic and participant observation methodologies to investigate social differences in the city, a practice that was picked up the late 1970s and 1980s by a number of other social geographers (e.g. Jackson 1983). Humanistic geographers, who eschew the theories of absolute space produced through the quantitative revolution, invest their social geography with a much more intersubjective and experiential view of space (Ley 1977; Ley and Samuels 1978; Rowles 1978b). Feminist geographers have also tended toward qualitative approaches, seeking to unpack and understand the gendering of space and spatial relations through a methodology that privileges the voices of the people they engage in the field (Jones et al. 1997). As England (1994: 82) suggests:

Most feminists usually favor the role of supplicant, seeking reciprocal relationships based on empathy and mutual respect, and often sharing their knowledge with those they research. Supplication involves exposing and exploiting weaknesses regarding dependence on whoever is being researched for information and guidance. Thus the researcher explicitly acknowledges her/his reliance on the research subject to provide insight into the subtle nuances of meaning that structure and shape everyday lives.

England goes on to suggest that the "intersubjective nature of social life means that the researcher and the people being researched have shared meanings and we should seek methods that develop this advantage." These methods are designed to "get at" experience, using descriptive and analytic approaches that help deconstruct and, perhaps, reconstruct how the gendered spatial organization of social life mediates bodily practices and performances. In general, then, feminist geographers push researchers to think about their social position within the research process itself.

Social geographers also use qualitative approaches to study representations of social groups, spaces, and processes, utilizing qualitative methodologies and approaches to investigate archival and textual materials to explain how social differences and inequalities have developed over time (see, for example, Sparke 1995, 1998, who uses a critical cartography framework to analyze sociospatial constructions of difference). As such, qualitative social geographers are constantly reconsidering the nature of the categories of race, sexuality, gender, and age by examining how these social categories are "increasingly refracted through the cultural" (Jackson 2003: 38): social categories of race are deployed in ways that affect social policy in particularly pernicious ways. Wilson (2005: 131), using an array of textual methods, examines how popular discussions of "black-on-black violence" by both so-called liberals and conservatives in the US have been "mobilized across America to create a villain, black youth, that had far-reaching penal and legislative ramifications. . . . This 'black-on-black violence' vision, like so many social ills narrated and accepted in the mainstream [culture], became central to the formation of social policy." In this way, social geographers, like Wilson, analyze data they consider important to their study of social difference and inequality, while engaging with approaches that are also present in other subdisciplines in geography.

The object of study in qualitative social geography is not as clearly delineated as it is in quantitative-based research. While qualitative geographers are interested in social distance, the spatial organization of social groups in and across space, or questions of social and physical mobility, they focus on how these processes are invested in certain social and cultural meanings and relations of power. This shifts the methodological attention from questions of aggregation and toward concerns with the use of language and social discourse, bodily practice and performance, and experiences of spaces. That said, qualitative social geography is guided by a number of broad methodological principles. These include a belief in the power of analytic and critical description. A rigorous qualitative social geography describes mundane performances and research practices, building a textual, and sometimes visual or experiential, "picture" of sociospatial relations. In working through a descriptive analytic framework, qualitative social geographers try to understand how certain spaces of exclusion and inclusion, belonging and desire, or community and identity are maintained and challenged through daily action.

To develop their "spatial stories" of everyday experience, some social geographers use ethnographic or participant observation techniques, immersing themselves in an extended period of engaged research. Other social geographers use interview techniques, both semi-structured and open-ended, to tease out the nuanced under-standings that a select group of individuals have about their place in the world. In both cases, the resulting materials – fieldnotes or interview transcripts – are coded through a dialectic process of reading and re-reading to investigate themes and nuances, with contradictions accepted as measuring the plurality of experiences. In many cases, these approaches to data collection are used together, to analytic-ally describe and interpret the use and practices of space and place. As Cloke et al. (2004: 198) explain, the use of an ethnographic approach "is supposed to pro-vide its readers with a vivid impression of 'being there'." In so doing, qualitative social geographers might focus their attention on the following questions and concerns:

> So how might we conjure up a sense of place of the locale(s) in which the research is based and how this might change over the minutes, hours, days, weeks and months of the research? How might we describe the rhythms and routines of those actors who inhabit and/or compromise that setting? How might we move from these observa-tions to describe our interactions in that setting with those actors, initially and as they develop over time? How might we describe not only what we are learning but also the often strange and strained circumstances under which that learning is taking place? How might we describe the differences this makes to the way the research seems to shaping up, where it can and should go, and what power we have over this? And how would we describe how this develops in and between the locales or our expanding fields? (ibid.)

Put simply, qualitative social geographers should never underestimate the value of experience no matter how simple or apparently straightforward. Description is a powerful analytic tool allowing social geographers to disentangle how differ-ences and inequalities are "mapped out" in and through the various landscapes of rural, suburban, and urban spaces, colonial and postcolonial contexts, or the global north and global south.

Across the divide: the challenge of mixed methodologies

In the previous two sections, I laid out two methodological frameworks, one quantitative, one qualitative. At first pass, it would seem that these methodologies are mutually exclusive because they draw on very different epistemological and ontological assumptions. Despite this apparent divide, some geographers employ both quantitative and qualitative methodologies in their work through what is called "mixed methodologies." Mixed methodologies suggest that it is possible to blend the analysis of both quantitative and qualitative data in the same study, using variegated sets of data and questions to "triangulate" one's findings (England 1993). McKendrick (1999: 44), for example, suggests that "in-depth interviews with senior decision-makers and the interpretation of briefing papers could be *cross-checked* and *interrelated* to provide a corroborated and more comprehensive account of the decision-making process" (original emphasis). For some, qualitative data exploration, through observations, may provide hypotheses that can then be tested quantitatively (LeCompte and Schensul 1999a, 1999b). Other researchers find it valuable to first map quantitative data across space, analyzing the relationships between various quantitative data sets, and then qualitatively investigate if those relationships are maintained on "the ground" (England 1993). Qualitative researchers might go even further, interrogating how the quantitative relationships they have mapped are subjectively experienced in place.

A mixed methodological study does not need to employ a range of quantitative and qualitative practices and approaches, but might also draw from an array of possibilities from within and across the range of these areas. Mixed methodologies might include qualitative surveys and interviews or quantitative surveys and secondary data analysis. In thinking about a mixed methodological framework, Valentine (2003) suggests that, first and foremost, one has to determine the research question being asked. For example,

> you might begin by carrying out participant observation to gain an understanding of the participants and their group dynamics, but then use individual interviews as a way to explore some individual motivations for participating [in certain social activities] and some of the tensions between members of . . . [your target] "community." . . . When multiple methods are used in this way, the material generated by each technique may throw up apparently very contradictory findings. . . . Such findings are not a problem but rather show how successful you have been in capturing the complexities, contradictions, ambiguities and messiness of human behaviour and everyday life (Valentine 2003: 45).

It is important, then, to revisit the distinction between methodology (as a theory of practice) and method or technique (as the actual practice). Methodologically, Valentine defines what she sees as the essential research questions to be answered and what data might best help answer those questions. Next, she turns her attention to the practicality of how to "go about" getting at those data. Understanding that her methodological questions are messy and complex, Valentine suggests the use of a two-pronged methodological strategy employing two methods or techniques: participant observation and interviewing. As she views the world as inherently messy her interest in a mixed methodological framework allows her to tease out the complexity and possibilities of everyday social interaction in and across space.

Brown et al. (2005) take a different approach by bringing together a complex array of methodological considerations in their study of electoral politics in Tacoma, Washington. They begin with a discourse analysis of the wider political debates about a gay right vote. Turning their attention to the vote itself, they utilize quantitative analyses to ascertain to what extent the vote was spatially correlated with different social categories: race, class, gender, age, and marital status, for example. As they explain, the mixed methods approach allowed us to unpack the black box of "context" in which Tacoma's electoral geography was situated. Juxtaposing qualitative discourse analysis and a quantitative ecological analysis allowed us to appreciate a wide array of forces at work that influenced the vote, and to confidently dismiss more locally insignificant ones. It also allowed us to appreciate the cultural interactions and saliencies of demographic variables at work. And so we would suggest mixed-methods might be a fruitful research trajectory in urban electoral geography – especially around the culture wars (Brown et al. 2005: 288–9).

Brown et al., while not offering this explicitly, suggest in their "mixed methodology" research framework that geographers can answer a number of different questions using a broad array of methodological tools (see also Del Casino et al. 2000). More than this, though, these authors, and others like them that engage in mixed methodologies (e.g. Dunning et al. 2007), suggest that no one approach can answer all questions. Instead, by mixing methods from across the quantitative and qualitative spectrum, researchers can make a number of "cuts" at any particular social problem, dissecting how differences and inequalities are sociospatially organized through a number of geographical processes.

There are challenges, however, to mixing methodologies. First and foremost, there is the possible tension that emerges when a researcher tries to employ different theories of space in one study (Del Casino et al. 2000). For example, the use of an abstract theory of space to map spatial patterns might rigidly fix the scale of analysis in a way that makes the view of space as social and contextual difficult to sustain (see Jones 1998). Further, certain methodological approaches are invested with political limitations because methodologies are embedded in epistemological and ontological presumptions about the world. It is sometimes hard to divest a certain methodological approach – say quantitative spatial analysis – from the notion that there is an objective and rational world that structures sociospatial relations and behaviors, while a qualitative analytic geographer might see the world as inherently messy and thus eschew any attempt to rationalize and order space. But, when done well and with thought, a mixed methodological approach may highlight limitations and the partiality of the research process through the very fact that each layer of a mixed methodology sets out only part of the story.

There is a further cautionary tale here. Mixed methods, when brought into a methodological framework grounded in a particular epistemological perspective – such as an objective science – may presume that the end point of the research process is generalizability. That is why many geographers have been critical of a methodological pluralism that suggests the end point of mixing methods is triangulation, or the process by which we verify the results of one data set with that of another. This is because methodological triangulation raises a key theoretical concern in any mixed methodological framework – how does one resolve the epistemological tension between the general and the particular, objectivity and subjectivity? It is thus valuable to detach method (practice) from methodology (theory of practice). In this way, then, one could use a particular technique – factorial ecology or social area analysis – to provide a broad but partial context for

Box 3.3   A "Note" on Thinking and Writing "Scientifically"

The decisions social geographers make are not only found in the methodology; they are reflected in the written product. What social geographers "do" with their data and how they write those data up is an essential part of social geography.

Positivist and critical rationalist social geographic research seeks causal explanation, highlighting in the writing process cause and effect as well as correlated relationships. Causal explanation and objective description of pattern and process are thus particular forms of analysis and a style of writing. Through the methodological process of testing hypotheses or visualizing certain patterns and relationships, social geographers explain the relationship between, say, the patterns of poverty and race. In another context, mapping the patterns of mobility and travel of people, social geographers might explain how (and why) spatial processes of inclusion and exclusion structure that pattern. The final written product would trace the social geographic patterns and processes being studied. Limitations come when a social geographer knows that the explanation is incomplete.

Social geographers working in post-positivistic frameworks assume their representations are partial and incomplete. The written product is centered on interpretation. "The task of interpretation requires building up a substantial stock of knowledge in order to frame an understanding of particular events [places, and experiences]" (Ley and Mountz 2001: 236). This means grounding writing in everyday experience, while teasing out the subtle plays of power, the subjective experiences of that power, and the individual and collective understanding of the relationship between space and identify, difference and inequality. When writing up, it is common to make the research process part of the story. There is much less urgency in generalizing to other contexts; it is the depth of a particular experience that is important in this form of writing.

In both cases, critical social geographic research can be published in different outlets – academic journals, reports, and newspaper or magazine articles. Social geographers can take advantage of their social position as academics to try and affect change. After all, "scientific research has tremendous legitimacy in the academia as well as a great deal of political currency in wider society, which is simply too powerful to ignore for those engaged in critical approaches" (Hickey and Lawson 2005: 97). In this light, labeling certain analytical approaches as scientific (e.g. quantitative geographies) and others as less-than-scientific (e.g. qualitative geographies) is ineffective and pointless. All critical social geographic has value because all critical social geographers are committed to "revisiting and re-examining initial assumptions and questions of reflexivity, open inquiry, and rigor in their research" (ibid.: 99). It is the commitment to thoughtful and self-reflexive (and appropriate) methodologies that makes writing so politically powerful.

Quick Exercise

Find a recent journal article in social geography and rewrite it so that it can be published as a newspaper article. How do you have to change the language and style of writing to make the research appropriate to the new audience?

an in-depth ground truthing of that context through open-ended interviews or participant observation. DeVerteuil (2003a, 2003b) does this in his study of homelessness in Los Angeles County, using social-area analysis to partially predict what areas of the city may be more amenable to homeless individuals. He then follows this with interviews with homeless individuals living in three different sectors of the city to see how their experience of those places vary in relation to the social-area analysis of the city. He created a set of qualitatively bound regions based on the analysis of a number of quantitative data, which he could then examine qualitatively through interviews to understand the relationship between the sociospatial organization of the city and the everyday experience of homeless peoples.

There are also institutional and disciplinary constraints that come with "mixing" methodologies. Michael Brown (2007: 208), for example, explains how "I . . . have a general sense of a queer geography where there is a not-so-subtle disciplining against *any* use of quantitative techniques and analyses or of GIS." Many researchers are deeply skeptical about thinking across the methodological spectrum. These institutionalized limitations might marginalize attempts to think "beyond" the traditional comfort zones of certain methodological approaches and types of data. That said, mixed methodological approaches can bring together researchers from across the spectrum of social geography by engaging in research that serves their broader political and intellectual interests – this might help to open up the concept of critical social geography and expand it in ways that have, until recently, been impossible because of the institutional investment in privileging one way of knowing over another.

From research to action through participation

For some social geographers, the methodological issue does not revolve around whether or not to employ quantitative, qualitative, or mixed approaches. The question is: to what extent can – and perhaps should – social geographers try to affect change with their research? Indeed, one could argue that social geography remains one of the central activist subdisciplines in geography, whose history includes the work of activist spatial scientists as well as radical Marxist and feminist scholars, among others. While there is a long tradition of debate around what social geographers mean by "action," social geographers continue to be interested in grounding their work in ways that positively affect change. It is not surprising, then, that the tradition of participant action research (PAR) is one that has come to hold sway recently in social geography. As Rachel Pain (2003: 652) suggests, "While many social geographers engage in forms of political activism, recent years have seen a sharp refocusing of interest in activism as an explicit strategy and outcome of research and vice versa. Earlier assumptions that academic endeavours and activism were quite distinctive and separate pursuits which had to be forcefully and problematically combined have been dispelled, and reflection on concrete examples of practice has led writers to confirm the muddying of the objectives and roles of academic/activist." Unlike mixed methodologies, where the tension revolves around questions of quantitative or qualitative research approaches, the tension here is between activism and academic textual production and reproduction, scholarly analysis and engaged policy research (Pain 2006).

The boundaries that may exist between academic and nonacademic communities and spaces are destabilized by social geographic research developed in conjunction with so-called research subjects. Indeed, PAR, and other participatory approaches, such as "participatory diagramming" (Kesby 2004), work against the narratives of research and researched, including participation from as many as possible, although this is not always an easy process (Doyle 1999). At the core of these participatory research projects is the presumption that it is necessary to become familiar with the concerns and issues of those with whom you want to work. This engaged intellectual intimacy certainly rubs against a distanced, objectivist aproach, which seeks to maintain a clear distinction between the researcher and the researched. It also differs from some qualitative methodological frameworks that develop thick descriptions of complex sociospatial relations without any clear suggestion of how the research product may affect direct change or result in a particular set of actions or policies. This is not to suggest, of course, that broader qualitative researchers do not reflexively consider the impact of their research on others (e.g. England 1994; Katz 1994), or that the products of academic research do not have broader engagement with those outside universities (Till 2001). It is to suggest that the "outputs" might, at times, be intended for different audiences and communities. Pain (2006: 253) argues, for example, that "In some parts of geography a certain paper radicalism has become mainstreamed, while consultancy and 'applied' contract research may have more positive political impacts." Pain's criticality is tied to her suspicion of what is sometimes thought of as "armchair" research, whereby the sociospatial relationship between researched and researcher remains a distant one despite what appear to be political intentions. For some, this is resolved through the production of both reports and academic publications that consider the variety of audiences that might want access to social geographic research (Doyle 1999). It might also be necessary to consider a multiplicity of presentation styles – verbal, visual, tactile, etc. – that can engage audiences that are not always literate or attuned to the production of relatively linear narrative structures.[3]

Social geographers might begin to "look past" the dualities that mark these intellectual tensions, and, instead, ask themselves how they can open up dialogue and engagement with multiple communities and groups through their projects. This demands that they consider the power relations embedded in their research projects, and think about their identities as both researchers and activists. "Put simply, the researcher needs to learn how to move between his/her various identities, and to be aware (and able to read) the effects of this movement on this research as a whole" (Fuller 1999). Social geographers all work in and through a number of axes of difference – based in class, race, ethnic, sexual, gender subjectivities and identities – that affect their relationships with others. It is impossible to escape, for example, the fact that academics are invested with certain sociospatial privileges. In policy circles it might be much more likely that those in power will "listen to" or "engage" with academics before the people for whom they claim to be creating policy. Researchers have to not only be cognizant of these relations of power; they also have to "think about" how they are also subject to the various plays of power that exist within their own research communities (Kitchin and Hubbard 1999; Smith 2000b).[4]

Developing participatory geography is, therefore, a didactic and iterative process of back and forth negotiation across a number of spaces and communities. It is also a geography that is considerate of the need to think about how geographers can be part of a larger ethics of care and social justice. That means that social geographers should promote alternative geographies of care that resist the "common tendency to privilege the local over 'distant strangers'" (Popke 2003: 300). Drawing on the social theoretical work of Levinas, Popke (2003: 303) suggests that "my being is always-already an occupation of the world . . . which impinges on others. . . . We thus incur an unpayable debt to the other." In considering ethics – not just research ethics but our own ethical position as people – social geographers need to rethink their relationship not only to the space of immediacy, the spaces of their own local context, but also to the broader spatialities in which they are also present (Popke 2006). This emboldens a social geography that is cognizant of the uneven sociospatial relationships that structure relationships between the global north and global south (Katz 2004) and the tendency to privilege "the local" in research projects (Pugh 2005). In this highly globalized world, the bounding of local spaces is never fully possible, and we are intimately connected through a myriad web of sociospatial relations to millions of others. So, even if research is developed in so-called distant places, researchers need to remember that what they are doing as social geographers has broader affects/effects. Researchers are "responsible" for the stories they tell with their research; and they have to reflect on the powerful representational politics of the writing process and how their work might be used to promote a broader empathy and ethics of care. This is a complicated notion, but one that animates an important aspect of social geography's longstanding commitment to engaging issues of difference and inequality, social justice and activism (e.g. Harvey 1972; Smith 1994; Miller 2000).

The question of what social geographers mean by social activism, action, and engagement will not be quickly resolved. There is no doubt, though, that critical social geography is broadly informed by a certain ethical consideration for both the "proximate" and the "distanced." In engaging this concern, social geographers often demonstrate a genuine concern with expanding the possibilities of creating a more just and equitable world. Methodologically, this means that social geographers draw from approaches that seek to minimize the distance between the so-called researcher and researched. Social geographers work across any number of axes of difference as well as through a myriad of spaces to challenge the broader structures of power and hegemony that structure inequalities.

Ready, Set, Go! "Doing" Social Geography

[W]hat constitutes and comprises the social? A generation after Margaret Thatcher, whose hateful, antisocial individualism evoked the famous outburst that "there is no such thing as society," and whose legacy still in many ways haunts contemporary neo-liberal policies around the world, and with global struggles again on the rise, asking the question of the social may just be a radical act (Smith 2000b: 28).

In this chapter, I have traced some of the broader methodological concerns that inform social geographic research. I ended with a suggestion that a critical social geography is interested in methodologies that engage in a broader ethics of care and challenge the structures of inequality mediating the lives of millions every day. In so doing, we have come full circle; it is clear that questions central to social geography remain not only current but also pressing. "[A]sking the question of the social . . . [is, indeed,] a radical act," one that we must take seriously. Social geography is aptly positioned to help us both understand and explain how the everyday struggles that take place in and around the world are intimately tied to the sociospatial construction of difference and inequality. And, it is possible that social geographers can draw liberally from a wide breadth of methodological approaches as they try to enact change through their social geographic research. At the same time, they also have to remember that there are a number of audiences "out there" that might find their research not only useful but applicable to their own interests; these interests might want to use their research to challenge the privileged position of the few who control access to the majority of the needed resources. Our social geographic research can thus draw on methodologies that allow us to construct spaces that celebrate difference and open up the possibility that people can develop intimate relationships in broadly conceived safe and healthy contexts. Societal relations and the important and intimate social relationships that we share with those who are both "near" and "far," "similar" and "different" are central to social geographers. It is important to engage in methodological questions and practices that promote multiple possibilities and challenge the presumptive and normative reification of the binary logic of "us" and "them," "subject" and "object," "quantitative" and "qualitative," "interpretative" and "explanatory." To that end, we now turn to an extended discussion of social geography in practice, grounding these social geographies in the everyday spaces of young and old, gay and straight, and healthy and ill, to name just a few.

Notes

1   The "weighty materiality" of everyday life sometimes gets in the way.
2   This does not mean that poststructuralist geographers are not interested in the materialities of everyday life. Poststructuralists are, in fact, very interested in how discursive formations create real (albeit temporary) effects of power that inhibit positive expressions of difference and maintain inequality.
3   Pink (2001) discusses a methodology for visual ethnography, which could be used effectively to engage an audience.
4   For many, that means engaging in the politics of the academy and its procedures and regulations for gaining full-time employment, tenure, and promotion.

Part II

Social Geographies across the Life Course

In this part, we examine social geographic questions related to health, communities, and organizations, as well as social activism, movements, and justice. Social geographers share a common interest with the issues discussed in this part regardless of their empirical focus on children or adults, boys or girls, men or women, young people or the elderly. This part begins with a discussion of health. It is argued that while not always explicitly, many social geographers ask questions related to health and healing, mental and physical wellbeing, or, more metaphorically, community and organizational health. Next, we turn to an examination of communities and organizations, raising questions of how social geographers provide a unique perspective on these important social objects. Finally, the part addresses questions related to social activism, movements, and justice. Many social geographers are intimately engaged with the struggles that they also study, and the final chapter in this part asks how geographers might remain connected with ongoing struggles related to social inequalities and the positive assertion of social differences.

Chapter 4

Social Geography and the Geographies of Health

- ■ When is Social Geography not about Health?
- ■ Defining "Health" and "Disease," the "Medical" and the "Alternative"
- ■ Critical Geographies of Disease and Health Care
  - ■ Disease ecology and the social production of (dis)ease
  - ■ Health care studies, investigating (un)healthy places
- ■ Critical Medical and Health Geographies
  - ■ Rethinking the spatialities of health, landscape, and identity
  - ■ Body politics and the geographies of disability
  - ■ Sexing medical and health geographies
- ■ Critical Geographies of Health, Inequality, and Difference

When is Social Geography not about Health?

Despite the optimism of the 1970s that infectious diseases would be eradicated through biomedical interventions (vaccines, inoculations, prevention outreach programs, etc.), the world today is still concerned with major epidemic infections transmitted from animal to human, such as malaria, as well as from human to human, such as tuberculosis. Many of these illnesses account for both tremendous social loss – with the death of family and community members from malnutrition – and new and emerging social stigmas and prejudices – with the powerful symbols attached to various diseases such as HIV. By mapping any number of epidemic diseases, it could be shown that different societies are more susceptible to certain infections than others (see Figure 4.1). It is then possible to compare these maps to ones that

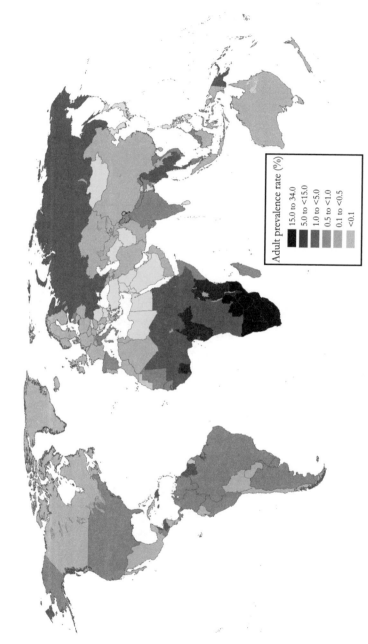

Figure 4.1 Global map of the percentage population living with HIV in 2006. (*Data source:* WHO/UNAIDS.)

Adult prevalence rate (%)

15.0 to 34.0
5.0 to <15.0
1.0 to <5.0
0.5 to <1.0
0.1 to <0.5
<0.1

illustrate social and demographic indicators, such as "life expectancy" and "infant mortality," and their variations both globally and locally. It is likely that certain infection rates would be correlated highly with lower life expectancies and higher infant mortalities. This should immediately raise questions for social geographers who are concerned with both questions of inequality (and access to needed health-related resources) and social difference (and how we conceptualize those who are "healthy" and "ill").

So, I return to the question above and ask, "When is social geography not about health?" This may seem an odd question, as many social geographers would rarely claim themselves to be studying health per se. Yet one could easily see how a lack of access to park space for children in urban inner city New York might encourage higher rates of injury (e.g. broken bones) among those same children (Katz 2004: 174–5). Examining the relationship between access to housing for the elderly in Spain, it is possible to investigate how people in certain income groups have better and more consistent access to health care than others (Costa-Font 2008). Or one could examine how the changing economy of China is producing a new set of problems in elder care as fewer families are offering the extended care they once did (Bartlett and Phillips 1997). Put more simply, the day-to-day struggles that many individuals go through to survive are intimately tied to questions of "good" and "bad" health (Moss and Dyck 2002). And, these patterns of "healthiness" are interrelated with any number of critical sociospatial processes – capitalism, heterosexism, and racism – that mediate, and sometimes regulate, how people gain access to needed resources related to their health. These sociospatial processes are not only about physical or bodily health but about mental and emotional health as well (Parr and Butler 1999).

Moreover, the meanings of health and illness vary quite dramatically across space and time. It was not too long ago that the social norm in many western societies was to think of disease as a product of an individual's "essential character" (Barnes 1995). In this historical context, diseases were considered the fault of the individual or even an entire class of people, such as the poor, and not a product of a bacterial agent. While "germ theory" – the belief that bacteria and other agents, such as viruses, affect the health of bodies – dramatically altered how people view disease and illness, social and collective meanings and practices have not always followed scientific knowledge and practice. As an example:

> In the historiography of medicine, the rise of germ theory is the great divide of the nineteenth century, in light of which all preceding and subsequent developments are interpreted. Where tuberculosis in France is concerned, the decisive dates have been 1865 and 1882, when Villemin demonstrated the inoculability of the disease and when Koch identified the tubercle bacillus, respectively. However, several significant elements of the pre- germ theory etiology of tuberculosis survived intact through the late nineteenth century. Among these elements are filth, stench, and overcrowding, all symptomatic of the underlying pathology of the city (Barnes 1995: 25).

Susan Craddock (2000b) illustrates similar practices in the context of San Francisco, where the plague was constructed by public health officials as a disease not only of the poor but of a particular ethnic poor, Chinese and Asian populations, whose social practices as "rice eaters" somehow compromised their immune systems and made them susceptible to particular diseases (Craddock 2000a: 130). There are modern-day parallels to the views of tuberculosis in France and the plague in San Francisco in the nineteenth century, such as the HIV epidemic in the late twentieth and early twenty-first centuries (Farmer 1992; Craddock 2000b; Raimondo 2003). The powerful stigma attached to HIV disease and AIDS remains despite vigorous awareness campaigns explaining that HIV is not transmitted through casual contact with HIV-positive individuals or the "things" (such as toilet seats) they may touch (see Patton 1990, 1994; Brown 1995).

There is value in asking social geographic questions about health and illness, health care and disease, and how certain social systems and practices of health and healing, medicine and disease, healthy and unhealthy, are intimately tied to everyday social geographies. It is not simply that certain social groups and peoples are more susceptible to particular illnesses or more likely to be associated with a particular disease; there is also an inextricable connection between someone's place in the world and their health (Gesler and Kearns 2002). This is why social geographers have long been interested in the relationship between the changing environment, both "built" and "natural," as well as the corporeal (or bodily) experiences of health (Moss and Dyck 1999). This means investigating how the changing historical and geographical definitions of the "the medical" – and what medicine means – affect the organization and experiences of health as well as illness and disease (Philo 2000, 2005b; Parr 2004). This chapter addresses these questions, asking how social geographers study health and disease as well as medical and alternative health care practices and spaces. It also discusses the spatiality of health and health care in relation to other nodes of difference, such as ability, race, class, gender, and sexuality.

Defining "Health" and "Disease," the "Medical" and the "Alternative"

No matter where you are today if you are thinking about your health you are considering more than whether or not you feel "good" or "bad." You are also taking account of the broader sociospatial context in which you are living (perhaps your country or nation), the rules and regulations about your health that are part of that space (perhaps your right to choose certain procedures or health care practices), and how you, as an individual, relate to that space and those regulations (how we submit or transgress laws that regulate our health and health care choices). From giving birth to a right to die, health and bodies are constructed and practiced through a complex web of social relations and a myriad of spaces, from homes to schools and churches to international associations, like the United Nations, which offer policy recommendations so that there might be "Health for All" (United Nations 1981). The regulation of health varies not only across time and space but across the life course: young babies across the globe are inoculated based on their parents' or the state's assumptions about their health, while public universities, such as those in the state of California, mandate that students both carry health insurance (either private or purchased through the university) and get hepatitis B vaccinations (among other vaccinations). Health is thus an interpretive process of engagement between the self and others, from parents to doctors to colleagues and friends to neighbors and politicians. It is also an interpretive process of engagement between the self and one's place in the world, from the clinic or hospital to the communal herbal garden to the pharmacy or to a friend's medicine cabinet.

Through these engagements, it is possible to see that the term "health" is highly contested, for understandings of what it means to be healthy vary depending on where someone is, who someone is with, and how they feel at any given time. It is, in fact, easier to define health as an absence of something else, disease and illness, than it is define the concept itself. Health is a fully relational concept, it is dependent on some "other" to ensure its own meaning. This is fairly ironic, since considerable time, energy, and resources are spent trying to maintain "health." Yet the terms "healthy" and "unhealthy" are very much moving targets. Smoking, after all, was once considered a good way to relax and maintain one's mental health. As the advertisement for cigarettes in Figure 4.2 illustrates, "It's a psychological fact: pleasure helps your disposition." Recently, new signs of being "unhealthy," like "erectile dysfunction" or ED, are rethinking the definitions of sexual health: a man is not "completely" healthy unless he can maintain an erection for an extended period of time (Del Casino 2007a, 2007b).

This would make us think, then, that the concept of "disease" might be straightforward given its importance to our definition of health. Alas, it is also highly complex. The definition of disease, like health, varies across geographic and temporal context. In its simplest form, disease is a condition that has been diagnosed (i.e. defined) by a medical practitioner. In the west, biomedical practitioners – or allopathic physicians – generally determine how a particular disease is defined. For many, a disease is something that can be defined biomedically, where the link between a cause and effect might be known. Illnesses, in contrast, may manifest themselves without any clear cause or disease etiology. It is common to have a cold without the presence of a "disease." If that isn't confusing enough, disease is not simply the absence of "health" because a person can live a perfectly healthy (and long) life with a chronic illness (e.g. Crooks 2006; Crooks and Chouinard 2006). But diseases are processes that mitigate how people might live. It is thus valuable to consider how diseases manifest themselves, how and why they might spread, where they spread, and how they might be contained. At the same time, diseases are not simply the responsibility of individuals; they are often tied to the dynamic changes taking place in sociocultural, political-economic, and environmental contexts (see different takes on the disease–environment relationship in Mayer 2000; Brown 2006b). It is also important to recognize that diseases are not isolated from one another.

Figure 4.2   Camel cigarette advertisement from the journal *Popular Mechanics Magazine*, 1955 (original in color). Image downloaded on June 6, 2008 from http://blog.modernmechanix.com/2007/05/27/camel-ad-pleasure-helps-your-disposition/.

In fact, co-infections or co-factors are common and can exacerbate the consequences of having certain diseases. Malnutrition diminishes the body's capacity to fight off common infections, which other healthier bodies might be able to handle. Immune-suppressing diseases, such as HIV disease, or autoimmune diseases, such as lupus, may make the body susceptible to other diseases or turn the body's immune system defenses on its own cells. No one dies from HIV disease (often called AIDS); they die from tuberculosis or malaria or even a common cold because their immune system is unable to produce antibodies to fight off the infection.

Despite the fact that biomedicine is *the* dominant cultural system used to define and know diseases, such as HIV or lupus, geographers of health study alternative definitions of health and healthiness as well as illness and disease in order to investigate the plurality of health practices. They have done so by investigating the mundane ways in which people practice their health and the relationship of these practices to particular places (e.g. Kearns and Gesler 1998b). Take, for example, the everyday practices of self-medication in which people engage: aspirin, cough medications, and over-the-counter diet pills are all used regularly by individuals to self-regulate their health and mitigate illness. Also consider elective surgeries, such as liposuction, which pulls fat directly out of the body, making someone feel lighter and thinner, and therefore they may believe they are healthier. Elective surgeries of this kind are becoming common globally. In some places, a thriving "health tourism" industry is emerging to handle elective surgery at much lower costs than one might find in the United States, Japan, or Europe (Goodrich 1993). Thailand and South Africa, among other places, are now global destinations for elective plastic surgery (Connell 2006).

There is also a growing field of "complementary alternative and medicine" (CAM), which consists of practices that are "outside" the realm of the biomedical, including herbal medicine therapies, massage, and herbal saunas (Andrews 2003; Andrews et al. 2004). In some cases, dominant health care institutions take alternative practices seriously; for example, the use of acupuncture is sometimes allowed and recommended by biomedical practitioners as a medical intervention for various chronic health problems (Clarke et al. 2004). And, geographers have become more interested in these biomedical alternatives, investigating the important relationship between healing and place (e.g. Gesler 1998). The relationship between a hegemonic biomedical (or allopathic) set of practices and an alternative (or holistic) set of health practices is not a straightforward one. In fact, these processes are complexly inter-related in ways that sometimes blur the distinctions between the two (Del Casino 2004). Social geographers can and should investigate the practices of "the medical" and "the alternative" not in isolation but in relation to each other, asking how certain practices may be dominant in certain places and not others. In order to under-stand the variegated ways in which social geographers might study health and disease, the medical and alternative, we now turn to a discussion of critical medical and health geographies. In so doing, we want to examine how social geographers might "go about" investigating inequality and difference in the context of health and health care, disease and illness, healthy and unhealthy bodies and spaces.

Critical Geographies of Disease and Health Care

Medical geography is a field interested in questions related to quality of life, access to health care, and the sociocultural and political-economic contexts and consequences of disease distributions and diffusions. Its twin research foci of disease ecology and health care studies offer important insights into critical geographies of health (Mayer 1982). Both of these areas came into contact with the quantitative revolution and the movement toward a more socially relevant spatial science in the 1970s, investigating how the spatial organization of societies impact the health and illness of a place's population. Moreover, both disease ecology and health care studies have engaged in the move from biomedical to social-ecological models of health and disease, focusing on the importance of human (and political) ecologies of disease on the one hand and the social production and construction of health care on the other.

Disease ecology and the social production of (dis)ease

Disease ecology is an area of inquiry rarely examined in social geography; but it offers insight into a number of important geographic relationships. Put simply, disease ecologists work through an epidemiological lens to investigate how our "place in the world" differently affects the distribution and diffusion of various diseases through the study of mortality (death) and morbidity (disease and/or illness) and the causal links between the two. Broadly speaking, the goals of any disease ecology are: (a) to understand why morbidity or mortality rates may rise or fall; and (b) to investigate how and why a disease may wane and how to control future spread. Disease ecologists do this through the study of the interrelationships between the social, biological, and (built and physical) environmental contexts of disease distributions and diffusions in the hope of determining how to reduce the spread and effects of particular diseases (Meade and Earickson 2000). Within these contexts, disease ecologists examine two broad categories of diseases: chronic and acute. Chronic diseases (or illnesses) are long-term conditions that may or may not require medical intervention, such as heart disease or high cholesterol. Acute diseases (or illnesses) are intense, short-term conditions, such as influenza or strep throat. Some chronic diseases are differentially intense, causing periods of decreased mobility or feelings of ill health (Crooks and Chouinard 2006). In other cases, chronic and acute diseases can be the cause of mortality. Some diseases are also considered infectious, spreading from one person (or animal) to another person (or animal) or even through one animal (e.g. insect) to another animal and then to a human (Mayer 2000). Often, disease ecologists are interested in understanding the vector of an infectious disease, the subject through whom a disease passes as it spreads. Some infectious diseases can be carried from an insect to a human (e.g. malaria), while others are purely human-to-human (e.g. HIV). Disease ecologists, like so many social geographers

Box 4.1   Methodological Note: Human Ecologies of Disease

Human ecology is a "framework" of medical geographic inquiry that "triangulates" different types of data to explain the "state of health" of a population. For Meade and Earickson (2000), human ecology is a holistic and synergistic approach to the study of health and disease, as it brings together data from the realms of biology, society, and the "environment." Figure 4.3 illustrates how human ecology's tripartite conceptual model of population (or biological), habitat (or environmental), and behavioral (or individual and sociocultural) data are triangulated to explain how and why the status of one's health varies across space.

While this model is not without its problems – the most obvious of which is the separation of "the social" from "social organization" – it does provide a methodological lens through which social geographers can investigate the processes that affect "state of health," as well as disease causation and distribution. This model can be adapted to include, under the broader category of "behavior," political and economic processes that also affect health and disease. This model is also valuable because it includes "the social" and "the biological," while also suggesting that social geographers remember the broader environments in which health is realized on a day-to-day basis.

Quick Exercise

Recent reports note that malaria is spreading in sub-Saharan Africa. Using common online search engines, identify the human ecological issues involved in this spread. What methodologies might help to identify aspects of this human ecology not currently being discussed? What would you recommend as the best approach to mitigate this spread in the short and long term?

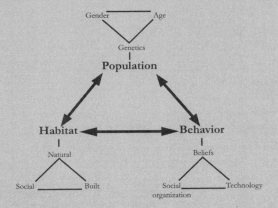

Figure 4.3   The triangle of human ecology. (Meade and Erickson 2000: 25, reprinted with permission.)

before them, are very much interested in the relationship between society and nature as well as among social groups and individuals.

When studying the spread of diseases, it is thus important to examine a multitude of factors, including the overall population that is impacted by a particular disease, the environmental context (broadly conceived) in which that disease is spreading, and the social behaviors or practices that might intensify or mitigate the diffusion of a particular disease. It is impossible to partition one of these areas out from the rest, and so it behooves social geographers to consider the interrelationships among the multitude of factors that intensify certain disease distributions and limit others. Moreover, it is critical that those studying diseases take into consideration the broader sociocultural and political-economic contexts that play such a crucial role in determining how certain diseases spread and why others may be stopped. Reclus's social environmental geographies already raised important questions regarding the unequal organization of and access to the world's resources. After all, one's access to clean and healthy spaces impacts one's everyday experience of health and disease. As an example, malaria eradication programs have been very effective in a number of highly industrialized economies, while this particular disease, spread via mosquitoes, remains a leading killer of people in many parts of the developing world (Klinkenberg et al. 2004). There is always a social geography that underlies any disease distribution or pattern, a geography based in the context of human–environmental and social relationships.

Social geographers can thus work through a disease ecology framework while offering a critical analysis of how sociospatial relations of power impact disease distributions. While the biological processes of disease spread are important, the broader sociospatial context may play an even more significant role in the daily lives of those at risk for certain infectious, chronic, or acute diseases, such as HIV, asthma, or influenza. There is no way to divest disease causation from its broader socio-spatial context. A social geographic approach to disease ecology, therefore, would investigate the distribution and diffusion of diseases as emerging out of the dynamic environment, much of which is based in human-induced change. As an example, recent studies have shown that dysentery rates, particularly among children in the developing world, are affected by access to clean water supplies and adequate public waste sanitation more than by the so-called "environmental causes" of the bacteria that cause dysentery (Emch 1999). As another example, shrimp farming and other aquaculture practices can produce in areas with endemic malaria or dengue hemorrhagic fever, such as Kenya, new sites of standing water ideal for the breeding of mosquitoes (Howard and Omlin 2008). These mosquitoes have the potential to further spread malaria or dengue fever. Recent studies have also shown that schistosomiasis – a parasitic infectious disease that develops in water-based snails and spreads to humans – can become endemic in new flood areas around dams (Sleigh 2006). The most recent example is that of the Three Gorges Dam area in China, where the expansion of water on the land may be linked to the potential for this disease to spread to multiple communities (Jackson and Sleigh 2000; Li et al. 2000). This is similar to what happened in Ghana in the 1970s along Lake

Volta, a human-created waterbody whose construction was linked to an increase in cases of schistosomiasis. The problem persists to this day despite the availability of medication to reduce the rates of this disease (Hunter 2003). Susceptibility to these various diseases, based in changes to the environment, are thus not without sociocultural and political-economic links. It is often the case that extended exposure to unsanitary spaces, malarial exposure via aquaculture practices, or contact with the parasites that cause shistosomiasis are more common among the working poor. In a similar vein, those who must get drinking water from rivers or the manmade lakes that might contain high levels of parasites because they have no running water are much more likely to encounter schistosomiasis. Further exacerbating these problems is the fact that dam construction displaces people from the land and disrupts the rivers that once served as important sources of economic and nutritional sustenance (Sleigh 2006).

There are other ways, however, that shifts in the ecology of certain places might lend themselves to the expansion of diseases. Take, for example, intensified urbanization. Proximity to freeways, ports, or industrial parks might increase the likelihood of having asthma (Corburn et al. 2006). Diseases of the skin and regular rashes are also common among those living close to these hazards. Crowded urban areas, particularly in poorer neighborhoods, have historically intensified the rate of tuberculosis or whooping cough infections, which are spread via the human respiratory system (Grineski et al. 2006). The recent outbreak of SARS (severe acute respiratory syndrome) was concentrated in major metropolitan areas, such as Hong Kong and Singapore, and was linked to wind flow patterns and poor water drainage in certain high rise complexes in Hong Kong, in particular (Li et al. 2006). As an airborne disease, SARS spread quickly and was quite dangerous to the most vulnerable, particularly children and the elderly. The close proximity of urban living and the built environment of the high rise itself partially accounted for the rapid spread of this particular disease. This means, as well, that certain ethnic and racial communities are more susceptible to certain diseases because of their proximate location to heavily polluted urban areas, factory areas, and freeway systems.

Ironically, there are also consequences when humans intentionally modify their own biological environments to reduce certain diseases. The hope that penicillin and other medicines more generally would put an end to infectious diseases in the 1970s has not come to fruition. Some of the most significant problems today stem from the fact that new forms of old diseases are emerging that are resistant to the prophylactics meant to stem their spread. Newly developed malarial medications have not been able to keep pace with the mutation of malaria. It is quite possible to contract a strain of malaria that is drug resistant. Antiobiotics, once seen as a panacea for all diseases, have been given in such large quantities for viral infections that they are becoming ineffective against bacterial infections as well. In some cases, antiobiotics have also destroyed the beneficial bacteria in the body, giving rise to a new regime of medications called probiotics, which promote bacterial growth in the body for bacteria necessary for digestion. Thus, despite the optimism that biomedical advances would rid the world of most diseases, a resurgence of older

Box 4.2   Geographies of (Dis)ease

The distribution of diseases and the fear attached to them can produce (dis)ease, a process of social and spatial stigma. Take, for example, bovine spongiform encephalopathy (BSE) or "mad cow disease." This disease, which can spread from a cow to a human who ingests that cow, significantly impacted the British beef market. Today, travelers from the UK are asked to report if they have been in a "rural area" when entering the US as a way to mitigate the spread of BSE in the US. Despite these efforts, there have been a few cases of BSE reported in the US, prompting the South Korean government to stop the import of US beef into its country. In another case, Haiti was identified as a key site for the spread of HIV, leading to the decimation of its tourist economy in the 1980s (Farmer 1992). Fear of SARS and avian bird flu has similarly hurt the tourism economies of Hong Kong and Thailand.

Other examples can be found throughout history (see Wolch and Philo 2000). Seen as unproductive and sometimes dangerous biological citizens (N. Rose 2007), certain populations were quarantined to minimize their impact on the larger society. Stigma is also fueled by misconceptions of how diseases spread in the first place, leading many to conflate the causes of one disease with the spread of another (Dear et al. 1997; Takahashi 1998b; Takahashi et al. 2002). Such confusion may have significant social implications, as people are marginalized because of misperceptions and not real risk. This is most classically seen in the case of Ryan White, a young boy in the United States who contracted HIV from a blood transfusion while being treated for a blood disorder known as hemophilia. Ryan White fought the stigma and isolation and became an important representation of how HIV was and was not transmitted. For those in marginal social positions, it is often difficult to fight against such spatial quarantine.

Quick Exercise

How have organizations, such as ACT UP and The AIDS Memorial Quilt (HIV/AIDS activist organizations), challenged the social and spatial stigma attached to HIV/AIDS? What are the differences in their organizational strategies? (See http://www.actupny.org (ACT UP) and http://www.aidsquilt.org (The AIDS Memorial Quilt of The Names Project Foundation) for information on these organizations. You can also find other local ACT UP organizations in major cities globally.)

diseases and the emergence of new diseases challenge the ways people live on a day-to-day basis. In this context, the social consequences of not protecting bio-diversity become even more important as people struggle to find ways to cope with both chronic and acute illnesses. In places where biomedical treatments are rarely available, the sociospatial organization of common property resources forms an essential place for the development of nonbiomedical treatments and medications to minimize the severe symptoms associated with many diseases. The intricate link between disease, health, society, and environment is thus more complex when we considering the invaluable significance of biodiverse ecoregions and their potential to provide short- and long-term mitigations of current and future diseases. This includes biomedical interventions, which continue to rely on both naturally and synthetically based medications that may help people cope with the day-to-day realities of trying to live healthy lives.

Health care studies, diffusing medical and alternative health care systems

In similar ways to disease ecologists, social geographers of health care have used spatial models to examine the distribution of medical services (Earikson 1970; Misra 1970; Shannon and Dever 1974; Shannon and Spurlock 1976; Pyle 1977; Phillips 1981). In the 1960s the "resurgence of social awareness" in the US (Pyle 1983: 87) prompted medical geographers to question the uneven distribution of medical care. Planning became an important point of intervention in debate about health care, as did critiques of free-market approaches to health care delivery (Pyle 1983). In this context, Pyle (1983) noted three major problems with 1960s medical care in the US:

1   Hierarchies of hospitals can be identified, but locations have not been deter-mined by principles of spatial equity with respect to access.
2   There are specific cultural and behavioural determinants of health-care facilities selection and use within the United States.
3   It is possible to utilize principles of location analysis in planning the locations of new health-care delivery facilities, but policy decisions often overshadowed "rational" solutions to location problems.

Shannon and Dever followed in this tradition with their text *Health Care Delivery: Spatial Perspectives* (1974). Using central place theory (Smith 1986), they modeled a hierarchy of health care facilities across an absolute space, thereby idealizing where health care facilities should be located to best serve local populations. They then took the ideal model and compared it to several places – the Soviet Union, Sweden, England – and compared those systems with that in the US. They conclude that issues of funding have prevented the US from implementing an effective "spatial and functional organization" of health care. They also argued that medical systems should be open to all people regardless of race, income, or religion: they suggest that the equal distribution of services across an absolute space would go a long way to solving uneven medical care. Pushing this further, though, Shannon and Dever strongly recommend the expansion of preventative medicine – outreach and education, for example – through a "regionally centralized administration . . . [which would] oversee a functionally and spatially decentralized execution of a coordinated and integrated system of medical service" (Shannon and Dever 1974: 33). As medical geographers, they also believe that the most effective preventative practices come from the field of biomedicine.

There are numerous studies that have followed in this tradition, tracing the spatial relationships between health care accessibility and health outcomes (e.g. Joseph and Bantock 1982; Halseth and Rosenberg 1988). At the same time, other medical geographers have pushed "beyond" a purely facilities location approach, asking how to better integrate sociocultural and political-economic processes into studies of both access to and decisions regarding health-care facility choice and practice (Rosenberg 1988). Scott et al. (2002) have interestingly shown how lower levels of economic development in KwaZulu-Natal, South Africa might be correlated with less health care accessibility, which may lead to an underreporting of cancer rates. This suggests that studies of disease distributions cannot rely simply on epidemiological data. Instead, to understand the geography of disease distributions, researchers must also trace the complicated geographies of health care. In a different study, Gage (2007) demonstrates the important relationship between distance and prenatal care for women in Mali, Africa. In this case, distance from services and a lack of transportation services limit accessibility to prenatal and antenatal health care visits, which may increase the mortality rates of both women and children.

Others suggested that social geographers examine health care as more than simply an issue of accessibility (Eyles and Woods 1983). Gesler (1991), for example, utilizes a diffusionist model to examine how biomedical language has moved through chains of health care facilities supplanting other forms of health and disease knowledge. Chiotti and Joseph (1995) outline how Toronto, Canada has been socially reproduced over time, creating a differential urban environment with areas of least and more resistance to the location of an AIDS hospice.[1] In this context, Casey House is shown to be located in a neighborhood characteristic of those that have little resistance to facility location – poorer, inner city spaces with high renter occupancy. But a facility location approach based on an analysis of social and economic context variables does not explain the entire story of Casey House. The siting of this AIDS hospice finds itself intimately connected with the meaning ascribed to the neighborhood itself, which has developed a shared sense of belonging and caring related to HIV. This is because:

the neighborhood within which Casey House is situated is host to a number of informal institutions associated with the gay community. . . . Once a year, the neighborhood is "encircled" by a unique community event, the gay pride parade. Being centrally situated within this cultural landscape, one can argue that at least in terms of proximity to the main at-risk population, the neighborhood is suitable for the location of an AIDS hospice (Chiotti and Joseph 1995: 137).

In this case, this neighborhood has developed a queer identity, which made it an appropriate and comfortable space for the location of this particular health care facility. This does not deny the important economic factors that made the neighborhood less resistant to the placement of the AIDS hospice. Instead, it suggests that a dialectic view of space that examines the mutual constitution of the social and spatial provides insight into how health care may be placed in the urban landscape.

Box 4.3   Methodological Note: Structure-Agency Methodology in Health Geography

In explaining the spatial organization of health care as well as health practices, some health geographers draw on both political economic (structural) and humanistic (agency) theoretical frameworks. This synthetic approach is exemplified in the work of Robin Kearns and Alun Joseph (1997: 23), who apply a structure-agency model to the study of rural health care "restructuring" in New Zealand among both Maori (indigenous) and Pakeha (European origin) peoples. Following Relph (1976), Kearns and Joseph (1997: 24) argue that "human experience of localities . . . [is] imbued with meaning and shared value" and that these meanings are collectively organized by communities through their readings of "the built environment . . . [of] hospitals, meeting halls, or schools." The restructuring of rural health care is tied to localized "senses of place." Indeed, Kearns and Joseph argue that hospitals are "more than health-care facilities; they are also part of the articulation of place" (ibid.: 28). At the same time, the struggles over health care accessibility and services are situated at the national level in New Zealand and are determined by broader economic (structural) factors.

In Figure 4.4, Kearns and Joseph outline the structural constraints on rural health care outreach in New Zealand, highlighting how the political economy impacts the services available through the rural health service. The restructuring of the political economy of health care is not without its contestations, as both Maori and Pakeha peoples construct "communities of interest" that can challenge the defunding of rural health care. Although physically separated in this model, "place" and the "cultural fabric" are conceptualized as interdependent. In short, Kearns and Joseph argue that while rural restructuring of health care is real, it is challenged by local communities that place symbolic value in the institutions of health care, which they see as "more than" hospitals and clinics. These spaces are viewed as part of the community, an

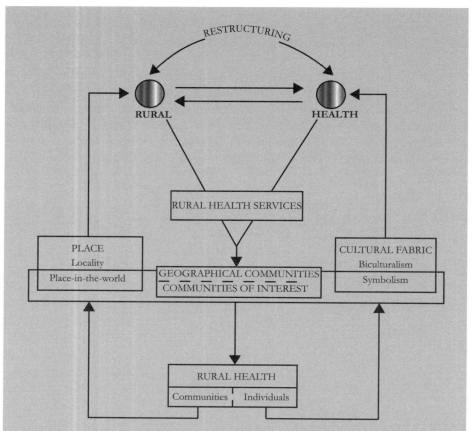

Figure 4.4   A framework for linking restructuring with rural health.
(Adapted from Kearns and Joseph 1997: 23, reprinted with permission.)

essential aspect of its characteristic as a place. The "threat to *local* health-care services was clearly seen as an assault on community itself. There were no divisions along lines of interest, by they socioeconomic, professional or 'racial'" (ibid.: 28). Methodologically, they show that there is value in studying the structural constraints on health care as well as the place-based values that "communities of interest" might share.

Quick Exercise

On a piece of paper, make a table with two columns. In the first column, list the structural constraints that might impact someone's access to health care. In the second column, list the ways in which individuals and groups can enact their own agency and work against these constraints.

In somewhat similar ways, I have traced the diffusion of alternative health care practices in Thailand, illustrating that the spread of HIV has led to the re-emergence of a self-defined "traditional Thai medicine" that promoted the expansion of a network of local healers who could work with people living with HIV and AIDS (Del Casino 2004). The resurgence of an alternative medicine happened in this case because biomedical interventions for HIV have been limited in a Thai context. As such, alternative approaches spread through the development of local healer groups and in biomedical facilities, such as hospitals and clinics, which came to rely on herbal medicines, meditation techniques, and herbal saunas to help people living with HIV and AIDS deal with the opportunistic infections they developed as a result of their compromised immune system. Such "alternative" approaches to studying health care in medical geography were prompted by the development of a series of intellectual challenges to the hegemony of biomedical-centered models of health care in geography, which questioned the need for one kind of health geography. It is to these new theories of the geographies of health, which rely on a conscious engagement with critical social theory, that I now turn.

Critical Medical and Health Geographies

While the development of disease ecologies and health care studies, which are sensitive to social inequalities and access to services, remains important to social geography today, the work of Gesler (1992) and others (Kearns 1993; Dorn and Laws 1994; Dyck and Kearns 1995; Eyles and Litva 1996) began to push the study of health and disease in geography in a new direction. These geographers did so by questioning the biomedical-centric nature of medical geography; they challenged the a priori assumption that a certain type of medicine and way of defining and knowing health, illness, and disease was always the best approach. Put simply, they wanted to expand the array of social theoretical approaches that medical geographers use in their investigation of health-related issues. And, they were interested in extending the study of health beyond the hospital and clinic and into the arena of the mundane, investigating the experiences of living with and experiencing disease (Del Casino 2009), the complicated dynamics of therapeutic spaces and landscapes (Smyth 2005), and the body as a space of health and disease (Parr 2002). New sites of inquiry developed within what Robin Kearns (1993) defined as a "reformed medical geography," and what Kearns and Gesler (1998a) would later call a "geography of health." Topics that had been heretofore marginalized within the confines of a critical medical geography were now being taken seriously, as social geographers interested in the intersections of health and place and health and the body drew from a wide array of social theories and social theorists in their research (e.g. Eyles and Litva 1996; Philo 1996, 2000). Importantly, this turn toward health and alternatives to biomedicine has not completely evacuated questions related to "the medical" from critical medical and health geography. As Parr (2002: 241) argues, "geographers of health do not need to 'do away with' the medical, but can continue to engage with it, albeit in a more critical capacity than has been the case previously within the subdiscipline." In this vein, there remains a need to engage and reflect on how "the medical" reworks notions of healthy and ill bodies and spaces. This section scratches the surface of this broader reform through a brief investigation of three areas of critical medical and health geography: (a) a rethinking of the spatialities of health, healing, and landscape; (b) the emergence of critical disability studies in geography; and (c) a new found focus on sexual health studies in critical social geography.

Rethinking the spatialities of health, landscape, and identity

The tensions that emerged between social and cultural geography in the 1990s directly impacted the study of health in geography. In particular, a group of health geographers turned to social and cultural theory to better investigate what they saw as the important "health–place relationship." For some medical geographers, it was time to "re-engage" with their social geographic roots (Eyles and Woods 1983; Kearns 1993), while for others it was necessary to expand their use of theory coming from cultural geography (Gesler 1991). As Kearns and Gesler (1998b: 5) explain, "one of the key implications of putting health into place is that a reinvented medical geography must be *social*, given that diseases, service delivery systems, and health policies are socially produced, constructed, and transmitted" (original emphasis). Within this resocialized medical geography emerged a focus on therapeutic landscapes, spaces, and networks (Smyth 2005). The focus on "the therapeutic" has been seen as a particularly important corrective to the highly medicalized nature of medical geography, which Gesler (1992) believed failed to acknowledge the diversity of spaces that might be considered healthful spaces of healing. The corrective Gesler offered also suggested that geographers of health could once again engage questions of society–environment relations through the study of "natural" healing places, such as hot springs (Geores 1998; Gesler 1998), as well as socialized healing spaces tied to religious systems (Smyth 2005: 489). This move also took a historical turn, as "geographers of health" began to investigate the longer-term traditions of the healing–place relationship as well as the commercial applicability of healing as a commodity. Geores (1998: 36) describes the history of "Hot Springs, South Dakota . . . [as] a town founded by entrepreneurs [who wanted] to sell a commodity called 'health.' Warm mineral springs were the core of place-making activities." Importantly, as the healing–place relationship developed over time in Hot Springs, the town founders called upon a biomedical legitimacy, luring clinics and physicians to the town to justify the long-term agenda of linking health to the hot spring. It is important here, then, to understand how the process of constructing a landscape of healing is intimately tied to the social construction of what is meant by "good health" and "medicine."

Importantly, social geographers cannot and should not conceptualize therapeutic landscapes as idealized places of healing alone. It is essential to examine the powerful ways in which the "therapeutic" is deployed as a mechanism of both individual heal-ing and social control. Wilton and DeVerteuil (2006), for example, suggest that the therapeutic landscapes associated with alcohol rehabilitation and sobriety operate simultaneously as "sites of control." In describing the development of therapeutic rehabilitation spaces in San Pedro, California, they suggest that:

> it is also important to understand that these programs are, by their very nature, sites of control. The social relations that exist between staff and clients and among clients are not neutral or devoid of power. . . . The commitment required of clients in these settings is substantial. It involves not only a change in one's relation to alcohol, but also a fundamental change in one's sense of self. Co-presence in the program space allows for surveillance as well as careful instruction to facilitate successful self-governing or self-care. Failure to follow programmatic requirements is grounds for immediate expulsion. Moreover, the relations that exist among individuals within the organization – as specific micro-scale technologies – are incorporated into, and come to reflect, the broader rationality of the political domain. The programs rely on the state for much of their funding and are subject to regulatory requirements and shifting political priorities. At the level of the broader political domain, the activities of these programs contribute to the management of alcoholism conceived not as instances of individual suffering but as a problem of the population requiring intervention (ibid.: 659–60).

Healing, in this context, might be a process imposed upon individuals by the state, which wants to control not only the mobility of drug users but their behaviors as well. These mechanisms of control are tempered by the diversity of spaces within the rehab landscape that serve the recovering drug user, including twelve-step pro-grams such as Alcoholics Anonymous. At the same time, Wilton and DeVerteuil describe the ability of the rehabilitation centers to impact the community in which they are sited through efforts to close liquor stores in close proximity to rehab centers. The spaces of healing, in this case, extend beyond the space of rehabilitation, and the therapeutic landscape of sobriety becomes part of the city of San Pedro itself. This might mean that the therapeutic spaces of these centers extend the powers of the government to regulate not only the behavior of the clients but also the behavior of the lower income, working people living in the surrounding community. In reflecting on this complicated process, it is clear that the landscapes of health are not independent of the broader context in which they are situated. They are thus subject to the plays of social and spatial stigma that maintain such landscapes in low-income residential and commercial areas with minimal organized resistance to their siting, as Wilton and DeVerteuil also describe (see Takahashi 1998b).

More broadly, thinking of health (and healing) as something that happens "beyond" the hospital or clinic is an important shift for social geographers. It signals, first and foremost, that studies of health can focus on more than the material spaces of biomedical power, such as the clinic or the hospital. In fact, the mundane spaces of healing, such as the home, and the extraordinary spaces of health, such as the hot spring, are legitimate sites of social geographic inquiry for medical and health geographers. What this research also suggests is that health and healing, illness and disease are "more than" simply medical terms or conditions. The meanings of these social categories are intimately tied to the politics of identity and subjectivity that are part of the ever-changing health–space relationship. The spaces of health and healing are thus understood only in the context of the various raced, classed, gendered, and sexed identities and subjectivities that we inhabit. Critical health and medical geography, taking their cue, in part, from the cultural turn in geography, have rethought the importance that sociospatial differences have in the everyday practice and use of the spaces of health care. This set of traditions draws from a broad array of social theoretical innovation, though, including critical humanist, Marxist, and feminist geographies, to: (a) expand the understanding of what is meant by health and healing; and (b) diversify the spaces that are considered within critical medical and health geographies. The focus on the relationship between spaces of care and social identities and subjectivities also suggests that social geographers open up new spaces of difference in their medical and health geographies. It is not suprising, then, that Gesler and Kearns (2002: 118) urge geographers "to consider how medicine and society focus on the body, the deviant body in particular. We need to be aware [therefore] of how 'the other' is stigmatized and marginalized and how bodies and 'the other' are labeled." To this end, I now turn to one of critical medical geography's main contributions to the study of difference, disability studies.

Body politics and the geographies of disability

In 1994, Dorn and Laws wrote a particularly important rejoinder to Kearns's earlier (1993) call for a "reformed medical geography." In their paper, they argued that a "reformed medical geography must acknowledge and critically assess its intellectual heritage which understands the body as a site invaded by a disease with a specific etiology" (Dorn and Laws 1994: 107). The body is, after all, "more than" flesh and bones; the body is also a contested political and social space (Schatzki and Natter 1996), which is regulated, disciplined, and practiced like other social spaces. Because the material space of the body is also a social body it is subject to the psychosocial "concept of abjection where we are simultaneously attracted to and repulsed by exotic bodily difference" (Dorn and Laws 1994: 107). In the process of abjection, societies, groups, and communities impose certain notions of the normal and abnormal, acceptable and unacceptable, and productive and unproductive onto individual or collective bodies. As such,

> The imposition of abject bodily identities must at least partly explain society's emplace-
> ment of certain people into particular environments: the lunatic asylum, the nursing
> home, the "sheltered" workshop for the physically disabled. Microgeographies of abjec-
> tion separate the deviant body so that it will not pose a challenge to established social
> [and spatial] norms.

Put simply, Dorn and Laws suggest that while the therapeutic landscape tradition in critical health geography offers an important corrective to the biomedical traditions of the diseased body, that tradition ejects from its analysis the body politics of living with and experiencing health and illness, disease and well-being. "[S]witching the gaze from a concern with the 'body-as-site-of-oppression' to 'place-as-a-site-of-oppression' does not eliminate the need to reclaim the body as a site of resistance" (ibid.: 107). In claiming the body as a "site-of-resistance," Dorn and Laws further argue that "deviant bodies, social institutions, and practices are inseparable from one another. Deviancy, as a cultural system for representing the impaired or abnormal body, is constantly up for grabs, as always being renegotiated through the exercise of political power" (ibid.: 108; also see extended discussion in Chapter 5). The meanings of ability and disability shift as individuals, social groups, and organizations struggle for broader human rights for the so-called deviant, ill, and diseased. Therefore, the social geography of ability and disability is marked by the very active and political process of constructing spaces of resistance to the hegemonic organization of exclusions that mark certain peoples and bodies as deviant and abnormal.

Dorn and Laws were not the first to work in the area of disability studies in geography (Park et al. 1998; Hansen and Philo 2007). Golledge (1993: 64), for example, argued that the "disabled live in transformed space. While the space in which most people live is certainly not homogenous, being replete with barriers and obstacles, and requiring effort to perform interactions, there is no doubt that this effort is magnified many times when one is disabled" (see also Golledge and Stimson 1997). Golledge's concern for the physical organization of space is complemented by the work of critical medical and health geographers interested in interrogating the interrelationship between disability as difference and the socio-spatial construction of inclusion and exclusion for those with both physical and mental disabilities or impairments. Imrie (1999: 26) refocuses attention on how disabled bodies are made to feel marginal to the physical spaces of the abled, particularly through "modern architectural conceptions of architectural form and the built environment [that] are simultaneously ableist and disablist by ignoring and/or denying the multiplicities of the human body." Physical space is not just problematic because of the "bumps in the road." For those with physical disabilities, the social privileging of the "abled" over the "disabled" means that the spatial organization of society limits the social and physical mobilities of certain peoples (Kitchin 1998a; Gleeson 1999; Kitchin and Wilton 2000). The dis-abling spatialities of everyday architectural forms reinforce the subjectification of people with physical impairments as disabled, abnormal, and out-of-place. As such, "many disabled people are denied the freedom to travel where and when they like" (Kitchin 1998a: 348). Within all these contexts, it is the social marginality of those with physical disabilities that limits them to certain spaces. These issues are intensified in contexts where there are few laws or regulations to provide services for those living with certain physical impairments or disabilities.

Of course, as critical medical and health geographers have long argued, the experience of living with physical disabilities and impairments is mediated by

Figure 4.5   Street sign marking out wheelchair "accessible" space in Guangzhou, People's Republic of China. Throughout the world, physical spaces are being adapted to the needs of those with different abilities. In Guangzhou, wheelchair parking is increasing access to certain spaces of the street. Such approaches to making the city more friendly to those with different abilities are far from ubiquitous globally. (Photo by author, 2006.)

various gendered (Valentine 1999) and sexualized (Butler 1999; Anderson and Kitchin 2000) identities and practices. In day-to-day practice and in our own social geographies, it is common to reduce people's identities to their disability, marginalizing the other axes of difference through which their embodied subjectivities are constituted (Anderson and Kitchin 2000). "In relation to disability and sexuality," Anderson and Kitchin (2000: 1164) have argued that "the common cultural representations are ones of asexuality, with disabled people uninterested or unable to take part in sexual activity, or as sexual 'monsters' unable to control their sexual drives and feelings" because of their disability (cited in Del Casino 2007b: 48). The tendency toward reductionism – "they are paraplegics" or "he is HIV positive" or "she is living with multiple sclerosis" – creates a twofold concern for social geography. First, when reducing experience to one node of difference, social geographers fail to recognize how corporeal (or bodily) practices are tied to a number of different structurings of space. Disability is not the only way in which people understand, practice, and experience their body through the spaces of the home, neighborhood, or even nation. Second, as the body is reduced to its disability, it is systematically

de-sexed, de-gendered, de-raced, and de-classed. This means that differently disabled bodies may not be recognized in certain community spaces, such as the gay
community, because they are seen as disabled and therefore without a sexual identity. As an example, "many disabled lesbians, gay men and bisexual individuals
(LGBs) feel the need to attend Pride festivals, not to support gay rights, but to draw
the LGB population's attention to their disabled members" (Butler 1999: 203). Spaces
can thus be socially and materially enabling, on the one hand, and disabling, on
the other. Fighting to de-straighten space through Pride might reinscribe an ableist
normativity that marginalizes people who do not meet the "idealized" vision of a
"perfect" queer body.

The social geographies of disability and disabled experiences are thus intimately
tied to the inextricable entanglement of space and identity, difference and inequality.
Valentine (2007) describes this process of identity-making as both an internalized
and externalized process in her discussion of D/deafness. "D/deaf is written in this
way to reflect that there are two dominant constructions of D/deafness: deafness as
a medical matter and Deaf as a linguistic minority" (ibid.: 15). Even though deafness
is ascribed from outside the Deaf community as a disability, within the spaces of
the Deaf disability might be tied to one's inability to use the linguistic conventions
of sign. By eschewing a reductionist biomedical philosophy that constructs deafness as a disability, it is possible to investigate how people perform their bodies,
temporarily privileging one way of knowing over another – disability creates different challenges and opportunities that may be unique but not unlike other challenges
and opportunities for so-called able-bodied individuals. And, social geographers
can interrogate how bodies are regulated through a process of "othering" certain
bodies as different. This means challenging reductionist practice that marginalizes
difference and structures spaces and identities in ways that maintain inequalities.
As such, social geographers should investigate the non-normative and resistant geographic practices of so-called disabled peoples as they live in and through spaces
that are, quite often, not of their own design.

The study of the space–disability relationship, of course, is not limited to the study
of physical disability (see Box 4.4). Social geographers have held a long-term
interest in understanding the spatialities of living with and experiencing mental
disabilities, illnesses, and impairments (Parr and Boyd 2008). "Whereas mental
health geography's 'first wave' was primarily concerned with the movements of
people with mental illness in the post-asylum era, its 'second wave' concerned itself
with questions of identity for people coded by society as mentally 'abnormal', and
the ways in which they are dealt with by people who identify as being 'normal' "
(Parr and Boyd 2008: 2). In the first wave, social geographers drew from the
rich tradition of radical geography to examine the problems associated with the
placement of facilities for those living with mental illness and the links between
deinstitutionalization and homelessness (Wolch and Philo 2000). As those with
mental illnesses were "released" from the asylum, the social safety net also dis-
appeared, leaving them with little choice but to find temporary shelter on the streets
of both rural and urban spaces. In this second wave, social geographers studying

Box 4.4   Hester Parr's *Mental Health and Social Space: Toward Inclusive Geographies?*

Mental health geographies have been influenced by an "institutional perspective," which focuses on the "medical," "the doctor," and "the asylum," with less attention paid to the people who are "living with a mental illness." Hester Parr offers a corrective to this perspective, tracing *both* the broader geographies of mental health *and* the day-to-day experiences of "people living with mental health problems" (Parr 2008: 23). This corrective pushes mental health geographies past the medicalized spaces of "care" and "exclusion" and into the everyday spaces of "the community" where many mental health geographies are played out. Parr enlivens mental health geographies, examining how people cope with and negotiate their way through both "medical" and "nonmedical" space.

Parr does this by tracing the history of therapeutic spaces for mental health "treatment" – community gardens, art projects, and virtual health forums – while placing these social spaces in contemporary context. Her goal: to investigate how such projects facilitate "inclusive" community geographies for people with mental health problems. Parr stresses that creating "inclusion" is not a straightforward process. In discussing art communities and art projects "for people with serious and enduring mental health problems," Parr argues that "While embodied artistic practice can (but not always) have stabilizing effects, and art project spaces can involve specific forms of social connectivity, engaging in artistic communities of interest in the wider city also holds differing and rather precarious opportunities for participants" (ibid.: 130–1). In her discussion of virtual health communities she also notes that members "still inhabit embodied offline worlds" (ibid.: 159), which impact personal experiences of their illnesses. Parr believes, however, that new spaces of mental health can expand inclusion. In her words:

> In predicting new future geographies of mental health, it is possible not only to discuss the very real need for comprehensive well-funded and equitable psychiatric and social service provision, but also to contemplate other innovations in public mental health. These innovative scenarios might see people with mental health problems as gardeners, artists, film-makers and community members who are networked and active in ways that connect with others who are not chronically ill or "mad" (ibid.: 184).

Quick Exercise

Using an archive of a local newspaper, search for debates and discussions about the location of mental health facilities. What are some of the issues and politics related to the location of these facilities? Are there any alternative treatment spaces available for people with "severe mental health issues" in your own area? If so, what kinds? If not, why do you think that is?

mental health have drawn from feminism and poststructuralism to rethink the space–identity relationship, particularly in the context of how those with mental illnesses are constructed through new narratives of difference as disabled, incapable, and unproductive. In many ways, the second wave of mental health geographies challenges the binary logic of mind and body, suggesting that minds are part of our bodies: mental health is a bodily and embodied process (Parr 2000, 2008). In this way, to a certain degree, mental health geographies parallel the work being done in physical disability studies. Wolch and Philo (2000) suggest, however, that both "first" and "second" wave approaches, which draw from different theoretical traditions, may be brought together to study the material landscape of mental health services and the processes at work that suture certain disabled mental health identities to particular spaces of the city, such as the street. Social geographers can also turn their attention to how denial and stigma marginalize mental health issues in rural spaces, where it may be difficult to attend to one's mental illness because "social visibility, rural gossip networks, fear of social stigma, and self-stigma may deter people with mental health problems from accessing services in rural communities" (Parr and Boyd 2008). Social geographies of mental health, illness, and impairment can transgress the arbitrary boundaries of urban and rural to consider how various social geographic processes – stigma, isolation, productivity, ability – work in and across the everyday lives and spaces of the so-called abled and disabled.

Sexing health and medical geographies

It is clear that the topics, approaches, and questions that make up the social geographies of health care and "the medical" are quite diverse. Despite this diversity, social geographers, particularly those interested in health and medical geographies, have remained rather limited in their engagement with questions related to sexual health (Del Casino 2007a, 2007b). Put simply, social geographers of health talk about sexuality but rarely talk about sex. It is not surprising, then, to see Philo (2005a: 328) argue recently that:

> It is an understandable unease, given deeply entrenched views about what comprises (il)legitimate subject matters and undoubted fears about being thought to have "unhealthy" interests, and yet it is arguably an *in*defensible unease because sex simply *is* so fundamental to the peopling, working and experience of the human world that is our study area.

Indeed, sex and sexual health are of concern to millions of people a year, as illnesses and diseases, such as HIV, chlamydia, and gonorrhea, continue to spread, and as transgendered, transexed, and intersexed peoples continue to negotiate mental health issues related to, for example, sexual reassignment surgery. Talking about sex, then, has never been more pressing and important, as Gwanzura-ottemöller and Kesby found in their study of sexual practice and risk among children aged under fifteen years in Zimbabwe (2005). Sex also takes place for many in spaces of complicated and ambiguous power relations related to the practices of gendered, sexed, raced, and classed bodies identities (Thomas 2004, 2008). That is why Thomas (2004) examines how girls practice sex and their heterosexuality in everyday spaces, complicating simple readings of girl–boy relations as constructed only through gendered relations (see Chapter 7). At the same time, social geographers can also investigate how sex can be violent and unwanted, used as a tactic of individual or social control. Rape is used every day globally as a tactic of war. And, rape and other forms of sexual violence directly affect the material, psychological, and social body through the tearing of flesh, the emotional crisis tied to forced penetration, and the ostracization that happens for women (and men) who may have been attacked.

Sex is also practiced as part of alternative sexual communities, networks, and spaces of alterity based in practices of bondage and domination or BDSM[2] (Herman 2007). The social regulation of sex means that certain peoples – e.g. those in BDSM communities – might "hide" themselves, however, causing both psychosocial pressures and physical risk. Higher risk sexual practices in this case are a result of trying to avoid detection by family, police, or friends. It is important to appreciate, then, that the practices and normalization of different ways of having sex are historically situated (Philo 2005a), as is what we mean by a healthy sexual body (Del Casino 2007a). And, this affects sexual health.

The recent upsurge of drugs to alter the body, such as Viagra, Levitra, and Cialis, which treat erectile dysfunction and make certain practices of sex possible for example, have a number of implications for the study of sexual health in social geography. First, the development of Viagra (and other sexuopharmaceuticals, such as Levitra and Cialis) has challenged what constitutes a healthy sexual body and altered how we interpret sexual health and sex more generally (see, for example, Loe 2004 and her discussion of Viagra, sex, and ageing among women). This has, subsequently, had an effect on the practices and performances of sex itself. By validating the erection as a key aspect of one's masculinity, it puts pressure on individuals to perform that masculinity in ways that may actually place them at risk, finding themselves in spaces and situations that they might not have considered earlier (Kochems and Del Casino 2004). For example, the bedroom, once a space of sanctuary and non-penetrative intimacy, may be reorganized as an erection- and phallocentric space of masculine desire (Potts et al. 2003). Bodily practices of provocative touching, whispering, and caressing may now be replaced with a reductionist form of sex set in a foundational penetration. Reciprocally, the use of such drugs might make new sexual opportunities available that were once denied, including extended arousal that may cause both pain and pleasure simultaneously. In BDSM playrooms or in other non-heteronormative contexts, Viagra might enhance sexual identity and provide release from the strictures of certain straight sexual practices. In this way, Viagra might promote a non-normative healthy sexual life that is not narrowly confined by the parameters of heterosexism and its missionary zeal. Viagra also "works" in the context of a conservative or progressive agenda, revivifying nonpenetrative or nonprocreational sex and virginity as positive aspects of a Christian premarital or marital ethic or, by contrast, promoting networks and communities founded around nonpenetrative sexual practices that do not require the erect penis as a prerequisite of satisfying everyone's sexual desire.[3]

Second, as drugs such as Viagra have entered the market,[4] they have taken on new and varied sexual meanings that work well beyond the initial notions ascribed to them by their makers. These meanings, and the use of Viagra in numerous, complicated sexuospatial contexts, have shifted the dynamics of risks related to the transmission of HIV and other sexually transmitted infections (STIs) (Swearigen and Klausner 2005). Their use, and the relationship to the transmission of certain diseases, however, is never a straightforward one. As Brown (2006b: 887) suggests, "sex can take multiple forms, and actions, each of which has a different degree of risk of exposure to different sexually transmitted infections." And, thus, the relationship among, say, Viagra use, sex, and HIV may only be significant when other drugs, such as methamphetamines (speed or crank), ketamine, or gamma-hydroxy butyrate (GHB), are used to practice certain sexualized and drug-using identities – as these reduce inhibition (or memory) and thus may increase risk for engaging in practices or conditions (spatial and temporal) that could lead to HIV transmission, such as unprotected vaginal or anal sex. Or, the link between Viagra, sex, and other STIs, such as chlamydia and gonorrhea, might only be significant when individuals leave a place of comfort (their home) and move into new spaces of desire, such as a resort in another country, and drink alcohol and/or practice sex in ways that put them at risk (e.g. having sex with anonymous sex partners without protection). Viagra, itself, might not be the drug that leads to unprotected sex, but it might engender a new body (part) that allows one to more actively engage in unprotected sex with individual or multiple sex partners and thus, potentially, increase one's risk for HIV or other STIs. The social meanings that work through Viagra's production and distribution – that penetration and/or erection are essential – do intersect with new sexuospatial practices and identities. In the case of the latter, male sex workers might extend their working day and service more clients, promoted by this drug's abilities to keep them hard. Party-and-play (sex and drug parties) situations might become more intense as sexuopharmaceuticals allow for extended sexual interactions. And Viagra might be critical if one is to maintain his place within such a context: losing one's hard-on might lead to (dis)placement. There is, of course, no essential link between sexuopharmaceuticals, other drugs, and risks related to HIV and STIs. But, sexuopharmaceuticals do change the dynamics of how one might perform in certain places that may increase the chances for such transmissions.

There is more to be done in the area of sexual health studies in social geography, suggesting that the study of sex can also explain how different spaces and practices reinforce and/or challenge certain gendered and sexualized identities. It is important to remember, then, that sex takes place in spaces often replete with relations of power that affect how people have sex, with whom they have sex, and why they have sex. All of this suggests, then, that social geographers should continue to sex the field of medical and health geography, asking questions that push how they conceptualize healthy bodies and spaces.

Critical Geographies of Health, Inequality, and Difference

> Medical rhetoric also extends beyond health care and is used to enhance the meaning of nonmedical phenomena, through such expressions as "the health of the economy," and "the sick society" (Gesler 1992: 741).

This chapter has discussed how social geographers who draw from the traditions of critical medical and health geography have relied on and contributed to a wide array of theoretical and methodological perspectives to study disease and health care distributions, the meanings we ascribe to health and disease, as well as the experiences of living with certain illnesses and impairments. Social geography, as a subdiscipline, has a strong affinity with questions of health and health care as well as disease and illness because of the strong interest in the study of difference and inequality. In the case of the latter, social geographers remain interested in the spatial extent of health care services and the problems of health care accessibility for people who are particularly marginalized. Social geographers are also interested in understanding how differences are constructed and maintained through socio-spatial relations of ability and disability, healthy and ill, while drawing upon a wide array of theoretical approaches – from feminism, queer theory, humanism, Marxism, psychoanalysis, or poststruturalism. They want to tease apart various health–place and health–identity relationships, simultaneously tracing how social and political bodies and subjectivities are maintained through these relationships. There is more to do, though, if social geographers are going to find new ways to expand services to those in need and open up new spaces where differences are constructed not through processes of abjection but through practices of diversity.

Notes

1   This work follows a long tradition of facility location studies in social geography (see Wolpert et al. 1975; Dear and Taylor 1982; Dear and Wolch 1987; Dear and Gleeson 1991).
2   BDSM stands for any combination of bondage and discipline, domination and submission, and/or sadism and masochism.
3   This can be seen in the rise of "teen virginity" campaigns (Mosher et al. 2005; Simon 2006) and with the development of new social networks organized around asexuality, such as the Asexuality Visibility and Education Network (http://www.asexuality.org/).
4   There are also numerous "nonbiomedical" drugs that claim to do the same thing, although these have not reached global markets in the same way as the biomedical drugs.

Chapter 5

Communities and Organizations

- On the Problematics of Communities and Organizations
- Experiencing Communities as Spaces of Belonging?
- (De/Re)Scaling Communities
  - Is there really a rural community?
  - Transnational communities, beyond/between the "nation"
  - Virtual community life and the spaces of possibility
- Organizational Geographies
  - The prison and the production of deviant geographies
  - Organizing bodies in and through homeless institutions and spaces
  - Development organizations as sites of resistance and authority
- Communities and Organizations, Any Difference?

On the Problematics of Communities and Organizations

At first glance, the concepts of "the community" or "the organization" appear fairly straightforward. After all, they are widely used in daily language. Yet, these terms are also highly problematic and contested, being operationalized and utilized in numerous ways. When people think of community they often have a vision of a very local space, such as a neighborhood or small rural town. As this text has already traced, though, these local spaces are linked and networked with numerous other spaces. They are also complicated by their own sets of social and spatial politics of inclusion and exclusion, belonging and difference. It is therefore important to ask how communities are formed as well as how they are circumscribed, sociomaterially, to construct both feelings of being "in place" and "out of place." Take, for example, the term "the gay community." This term suggests a unitary whole to this social grouping, that all those who identify as gay see themselves in one community. Delving a little bit deeper and unpacking the complicated social identities that make up this so-called community, it is clear that the "gay community" includes people who identify in a number of different ways as lesbian, gay, bisexual, transgendered, queer, or intersexed (LGBTQI).

In similar ways, organizations might be conceptualized as individual units, bracketing a set of consistent social relationships and practices. Studies of corporations, schools, or hospitals belie this simplistic reading of organizations. At any given moment there may be numerous social networks operating in any given organizational space. This might be "structured" right into the organization itself: imagine a transnational corporation, its subsidiaries, and all its divisions (sales, marketing, research and technology, etc.). These suborganizational groupings may be in a struggle over resources internal to their organization. This is most classically represented in the space of the public university in which some of you might be sitting right now, where departments and other units compete for a finite amount of resources (see Roberts 2000). Those who work both inside and outside organizations may discursively construct these spaces in differing and competing ways. Organizations are thus replete with sets of resistant practices that may work for or against the larger agenda of the organization. In general, then, organizations both produce certain geographies – corporate firms like WalMart literally construct retail space – and are produced by certain geographies – the broader flows of social discourses, networks, and relations that are part of the broader space in which the organization is embedded.

What make both communities and organizations real are the social geographic practices used to construct and produce community and organizational spaces. Communities and organizations can thus be enabling and disabling, productive and counterproductive, hegemonic and resistant, depending on the ways in which they are sociospatially constituted. Both concepts, though, regardless of how one might study them, are central to people's everyday lives. There is rarely a day when people do not engage in (or with) communities and organizations of which they claim that they are (or are not) a part. These spaces are thus tied to how individual identities are practiced as well as how inequalities are distributed in and across space. This chapter examines these important geographic objects/subjects, tracing the different ways in which social geographers have examined questions related to communities and organizations. It does this while tracing exemplars of some of the community and organizational practices that have been closely analyzed in social geography.

Experiencing Communities as Spaces of Belonging?

Community in its simplest sense is about belonging. That belonging means that there is some sense of commonality, some shared experience to which members of the community can cling. Community is thus about similarity and singularity (Panelli and Welch 2005). Yet communities are social processes that are also based in exclusions, either overt or covert. Communities are therefore also about difference. While this might seem oxymoronic – how can a concept based in similarity also be about difference? – it is possible to think of communities as contested spaces where competing notions of what it means to be (or not be) a member of a community are negotiated (Gibson-Graham 2006). Communities are thus structured through difference because of the exclusionary practices that go hand-in-hand with their construction. Communities are dependent on defining who belongs (their singular definition), and thus who does not belong. This is why Anderson (1991) analyzed the concept of "the nation" as an "imagined community." In his discussion, he argues that the nation is imagined and constructed through language and linguistic conventions. In arguing for conceptualizing a national community as imagined, Anderson (1991: 6) points out that the community "is *imagined* because the members of even the smallest nation will never know most of their fellow-members, meet them, or even hear of them, yet in the minds of each lives the image of their communion" (original emphasis). An imagined national community can promote equity but it can also lead to a strong sense of nationalism and patriotism that pits one nation (or national identity) against another. It can create exclusionary practices based in assumptions of what it means to be German or Turkish, British or Argentinian, American or Mexican. The practice of constructing a community as both "belonging and difference" and "exclusion and singularity" has the potential to create inequities across social spaces and groups: those who do not belong have no access to the organizational resources found in the community (e.g. a referendum in California in the 1990s (Proposition 187), which was eventually ruled unconstitutional, stated any person of any age who was not a citizens of the US was ineligible for social services).

To be part of a community has also historically meant to be "in place" (Cresswell 1996), to engage in the proper social practices that engender the belonging necessary to have a community. As Cresswell (1996) argues, though, if there is an "in place" then there is also an "out of place," social practices and peoples that are meant to be spatially excluded. These exclusions structure what and who belongs in a communal space. There is thus a certain groundedness and materiality to the concept of community, an apparent permanence structured through a collective experience of place. In Cresswell's terms, "place reproduces the beliefs that produce it in a way that makes them appear natural, self-evident, and commonsense" (ibid.: 16). In similar ways, when "in place" the general practices of being a member of that community become engrained in daily action: communities work because people do not necessarily "think about" what it means to belong to them. "Kneeling in church is an interpretation of what the church means; it also reinforces the meaning of the church" (ibid.). To be a member of a church community you follow the rules inscribed in the spaces of that community and these usually become normalized and routinized sets of practices.

The emergence of the "suburb" provides an excellent example of the imaginary and material social geographies of community in practice. In the US, the development of Levittown, Pennsylvania was premised on the notion of a certain type of community space, one that catered specifically to a heterosexual, white, and working class family centered on the single-family home (Hayden 2002; Blunt and Dowling 2006). With connections to the urban core through road and rail, the US suburb grew dramatically and a new social geography emerged, which constituted a suburban white space, on the one hand, and an urban black space, on the other. In these new suburban communities certain rules about privacy were also imposed: the single-family home came with a clear delineation of where one property ended and another began. Community-based organizations, such as the Boy and Girl Scouts and parent teacher associations, reinforced certain rules of what was proper and appropriate suburban (and by extension national) behavior. Community "loyalty" and commitment were reinforced through home ownership; housing prices maintained a class-based exclusionary practice that also translated into race-based segregation. Within suburban communities in North America more generally public behavior has also been highly regulated (Cowen 2005). Laws against loitering as well as other "out of place" activities remain highly prohibiting, even more so than one might find in cities (Mitchell 1997). Although not always explicit, the new communities of the suburbs reconstructed a highly divisive social geography based largely in segregation (Wilson 2000; Hayden 2002). The sense of "imagined community" that has developed around the suburb has, therefore, also meant that much more insidious social practices of difference and inequality are constructed not only through formal laws but also through mundane practices of community-based prejudice and social exclusion.

(De/Re)Scaling Communities

The emergence of any given community is also spatial. This is because, first and foremost, this object is situated somewhere in terms of both its material and immaterial geographies. It is often circumscribed and bounded by certain socio-spatial relationships, although it is very often networked with other communities. Importantly, communities are continually being "stretched" across a greater expanse of space, as diasporic experiences – those of North African migrants in Europe, for example – expand the geographies of certain identities and practices. More informally, communities are emerging in new spaces – for example, in online Internet environments – constructing mutual identities based in any number of social relationships. International "gaming" communities – where people literally create new communities online through interactive games – have developed as individuals construct new identities around their gaming practices. Communities also develop around the everyday practices of "being in place," making it possible to trace the expanse of communal relations through a study of the spatial patterns of travel behavior that bring people together. In all cases, communities are subject to important social relationships that are subject to political, economic, and cultural processes.

Politics in this case might be thought of both as a community practice – the development of community policing networks – and as a set of informal processes that develop between individuals working and living in certain community spaces. Investigating these connections and the ways in which certain sociospatial relationships help to invest places with symbolic meaning as communities is an important aspect of social geography.

The remainder of the first half of this chapter will trace the study of communities in and through a discussion of a number of political practices, both overt and covert. While communities are often conceptualized as structured from the top down or bottom up, as a set of arboreal (vertical) relations – from the local to the global – they might also think be theorized as a set of rhizomatic (horizontal) relations – as connections and networks without any clearly defined beginning or ending (Deleuze and Guattari 1987). Social geographers commonly think in terms of vertical relations produced by and through scale(s), using the concept to illustrate either (a) that scales are fixed as they get larger to encompass more and more space (Taylor 1982) or (b) that different sociospatial processes are nested within a hierarchy of scales, from the local to the global (Brenner 2001; Swyngedouw 2004). The latter concept of scale is the most commonly deployed in social geography today because it takes as an assumption that scales are human constructions developed through the deployment of social power (Swyngedouw 1997; Howitt 1998, 2003; Jones 1998; Marston 2000; Smith 2000a; Herod and Wright 2002; Sheppard and McMaster 2004; Mansfield 2005). As an example, the local as a scale is actively constructed through the material and social bounding of that space; it is thus organized as different and unique from other scales – the body or the nation. Local scales are invested with meaning, subject to the plays of power that are found in all spaces.

Scale as an analytic social construct is thus an object that is made real through human intervention: scholars arrive at a number of scalar relations that appear to constitute a verticality to the sociospatial world. Recently, there has been quite a bit of debate about this approach to scale, with some geographers suggesting that social geographies are made up of horizontal relationships with little explicit structure to them (Marston et al. 2005). A horizontal view does not necessarily deny scale as an analytic tool but it does suggest that sociospatial relations and networks develop in much less orderly ways through ongoing interactions (Marston et al. 2005 might disagree). Using the concept of the rhizome – a term used to describe the subterranean unorganized horizontal root structure of certain plants – Deleuze and Guattari (1987: 6) have suggested that "any point in a rhizome can be connected to anything other, and must be." In Deleuze and Guattari's language, communities emerge "in very diverse forms, from ramified surface extension in all directions to concretion into bulbs and tubers" (ibid.: 7). Social geographers have historically studied the community as the tuber or potato – using the concepts of "place" (e.g. Cresswell 2004) and "locality" (e.g. Cox and Mair 1988) – while sometimes marginalizing or ignoring the roots and rhizomatic possibilities. This chapter examines both the tuber and the root, the structured and unstructured community. Thus, while social geographers might map how people travel through certain community spaces, they should not think that those community spaces are bound by those patterns of travel.

If communities are made real through their social production, then it also makes sense that communities can emerge around different moments in the lifecourse. This could include a community of church youth group members, a community of academic scholars, or a retirement community. A self-identified community might develop out of an online chat room or through an international online distance-learning context. More often than not, though, communities, even when they are constructed as spaces based in certain definitions of childhood or adulthood, cannot deny the existence of "the other." What this means is that a children's community center is not a child-only space because it is regulated by adults. Retirement communities depend on both non-retired labor, which may come from any number of age ranges, and broader social networks, such as families of children and grand-children, to sustain them. So, while the identification of a community might be coupled with a clear demarcation of space, a community almost always depends on its interconnections with other spaces and people to survive. Moreover, communities are sites through which various processes take place that push past the apparently rigidity of any bounded space. Taking the lifecourse into consideration means think-ing about how communities are experienced by children and adults differently. This is complicated by the fact that all people are subject to other social processes of ability, ethnicity, race, age, gender, and sexuality and that the concept of community is often constructed through a variety of differences and inequalities.

This section reviews three exemplary moments of social geographic studies on communities. It begins with a discussion of rural communities and the problems associated with assuming that such spaces are socially and spatially uniform. Next, it asks how communities work "beyond" national boundaries through the processes of transnational migrations and networks. Finally, it moves from the transnational to the virtual, asking how community spaces are constituted in and through the spaces of the Internet and other mobilizing technologies.

Is there really a rural community?

> Somewhere deep down in the early twenty-first century psyche there seem to remain long-standing, handed-down precepts about rural areas, marking them as spaces enabled by nature, offering opportunities for living and lifestyle which are socially cohesive, happy and healthy, and presenting a pace and quality of life that differs from that in the city (Cloke 2003b: 1).

So begins the first chapter of *Country Visions*, a volume of essays on rural geographies edited by Paul Cloke. From the outset, this group of rural (social) geographers teases apart the complexity of rural space, asking how the cultural construction of "the rural" as "idyllic" is complicated by the social relations found in rural commun-ities. The problematic mapped onto the rural is their often singular construction as isolated, independent and autonomous communities. And, in the context of every-day representations of rural communities, homogeneity has been assumed over complexity. As Panelli and Welch (2005) point out, this notion of homogeneity (what they theorize as singularity) is part of how people in some rural communities think about their own relationship to the wider rural community space. In day-to-day speech acts, people may talk about the community as unified, coherent, and singular. Digging below the surface, though, rural community spaces are subject to a complex set of body and identity politics, which illustrate that "rural areas are indeed characterised by sharply delineated gendered and racialised assumptions about what kind of labour is appropriate to individuals" (Dixon 2003: 120). Tracing the gendering and racialization of rural space in eastern Carolina, Dixon (2003) suggests that changing demographic patterns and employment strategies have altered the practices of crabbing – the practice of unshelling crabmeat – and community in the region. The influx of legal Mexican female labor into the industry has created a new sense of community among the local population (both white and African-American), which resents the new immigrants and constructs them as "outside" the "real" rural community. While this might not always lead to direct challenges to the presence of Mexican women in eastern Carolina crabbing, "their social presence is barely acknowledged" (ibid.: 130), long-term residents sometimes "bemoan the gradual erosion of a distinct 'down east' way of life" (ibid.: 128). The social construction of "down east" as an idyllic (and singular) community space helps to maintain social differences (and inequalities) between local women and Mexican immigrant labor.

Sibley (2003) uses psychoanalytic theory to further explain the exclusionary practices associated with a notion of rural community in England and Wales. He draws particularly on the notion of "splitting" to describe the development of "psychotic anxieties." This is a process by which people create a physical and social distance between themselves and others, as the community elite define difference through notions of the "disruptive" and "chaotic" outsider. In the context of rural community space in England and Wales, this has merged with real laws regulating socially constructed deviant and mobile Gypsy (or Traveller) populations (Belton 2005). In this case, ethnic Gypsy peoples are seen as outside the norms of everyday English and Welsh societies. They are disruptive of the bucolic rural norms because, as mobile subjects, they are not perceived to be tied to place in the way that other rural peoples may be. Cresswell (2001: 14) traces a similar process in the US, where turn-of-the-century constructions of "the tramp" were "threatening to undo the cosy familiarity of place-based communities and neighborhoods." Mobility is thus a "threat to the rooted, moral, authentic existence of place." It is not surprising, then, that other "foreign bodies," such as non-British asylum seekers, are constructed as anathema to rural British communities as well. The movements of foreign bodies disrupt homogenous notions of rural space: "One resident suggested that 'what people are worried about is the fear of the unknown. There are no ethnic [*sic*] people in the village'" (Sibley 2003: 227; citing Gibbs 2000). The "anxiety" created by these new bodies in a demarcated rural space of apparent ethnic homogeneity thus locates certain peoples and practices as out of place.

If rural communities are, on the one hand, constructed through exclusionary practices of who does not belong, they must also, on the other hand, be socially produced through the active practice of defining who does belong. Indeed, the changing nature of rural life in many parts of the global north – increasing outmigration and economic underdevelopment – means that certain norms of rural life need to be actively protected. Such is the case of the norm of heterosexual relationships in the rural communities of the United Kingdom and New Zealand, where commercial projects have been put in place to address the "real social problem" of female outmigration and the decreasing number and size of farming families (Little 2003: 409). Underlying these campaigns is a deep held assumption that rural communities are made up of heterosexual and married couples, with nuclear families living in single-family households. In the context of this assumption of rural community space, women should be "'suitable' partners . . . who had a clear comprehension of what it mean to run a farm" (ibid.: 411). And, they should be willing to participate in a household economy that has clearly demarcated gendered boundaries and practices. As Little further explains, "The requirement was not necessarily for someone who had the scientific or technical knowledge to contribute to a farm business, rather it was for someone who appreciated the difficulties of running a farm and could understand that [male] farmers had to prioritise the farm over a relationship" (ibid.). As heterosexuality is being practiced in these campaigns, then, women are gendered and sexed as part of the farm; they are entering a community of male farmers that run the economy and support the rural household. This is not a complete process, however, as rural communities are often practiced in ways that complicate any straightforward reading of them as unitary and singular spaces (Panelli and Welch 2005). People actually work through their notions of themselves and community as they deal with their differences. Indeed, as Panelli and Welch (2005: 1603) describe in their study of community in Newstead, Australia, individuals use the spaces of community "when they need to engage a sense of being part of community." This suggests that communities emerge through the social engagements within them. There is utility, then, in investigating how people employ concepts of "community" and "belonging" as they negotiate their own identities as rural subjects and citizens.

Transnational communities, beyond/between the "nation"

Conceptually, transnationalism, unlike rurality, denotes crossing, mobility, and movement between national spaces. It would appear, then, to be antagonistic to the concept of community, which appears rooted in place (Cresswell 2001). But, as was already demonstrated, community – particularly in the context of transnationalism (Mitchell 2003) – is a complex concept that belies any simple reading of it. Communities are "sites of belonging," but belonging does not mean that members are always physically proximate. It could mean that communities develop across the experience of global or regional dispersal, through the development of an identity as a diaspora. Social geographers thus investigate the relationship between transnational movements and new forms of community, examining how these border crossing practices do not necessarily negate a sense of belonging or connection to either one's place of origin or one's place of current living. In this way, transnationalism may be theorized as a space of "in-betweeness" (Mitchell 2003: 74). At the same time, transnationalism is cut along many axes of difference, which suggests that the need and ability to move is structured through various gendered, race, classed, sexualized, and ethnic social politics (Pratt and Yeoh 2003). For example, within the Asia-Pacific world region, internal migration dynamics from areas of relative poverty to areas of relative wealth – from rural Philippines or Indonesia to urban Hong Kong or Singapore, for example – are tied into important networks of domestic labor recruitment (Boyle 2002). Transnationalism intersects with community in this context as migrant workers negotiate their place in "two worlds" (see further discussion in Chapter 8). On the one hand, they connect "back home" through the practice of remittances – sending money to home communities – and by sending letters and packages to families (Pratt and Philippine Women's Centre 2005). On the other hand, they create new transnational community spaces and homes in the so-called "host" spaces as well (Trotz 2006).

Voigt-Graf (2004) historicizes the movement of people out of India into wider transnational global networks beginning in the British colonial period, further complicating the relationships between transnationalism and community in a number of important ways. First, transnationalism should not take "the nation" as a unified whole. In the case of India, Voigt-Graf shows how different Indian ethnic communities also have different trajectories of transnational movement and experience. Punjabis in northwestern India were tied into colonial networks of movement in ways that were different from other parts of northern and southern India. The latter group includes those migrants who were moved to Fiji, an island in the South Pacific, as indentured servants. Because of the nature of their movement, Indians in Fiji developed social identities as Fijian-Indians with no real connection back to India proper. Second, the relationship between the historical context of one group's movements and the class-based politics of transnational migrants need to be interrogated. Kannadiga ethnic peoples from southern India often have an "urban professional background" (Voigt-Graf 2004: 33) but, as recent transnational migrants, remain strongly tied to the home space of India. "Kannadigas are parochial metropolitans whose skills are sought after in global cities but who remain culturally encapsulated and conservative" (ibid.: 34). People of Punjabi ancestry in northern India, however, have a much longer history of transnational mobility tied to primary economic activities, such as agriculture. Over time, then, they have developed a multiplicity of transnational connections that link them to a number of nodes in the larger Punjabi community globally. Third, transnational community connections vary quite dramatically depending on the relationship between ethnicity, class, work experience, and time and place of movement. As Figure 5.1, shows, the transnational spaces of Punjabi migrants on the one hand, and Kannadiga migrants on the other, are organized differently. Punjabi transnational migrants

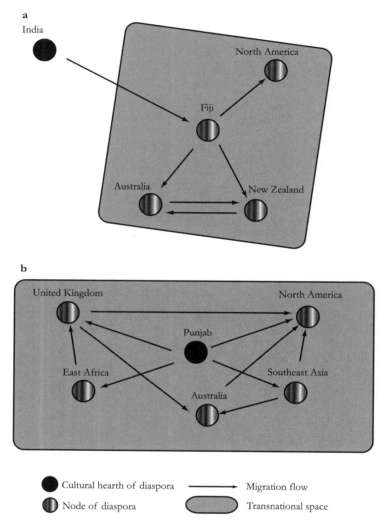

Figure 5.1   (a) A model of the Indo-Fijian transnational community. (Adapted from Voigt Graf 2004: 37, reprinted with permission.) (b) A model of the Punjabi transnational community. (Adapted from Voigt Graf 2004: 34, reprinted with permission.)

have constructed a globalized community space with multiple nodes and flows, none of which reach back to India, whereas the Kannadiga are routed in transnational networks that begin and end, almost always, with India.

Transnationalism is a process, therefore, that involves the movement of people not only between two national spaces; it also includes multiple nodes and networks. As these nodes and networks develop so to do new senses of transnational and national community identity (Trotz 2006). Indeed, new mechanisms of community building and identity emerge as people engage in transnational movements. "In the case of Guyana [a country in South America] . . . where more Guyanese live outside the country than inside the country, it is perhaps not surprising that so many overseas organizations [through which people of Guyanese ancestry can engage each other] exist" (ibid.: 46). In this case, community networking is happening in Toronto, Canada and not in Guyana itself. In the case of Guyanese transmigrants living in Canada, however, their experiences of community are complicated by class- and race-based differences that are transferred into the Canadian-Guyanese social context from Guyana. "The racial polorization of Guyana's political landscape also characterizes some of the overseas institutional affiliations, most obviously in political organizations (which tend to follow the two main political parties and thus largely to be racialized between [indigenous North American] Indians and African Guyanese) and hometown associations (given the historic patterns of racialized residential segregation in Guyana)" (ibid.: 49). Transnational communities are subject to relations of power similar to other forms of community, although these might be reconfigured as people move from one space to another and begin to enact new understandings of themselves and their identities as international workers or newly recognized citizens of another country.

The case of Guyanese migrants to Canada points to another important aspect of transnationalism and transnational communities: the networks and spaces that constitute these connections are also subject to the social and spatial practices of inequality and difference. As Mahler (1999: 712; cited in Pratt and Yeoh 2003: 163) argues, "transnational processes may produce new spaces, but this does not mean that actors within these spaces are set completely loose from their social moorings. The tether [including that of place] may be loosened, redirected, and perhaps frayed but not lost." Pratt and Yeoh (2003) therefore analyze the complex interplay between gendered identities and transnational experiences of place (and community). In some cases, such as Singapore, Pratt and Yeoh recognize that transnational migration out of Singapore is a predominantly "masculinised practice" (ibid.: 162), which does little to disrupt the gendered practices of home and community in Singapore. Movement and transmigration do not necessarily mean, either, that migrants will adopt themselves to their new cultural context, and certain gendered social practices may very easily be maintained as people move from one place to the next. Walton-Roberts (2004) shows that the use of medical technologies, which allow for prenatal sex selection among Sikh Indian communities living in Canada, parallels a similar practice in northern India, where preferences remain strong for male children. The gendering of the birth process thus does little to challenge the patriarchal norms that have been established in one context – India – as people move to another context – Canada. Elmhirst (2007) notes that men who remain "behind" in underdeveloped regions, such as Lampung, Indonesia, because women are being drawn into a larger and larger international division of labor, are reasserting their masculinities and power within their local community. Transnationalism may open up possibilities for some to participate in new community spaces that give them access to certain social, economic, and political resources. In other cases, however, transnationalism may impact the social organization of a number of other community spaces that force people within them to rethink their social position relative to the changing community in which they are embedded.

Virtual community life and the spaces of possibility

Across many global spaces and networks, individuals also engage with new communication technologies, collapsing the social distance that exists between places. While access to the technologies of mobile phones, computers, and the Internet is far from ubiquitous, there is no doubt that new communities are emerging through these technological interventions. MySpace, Facebook, and YouTube provide space for new communities through interactive chat rooms and asynchronous discussion boards. Alternative communities are also developing in similar ways. XTube provides an adult "alternative" to YouTube, the latter of which strictly sensors sexual content on its site. Geographers of all stripes use online community bulletin boards and listservs organized around their identities as critical geographers, urban geographers, leftist geographers, feminist geographers, and sexuality and space scholars. The emergent act of "blogging" – posting narratives, images, and other content on blog websites – has also opened new community possibilities. "Blogging is an activity which both takes place in and produces community," Crampton argues, as "Bloggers link to each other, comment on each other's sites, mention each other in their blogs, create 'fansigns' (buttons or cool graphics mentioning the site's name, or webcam pictures with the site's name inscribed somewhere on the body) thus creating friendships and mutual support" (Crampton 2003: 96). Some of these communities are fleeting, with little long-term connectivity, others emerge and submerge as issues and concerns are raised, while others still are sustained over a longer time period (Thurlow et al. 2004). Membership varies, as some virtual interconnections are linked to certain costs, while others are "relatively" free (if you don't mind the bombardment of advertisements that often accompany some websites). Indeed, the material costs of being a community member in virtual or cyberspace can be prohibitive, and, as geographers have noted, there remains a need to be somewhere when you are connected (Kitchin 1998b; Walmsley 2000), although wireless networks are making access more spatially diffuse, as are satellite and cellular connections to the World Wide Web (WWW). In this way, though, "Cyberspace might have annihilated distance, but not place" (Walmsley 2000: 17). At the same time, virtual spaces, because they can be invested with certain degrees of anonymity, might be important sites for the defense of one's own imagined place-based religious or national community. That is why Adams (2005: 174) argues that "the distanciated context does not simply reduce people's reluctance to enter into an argument; it removes the communal framework that would preserve the creative labor of achieving consensus."

With that said, virtual spaces are not necessarily anti-communal, as they can be sites through which social connectivities are made possible beyond the limits of distance (and time) (Adams 2005: 175). The Internet can create spaces of dissent and resistance, for example. Froehling (1997) demonstrates how the Internet – e-mail networks and the WWW – effectively supported the Zapatista efforts of indigenous resistance against the Mexican government in their home state of Chiapas in southern Mexico in the 1990s. The diffusion of information on the uprising in southern Mexico reached other parts of North America through e-mail connections, eventually leading to "fax protest campaigns against Mexican consulates," which "were supplemented by direct action, including concerted demonstrations in February 1997 in front of thirty-six consulates in the United States" (ibid.: 302). A virtual community organized around its defiance against the Mexican government's mistreatment of indigenous groups in Mexico thus merged with physical challenges to the spaces of the Mexican government in the US (see also Warf and Grimes 1997; Dodge and Kitchin 2001 for further discussion of resistance through virtual spaces). The Zapatista movement has been stretched through a number of rhizomatic connections with activist communities across North America (Froehling 1997).

Virtual spaces are not autonomous from other spaces, as people can (and do) negotiate their social identities and community relationships through a mix of so-called virtual and physical interactions (Turkle 1995). Indeed, as Dodge and Kitchin (2001: 55) suggest, "significant usage [of virtual community spaces] consists of supporting social networks outside of cyberspace rather than the creation of new networks." Students in educational settings are being asked to "blend" their classroom practices, working back and forth between online and face-to-face instruction (Maintz 2008). And, as Maintz (2008) outlines, students have found the face-to-face meetings critical to their developing sense of educational community because bodily cues and gestures are often missed in online communication. The expansion of virtual networks also puts additional stresses on individual members of a community; they must be available because they have technologies, such as mobile phones, e-mail, or a webcam. This intensifies the expectations of participation in certain communities, as members negotiate the "co-presence" of others through a ringing phone or the sound of an incoming e-mail or text message.

This all suggests that virtual community spaces, like other spaces, are subject to social relations of power, to pressures to conform to certain socialized norms, and to sanctioned rules appropriate to a particular community. The practices of virtual spaces can be highly regulated, and they can produce knowledge that targets particular populations within the community. Crampton (2003) demonstrates how GIS-based Internet maps locate certain populations and practices – sex offenders, gun violence, drug crimes – that might be "outside the norm" (ibid.: 131) within the material community spaces of the city. Geographic positioning systems (GPS) can also be used to mark criminals and track them virtually, ensuring that their virtual signal does not cross over into "safe" (material) community spaces. Cutting across this issue of surveillance of community spaces are issues of community access. As Crampton effectively demonstrates, access to the virtual, particularly Internet spaces, varies dramatically across global and local spaces. In 2002, for example, 55.9 percent of people in the US and Canada had access to the Internet, whereas only 1 percent of people in Africa had the same level of access (Crampton 2003: 146).

Within the US, Crampton further demonstrates that census tracts with a high percentage of "white, non-Hispanic" were almost twice as likely to have Internet access as those in tracts with a high percentage of "black, non-Hispanic" and "Hispanic" (ibid.: 165). In real terms, there are localities and communities that, therefore, have little to no access to the virtual community spaces of cyberspace. This reality is brought home in the words of Mr Kenyada, with whom Crampton discussed this digital community divide. In Crampton's words, "Mr. Kenyada in DeKalb County, Georgia . . . is not interested in a 'postmodern' interplay of endlessly varying identities in chat rooms . . . but rather helping a child do some homework, and perhaps through that child getting their grandparents to learn how to use a mouse" (ibid.: 167). A critical social geography of virtual community spaces must be cautious to remember the inextricable interconnection between so-called virtual and real space. There may be an exciting array of communities in which individuals may reformulate their identities or create new networks and connections. But not all communities can form such relationships, and a "divide" remains as an important marker of difference and inequality in the spaces of the virtual.

Organizational Geographies

If community spaces sometimes appear ethereal, organizations often appear concrete. After all, organizations dot the landscapes of our town and cities. They mark out spaces of identity and subjectivity, linked to the performances of capitalism (the firm), collectivism (the union hall), health care (the hospital), crime and criminality (the prison), education (the university), religion (the mosque), or informal mundane social networks (the café). At the same time, they are much more than the "bricks and mortar" associated with their material structures. Organizations are produced by and productive of various discourses and practices of social relations, identity, and subjectivity. Put simply, building an educational structure and filling its rooms with chairs, desks, chalkboards, and technologies only goes so far to producing an educational space. There must also be rules, regulations, practices, and social norms that make use of those material geographies. Without those social mechanisms, a classroom would not necessarily be a space of education. Importantly, though, the rules and regulations of the classroom are not simply produced in that space. Children in public education in the US are taught to say the pledge of allegiance, while students in Thailand all listen to the King's anthem each morning before they start their day. In this way, the spaces of education are also the spaces of citizenship and national identity. Once taught the mechanisms of citizenship and national identity, students can take those lessons with them "out into the world" beyond the school.

Organizational spaces also overlap through the networked relations among and between them. Nongovernmental organizations, which by their name declare themselves as "not the government," often do their work in governmental spaces and in conjunction with government workers. Wolch, therefore, referred to the nonprofit (or nongovernmental) voluntary sector in North America and Western Europe as the "shadow state" because "State-imposed pressure to plan, manage, and evaluate have altered the internal organizational practices of many voluntary organizations" (Wolch 1990: 215). Organizations are also not contained by the space in which they might be materially located. Appalshop, a nonprofit documentary film organization that produces films in and about the Appalachia region in the eastern US, relies on a broad network of national fundraising efforts and participates in workshops and festivals across the country (Del Casino et al. 2000). In so doing, this organization's long-term efficacy is very much dependent on its relationship to both governmental and nongovernmental funding and support resources (see Figure 5.2).

There are numerous ways in which one might theorize the social geographies of organizations, working across any number of methodological approaches – from spatial science to radical geography to poststructuralism (Del Casino et al. 2000). This section will rely on the social theoretical work of Michel Foucault, whose theories about space and spatial practices have had a strong influence on social geography (see, for example, the essays in *Space, Knowledge and Power: Foucault and Geography*, by Crampton and Elden 2007). Foucault was particularly concerned with systems of power and knowledge and the ways in which particular architectures of, for example, the hospital produce certain regulatory regimes, such as biomedicine and what Foucault called biopower – a system of knowledge that comes to dominate how people know themselves as biological beings (Elden and Crampton 2007). Foucault employed a variety of historical methodologies to trace out the processes by which organizations produce "docile bodies" through mechanisms of surveillance and governmentality (or "effects of government") (Philo 2004). This term is most simply defined as "the conduct of conducts," which specifically includes governmental "discipline over bodies ... 'police' supervision of the inhabitants of the sovereign territory ... the biopolitical regulation of the 'species life' of a population ... and self-formation through ethical care of the self" (Huxley 2007: 187). The effects of government are found in organizations and can be traced through both the discourses organizations produce – psychiatric medicine – and the self-regulatory practices people take on as individuals living in and through these organizations – "self help" (ibid.: 188). Governmentality can also be examined through what Hannah (2000) describes as the mechanisms of the state, such as the census (see also Thongchai 1994), wherein racialized social categories are used to create regimes of control and regulation. Put simply, organizations such as the US Census Bureau produce certain knowledges about "proper" conduct and identity. In this way, power is productive – it literally produces how people know and think about sociospatial relations, identities, and subjectivities. Individuals incorporate that conduct into their own personal regulations of "the self" and "the other." Organizational life, in this way, stretches beyond the material boundaries of the architecture of the hospital or the prison and becomes part of everyday practice. This is not to deny the possibility of resistance. In fact, Foucault was

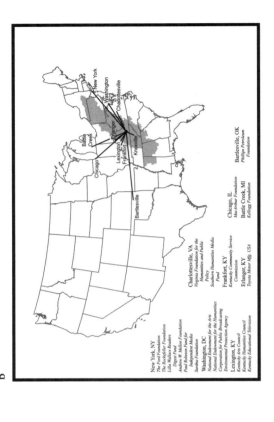

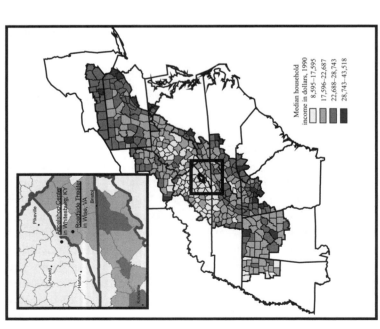

Figure 5.2 (a) Appalshop in the Appalachian Regional Commission Area. (b) Appalshop's major government and corporate funding sources, 1996–7. Appalshop is a regional nonprofit, documentary film organization, which produces films about the Appalachian region. These maps illustrate the way that an organizational geography might begin by "mapping" the absolute and relative location of an organization and then investigate the connections that organization has across space with other organizations. In this case, (b) shows the range of Appalshop's ability to draw funds from across the eastern USA. (*Source*: Del Casino et al. 2000: 531–2; cartography by Stephen P. Hanna, Mary Washington College; reprinted with permission.)

Box 5.1   Methodological Note: Foucault's
Archaeology and Genealogy

Chris Philo has written extensively about Michel Foucault's contributions
to the discipline of geography, providing insight into his methodological
approaches and their value to social geographic research (Philo 1992, 2000,
2004, 2005a). Foucault remains one of the most important social theorists
for geographers (Philo 1992: 138), although his writings are sometimes dense
and challenging for geographers just starting out in the field. Social geographers
are interested in the study of "discourse" – or "organized bodies of knowledge"
– and "power" – or "the mechanics" of authority, around which Foucault
organized most of his writing (Philo 2004: 122–3). In explaining Foucault's
methodological approaches, Philo describes the following:

> Foucault's first four major texts are usually cast as *archaeologies*, wherein the
> ambition is to excavate for critical inspection the "discourses" (or organized
> bodies of knowledge) that have emerged within European history as the
> foundations for both intellectual orthodoxy and practical endeavour (ibid.: 122,
> original emphasis).

> Foucault's next four major texts are usually cast as his *genealogies*, wherein he
> decided that the real "object" of his inquiries was less discourse and know-
> ledge and more the mechanics of power, in which case his earlier archaeologies
> also became available for re-reading as more critical offerings charting how
> order (conceptual and substantive) arises and is maintained in the human realm
> (ibid.: 123, original emphasis).

Applying a Foucauldian archaeological or genealogical methodology is not an
easy task. It demands a deep and intensive reading of the data to discern how
power is being conceptualized and organized. Yet, as Philo notes, Foucault's
work informs a wide array of social geographic topics, including health and
medicine (Philo 2000) as well as the study of "population" (Philo 2005a). Thus,
while Foucault's own work is historical and archival, his attention to questions of how power works can be applied to the study of contemporary social
geographic issues, including health, community politics, and organizations.

Quick Exercise

Identify a global problem of current interest. Based on Philo's brief discussion of Foucault's methodological approaches, what sorts of questions might
you ask of that problem you have identified? How might a social geographer
using Foucault's methodologies go about answering those questions? What
sorts of data would she or he need to collect?

very much interested in resistant practices (Foucault 1999). But resistance does not operate in organizational life simply through direct opposition. Resistance emerges because no system of power or authority can ever constitute a totalizing authority – governmentality effects are, at best, partial and incomplete.

The remainder of this section examines three kinds of organizational spatial practices: the prison and the production of deviant geographies, homeless institutions and the regulation of non-conforming bodies, and the development organization as a conflicted site of resistance and domination. In so doing, it provides an overview of how the material spaces of various organizations are stretched out into other social spaces as broader discourses of what is meant by "the prison," "the homeless institution," or the "development organization" merge with other social practices of surveillance, regulation, and control, as well as resistance.

The Prison and the production of deviant geographies

In February 2008 it was reported that the US government had hit a new milestone – approximately 1 in every 100 people in the country was in prison (Pew Center of the States 2008). Indeed, the United States has the highest rate of incarceration in the world today. And, although rates vary across the country, it is estimated that "1 in every 15 state general fund dollars was spent on corrections in 2007" and that "between 1987 and 2007, the amount states spent on *corrections* [+127 percent] more than double[d] while the increase in *higher education* [+21 percent] spending has been moderate" (Pew Center of the States 2008: 14–15, emphasis added). The total prison population, when disaggregated, appears quite diverse across the categories of race and gender. For the population aged eighteen and over, 1 in 106 white men are in prison, while 1 in 15 Black men and 1 in 36 Hispanic men are currently in the "corrections system." In looking just at Black men between the ages of twenty and thirty-four, it appears that 1 in 9 are currently incarcerated, demonstrating that young men, particularly young Black men, are highly likely to spend time in prison. Among women, particularly those between the ages of thirty-five and thirty-nine, 1 in 355 white women are in prison compared to 1 in 297 Hispanic women and 1 in 100 black women (Pew Center of the States 2008: 6). If we look at the data on the "percent change in state prison populations in 2007," we also see that the increases in incarceration vary spatially (a parallel phenomena can be found in death penalty executions, see Figure 5.3). "The South led the way, with its population jumping from 623,563 to 641,024 – a rise of 2.8%. Only three of the 16 states in the southern region reported a drop in inmates, while nine experienced growth exceeding 4 percent. . . . All told, 36 states reported higher numbers as 2008 dawned" (Pew Center of the States 2008: 7). In real economic and social terms, the costs of this massive expansion of the US prison system are staggering. The gap between rich and poor and across racial groups will widen even further as more people of color are imprisoned, and as harsh penalties are enacted differentially across the country (see Figure 5.3).

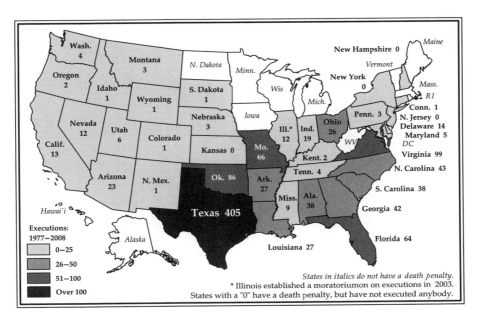

Figure 5.3 Map of death penalty cases in the United States between 1977 and 2008. (Cartography by James Woods, CSU, Long Beach, Department of Geography.)

The material effects of this expanding prison economy are important sites of analysis for social geography. And the spatial expansion of prison over education should give pause, as should the deeply racist geographies that undergird prison growth. But these massive infrastructural developments also point to a more general concern, which Foucault articulates in *Discipline and Punish: The Birth of the Prison*. This expansion is representative of a larger tactics of power; one tied to the surveillance and regulation of social spaces and social bodies. It is an attempt to produce what Foucault calls "docile bodies," bodies that self-regulate for fear of being seen and identified and thus imprisoned. In a historical sense, the prison functions to "break up collective dispositions; analyse confused, massive or transient pluralities. . . . Its aim was to establish presences and absences, to know where and how to locate individuals, to set up useful communications, to interrupt others, to be able to at each moment to supervise the conduct of each individual, to assess it, judge it, to calculate its qualities and merits" (Foucault 1995: 143). The prison is more than a spatial expansion of imprisonment; it reflects the deeper expression to control and regulate space (Herbert 1997b). In this light, it is not surprising that the prison might be viewed as a racist institution, which spatially identifies non-white groups living in "inner cities" as socially and economically unproductive and therefore in need of imprisonment (see Box 5.2).

It is thus not only the organizational space of the prison that places distance between the "general population" and its "deviant other." The "idea of the prison" is being extended out into society as surveillance intensifies a hegemonic social

Box 5.2   The Geographies of Racism and
"the Prison" in California

Ruth Wilson Gilmore (2007) demonstrates in *Golden Gulag: Prisons, Surplus, Crisis, and Opposition in Globalizing California* that "crime" and a "criminal" are fluid and historical processes. Working through a political-economy framework, Gilmore argues that the explosion of prison space in California is not an "accident" but a result of a conscious effort to fill the economic gap in the state with a new economy – the prison – while also addressing the "moral panic" of fear and concern over growing social instability – particularly related to "gang" violence. Over the course of the 1970s, 1980s, and 1990s the state of California instituted a number of laws to "get tough on crime," including extending prison sentences of "known" gang members, expanding the criminality of nonviolent crimes (e.g. drug possession), and intensifying repercussions for recidivism through the "three strikes" law (e.g. anyone incarcerated three times would be imprisoned for life). As a result, certain spaces of California – particularly inner city spaces for young men of color – are now targets of anti-criminalization campaigns. The leads Gilmore to argue that: if "[r]acism is the state-sanctioned and/or extralegal production and exploitation of group-differentiated vulnerability to premature death," then "Prison expansion is a new iteration of this theme. Prisons and other locally unwanted land uses accelerate the mortality of modestly educated working people of all kinds in urban and rural settings and show how economic and environmental justice are central to antiracism" (ibid.: 247).

At the same time, Gilmore points toward resistances to this expanding geography of imprisonment. Tracing the Mothers "Reclaiming Our Children" (ROC) campaign, Gilmore shows how organized resistance is also invested in a historical geography of gender politics and African American cultural experience. Mothers ROC members, she suggest, use "techniques developed over generations on behalf of Black children and families within terror-demarcated, racially defined enclaves . . . to choreograph interracial political solidarity among all kinds of caregivers losing their loved ones into the prison system" (ibid.: 236–7). Moving beyond the divide of Black, Latino, and white the Mothers ROC have been able to "reach across social and spatial divides" by recognizing the "ideological power of motherhood to challenge the legitimacy of the changing state" (ibid.: 246). In sum, "The racial and gendered social division of labor required mothers of prisoners to live lives of high visibility; ROCers turned that visibility to a politically charged presence, voice, and movement against injustice, such that their activism became the centerpiece of their reproductive – and socially productive – labor" (ibid.: 238–9; also see Chapter 8).

Quick Exercise

Using Figure 5.3, provide the following: (a) a description of the national pattern of death penalty executions in the US between 1977 and 2008; and (b) a set of hypotheses that might help explain the pattern. What other data might help you further test your hypotheses as to why the pattern looks the way it does?

order – where the poor and socially marginalized are further isolated and institutionalized. It is not surprising, then, that the government of the US continues to invest massively in instruments of surveillance at the national and local levels (Crampton 2003). Indeed, as Peck (2003: 226) argues, "the explosion of incarceration rates can be seen to represent a racialized strategy for brutally reregulating the urban poor." The disproportionate investment in technologies of surveillance – police forces, national guard, border police, cameras, videos, etc. – occurs in spaces on the margins – the inner cities with much higher rates of poverty and people of color. That is why, for example, challenges to the authority of the police are met with quick attempts to re-regulate space (Herbert 1997a). Driving this intensification of a geo-surveillance society is fear – fear of bodily crime, fear of the poor or the homeless (Del Casino and Jocoy 2008), fear of terrorism (Sparke 2007), fear of the illegal immigrant (Coleman 2007; Gilbert 2007), or fear of disease (Braun 2007). Fear is actually an essential aspect of control; it reproduces the legitimacy of the state and submission of its citizens to its order. Fear also provides the state with the authority to produce "spaces of exception: spaces where people can be controlled, coerced, tortured, or even killed with impunity because their geographical location is imagined and administered as somehow beyond the reach of justice" (Sparke 2007: 339). Guantánamo Bay – where so-called "enemy combatants" in the US "war on terror" are detained – is maintained as a critical "space of exception" for the government (Agamben 2005). It is a space where the rights of prisoners under either the laws of the US or international law set out in the Geneva Convention have been abrogated.[1] Indeed, "President Bush's order [in 2001 to indefinitely detain all terrorist enemies] . . . radically erases any legal status of the individual, thus producing an unnamable and unclassified being" (Agamben 2005: 3). In this way, then, Guantánamo Bay is vital to the maintenance of the new world social order, wherein "spaces of exception" become essential in sustaining a strict imperial order (Reid-Henry 2007).

To understand these fears it is necessary to ask how the broader social context in which fear of crime and criminality is produced. This includes understanding how fear produces crime itself. Take hate crimes against people of color, religious minorities, or gay, lesbian, transgendered, or bisexual peoples (see case studies in *Spaces of Hate*, edited by Flint 2004). Deeply invested in these crimes is a sense of surveillance, regulation of the so-called norms of society, at least as perceived by those who commit these crimes. Hate crimes are about saying who belongs where and when; they are a spatial effect of bigotry and social prejudice as well as fear of the unknown. In discussing hate crimes against gay and lesbian peoples in Columbus, Ohio, for example, Sumartojo (2004: 89) argues:

> Perpetrators of hate crime draw from their own normative understanding or beliefs about what type of person is "out of place" in a given setting. If these rules are breached, their understanding of place is challenged. Studies of hate crime have suggested that perpetrators of hate crime may identify with a place such that their sense of place makes them feel licensed to defend it from intrusion. In doing so, they affect the interaction with, and sense of place of others, including victims, whose previous identification with a place may be challenged.

Foucault would not find these acts surprising in societies where "citizens" see it as their right (and duty) to regulate social space and relations in ways similar to that of the prison. In fact, hate crimes, and other violent crimes such as rape (which can be part of strategy of war as in Darfur, Sudan), extend the rationalities of the prison and its systems of surveillance out into a wider social space of the everyday in ways that are quite problematic. The recent experiences of Iraqi and other Muslim men who were tortured at Abu Ghraib illustrate how prison spaces reflect wider systems of violence, hate, and prejudice. In this way, the logics of the prison are refracted through other social relations of power and authority found in the everyday spaces of hate.

At the same time, the "idea of the prison" and its regimes of self- and community-regulation are incomplete processes. Not only are laws regularly transgressed but laws are also challenged and disrupted through the active reuse of space, as when people consensually transgress legal boundaries in certain sexual practices, for example. Resistances also emerge against hate crime or rape through the production of counter-organizations, such as gay rights networks and crisis centers, or through the spatial practices of protests, such as "Take Back the Night Marches," which seek to reclaim streets as safe spaces for women.

Organizing bodies in and through homeless institutions and spaces

Homelessness is a process that works through a variety of organizational spaces in ways that make it similar to the regulation of imprisonment. In some cases, homeless people find themselves in actual prisons, where they are kept because no other organization is available to handle their care. For many, though, homelessness is a diverse experience complicated by their health, ability, age, race, ethnicity, sexuality, and gender, as well as the complex landscape of organizations serving homeless people. The regulation of homeless bodies in the spaces of both the "city" and the "country" is thus difficult to generalize, as there is no one universal experience of being without a home. Homelessness can be thought of as a long-term state of being without shelter or a permanent home, or it can be conceptualized as a temporary, sporadic, and transient experience of being in and out of a home (Del Casino and Jocoy 2008). The experiences of homelessness also vary quite dramatically across global space. The temporary shelter of someone living on the street in urban Los Angeles is distinguished from the couch of a friend in rural England or the shantytown, or temporary shelter, in Buenos Aries or Manila. The regulation of homeless subjects in the city or the country, in the global north or global south, varies as well. In some cases, punitive action against the homeless has led to laws to clear them from the streets. This is particularly true in the context of cities, such as New York and San Francisco (see Smith 1992; Mitchell 1997). In other cases, homelessness in seen as something to be managed through the expansion of services, although the location of those services might vary quite dramatically depending on the nature of the neighborhood or town in which they are located. This is exemplified in recent efforts by the British government to provide "soup runs" for homeless people, which involve locating food support in open air spaces throughout cities (Johnsen et al. 2005). In many cases, individuals and collectives manage their homeless experience through the development of their own organizations. This is true in the case of South Africa, where the South African Homeless People's Federation or uMfelanda Wonye ("we die together") has developed new community networks in the post-apartheid period (Khan and Pieterse 2004: 2).

In Foucauldian terms, the management of homeless bodies is about regulating their social and physical mobilities so that they do not transgress the normalized spaces of the homed population (Foucault 1973). In *The Birth of the Clinic: An Archaeology of Medical Perception*, Foucault argues that "deviant bodies," particularly those seen as diseased, are identified as dangerous to healthy society. The expansion of this medicalized logic of the diseased and healthy body, as Takahashi et al. (2002: 302) suggest, is taken up in broader social discourses resulting in the "partition [of] society into groups, where stigmatized groups over time embody devalued traits, such as disgrace, laziness, criminality, or mental disorder." Pushing this Foucauldian notion of stigma further, Takahashi et al. argue that "stigmatization also partitions space, where the social attributes of stigmatized groups become manifest as spatial boundaries of disorder" (ibid.). These boundaries produce powerful systems of marginalization. For women with children in Orange County, California, for example, "the transitional shelter served to reinforce the social identity ('homeless woman') from which they were trying to escape" (ibid.: 308). DeVerteuil (2003a) examines the experiences of single homeless women as they "cycle through" the various spaces of homeless services in Los Angeles, demonstrating how some "women . . . suffered both residential instability and institutional dependency" (ibid.: 369). while others "had stable residential patterns because of their significant institutional dependence . . . because they spend so much time in highly controlling and long-term institutional settings such as prisons" (ibid.: 371). DeVerteuil's work importantly points out that women who are experiencing homelessness may also

Box 5.3   Methodological Note: Mixed Methodologies
and the Study of Homelessness

Social geographers utilize different techniques in the study of homelessness. In some cases, they choose to use "mixed methods." Lois Takahashi (1998b), in *Homelessness, AIDS, and Stigmatization: The NIMBY Syndrome in the United States at the End of the Twentieth Century*, examines national survey data and open-ended interviews to study the "attitudes" toward homeless people as well as the experiences of stigma by the homeless themselves. Drawing from data collected through a national survey, Takashi illustrates spatial variation in acceptance of facilities for homeless individuals and for people living with HIV and AIDS nationally. To do this, she draws on a statistical analysis of a large data set and employs mapping techniques to visualize spatial patterns.

Takahashi also explores other data sets to "tease out" the relationship between stigma and NIMBYism (Not In My Backyard politics). This methodological shift demands a spatial shift; her focus moves from the national level to a local one. In-depth interviews demand more time and less breadth. Focusing on Orange County, California, Takahashi explores the interrelationships among race, HIV, and homelessness through an analysis of Vietnamese and Latino community attitudes toward people living with HIV and AIDS. In particular, she interviews "opinion leaders . . . identified using local newspaper articles and interviews with researchers and community leaders. A snowball method was used to identify Latino and Vietnamese persons holding significant public influence. Local newspaper articles and researchers were used as initial contacts to identify seven individuals. . . . From these seven individuals, twenty Latino and Vietnamese informal opinion leaders were identified and contacted for interviews" (ibid.: 132).

Through the national analysis, Takahashi draws conclusions about the variegated geographies of "acceptance" for people who are homeless or HIV positive, while in the local analysis she offers a nuanced and complex reading of the "coping strategies" (ibid.: 143) that people employ to deal with their prejudice against people who are different and their responsibilities to familial and community members who may be ill.

Quick Exercise

In a group of two or three people, design your own mixed methodology study that addresses an important social geographic question. Outlining your questions, ask the following: (a) what types of data will you need to gather; (b) where will you find those data; and (c) what training will you need to complete the study?

deploy similar notions of stigmatized space as they move throughout the city. As one participant in the study said, "I didn't really want to go downtown. I really didn't. It's so dangerous down there" (ibid.: 376). That said, their spatial choices were mediated by the spaces of the city itself, as most homeless service organizations were located in Los Angeles's poorest neighborhoods. And, as cities reinvest in downtowns homeless organizations and peoples will also be moved – either forcibly or by the movement of service organizations themselves.

The regulatory regimes of homeless stigma operate in rural spaces as well, where "certain kinds of mobility . . . serve as negative signifiers" (Cloke et al.: 23). Problematically, then, within rural spaces homelessness is seen as exisiting "outside" rural life. And, because it is not part of rural life – rural spaces are too idyllic to have homelessness (see discussion above) – homeless people must be coming from somewhere else. This is a powerful spatial discourse that constructs all homeless people as an "other," resulting in real policy implications: "the exclusive and exclusionary nature of some rural areas . . . [means there is a] reluctance to provide assistance particularly . . . where homeless people are deemed 'other' not only in terms of their origin from outside the community but also in terms of their lifestyle and apparent non-conformity to societal norms and expectations" (ibid.: 33). Despite the desire to construct a unitary mobile (and deviant) homeless subject, empirical work in rural England demonstrates that the mobility of the homeless is complicated as they move "out of rural areas," "within rural areas," "to rural areas," and "through rural areas" (ibid.: 24). The spatiality of services is often urban-based, forcing those who are homeless to leave rural areas in search of accommodation and social services. For some, however, rural "country" spaces provide anonymity and distance from the regulatory regimes of homeless organizations themselves. As one respondent in the Cloke et al. (2003) study suggests, "I prefer the country because it's quiet and you can do what you want out there you know you haven't got people nosing, nosing about and seeing what you're up to" (ibid.: 27). Materially, then, it is difficult to find the "bricks and mortar" of homeless-oriented services in some rural spaces because certain notions of rurality fail to appreciate difference along the axes of homed and homeless. This produces a landscape of inequitable resources, which creates daily push factors out of some rural areas and into other rural and urban spaces. In general, this illustrates the complexity and diversity of homeless experience; it also suggests the need to further interrogate how stigma toward the homeless is produced through discourses of, for example, "Not In My Backyard." In Foucauldian terms, homeless bodies are produced through discourses of power; they are "made real" through the processes of identification that mark them as transient, deviant, and problematic (Lawrence 1995). These regimes of power operate spatially through the production of spaces where the homeless are supposed to locate. But studies of homeless mobilities also suggest that the actual practices of being without a home complicate any straightforward reading of homeless experience. Homelessness as a sociospatial process, then, is experienced through both locality and mobility as people work their way through and across any number of organizational spaces and boundaries.

Development organizations as sites of resistance and authority

Foucault reminds us that organizations are "more than" material constructs because they are sites from which important social discourses and practices emanate. Indeed, it is clear that prisons and homeless service organizations are both produced by and productive of certain practices that regulate how people think about various forms of deviance. In somewhat different ways, development organizations – organizations designed to provide social and economic support and services for poorer communities in the global south – also serve the regulatory functions of "the government." This might seem odd to consider, as most of these organizations are thought of as nongovernmental. But development organizations are structured through a number of local and global networks that make them conduits for government-alizing practices of what is "appropriate" and "inappropriate" development. It is not surprising, then, that Escobar in *Encountering Development* argues that:

> We must analyze how peasants are constituted by the work practices of development professionals; that is, how the former's concrete experience is elaborated upon by the professional discourse of the latter, separated from the context in which the peasant's problems arise and shifted to that in which institutions speak and act. This work of abstraction is a necessary condition for development to work in the process of describing, inquiring into, interpreting, and designing treatment for their clients and beneficiaries. Although most times this process of abstraction and structuring – which goes on in large part unconsciously – takes place at the top (international or national levels), it inevitably works its way down to the local situation, where most of the work is done. The local level must reproduce the world as the top sees it, so to speak (Escobar 1995: 111).

Escobar's critical analysis of development organizations that work in the global south has had a strong impact on social geographers who are interested in investigating the complex plays of power that operate through these organizations. Broadly speaking, social geographers of development want to understand how these organizations socially structure people and places through their discourses and practices of development. Theoretically speaking, development is not a "thing" or an "end product" but a process, one that is productively organized through systems of power and knowledge.

Thus, while the work of Foucault has been criticized for its focus on European organizations and places, Escobar draws on it in his analysis of the governmentality effects that operate through professionalized development organizations. In so doing, Escobar starts to untangle how development is wrapped up in capitalist and western-centric notions of progress and advancement, which structure the world as "underdeveloped," "developing," and "developed." Dominant models of development, he argues, are spatially located in the global north. And, millions of people have to engage that model on a daily basis through their contact with development organizations. While many organizations want to provide help for people who might be hungry or poor, they still tend to structure space in ways that facilitate the flows of power from the global north – where many development organizations begin – to the global south – where the "recipients" live.

The relationship between organizational authority, vested in nongovernmental development organizations or NGOs, and the so-called recipients of that development is brought to bear quite powerfully in *Playing with Fire*, a collective autobiography of eight women working in and researching women's empowerment organizations in India. Writing in the collective voice, "we," they argue: "We wondered why those who live and do the most challenging work with Dalit [untouchables] and the poorest communities are rarely the ones who are invited to participate in conversations about that work or to prepare the reports, articles, or books on it" (Sangtin Writers 2006). The Sangtin Writers argue that NGOs remain firmly invested in local (and global) social relations of gender, class, and, in this case, caste. The professionalization of these organizations creates social and spatial identities that construct a new social binary around the development "expert" and the development "client." This is, in many ways, "hardwired" into the organizational practices of the NGO and its workers, which see no problem in constructing their work in relation to an "us" (NGO professionals) and "them" (clients or consumers). This is why Walker et al. (2007: 427) argue that in Mexico, "Many mainstream conservation and development organizations frame their projects and programs in terms of empowering poor and marginalized people. In practice, empowerment is "technical assistance." Typically offered in the form of workshops designed to impart certain information or methods (e.g. of forest management), technical assistance is the on-the-ground practice many NGOs enact to "strengthen civil society" or "build social capacity." I have found similar practices among locally based NGOs in Thailand, whose work on "capacity building" with people living with HIV and AIDS groups is dependent on teaching them how to best complete for government-based grant and funding applications (Del Casino 2006).

Dolhinow (2005) traces a similar process in the rural US southwest, where NGOs reinforce certain notions of "self help," catering to a model of development in which collective responses are marginalized in favor of individual (household) approaches. Because nongovernmental development organizations are bound into the webs and networks of funding agencies and donor organizations, they can become complicit in the deepening of governmentality effects and the regulation of individual and community conduct in development practices. This is made worse by the fact that development organizations need to focus on the constant process of fundraising for their efforts. "NGOs must be highly competitive," Dolhinow (2005: 574) argues, because "Not only are NGOs now expected to be experts and professionals, but they are also expected to compete like full-blooded capitalists – even though they are usually not supposed to make a profit." The irony, then, is that the focus on maintaining funding networks and relationships intensifies the vertical organizational structure of donor organization and development organization, while limiting the horizontal structures across communities through "political awareness" campaigns and "empowerment" (ibid.: 575). McKinnon (2007) further avers that the professionalization of development organizations restructures the relationships between "the community" and "the state," as NGO efforts create new mechanisms of surveillance for the government. In northern Thailand, for example, local NGOs work in coordination with UNICEF (United Nations Children's Fund) on their "Sentinel Surveillance Program," which is designed to "combat child trafficking" (McKinnon 2007: 781). What appears on the surface as a positive and constructive program to "train individuals from border communities . . . to do research on such issues as HIV/AIDS or migration patterns in the community" could also be used by the Thai government to track people who do not have "citizenship papers or title to their land" (ibid.). In this way, NGOs function to extend the governmentality effects of state surveillance of Thailand's border regions, which is peopled by ethnic minorities who have few civil or legal rights.

As McKinnon also argues, though, the organizational connectivities between the governmental and nongovernmental sectors produce new resistances. Issues that are rarely on the radar of Thai government officials might be brought to light within a surveillance program. I found similar processes at work in the spaces of health care in Thailand, as NGO outreach facilitated the flow of new knowledges and practices from the community and into the state health care sector. This problematized a narrow and straightforward reading of health as something that could be measured purely by biomedical science, as "alternative" traditional Thai medicine (*phaet phaen thai*) practices were becoming more commonly used in rural hospitals and clinics (Del Casino 2004). That said, the spatial extent and power of the government to regulate life through any number of organizations remains powerful, even as those organizations claim to be working, themselves, "beyond the state."

Communities and Organizations, Any Difference?

This chapter has discussed a number of different community and organizational spaces, examining how these two social geographic objects/subjects are complexly related to the power dynamics found in everyday society. Although rural, transnational, and virtual communities may occupy different spaces and networks, they are all subject to the practices of broader social relations. More than this, these communities are constituted spatially through the production of them as "imagined." This doesn't make communities any less real. It simply means that their spatialities are actively produced and created through the practices of inclusion (and exclusion) as well as similarity (and difference). In contrast, organizations were discussed as "more than" their material foundations; they are produced by and productive of discourses and practices of power. Using the work of Michel Foucault as a base, this chapter examined how "the prison," "the homeless service organization," and "the development organization" are structured to reproduce certain governmentality effects. In this way, the organization was theorized as a site through which certain social discourses and relations flow. The prison may be a material space of exclusion but its power to regulate everyday life is also powerful. Homeless people also find themselves moving in and out of a number of organizational spaces, which seek to regulate their mobilities in urban and rural space. While development organizations working in the global south may make claims to produce cooperative and participatory structures, they can also produce new forms of regulation and conduct that favor the knowledge of development that emerges from the global north. Or, as in some cases, NGOs and other development organizations can function as sites of control and surveillance directly for governments in the global south. In both cases, though, communities and organizations are useful starting points for social geography. They help to ground research questions in an empirical set of processes that can say a lot about the structuring of space, the inclusionary and exclusionary practices of social groups, and the functions of broader discourses of power and authority. There is hope, of course. And the next chapter traces how social geographers resist the structuring authorities of regulatory communities and organizations through a number of overt and covert anti-authoritative practices.

Note

1   This may change with several key US Supreme Court rulings that have upheld *habeas corpus*, the right to appear before a judge (in a timely manner).

Chapter 6

Social Activism/Social Movements/Social Justice

- Social Activism/Social Movements/Social Justice
- Does Social Geography have a Moral and Ethical Compass?
- Everyday Resistances, Organic Possibilities
- Active(ist) Geographies
  - Queering resistance, activism(s), hetero- and homonormativities
  - Challenging racism in/through geography
  - Toward a public participatory geographic information systems (PPGIS)
- Movement Geographies
  - Rethinking citizenship, HIV, and social subjectivities
  - Postnational social networks, emerging anti-globalization movements
  - An alter-movement movement, poststructuralism's new spaces of engagement
- Social Geography, Social Justice(s)

Social Activism/Social Movements/Social Justice

Social geographers have a longstanding commitment to studying and challenging inequalities. It is not surprising, then, that they also find themselves intellectually and politically interested in social activism, movements, and justice. Part I of this book examined how social geographers can and should effect change with their research. This is part of the rich tradition of the subdisicpline, as is the genuine interest in going beyond research into the realm of direct action and engagement. For some, that means formulating questions related to activism and resistance as a central component of their research. For others, it means researching and writing on topics that are both timely and pressing. For some others still, there is a strong interest in tracing the longer historical geographies of difference and inequality, focusing attention on the contested, transient, and unstable nature of the social and spatial categories and identities used to maintain spaces of differences, sites of exclusion, and places of stigma. The work and activism of social geographers is not always "direct," in that there also remains a strong interest in investigating the subtle and mundane, but no less important, day-to-day practices of struggle that are part of so many people's lives. The results of social geography's activist project are diverse and variegated, working through networks and nodes both "close by" and "at a distance" to engage in broader social concerns.

Social geographers are uniquely placed to engage in broader activist practices because they draw from a methodological toolbox that is malleable, capable of addressing a wide range of questions and concerns. Social geographers can learn from spatial science and the social relevancy debates, which have merged with critical spatial science and participatory GIS today. They can also draw from the methodological pluralities of radical, critical humanist, feminist, queer, and poststructuralist geographers, who work across a number of practices – from ethnography and participation observation to interviewing and focus groups to action research and mixed methodologies – and call into the question the power relations that structure spatial relations across important nodes of difference. This chapter investigates a number of social geographies, which trace out the day-to-day politics of "the social." It begins with a discussion of "moral and ethical geographies," examining the different ways that geographers have conceptualized the relationship between questions of the "moral," the "ethical," and geography.

Social geography, with its focus on "the social" and society, logically has an interest in broader questions of morals and ethics. While much of the earlier work on moral geographies was informed by humanistic geography, Marxist, feminist, queer, and poststructuralist geographers also engage in the question of moralities and ethics today. Indeed, there have been several calls over the past two decades for geographers to more seriously engage questions related to morality and ethics (this is evinced by the journal *Ethics, Place, and Environment* and in the work of geographers such as Smith 1994; Proctor and Smith 1999; Popke 2003, 2006, 2007). The chapter turns from a discussion of morality and ethics to resistance, with particular reference to the work of Antonio Gramsci, a twentieth-century Italian Marxist who theorized the relationships among, for example, education, organizing, and power.

Following these two conceptual sections, this chapter focuses on activist geographies through a discussion of different points of resistance to broader dominant politics and practices. Activism is sometimes thought of as overt and "in your face." Social geographers demonstrate, though, that activist sensibilities – developed through an interest in challenging inequalities and the marginalization of certain forms of difference – can take place in a number of ways. The final section of the chapter concentrates on social movements. Social movements are often thought of as "large-scale" organized forms of action that engage global problems or processes. This problematically sets up activism as "action" at the local level and movements as "moving" at the global level. While I certainly trace "globalized" forms of action in this section, I also resituate movement geographies in other resistance spaces, such as those that work "outside" the operations of capitalist social relations. Social movements and social activism are both concerned with questions of social justice, and therefore both social activism and social movements are critical to social geography.

Does Social Geography have a Moral and Ethical Compass?

[W]e now know a good deal about the more economic dimensions of residential segregation – we understand much about the workings of housing, land and labour markets, as keyed into the dynamics of capital accumulation – but we need to combine this knowledge with careful inquiry into the moral frameworks underlying group formation and its spatial expression (the categorisation of human groups from both within and without; the strategies of inclusion and exclusion that they pursue and which are pursued by others in relation to them) (Social and Cultural Geography Study Group Committee 1991: 17).

Over the past two decades, social geographers have drawn from a broad array of political and theoretical traditions while asking their questions of and about social justice (Smith 1994). Indeed, the Social and Cultural Geography Study Group Committee of the Institute of British Geographers suggests that the focus on economic difference and inequality has marginalized the discipline's concern with social difference and inequality. Changing the economic conditions of production and reproduction might go a long way to address questions of class but this might deprivilege issues of race, ethnicity, gender, sexuality, and ability that are also important nodes of difference (and inequality). Scholarship concerned with questions related to social justice should not forget questions of class and economy. At the same time, these are certainly not the only ways in which difference is constructed – from within and without – nor inequalities experienced – through the processes of inclusion and exclusion.

To this end, social geographers have engaged with moral and ethical philosophy[1] in their attempts to conceptualize social justice. In particular, social geographers continue to return to Immanuel Kant, whose "own moral philosophy . . . pivoted between a sensitivity to everyday moralities and the attempt to establish what a more transcendental morality (an 'ideal type' morality) possessed by the 'fully rational being' would look like" (Social and Cultural Geography Study Group Committee 1991: 15). Kant was particularly concerned with "common moral talk" and the "moral assumptions that all of us routinely make in our everyday lives in order to establish what should be done, who should be trusted, where we should go" (ibid.: 16). For Kant, then, the everyday geographies of location – in both a material and a social sense – is a critical component of how to conceptualize *individual moral practices* of "conduct or behavior" (Popke 2009). Put more directly, Kant's moral geographies are intimately tied to the practices of what is "good" and "bad." More recently, Popke (2007) has returned to Kant in his discussion of a broader *social ethics* of "cosmopolitan responsibility," asking how to "cultivate alternative geographical imaginations" that "respect their specificity while also fostering a wider sense of ethical responsibility toward . . . open-ended outcomes" (ibid.: 515). This responsibility, Popke argues, is tied to Kant's notion that we are " 'woven together' with geographically distant peoples and places," which "impels us . . . to work toward a more cosmopolitan stance that would transcend our narrow nationalist or sectarian interests" (ibid.: 510). This is not an easy place to be; it demands working back and forth across categories of "near" and "far," "inside" and "outside," to embed ethics in new networks that promote equity and justice across spaces without privileging one way of knowing or doing those moral geographies. In short, a cosmopolitan ethics or justice will fail if it is compelled by a neoliberal discourse that promotes individualism and conspicuous consumption over "communalism and ethical responsibility" (ibid.: 515).

Popke rightly notes, therefore, the limitations in Kant's theorization of cosmopolitan responsibility, which is embedded in Eurocentric notions of universal rights and laws. In Kant's formulation, "hospitality was . . . limited: his cosmopolitan right was not permanent residence, only temporary sojourn" (ibid.: 512). It is not surprising, then, that other social theorists have questioned Kant's definitions of hospitality and cosmopolitan responsibility:

> Derrida points out that an offer of hospitality – a welcome into my space, my household or territory – requires that I maintain a measure of sovereignty over my home. Hospitality is, therefore, always-already *conditional*. . . . To this Derrida contrasts what he called an unconditional or absolute hospitality: "absolute hospitality requires that I open up my home and that I give not only to the foreigner . . . but to the absolute, unknown, anonymous other, and that I *give place* to them" (Popke 2007: 512 quoting Derrida's (2000) *Of Hospitality*, original emphasis).

Derrida, whose poststructuralist philosophy has informed a wide array of geographic research on identity politics and ethics, suggests moving "beyond" geographic notions of place-based rights in order to truly welcome and respect others. This is a difficult notion because it suggests, on the one hand, a need to respect difference, and, on the other hand, to welcome those differences into the "home." The "home" itself, though, is a social space that privileges certain practices and ways of knowing (Blunt and Dowling 2006). In "accepting" difference, then, it is necessary to understand that the day-to-day practices of home spaces – in both the literal material sense of our home and the metaphorical notion of home as nation – are complicated by our practices of inclusion and exclusion. Popke's reading of Kant is certainly not the only reading of morality and ethics in geography, therefore. Indeed, as he suggests, feminist and poststruturalist, as well as Marxist and postcolonial, geographies inform social geography's conceptualizations of ethics (responsibility) and by extension moralities (conduct).

What this reading of Kantian philosophy does suggest, however, is that social geographers respect difference in their attempts to mitigate inequalities. Engagement across boundaries and with the so-called "other" continues unabated in this globalizing world of virtual and material connections and networks. It is very difficult to imagine complete disengagement from the world, although those in power, ironically enough, have more power to disengage than those who have less power and authority. This is true for social geographers as well, who have the power to go out "in the field" and then return "home" again (Robbins 2006). In this light, social geographers must use their explanatory and interpretive methodologies to answer questions that are important to more than themselves. Social geographers may not always be able to affect policy on the ground but then can raise questions, work with others to challenge power, and celebrate difference in their social geographies. To that end, I now turn to a discussion of resistance in the social theoretical work of Antonio Gramsci.

Everyday Resistances, Organic Possibilities

Social geographers have long been familiar with the work of Antonio Gramsci, a twentieth-century Italian Marxist, whose theorizations of hegemony extend classical Marxist theories, which assume that power and authority are regulated through economic and political organizations tied to the economy and the state. Gramsci argued, instead, that power is not only vested in the state (political) institutions; it is also reinforced through social and cultural (civil) organizations and institutions, such as the church and the educational system. Hegemonic power operating through civil society is a critical aspect of the economic domination by elite classes, in fact, because "Hegemony mystifies power relations, public issues, and events, and encourages fatalism and political passivity, and justifies system-serving sacrifice and deprivation" (Peet 1998: 129). As Peet goes on to note, many geographers have found Gramsci's theorizations of hegemony valuable to their work (see Peet 1998: 129–37 for details). In the area of cultural geography, Don Mitchell's book *Cultural Geography: A Critical Introduction* relies on Gramsci's theories of hegemony to critique mainstream cultural geography. Mitchell argues that there is "no such thing as culture," there is only politics about something we call "culture" (Mitchell 1995). For Mitchell, Culture with a "big C" is a blinder constructed by elite classes to promote the "political passivity" of which Peet speaks. Culture reinforces authority and domination, i.e. hegemony.

The import of Gramscian theory is important for social (and cultural) geography, because it helps to theorize and explain how certain social groups and practices of exclusion and inclusion are sedimented in culture and cultural representations. Mitchell's analysis of cultural geographies thus "effectively socialized cultural geography" (Del Casino and Marston 2006: 998) by arguing that it is through social (class) relations that culture is produced. It is not surprising, then, that Smith (2000b: 28) argues, "Culture doesn't just happen. Culture is work. And work is a social process." But how can people resist hegemony if it is ubiquitous, shaping everyday social experiences through the continual reproduction of dominant cultural representations and spaces? Thus, while understanding hegemony is important, to understand resistance means turning to other aspects of Gramsci's conceptual toolkit. Indeed, it is "the intellectual," not "hegemony," that is the first concept introduced in the edited collection *Selections from the Prison Notebooks* (Gramsci 1971). The social organization of intellectuals is of primary concern to Gramsci because he was particularly interested in expanding adult education to build resistance through new civil organizations and groups. His own direct action with the factory worker councils of Turin, Italy and in the area of adult education attest to the value he placed on the education of what he called the "subaltern" strata of society and its intellectual capacity (Mayo 1999). Gramsci's discussion of intellectuals, and their role in society, helps to explain how the power of the elite classes is productive of social relations of class. As Stuart Hall (1996) argues, through a reading of Gramsci, social class is not a "fact" of the economy:

> The important thing here is that so-called "class unity" is never *assumed, a priori*. It is understood that classes, while sharing certain common conditions of existence, are also crosscut by conflicting interests, historically segmented and fragmented in this actual course of historical formation. Thus the "unity" of classes is necessarily complex and has to be *produced* – constructed, created – as a result of specific economic, political and ideological practices (Hall 1996: 423, original emphasis).

The question for Gramsci, then, is: how is it possible to produce class unity? The answer is to expand the "organic" intellectual capacity of the subaltern classes by creating new spaces of education and engagement. Everyone has certain knowledges and experiences, and these can be exploited to expand class unity and consciousness. "There is no human activity from which . . . intellectual participation can be excluded" (Gramsci 1971: 9). Resistance is dependent on the ability of social groups to expand on alternative forms of intellectual engagement that operate despite not because of "traditional" intellectual education in schools and churches. This includes, the "element of 'spontaneity'," which Gramsci argues should be cultivated in all forms of resistance. "Ignoring and, even worse, disdaining so-called 'spontaneous' movements – that is, declining to give them a conscious leadership and raise them to a higher level by inserting them into politics – may often have very bad and serious consequences," avers Gramsci (1996: 50–1). Spontaneous resistance is important because it challenges the hegemonic production of everyday spaces, identities, and subjectivities as well as uneven social relations of power.

Returning to the concept of hegemony, Gramsci theorizes hegemony as a process of building compliance through "traditional" intellectuals, who teach allegiance to the state and dominant culture through key civil organizations, such as the school or church (Gramsci 1996: 114–15). Resistance, in contrast, operates spontaneously and "organically" through new forms of engagement, learning, and organizations, such as unions. Intellectual capacity and intellectualism are essential characteristics of Gramsci's project, therefore, because "Every trace of autonomous initiative is . . . of inestimable value" (ibid.: 21). There are certain limitations to Gramsci's theories, however. First, as a Marxist, Gramsci argues that social relations are determined by economic (and class) relations. Second, because Gramsci believes the economy is *the* essential marker of all social relations, other forms of resistance, tied to the politics of ability, ethnicity, gender, sexuality, race, or ethnicity, are marginalized in Gramsci's theorization of "the intellectual" and "hegemony." Third, Gramsci is working from a European context and his reading of resistance can be considered Eurocentric.

Despite these limitations, social theorists have built upon Gramsci's critical examination of "the intellectual" to expand how they think about resistance(s) and hegemony (Laclau and Mouffe 2001). Poststructuralist theorists offer a "reinterpretation of hegemony . . . as a never-ending process of political struggle that occurs not just in the domain of formal politics (political parties, elections, revolutions, political protests, etc.) but also as part of relationships of power across all social relations" (McKinnon 2007: 778). Organic intellectualism, emerging both spontaneously and through activist politics, can work across any number of nodes of identity and subjectivity, producing new possibilities and alternative spaces, organizations, and networks. Poststructuralists situate hegemony in the work of all social groups; organic and spontaneous resistances create temporary, new, and alternative understandings and spaces as social groups compete, albeit on a very uneven terrain, over social (ideological) and material resources. Activism is thus "a field of social struggle and a zone of political engagement" (McKinnon 2007: 779), an ongoing process with no clear end point but lots of possible outcomes.

Theorizing resistances as operating through a number of networks and nodes breaks down the arbitrary boundaries of state (political) and civil (social) spaces and organizations. Resistance (and domination) operates in both spaces simultaneously, through the organic and spontaneous connections that happen as human beings co-construct space (Del Casino 2006). Indeed, "resistance is woven into the heart of the state apparatus itself, in part because state power is based upon different axes of power – economic, military, informational – which do not always work in perfect consort" (Sharp et al. 2000: 7). Domination and resistance are not oppositional forces. They work relationally and contextually: domination produces resistances and resistances produce domination. Put more simply, while in certain spaces resistance may challenge ethnocentrism or neocolonialism, the processes of heterosexism or patriarchy may be simultaneously reinforced in that same space (Radcliffe 2000). There is a need to trace how resistance *and* domination operate in certain spaces, as various social groups and peoples struggle to define alternative identities and subjectivities.

Active(ist) Geographies

On a day-to-day basis, individuals and collectives resist broader structures of power and authority. Sometimes this takes the form of direct protest or action, at other times it takes place through mundane and spontaneous social and spatial interactions. In the first instance, there might be a service union protest against a hotel chain. In the second instance, there could be two men holding hands and kissing on a public bus, challenging the presumptions of what is "appropriate" in that heterosexualized space. In this section, I want to turn to the different ways in which social geographers have discussed and thought about activism, broadly conceived. I focus, in particular, on how activism(s) within geography has forced shifts in how social geographers think and write about difference and inequality. It is important to note that geographers have long challenged the presumptive norms and disciplinary myopia, defining the discipline's problematic gender-blindness (e.g. Monk and Hanson 1982) or ignorance related to class-based issues and concerns (e.g. Harvey 1973). Many social (activist) geographers have thus drawn on feminist and Marxist theories and practices to raise questions and concerns related to gender and class politics in the discipline of geography. Moving in and out of the tensions present in the discipline today around how to enact change within (and beyond) the academy, this section traces the ways that social geographers actively challenge and resist heterosexism, racism, and academic elitism. It is important to recognize that these challenges are not exclusive to one set of scholars – queer, critical race, or critical GIS theorists. Instead, they are informed by the longer tradition of feminist and Marxist scholarship that has been working to open up geography and geographic practice to its own differences and potential inequalities. In this light, I begin with a discussion of everyday resistance through queer challenges to heterosexism. I follow this with a discussion about race and racial politics in/through geography. Finally, I ask how social geographers might utilize recent advances in geographic information technologies to open up democratic and participatory possibilities for community groups and organizations that can work with academic social geographers.

Queering geographies, activism(s), hetero- and homonormativities

The queering of geography is an ongoing process of, on the one hand, challenging the presumptive heteronormative assumptions of the discipline of geography, and, on the other hand, doing critical and engaged research that expands what is important and "legitimate" geographic research. In the first instance, queer geographers have been trying to overtly "queer" the discipline since, at least, the 1970s, providing space for both lesbian, gay, bisexual, transgendered, queer, and intersexed (LGBTQI) geographers specifically and sexuality studies researchers more broadly (Brown and Knopp 2003; Elder et al. 2004). This has not always been an easy

Box 6.1   Methodological Note: Mapping Women's
Experiences in/across Space

In 2003, Joni Seager published a third edition of *The Penguin Atlas of Women in the World*. This atlas is an excellent example of how to use cartographic principles to display social geographies of gender and sexuality at a global (and regional) scale. In particular, Seager traces the geographies of women's experiences of "families" (e.g. lesbian households, domestic violence, and marriage and divorce), "birthrights" (e.g. motherhood, contraception, son preference), "body politics" (e.g. breast cancer, HIV/AIDS, beauty), "work" (e.g. working for wages, unpaid work, migration), "having" (e.g. literacy, school, property), and "power" (e.g. the vote, women in government, and feminist organizing). Seager (2003: 8) also notes the problems of trying to balance "commonality and difference." The volume uses cartographic and statistical representational principles and practices – choropleth (shaded relief) maps, charts, symbology, arrows to demonstrate movements – to provide a global picture of the commonalities women share but also, perhaps more importantly, the differences. After all, as Seager aptly notes, "Improvements in one place are not necessarily transferable to other places: we remain a world divided" (ibid.: 7). Cartographic representation is thus a powerful descriptive and analytic tool for Seager's global social geography:

> It is as a geographer that I have found a way to strike a balance between the demands of acknowledging both commonality and difference: at its best, mapping can simultaneously illuminate both. Mapping is a powerful tool; in showing not only what is happening where, patterns are revealed on maps that would never be apparent in statistical tables or even in narratives. The similarities and differences, the continuities and contrasts among women around the world are perhaps best shown by mapping out – literally – their lives. It is my hope that this atlas raises as many questions as it provides answers (ibid.: 8).

Quick Exercise

Go to the Population Reference Bureau website (http://www.prb.org/) and download the free "World Population Data Sheet." Locate a variable that is relevant to the study and experience of women's lives globally. Using a GIS, or another computer cartography program, create a choropleth map of those data. What does the map tell you about the different experiences of women globally? (An example of a choropleth is found in Figure 5.3.)

proposition, as there have been direct challenges to the work of geographers studying sexuality (and sex) in the discipline, particularly in the Association of American Geographers (AAG) (Bell 1995a, 2007). An author in *The Professional Geographer*, for example, once exclaimed: "When engaging in their gay behavior they are not acting as geographers" (Carter 1977: 102; cited in Elder et al. 2004: 200). His concerns were raised after learning that a group of geographers had organized a "gay caucus" at an AAG national meeting. Despite the hegemonic scripting of geography as an asexual discipline and the outright hostility by some toward those interested in the study of and activism related to queer subjectivities, queer geographers have engaged some of the discipline's myopic readings of sexualities through publication as a form of disciplinary activism (Bell and Valentine 1995; Valentine 2000; Browne et al. 2007). Gill Valentine (1998), for example, published an important paper in *Antipode: A Journal of Radical Geography* about her disciplinary "outing" and "harassment," which plagued part of her career in the 1990s. As she writes, the harassment she faced not only challenged her professionally and emotionally, it challenged her own understanding of her research as a queer scholar.

> Although the choice of geographies of sexualities . . . as research topic at the beginning of my academic career was largely motivated by my own personal experiences, most notably as a lesbian, I never set out to "come out" within the discipline. While my sexual identity was constituting my research, I never intended this relationship to be mutual. Indeed, I rather naively believed that I could walk a tightrope of ambiguity in Geography about my own sexuality, while still writing about lesbians (Valentine 1998: 306).

Her "outing" in the public spaces of her discipline meant that she had to reconsider her relationship to her various social identities – as a woman, a lesbian, an academic, for example – and to other spaces, including those of her family where she had remained "closeted" (ibid.: 326).

Violence, particularly against people who occupy so-called different bodies and spaces, can be both emotional and physical. The degree to which those violences occur has been the center of much geographic research on gay and lesbian sexualities in geography. Within this work there has been a pronounced attempt to understand how spaces are mapped as "straight" and normatively heterosexualized. Glen Elder (1995) describes how white and black homosexual men in apartheid South Africa occupied different spaces and were regulated differentially by the state. Whereas black men who had sex with other men were contained in the spaces of mining, and thus posed little direct threat to the heterosexual order, white gay men "threatened the very existence of a patriarchal apartheid system" (ibid.: 62) because they were "out" in public (white, straight) spaces. In a different context, Brown (2000: 72) traces how "the closet" operates in the urban space of Christchurch, New Zealand, arguing that "typically gay spaces (bars, saunas, and cruise clubs) are entirely inconspicuous in the urban landscape." The operation of the closet in urban space is important because "men depend on the invisibility and anonymity produced in that space in order to have sex with other men" (ibid.: 77). The closet in this case acts as a space outside the regulations of a heterosexual norm. On the one hand, the closet marginalizes certain nonheterosexual practices and identities, while on the other hand it provides a safe (and resistant) space to be gay without physical or emotional reprisal.

Queer geographers have also traced more direct forms of resistance to heterosexual norms through, for example, "pride parades" (Browne 2007a; Johnston 2007). Pride parades, where nonheterosexualities are celebrated through the overt use of public space, have become more common across a number of globalized spaces, particularly cities, since the late 1960s (Johnston 2005). Although Pride was initiated to raise questions related to political (civil) and social human rights, "contemporary Pride politics in countries such as the UK and Ireland have been read in terms of resisting hegemonic normative heterosexuality through playful 'deconstructive spatial tactics' rather than demanding civil rights or legislative change" (Browne 2007a: 66). At least in the spaces of Europe and North America, the politics of Pride has as much to do with the complex relationships across so-called nonheterosexual subject positions (e.g. lesbian, transgendered, gay) as it does with contesting heteronormativities. In this way, the practice of a "queer politics" does more than simply challenge heterosexism; it "celebrates gender and sexual fluidity and consciously blurs binaries" (G. Brown 2007: 197) across a number of different spaces. As such, "radical queer organizations," such as "Queeruption," are making "conscious attempts . . . to work with groups in the Majority World":

> To this end, work has been undertaken with radical queer groups in Argentina (Espacio ReSaCA – Space for a Sexual and Anti-Capitalist Revolution), Israel/Palestine (the Black Laundry, a queer group opposed to the Israeli occupation of Palestinian land), Serbia (the organizers of the aborted Belgrade Pride) and Turkey (KAOS-GL, a lesbian and gay anarchist group). These are all organizations that, to varying degrees, are not simply attempting to create a space in their respective cultures for American and Western European style gay rights, consumption, and "lifestyles," but are experimenting in their local contexts with different anti-capitalist means of living autonomous queer lives (G. Brown 2007: 199).

Queering space is a set of practices that thus deals with "much more than" sexuality. Queer activism(s) engage in a wide array of political possibilities, creating allegiances and networks across nodes of difference that challenge a variety of inequalities. This work also suggests that social geographers work across the global north–global south divide by critically reflecting on the relationship between a queer sexual politics and an emancipatory ethnic politics, for example.

Importantly, then, queer geographers challenge not only heteronormativities with their writing and activism but also homonormativities – the normalized stabilization of a certain "homosexual subject" that "stands in" for all queer subjects (Nast 2002; Sothern 2004). Puar (2005, 2006), for example, offers a critique of "queerness" and the complicity between homonormativity and US-based geopolitical exceptionalism. In a provocative critique of foreign policy, Puar argues:

Queerness colludes with US exceptionalisms embedded in nationalist foreign policy via the articulation and production of whiteness as a queer norm and the tacit acceptance of US imperialist expansion. For example, national LGBTQ organizations such as the National Gay and Lesbian Task Force (NGLTF) and the Human Rights Commission (HRC) have been far more preoccupied with gay marriage and gays in the military than the war on terrorism or even the "homosexual sex" torture scandal at Abu Ghraib [in Iraq] (Puar 2005: 124).

Puar's critique of homonormativity is picked up by other queer geographers who want to challenge the normalization of a singular gay or homosexual subject (Nast 2002), although social geographers must be very careful not to create a new binary of homonormative and non-homonormative in the process of critical resistance (Oswin 2004; Lim et al. 2007). This is why Oswin (2004: 84) cautions that "the maintenance of a distinction between non-complicit and complicit queers suggests (however unintentionally) a corresponding distinction between authentic and in-authentic queers." What all this suggests is that queer geographers (and geographies) challenge the centering of identities and subjectivities in a singular narrative or in one place. Queer geographies thus "make space" for a wide array of difference(s) within both academic geography as a discipline and academic activist research in/with/through queer communities.

Challenging racism in/through geography

Throughout the post-Second World War period, social geographers have examined questions related to race, particularly the study of racial and ethnic segregation. This work has provided a unique opportunity for social geographers to continue the "tradition of mapping racialized migration flows, residential segregation, poverty and political participation" (Nash 2003: 638). While this work remains vitally important, particularly as social geographers try to challenge inequalities through public policy advocacy, there are inherent problems of race and racism within the field of geography. This is evinced both by a historical lack of race studies (Dwyer 1997) and in the very low representation of people of color (Pulido 2002; Kobayashi 2006) in the discipline. These critical examinations of geography's disciplinary context are important for two reasons. First, they break down the binary logic of academy and society. Instead of thinking about the academy as an "ivory tower" removed from everyday life, they examine the academy (and geography within it) as embedded in societies and social relations of class, ethnicity, race, gender, ability, and sexuality. Second, these critical reflections interrogate how geographers promote social justice and civil rights issues within their own intellectual community. Are social geographers simply criticizing racism "out there" beyond their own walls? If so, they may be reinforcing the image of a distanced and objectivist academy that fails to interact with the broader spaces in which they live their everyday lives. If social geography seeks to be antiracist, it has to critically reflect on itself.

One way to address these issues is to turn the social geographic lens on the discipline. Mahtani argues, for example: "In my own research interviewing women of colour in geography . . . I discovered recurring patterns of both racism and sexism that suggest inequities are increasing, not decreasing" (Mahtani 2006: 23). Mahtani is not alone in her assessment of the field. Sanders (2006: 50–1) offers a critique of the discipline's postmodern turn and its focus on difference; she believes this turn has done little to pry open the "black box" of academic geography for people of color. "Unless non-essentializing discourses can 'do something' with (and for) the multiple voices they acknowledge; there is simply no *there* there; and at the end of the day, the academy can be viewed as being duplicitous with other conservative institutions by merely reproducing what is." And, Akinleye (2006: 28) suggests, "it has been my experience that in geography research on social equity issues has not necessarily led to a more equitable treatment of those within the discipline who have historically been marginalized." This is an ironic moment. On the one hand, social geographers are interested in the study of social difference and, on the other hand, they sometimes do little to sustain diversity in their own field. Embedded in all of these concerns is the notion that within the discipline – although this is certainly not exclusive to geography – "systematic racism" leaves scholars of color in a "situation that can be very isolating, and the individual researcher of colour often feels like a 'poster child' for an entire 'race'" (Kobayashi 2006: 36; referencing Pulido 2002). Such commentary suggests that within geography departments, it is necessary to open up more space for colleagues to explore topics related to race/racism as well social justice and civil rights. While this will not automatically attract people of color to the discipline, it may effect some "local" change. And, it may be a way to build what Pulido (2002: 45) calls a "critical mass" of scholars who can "generate an intellectual synergy around race" (ibid.: 46). Pulido, and others, suggest that this does not mean excluding "white geographers" from the study of race. Instead, simply put, "more geographers of color would enhance our disciplinary discourse on race" (ibid.: 45).

Despite the discipline's apparent hegemonic whiteness, social geographies of race and racism have increased over the past two decades. This is reflected in a number of special journal issues, including *Social and Cultural Geography* (1.2, 2000), *The Professional Geographer* (54.2, 2002), and *Gender, Place, and Culture* (13.1, 2006), dedicated to the study of race in and beyond the discipline. In this context, Peake and Schein (2000: 133) note that "There appears to be a renaissance regarding questions of 'race' and racism within geography in general, and within North American geography in particular." Within this renaissance is a critical evaluation of race as a social and spatial process of becoming. Race is not a natural a priori fact of life; it is constructed through everyday practice and realized in discourses about race. "Much of this work has been informed by anti-essential perspectives on race which deconstruct race as a naturalized hierarchy of biologically distinct human groups while exploring processes of racialization which places individuals and groups within racial categories and have material effects in terms of the unequal distribution of power and wealth" (Nash 2003: 639). This doesn't make race and racism any less real (Wilson 2005). Moving from the study of race as a biological fact, to race as a process of making and remaking social meaning allows social geographers

Box 6.2   Race/Immigration/Geography

In the post-9/11 world, debates about "the border" and "immigration" are intensifying. This is not a phenomenon unique to the US, as many countries are embroiled in conversations about who belongs "inside" and "outside" the imagined spaces of the nation. These debates and conversations are often entangled with the politics of race. In the US, increasing in-migration has created tense situations along the border with Mexico, particularly in states such as California, Arizona, and Texas, as new social movements emerge to either assist those crossing the border or to try and stop people from entering the country illegally. In other parts of the US, such as the south, " 'unauthorized' immigration" (Winders 2007: 920) is changing how people construct the spaces of the nation and the community. Social geographers have increasingly turned their attention to the intersections between the politics of race and immigration, attempting to understand how new migration streams are affecting the sociospatial organization of race and racial segregation.

Jamie Winders (2006, 2007, 2008) explores the contested and complex relations of race through an extended discussion of Latino/as in-migration to the US south. In her analysis of Latino/as in Nashville, Tennessee, Winders (2008) argues that the in-migration of a "third" racial group – non-white and non-Black – has made the politics of race in this southern city more complex. "With near-perfect repetition, 'Latino/as and race' translated into Latino/as and African Americans, as White Nashville was discursively removed from framings of race relations and largely absolved of responsibility for adjusting to the city's new racial grammar" (ibid.: 253). In other southern states, the growing number of Latino/as, particularly families, is causing greater anxiety, particularly among the white elite of the region. In some cases, new laws, discursively tied to protecting the nation in a post-9/11 world, are increasing the scrutiny over migrant populations viewed as "dangerous" and "destabilizing" to the spaces of the south. The "slippage between racism and patriotism," Winders argues, "carries new currency post 9/11 and allows the South's anti-immigrant discourses and practices to cloak the workings of racism by drawing on a national reservoir of post-9/11 border anxieties. This racism is further masked by recourse to the South's specific historical practices and formations. Protecting state resources from 'illegal immigrants' in Georgia and Mississippi, for example, becomes protecting 'southern hospitality' and ways of life" (ibid.: 934).

Quick Exercise

Using archival information, trace the laws that have been either locally or nationally enacted to regulate immigration since 2001. What are some of the reasons given for the development of such regulations?

to investigate the complexities within races as well as social categories typically not scrutinized, such as whiteness (Dwyer and Jones 2000). The study of whiteness within geography is a direct attempt to construct an antiracist geography, while pushing geographers not only to examine "the social location of 'others' but also . . . to name one's own location" (Kobayashi and Peake 2000: 400).

The move toward constructing antiracist geographies of difference and inequality is also strongly and intimately tied to the growing dialogue between postcolonial theory and social geography (Blunt and McEwan 2002). Postcolonial geographers are particularly interested in rethinking the relationships between a global north and global south, between a colonizing geographic gaze and an emancipatory politics that challenges globalized racism. This is, of course, not an easy task, as it demands engaging with the voices of those who have been marginalized by colonialism and/or postcolonial development (Blunt and Wills 2000). It also demands that social geographers "analyze the languages of imperialism and empire" along with how "bringing 'democracy' and 'freedom' (or more precisely free market) to Afghanistan and Iraq . . . [and] 'making the [US] homeland safe' has involved the militarization of daily life, increased surveillance and detention of immigrants, and a [produced] culture of authoritarianism" (Mohanty 2006: 9). The deeply racist practices of US imperialism in the post-9/11 period draws on a broader colonial spatial imagination, which constructs the spaces of the "Middle East," or of "Islam" more generally, as backward, regressive, conservative, and conflictual (see Gregory 2004). This disciplinary activism thus asks social geographers to think more critically about nonwestern spaces when "doing" their research and theory (Robinson 2003) so that they can interrogate the deeply embedded racist ideologies of colonialism and postcolonialism that maintain boundaries between a so-called "developed" global north and an "underdeveloped" global south. Of course, postcolonial social geographers also point out that their examination of race relations can advance studies of racialized politics within the so-called colonial/postcolonial center in Europe and North America. In this case, the focus is on the uneven power relations within the categories of whiteness – through an investigation of British colonial practices in Ireland (Gilmartin and Berg 2007) – as well as immigrant and immigration politics – through analyses of the activist networks emerging in and across "native" and "migrant" communities in Italy (Merrill 2006). There is no simple way to enact antiracist social geographies. It is important, however, that social geographers continue to interrogate the spatialities – distances, networks, locations – that mark race and racism within and beyond the academic field of geography.

Toward a public participatory geographic information systems (PPGIS)

Activist social geographers critically reflect not only on their own subject but also on their place within a broader set of community spaces. As geographers have advanced their technological expertise – through developments in computer cartography, geographic information systems, and remote sensing – they have also tried to to break down the arbitrary boundaries between academic geography and local community politics. To this end, some geographers have been advancing public participation in the use and development of GIS databases and tools in the day-to-day activist work of community groups and organizations. This growing field, known as public participation GIS (PPGIS), has a number of "characteristics." These include:

1) emphasis on the role of participants in creation and evaluation of data; 2) accommodation of equitable representation of diverse views, preserving contradiction, inconsistencies, and disputes against premature resolution; 3) system outputs redefined to reflect the standards and goals of the participants; 4) capabilities for managing and integrating all data components and participation contributions from one interface – technologically sophisticated but easy to use; 5) preservation and representation of the history of its own development and be more capable of handling time components than existing GIS; and 6) embedment of the condition that "Public Participation GIS" is not primarily enabling technology focused but is primarily an ongoing "process" of self-determination by self-defining communities (Onsrud and Graglia 2003: 5–6).

This trend toward creating participatory uses of new technologies and increasing access to technological advances parallels the broader interest social geographers have in activist participatory action research (Pain 2003, 2004, 2006). The practice of PPGIS starts from the assumption that knowledge and knowledge production are not uniquely situated within the academy; spatial imaginaries are present in all communities. In Gramscian terms, the organic capacity of the intellectual is "present" already in community groups, who merely need the tools at hand to produce new ways of analyzing and knowing their geographies. The use of geographic information is thus not limited to certain peoples and spaces, but could and should be used broadly to address social geographic concerns and inequalities.

In this context, Drew (2005) suggests that PPGIS can be employed in interactive Internet environments to increase the transparency in decision-making processes. Using the example of environmental decision-making around Hanford, Washington, a post-nuclear facility space that has been the subject of a massive cleanup effort in the region, Drew concludes that both governmental and nongovernmental organizations and actors can engage in debate and discussion about important social and environmental concerns using these new technologies. Ghose and Elwood (2003: 17), while excited about the possibility of PPGIS, also argue that "local political context encompasses a complicated set of factors, involving multiple actors and institutions playing interconnected roles in shaping the processes of participation and of PPGIS production." It is not enough to simply assert participation; social geographers have to critically analyze the sociospatial relations and contexts through which participation is enacted. What Ghose and Elwood show through a case study of the use of PPGIS in inner city Milwaukee, Wisconsin is that "local government entities hold a more powerful position than the community organizations and have established modes of participation that community organizations are compelled to accept if they wish to receiving funding" (ibid.: 20). They do note, however, that community organizations have taken advantage of technologies designed to meet one need – urban revitalization programs for poor neighbhorhoods – and have used those same technologies in "demonstrating to other federal, state, or local agencies, and to private foundations and entrepreneurs that the community has clearly articulated revitalization goals and strategies" (ibid.: 21). When using PPGIS, academics and activists thus have to consider the "key organizational factors (such as knowledge, stability, capacity, and leadership) . . . differentially affecting the ways in which community organizations in Milwaukee are engaging with local political structures and GIS opportunities in their PPGIS activities" (ibid.). This points to the continuing need to contextualize the place-based social relations that impact the use of PPGIS.

While a critical analysis of the use of GIS in public and participatory contexts is an important aspect of an activist GIScience (MacEachren 2000), other geographers have demonstrated how GIS might be employed directly in community activism. The Syracuse Community Geography project is one example of geographers working across the academic–community divide using the technologies of GIS. This project brings together the skills of student and staff with the work of community workers and leaders to answer important geographic questions. One key example is the Syracuse Hunger Project (Johnson and Mitchell 2004), which utilizes a GIS to broadly map the spaces of both hunger and the services for those who are poor in Syracuse. Unlike a research project that has a clear question and testable answer, the authors of the project's report suggest that it "should be viewed as a work in progress. . . . When we began, we were not absolutely certain where the Project would go, believing once things got started, it would probably take off in new directions that could not be planned in advance" (Johnson and Mitchell 2004: 3–4). At the same time, GIS can be a powerful tool for collecting, collating, and analyzing a wide array of geographic data. It is also a mechanism through which social geographers can visualize the processes of hunger and service provision in and across the city.

> When we start to pay attention to the geography of hunger something new emerges – new ways of seeing the problem and, we think, new ways of addressing them. For the first time, with the development of Geographic Information Systems and other mapping technologies, we can really begin to map hunger – and its amelioeration – in all its complexity. GIS allows us to see hunger in a new way. And engaging in a community mapping of hunger, allows us to collectively appreciate not only the scope of the complexity of the problem, but also all that we have done right – and wrong – to address it (Johnson and Mitchell 2004: 6).

In Figure 6.1, we see one example of this project's output, a map with individual level data of "food stamp cases" and a quarter-mile radius that surrounds each "Food Pantry" in the city of Syracuse. The map allows for a visual comparison of "need" – hunger – and "resources" – food pantries. This map is only possible because of the collaborative context in which these data were collected and then mapped. In fact, the Syracuse Hunger Project demonstrates the inextricable link between a social geography interested in enacting change and a community politics invested in addressing the needs of those living in poverty. The project further advances its critical geographic project through its outputs, which are all available freely on the Internet. More than this, the project's final product – a written report and slide presentation with maps and broader explanation – demonstrates that activism does not need to take only one form of presentation – a journal article. Instead, it may be possible to communicate across the spaces of the academic–community divide through the use of multiple media and outlets. It is important to recognize, of course, that access to such resources, no matter how "cost free" they may appear, is limited by the geographies of technological connectivity. Social geographers have to remember, then, that they may need to produce their final product in multiple forms so that it can privilege the largest amount of users possible.

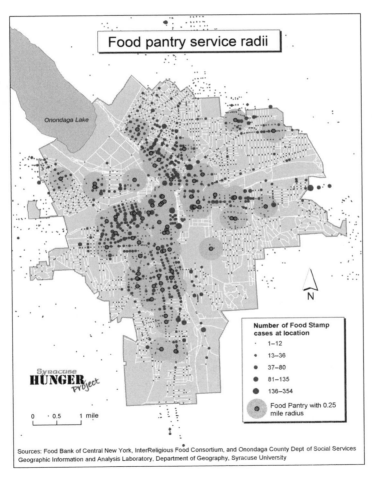

Figure 6.1   Food pantry service radii, the Syracuse Hunger Project. (Cartography by the Geographic Information and Analysis Laboratory, Department of Geography, Syracuse University, reprinted with permission.)

Movement Geographies

While geographers remain interested in activism within and beyond their own disciplinary spaces, social geographers are also concerned with tracing the emergence
of what are called "social movements". As Miller (2000) points out, social movements are inherently spatial processes, as they involve strategies that contest,
control, or rethink the use and organization of space. From union efforts to
control the shop floor and change working conditions, to anti-globalization and
anti-free trade efforts, to protests against a US presidential inauguration, social
geographers can contribute to these movements – in both their study of and participation in these activities. This section discusses just three broad sets of movement
geographies. The first centers on the relationship between national citizenship and
"biological" and "genetic" subjectivities. In particular, I examine how geographers
have studied the politics of the (dis)eased body, health care accessibility, and social
movements to improve the health of those living with HIV in the context of the
ever-changing technologies of the body. Next, I focus on anti-globalization (and
anti-free trade) movements and how these work through both national and postnational identity politics. Finally, I turn to poststructuralist theories of protest through
nonprotest, particularly in attempts to work "outside" the structures of capitalist
social relations. I focus, in particular, on the theoretical possibilities offered to us
by J. K. Gibson-Graham, whose poststructuralist feminist spatial politics offer a
counter to both capitalist economic practices and what she calls "capitalocentric
discourses." All these discussions are focused on how these movements engage social
justice research and practice.

Rethinking citizenship, HIV, and social subjectivities

The changing social and spatial processes of disease can intersect with identity
politics in ways that create new moments of social and collective action. Such is the
case with the spread of HIV and the advent of AIDS, whose diffusion beginning in
the 1980s intersected with an already activist sexual politics located in the broadly
defined gay community of the global north. Even before HIV was medically identified
and defined, collective action coalesced to challenge the ways that HIV became
stigmatized and marginalized in certain communities and spaces. And new programs
of care developed over time to effect change for those most directly impacted by HIV
(Brown 1997). This is evinced in the emergence of activist groups, such as Act Up,
which use direct action protests and civil disobedience to push governmental and
nongovernmental organizations to take HIV care and prevention seriously (Altman
2001). As HIV has continued to diffuse globally, it has intersected with other
localized social and spatial relations in unique and complicated ways that deny any
straightforward reading of its politics (Craddock 2004; Grundfest Schoepf 2004; Del
Casino 2006). And, the advent of new technologies to combat HIV disease, such as

antiretroviral drugs, is changing the landscapes of health and healing for those living with the virus, although access to these technologies varies quite dramatically across the globe. HIV disease is, in fact, not only biologically mutable – there are numerous different "strains" of HIV – it is also socially mutable – the meanings ascribed to HIV and to HIV positive (and negative) bodies have changed over time (Craddock 2000b). Drawing inspiration from health geography, it is vital that social geographers not forget that there are material biological consequences that come with HIV, even as they tend to privilege "the social" in their analyses (Parr 2002).

Wrapped up in the social geographies of HIV is a politics of responsibility, ethics, and citizenship. Who is responsible for the spread of HIV or for the care and treatment of those who are HIV positive? While citizenship is a term often used in political geography, it also has a clearly social definition tied to a "sense of belonging," "a sense of collectivity," and a "sense of rights" that intersects with questions related to ethical obligation. And, more and more, notions of citizenship are being rescaled away from the national and toward the global[2] and the local. As citizenship is being rethought, geographers are investigating how "citizens" are defined by their allegiance to new global and local normative subjectivities. People are not only political citizens, they are sexual citizens, for example, whose rights are defined at the level of the sexed body (Bell and Binnie 2000). Brown (2006b) notes that sexual citizenship is tied to social obligations designed to regulate individual public (and private) practices through laws against various sex practices, such as oral or anal sex. Nicholas Rose (2007) further suggests that the social obligations tied to these new notions of "citizenship" are also regulating bodies at the level of the molecular – at the scale of the biological and genetic. People are not only political or sexual citizens, they are also biological citizens, obligated to perform their bodies in ways that protect others from the spread of infectious diseases. As "good" biological citizens there is an ethical obligation to protect others – e.g. to not spread disease from one body to the next – grounding responsibility squarely in the individual citizen (Braun 2007). This is highly problematic because it recenters responsibility in certain bodies and spaces. So, in the case of HIV in Los Angeles, California, new HIV prevention campaigns called "HIV is a Gay Disease" and "HIVStopsWithMe.Org" center HIV transmission in, predominantly, gay male HIV positive bodies. It is thus the responsibility of those who are positive to protect those who are negative; those who do not participate in this new form of responsible citizenship are thus marked as biologically deviant (i.e. outside the social norms practiced in certain places).

New ways of thinking about biological citizenship and obligation, however, have also produced new forms of activism and resistance around what Nicholas Rose (2007) calls biosociality – social communities organized around a similar set of biological identity markers. Biosociality may be organized around one's HIV positive status through a support group or direct action, such as the protests organized by Act Up. Biological citizens, organized around their new biosociality, can also call upon their membership in national and global spaces to gain access to needed resources, such as medications or research and development. This occurred recently in Thailand, where a battle over a free trade agreement negotiation between the US and Thai governments culminated in a protest against patents on life-saving HIV-related medications. In this case, HIV positive individuals organized with other social groups – farmers' groups, environmental organizations, local business associations, and economic cooperatives – to directly combat what they saw as an unfair incursion of global protections for multinational corporations within the national space of Thailand. Free trade agreements that protect patents on antiretroviral drugs, making them too expensive for most Thais, therefore, have been constructed as an attack on the sovereignty of the citizenry of Thailand. New forms of biosocial organization – developed around an HIV positive identity – and globalizing knowledge about antiretroviral medications have coalesced in Thailand into a movement against free trade. These challenges are enhanced by the expansion of a broader HIV positive support group effort, which operates at the national (Thai), regional (Asia Pacific), and global levels. The biosociality of HIV can thus transgress the boundaries of the nation through the expansion of knowledge networks and activist exchange. In this way, biosociality may be thought of as rethinking citizenship through new models of care and ethics that work across national sites of difference. In Popke's (2007) terms, this might help further develop a new ethics of care that takes into consideration those who are both "near" and "far."

The global AIDS pandemic, as we know all too well, is not evenly distributed across the globe, and the broader social movement to address both prevention and care for those living with HIV remains a pressing issue for social geographers, particularly those working in many parts of Africa, Latin America, and South, Southeast, and East Asia. The struggle to provide appropriate care for those who are HIV positive is regulated not only by local social practices but also be global politics – George W. Bush has tied US funding for HIV and AIDS prevention to abstinence-only programs in parts of Africa. There is a constant vigilance to ensure that people are treated with dignity and ethically in places where access to health care and educational programs remain limited. Yet, the uneven politics of access to care is particularly acute in the area of drug development, testing, and production. "According to a recent World Bank report, most of the money for AIDS vaccine research is allocated for HIV subtypes more common in North America. . . . Yet people in poorer countries make better participants in trials and testing the efficacy of those vaccines both because they are 'treatment naïve,' meaning they have not been exposed to drug regiments, and because, apparently, it is acceptable for them to be exposed to HIV during the course of a vaccine trial" (Craddock 2004: 247). In this case, vaccine trials have been located predominantly in Sub-Saharan Africa. Global and local pressure is being brought to bear to change the practices of private pharmaceutical companies that, unlike their university counterparts, are not obligated to pass any test of research ethics before engaging in such research outside their home country. Today, corporations and governments are assigning biovalues to global citizens. Those values are being unevenly allocated, as are the resources tied to those values. The global fight around HIV care and prevention is thus tied to wider social movements resisting globalization and the global regulation of biomedical technologies through institutions, such as the World Trade Organization, and its policies, such as the Trade-Related aspects of Intellectual Property Rights (TRIPS), which protect corporation patents over life-saving medications across national boundaries at the expense of those most in need. These fights, therefore, continue on a number of fronts and across a variety of spaces.

Postnational social networks, emerging anti-globalization movements

In 1999, a dynamic set of anti-globalization protests emerged in Seattle, Washington to combat the World Trade Organization's broader global economic agenda (Herbert 2007). This was certainly not the first anti-globalization protest nor was it the last. What is significant about these protests is the extent to which they transgressed a number of historically diverse social identities:

> Mass mobilization to put pressure on the World Trade Organization during meetings held in Seattle, USA, during late November/early December 1999 caused great excitement around the world. Thousands of activists from different persuasions found the time and place to cohere around a common set of demands about the politics of globalization. Here was the embryo of a genuinely international mobilization and solidarity as Indian farmers' organizations, environmental campaigners, women's groups, trade unionists and black rights groups formed coalitions over common concerns (Wills 2002: 94).

The challenge, of course, for new anti-globalization social movements is the ability to sustain these networks across various nodes of difference. It is not surprising, then, that Wills (2002: 95) further argues that "Transformative politics . . . depend on bringing together different interest groups to find common cause and cement alliances, without masking differences between them." Challenges to inequalities, particularly ones produced by global organizations backed by a tremendous amount of national political and economic power, are difficult enough. They are even more difficult when one considers the need to work across social group and organizational identities (these complexities are discussed in the collective essay by geographers at the University of Washington; see Fannin et al. 2000).

The emergence of protests against globalization intersects with other important social geographic processes – informal and formal Internet organizing, spontaneous and planned travel and migration, and the contextual identity politics of multiple places – further complicating a simple reading of this movement. Activists are "more than" just activists, they are also community workers, government officials, or, even, tourists (Shields 2003). While the latter group might seem the most unusual one to use when conceptualizing protest, it is the case that "the manner of travel, demands on services, and activities outside of protest rallies per se are all common elements with many other types of tourists and forms of tourism" (ibid.: 1). Shield's analysis of "activist tourism" during the Free Trade of the Americas (FTAA) meeting in Québec City, Canada in 2001 highlights how activism and tourism intersect for those protesting the expansion of free trade across North and South America. He does this through an examination of a common artifact of tourism, the map. He begins by explaining that "In anticipation of the protests, a 3-meter (9-foot), 3.8 kilometer chain-link fence was erected – almost a parody of the eighteenth-century Ramparts surrounding the inner city of Vieux Québec" (ibid.: 2). The fence served as both a material and a symbolic barrier between those participating in global free trade and those who opposed the expansion of unfettered, US-dominated economic expansion. A formal map of the new spatial organization of the city was developed by local authorities to show how the fence would disrupt movement and mobility across the city. "Although the map of the Fence is intended to report and inform, it became a required text for protesters who needed local knowledge" (ibid.: 5). The map thus served as both a representational space and a space of practice as different social groups and organizations used it to situate themselves in relation to the fence. "Different groups [within the protest] traveled on different routes and congregated at different points along the Fence. Moderate mainstream unions and non-governmental organizations sponsored marches that avoided going near the Fence. Many others participated in a pre-summit 'People's Summit' in the parliamentary district, while the 'black bloc' of anarchists and proponents of direct action attacked the Fence and succeeded in pulling part of it down" (ibid.: 5–6). What these protests suggest is that activism involves other social activities and practices that are not only about protest: activists traveling to foreign countries or new cities have to locate shelter, eat food, and network with other activists. They thus rely on the spatial organization of urban space designed to accommodate a broader array of touristic and activist possibilities.

Anti-globalization movements in the urban global north are not exclusive to either "the north" or the "urban." Social movements against globalization are found across a variety of local spaces. As a result, rural spaces in the global north and global south are being invested with new forms of protest and activism that "are concerned with social transformation as much as political transformation. . . . [These movements, though, like their urban counterparts] do not aspire in themselves to seize power" (Woods 2008: 129). These transformations, while having global connectivities, are also localized and related to sociospatial relations found in particular places. In this way, as Woods (2003) suggests, it is better to speak of rural social *movements* rather than one rural social movement, even though many broadly defined rural movements struggle with questions of identity and rurality – what is rural and how should people practice rural life? The spatial expressions of protest and activism among rural social movements is also varied, working in and against broader shifts in national or international policy and through localized forms of power and knowledge. In Mexico, the emergence of La Vía Campesina – a peasant farmers' movement – relies not only on direct protest but on education and advocacy (Desmarais 2008), in ways similar to what Gramsci advocated. Working through both globalized and localized informal and formal social networks

Box 6.3 Methodological Note: Studying the "Far Right"

In *On the Fault Line: Race, Class and the American Patriot Movement* Carolyn Gallaher (2003) examines the class- and race-based politics of a growing "patriot" political movement. As a "social movement," Patriots are diverse group of politically "far right" activists, whose goals vary but whose basic tenets are to maintain the integrity of the US in the wake of the growing "new world order" defined as a "conspiracy of actors and organizations whose goals is to eliminate national governments, replacing them with one world government" (ibid.: 16). Gallaher employs participant observation and interview techniques, along with archival research, to construct a "picture" of the Patriot Movement as well as its identity politics. While all such studies are fraught with tension, including questions and concerns of ethics, Gallaher faced the problem of how to treat her research informants "fairly." In her own words:

> while studying the Patriot Movement does not produce the most sympathetic pool of research informants, I still worried about how to depict them fairly. I knew it would be easy to represent them through well-worn tropes, as "angry white men with guns," as "malcontents," or as otherwise "cracked and loaded." This is how many people viewed them, even in the academy.... If I was to dispel any of these notions, I knew I would have to be open to listening to my informants and not prejudice them, and that I would have to focus on how and why they saw things as they did, rather than condemning their point of view up front (ibid.: 239).

As Gallaher discovered, taking a position of openness also comes with an ethical responsibility to protect oneself as a researcher. This includes critically reflecting on the desire to "put aside our biases" and "to see the world for a brief while as they saw it" (ibid.: 244), typical tenets of qualitative research projects. In her interest to "get into the worlds of patriots" she allowed herself, albeit briefly, to be manipulated for the political ends of a few patriots. She chalks this up as both a hard life lesson and a problem with the literature in qualitative research, which fails to explain how to study those with whom we don't necessarily agree. "[W]hile the idea that you can be objective (and distanced) from your research subjects has been debunked ... there is, I believe, a place for the researcher that lies between the vista from above and the view from the trenches that a fully imbricated researcher working for the cause can provide" (ibid.). Finding that middle ground, however, is a challenge for any researcher but particularly for qualitative researchers who have a vested interest in developing relationships and gaining "insider" knowledge and experience.

> ### Quick Exercise
>
> Think back to a moment in time when you disagreed with someone at an ethical or political level. Write a brief reflective piece asking yourself how you might engage that person were you a researcher and interested in finding out how and why they thought the way they did.

and relations, this movement draws from the experiences of other peasant movements globally. Refracting itself through the practices across social movements globally, La Vía Campesina "has guaranteed gender parity in its leadership" and "is also acutely aware of the importance of youth to maintaining vibrant rural cultures and peasant communities" (Desmarais 2008: 146).

At the same time, not all anti-globalization social movements come from those on the so-called left of the political spectrum, and other groups challenge the globalizing processes of the World Trade Organization and the United Nations from the "far right." As Gallaher (2003) effectively points out, the Patriot Movement in the US – a loosely structured social movement whose central tenets include an anti-global pro-US-centered political and social philosophy – is critical of global forces and processes, although for quite different reasons than peasant social movements in the global south. The Patriot Movement fights against what it fears as "one world government" (Gallaher 2003: 170, citing Environmental Perspectives, Inc. 2001), as well as local government regulation, which it sees as driven by multinational corporations and international organizations, such as the United Nations. Gallaher traces a unique set of protest moments for Patriots in Kentucky, who oppose government regulation of the environment (through protests against biosphere reserves), agriculture (through the production of tobacco and hemp), and constitutional rights (through the protection of rights to bear arms). Unlike social movements from the so-called left, which depend on an identity politics grounded in class, race, gender, or sexual subjectivities, the Patriot Movement in Kentucky grounds its identity politics in nationalistic and racial subjectivities. Gallaher illustrates that the Patriot movement's appeal is to the protection of US spatial sovereignty as well as "white culture." Identity politics in this case are powerful markers of inclusivity and exclusivity, national identity and cultural protectionism. This thus raises the important question of who challenges globalization, why, and to what extent these are coordinated with a broader sense of social justice, equity, and respect for difference.

An alter-movement movement, poststructuralism's new spaces of engagement

Thus far, social movements have been conceptualized as movements based in an "anti"-politics: social movements fight against the social and spatial organization

of capitalist class relations or against the concept of citizenship as individual responsibility. There is another way to think about movement as non-movement or, to
paraphrase Pickerill and Chatterton (2006), as alter-movement. If "alter-globalization
. . . emphasizes anti-capitalist and social justice movements' creativity, celebrating
the movement's transnationality and their solidarity networks" (ibid.: 731), then it
is conceivable that alter-movements can operate beyond unequal social and spatial
relations. This is, in part, what Marston et al. (2005) are arguing when they suggest
a new geographic vocabulary for the discussions of scale. Scale in geography has
always implied a vertical set of spatial relations – from the body to the local to the
global – with power (and domination) assigned at the highest scales of analysis. But
if the concept of scale is removed from our theoretical and political vocabularies,
it may be possible to "recover the local as a site of significant practice" (ibid.: 427).
This means retheorizing "the local" and "the global" as well as the conceptual and
practical relationships between autonomy and geography (Pickerill and Chatterton
2006). And, it means understanding that the social and spatial relations that happen
"out there" are not all tied to a globalized and hegemonic capitalism (Gibson-Graham
1996, 2006).

Let's ground this theoretically heady stuff for a moment in some practical
examples. Gibson-Graham (2006) explains that feminists have, in fact, effectively
demonstrated that noncapitalist social relations are present in the everyday practice of (mostly) women working in the home. "Empirical work on the subject
has established that, in both rich and poor countries, 30 to 50 percent of economic
activity is accounted for by unpaid household labor" (ibid.: 57). Gibson-Graham
thus offers a new vocabulary to replace the hegemonic concept of Economy (i.e.
Capitalism) with the concept of "the diverse economy" (ibid.: 60). The goal is to
trace the myriad expressions of economic (social) relations that are "nonmarket"
– such as gift giving or poaching (ibid.: 61) – "unpaid" – housework, volunteer
work, neighborhood work (ibid.: 63) – and "noncapitalist" – communal or independent (ibid.: 65). The goal here, then, is not to "fight against the machine" of
global capitalism and the uneven production of its social relations, but to recognize
the already diverse and complex (and incomplete) sets of social relations that are
economic (and non-economic) operating every day in local spaces. Producing such
a vocabulary, however, is not enough, so Gibson-Graham "entered into conversations with people who were willing to entertain the idea of a different economy"
(ibid.: 131). In one such context, Jagna, Philippines, Gibson-Graham worked with
local community members to collectively produce an "audit of livelihood practices"
(ibid.: 178), with the goal of challenging the normative discussion of development
in this region. Global development organizations insist on promoting international
labor migration out of the Philippines and into wealthier parts of Asia, thereby
enhancing remittances, or monies sent from work locations back home, as *the*
form of local economic development. The process of doing the audit "allows for
reflection on what the community is nourished by (rather than what it lacks)" (ibid.);
it focuses attention on the possibility of what can be accomplished through a rethinking of everyday social relations of production and reproduction. In Jagna, then,

Gibson-Graham worked alongside community groups to expand the community economy through new and alternative economic practices, also providing valuable knowledge from other local spaces where cooperative practices have been effective and community economies developed.

There are shades of anarchy (see Chapter 2) in the work of Gibson-Graham, as there are in the work of Pickerill and Chatterton (2006), who propose a vocabulary based on autonomous geographies. "More than a reluctance to take power," Pickerill and Chatterton suggest that "autonomy is a commitment to freedom, non-hierarchy and connection and a desire to eliminate (or reduce) power relations" (ibid.: 739). In examining how autonomous spaces operate, Pickerill and Chatterton discuss the emergence of "social centers" in Europe. These cooperatively organized spaces are established through the practice of "squatting," whereby people inhabit an unoccupied space without formal ownership of it. Social centers do more than simply occupy the space, though, as the members try to hold the space "in common" (ibid.: 741). In some cases, social centers exist, as they do in parts of the United Kingdom, because of "wealthy benefactors, the use of central government and lottery funding, and long-standing ethical property owners (such as church groups and the Ethical Property Company)" (ibid.: 742). The spatial stability of these centers tends to be limited, as they are often moving from one place to the next, but social networks and the broader logics of these autonomous spaces, by "experimenting with new decision-making methods, extending critiques of social and economic relations, and self-management and not-for-profit accessible activities" (ibid.), do allow for longer-term resistances and new forms of social cooperation.

All these authors, who challenge the presumption of a monolithic space economy structuring all social relations, also note the problems with complete autonomy or absolute noncapitalist practice. In fact, all would argue that the spaces of autonomy and community economy likely work through both capitalist and noncapitalist space economies. What this body of work does suggest, however, is that social geographers need not deny alternatives, nor should they marginalize the spontaneous possibilities that Gramsci urged. Resistance is a fluid and dynamic process, as is domination. Social geographers have to consider the possibility, therefore, that at different points in time and space new ways of knowing, interacting, and doing may be possible. This might suggest the need to wage a massive protest against globalization or it might mean developing a local cooperative. Or, more likely, it might demand both. In either case, someone, somewhere, is likely doing something about it right now, in ways that rethink how we think about our place in the world.

Social Geography, Social Justice(s)

This chapter has traced a wide variety of activist and movement geographies. Social geography has a longstanding commitment to social change and social equality. This critical lens, which informs an interest in social justice, examines not just the world "out there" but the disciplinary position and context of geography. In this way, social geographers break down the boundaries between the spaces of the academic and the spaces of society in which their universities and professional organizations are embedded. Geography as a discipline is not a perfect and idealized utopia. There are problems associated with how differences are constructed within the context of geography's own intellectual "home." Feminists, working from the 1970s onward, began to challenge the hegemonic patriarchy of the discipline. Queer geographers and geographers of color (as well as sexuality researchers and critical race scholars in the discipline) further punctured the idealized picture of the discipline's sexuality and race blindness. Social geographic studies of sexuality and race are more common in the discipline today, although there are still limitations and prejudices that need to be addressed. Social geographers need to expand on (and relish in) their own differences, addressing the unequal treatment of subjects considered "relevant" to their social geographies. They also need to continue to "break down" the boundaries between the so-called "ivory tower" of the academic and the social "real" world out there. PPGIS is one way they might do this, through a cooperative and active engagement with people whose lives are most dramatically impacted by racism, sexism, classism, ableism, or heterosexism. While PPGIS might not address all of these issues right now, projects, such as the Syracuse Hunger Project, can help to expand the imagination when it comes to how to think about our use of geographic technologies and to what end.

Social geographers have also been part of an expanding set of movement geographies that call into question the ethical and political implications of how to think about diseased subjects and the politics of access to medication and other necessary health-related resources. HIV disease is a significant global pandemic affecting millions of people every day. Social movements to address the needs of those living with HIV and those at great risk of contracting HIV are being energized by local challenges to medicalized authorities, such as pharmaceutical companies. In some ways, we can all imagine the challenges posed to our new biological identities and obligations as citizens within larger struggles against globalization. The anti-globalization movements developing across both urban and rural space are important sites of inquiry for social geographers, particularly since they are interested in asking how such movements can address social justice concerns. Social geographers also have to be cautioned, however, to not continually gaze at their own progressive belly button. Those on the "right" of the political spectrum also engage in anti-globalization practices that close off difference instead of opening up diverse possibilities. Social geography ignores these movements at its own peril. As such, social geographers must not forget that while they continually focus their attention on the dominating forces of global capitalism, and its structuring of social relations of production and reproduction, there are alternative and autonomous spaces out there where individuals and collectives are rethinking social and spatial relations by recognizing and acting on noncapitalist practices. Totalizing narratives fail to capture the subtlety and nuances of everyday practice that work horizontally across places and networks. Social geography need not privilege hegemonic visions that deny spontaneous and organic resistances and practices. In this way, social geographers should think of social justice(s) just as they think about social geographies.

Notes

1   In discussing the relationships between morality and ethics, Popke notes that "our notions about what society is, as well as the ways in which the social is constituted and enacted within particular spatial contexts, are underpinned by a complex set of understandings about what is good or proper (morality), and about the nature, scope and geographical scale of our obligations and responsibilities toward various others (ethics). Note that this distinction – between a moral sphere of individual conduct and an ethical realm of responsibility and solidarity – is itself an ethical matter, and the outcome of cultural and political negotiation" (Popke 2009).

2   For example, notions of a global citizen are used to describe both nations and individuals in the context of not just HIV-related responsibilities – the development of a global AIDS fund – but other discourses of responsibility and citizenship – such as the "the global war on terror."

Part III

Social Geographies through the Life Course

In this part we examine differing social geographies across the life course. It is broken down into three chapters, which cover children's geographies, the geographies of the "mid-life," and the geographies of ageing. As people travel through the life course it is possible to discern a unique set of social geographies. This "periodization" of the life course is not without its problems, of course, as children's and adults' geographies vary quite dramatically depending on temporal and spatial location. Additionally, social geographers have noted that there is no "neat division" between young and old, child and adult; social geographers should think more about intergenerationalities. So, it is important to keep a critical eye on how social geographers might further complicate their own social geographic analyses as they work their way through the life course.

Chapter 7

On the Geographies of Children and Young People

- The Importance of Life Course Studies in Geography
- The Spaces of Childhood and Youth: Thinking Geographically
  - Setting an agenda
  - Across the north/south divide in children's geographies
  - Young people, identity, body spaces, and "child development"
- The Space(s) of Child Development(s)
  - Regulating and contesting the spaces of play
  - Organizing the social body of children through education
- Teen/Youth Spaces and Places
  - Sex, sexualities, and the body politics of teen life
  - Constituting the spaces of youth as spaces of danger
- Ethical Geographies/Children's Geographies

The Importance of Life Course Studies in Geography

Social geography has been, for most of its history, fairly blind to the diverse geographies that take place across the life course. In fact, most social geography focuses specifically on what might be considered "adult" activities and spaces. More than this, social geography has tended to ground its studies in the lives of an adult subject, who is often defined by a broadly conceived middle age, while largely ignoring children, younger and older people, and the elderly. This means that social geography has tended to deny the complexity of how people's views, use, and construction of space differ and change as their bodies grow, perceptions shift, and experiences lead them to engage in new sets of social relations and networks. Many social geographers[1] ignore the complexity of the life course, utilizing categories of difference – such as ability, race, ethnicity, gender, and sexuality – with little regard for the differences that "age" makes. This is fairly ironic given the fact that in many of the places social geographers study a vast majority of the population is either quite young (e.g. Afghanistan) or quite elderly (e.g. Japan) and that concepts of social identity and subjectivity are both perceived and experienced differently across the life course.

Of course, age, like all social categories, is a geographically and historically situated concept. In many places – from the "inner city" of the US to the slums of Mumbai to the barrios of Mexico City – children and young people take on the tasks often assigned to "adults" of working age, providing income and caring for siblings, parents, and grandparents. In other contexts, grandparents are asked to take on the role of parent to their grandchildren because of the premature death of their own children, the result of an AIDS-related illness. This is creating a demographic "nightmare" in many countries of the global south, where HIV is prolific. Countries as diverse as Thailand and Zimbabwe are finding themselves in a crisis of care – care for those who are living with HIV and care for those "left behind" by the epidemic. It is almost impossible to simply assign one set of practices to any one "age group" (Harker 2005). If age – and the social meanings and practices attached to age – is constructed depending on where (and when) someone is, then it is probably also correct to assume that the spaces conceptually assigned to people of varying ages – playgrounds, retirement communities, the mall – are also contextually produced. Put simply, a playground space, which might be typically understood as a child's place, is also an adult space because of the ways in which adults participate in its construction and regulation. Reciprocally, younger people can transgress adult spaces – such as age-regulated bars – bypassing adult-imposed systems of authority.

Despite all the complexity of how best to identify a child's space and an adult's space, there are certain sociospatial processes at work at different stages in the life course. These are made real through both the regulation of certain spaces – the construction of schools for children and laws that regulate young people's mobilities – and the resistances to these controls – manifest in the ways that children and adults allow "play" to transgress normative boundaries of "work." Also, certain key areas of social geographic inquiry – homelessness and housing, ability and disability, crime and criminality, sexuality studies, social and economic development – take on new meanings at different points across the life course. Homeless children's experiences of the street may be different than those of adults, who occupy and use urban space differently. This becomes even more complex when considering the interrelationship between age, homelessness, sexuality, and gender. Age and ageing also affect experiences of home and community, as well as organizational spaces more generally. And, mental and physical abilities shift and change over the life course, creating new possibilities and challenges as people age and experience spaces of home and work or public and private spaces differently.

This chapter focuses on the geographies of children and young people (see the definitions in Box 7.1). It does so with the caveat that children's and young people's

Box 7.1　Defining Children and Youth,
Childhood and Young Adulthood

How do we define the terms "child" and "adult"? When does "childhood" end and "adulthood" begin? How is this binary between the child and the adult further complicated by the categories of "youth" and "young adulthood"? Gill Valentine (2003: 38) argues that "while the transition from childhood to adulthood is often assumed to be linear as young people move from school to work, leave the parental home and so on, many do not move neatly from a state of dependence to a state of independence." She concentrates attention not on the definitional breaks that might apply to "children" and "adults" but on the transitions between childhood and adulthood through "the liminal period of youth" (ibid.). In her analysis, Valentine appeals to the complications of geography: these transitions vary from space to space for individuals and social groups. In short, one might be transitioning out of the familial home but still be in school. In this case, a person is an adult because they no longer live with their parents but a "child" because they are still in school. In many parts of the world, children never leave their familial home, and adulthood is marked not by the experience of leaving but by the experience of taking on new tasks and responsibilities of care and responsibility for both children and parents.

　For some social geographers, there is a need to create a discrete category of "the child" based on age (e.g. those five- to sixteen-year-olds in primary and secondary school). This can differentiate "the child" for methodological purposes. It can also reinscribe a linear developmental model on one's research subject(s). There is a problem with any definition, as it may deny the social and spatial practices of what it means to be young or "a child." In this chapter, then, the terms "child" and "youth" are applied rather loosely, and their uses and definitions are allowed to emerge from the experiences and data generated by the researchers and their subjects – children – themselves.

Quick Exercise

The terms "child" or "child-like" are commonly applied to people, practices, and places. In a group, think about how "being a child" or "being childish" is used as a metaphor for practices that are deemed socially inappropriate in your community. Broadening this out, how is the metaphor of childhood used in everyday practice to differentiate spaces (e.g. "the economy of so-and-so country is immature")?

lives are fully contingent on and related to the lives of adults. But, this is a vibrant time for the study of children and young people in social geography. The publication of the journal *Children's Geographies* demonstrates how the discipline is evolving to ask new and important questions and challenge old assumptions about how people experience, construct, and live in various spaces. The study of children and young people in social geography importantly challenges some of the basic assumptions about the organization of space, the construction of social networks, and the everyday material and immaterial geographies that constitute the lifeworld.

The Spaces of Childhood and Youth: Thinking Geographically

This section begins by turning to the work of Bill Bunge, whose early "expeditions" in Detroit (and Toronto) set the stage for a radical social geography of poverty, racism, urban life, and childhood and young adult life. His ideas still resonate today with many of the concerns and questions that remain pressing to social geographers. Moving from Bunge in Detroit, I shift gears slightly to a comparative look across the global north and global south through the pioneering work of Cindi Katz. Katz, whose ethnographic research on children's experiences of rural and urban space in Howa, Sudan and Harlem, New York City suggests that the social geographies of childhood and youth, while variegated across the north–south divide, also resonate with similarities. Her Marxist and feminist political economy perspective draws parallels to Bunge's radical work and extends that work through an on-the-ground analysis of children's cognitive understandings of their environments through which they work *and* play. Importantly, Katz suggests that certain processes of global capitalist accumulation are remaking social relations every day in places that appear different but demonstrate certain similarities and effects. Finally, I address Stuart Aitken's contributions to the "geographies of young people." Drawing from a wide array of theoretical inspirations – feminist, poststructuralist, and psychoanalytic – Aitken continues a long tradition of social geographic scholarship concerning young people. He also offers a core set of conceptual tools that can be brought to bear on studies of identity and body politics in children's and young people's geographies. This is not the only way to read the intellectual trajectory of children's geographies. But these three moments do provide a critical set of tools for studying the everyday geographies of childhood and youth and "set an agenda" for the geographies of childhood and young people.

Setting an agenda

Geographers began to "think about" children and their geographies explicitly in the 1960s and 1970s within the context of a broadly defined scientific geography, which was concerned with both how certain spaces disenfranchised children and young people (Bunge 1971, 1977) and children's mapping abilities and spatial cognition[2] (Blaut and Stea 1971, 1974; Blaut 1997a, 1997b). Bunge, in particular, advocated a scientific geography that was engagesd and grounded in the lives of real people and their experiences of poverty and racism through what he called "expeditions" into the urban landscapes of Detroit and later Toronto. "Bunge's expeditions employed a myriad quantitative and qualitative, aggregate and individualistic geographic approaches to the study of spatial structure and interaction without losing sight of the central theme of children's oppression" (Aitken 2001: 12). In *Fitzgerald: The Geography of a Revolution*, Bunge (1971) offers a nuanced reading of Fitzgerald, a neighborhood in Detroit experiencing social and economic marginalization. Through individual life history interviews as well as cartographic and spatial analysis, Bunge argues that the social and spatial organization of everyday life in the poor urban spaces of Fitzgerald reinforces race, gender, and class inequalities. In providing a comparative narrative of children's and young people's experiences, Bunge complicates their social marginalization and the relationships between poverty and racism. "Younger children," Bunge (1971: 205) urges, "are often more fortunate than older ones in terms of quality of life. Very young urban children are at least welcome in the neighborhood. . . . But the urban teenager feels the full hostility of the adult American society. Unlike most college kids' fraternity pranks, urban teenagers' revolts are not considered highjinks." Implicit in this discussion is the importance of race as a social force structuring experiences of the city, with differing and dueling perspectives on the practices of differently raced and classed social groups. While white fraternity members are seen as "pranksters," black teenagers in the same city are constructed as "dangerous thieves" (a point we will return to below).

Bunge also interrogates how the urban spaces of Fitzgerald are constructed through adult-centrism (see Figure 7.1). In his own words:

> The adults provide plenty of places for their own amusement, numerous taverns, supper clubs, and even go-go houses, but the teenagers have none. They are the neighborhood nomads. As long as they keep moving down the street or stay in their home they are not harassed. What is "their place," to which they must keep? The teenager population has literally gone underground, in the basements of some of their friends whose parents are not too hostile toward them, or are not at home or are simply indifferent. . . . The teenagers have a whole secret geography of their own, of little places they have found, a garage here, an abandoned car there. The teenagers' lack of territory means a lack of freedom and a suffocation of dignity. Every teenager in the community is a foreigner (Bunge 1971: 205; also see Figure 7.1).

In his work, Bunge highlights a number of important issues that resonate with current studies of children and young people. First, Bunge argues that the experiences of childhood are not uniform across space; clearly poor inner city experiences of youth vary quite dramatically from suburban experiences. And, as Bunge demonstrates,

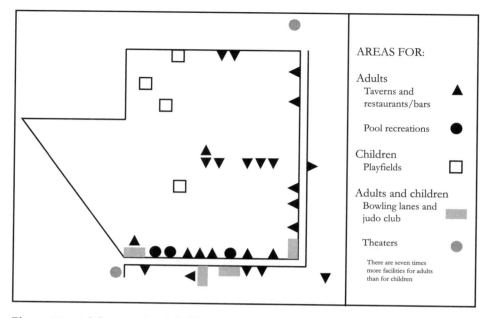

Figure 7.1 Adult recreational facilities in Fitzgerald, Detroit. (Reproduced from Bunge 1971: 154.)

these experiences are deeply raced and classed. Second, Bunge analyzes how adults structure space by imposing order and minimizing the mobility of young people; these everyday social geographies are adult-centric. Third, he suggests that multiple geographies operate in the same urban space. Young people enact their own "hidden landscape" (Bunge 1977, cited in Aitken 2001: 14), tracing new worlds in the cracks and margins of urban space. Fourth, Bunge shows how important a life course framework is for social geography. Children, young people, and adults all experience the social spaces of the city in dramatically different ways. What Bunge's research alludes to more generally, then, is that "childhood is a social rather than a biological phenomenon – which varies between social groups, societies, historical periods" (Holloway and Valentine 2000: 5). And, it varies in and across the spaces of city and country. In fact, the spatial organization of the everyday social world defines childhood.

Despite the work of Bunge and others, some geographers in the 1980s and into the 1990s felt marginalized because of their focus on children's geographies. As Cindi Katz explained in an interview, "When I published my *Annals* article (1991) I didn't want the word 'children' in the title because I wanted people to read it" (Del Casino et al. 1997: 43). Holloway and Valentine echo this sentiment in the introduction to *Children's Geographies*: "for the most part this work [on children in the 1970s and 1980s] has been largely ignored within an adultist discipline, such that James was still able to ask in 1990, 'Is there a place for children in geography?'"

(Holloway and Valentine 2000: 8). Bunge's impassioned call for a revolutionary new social and spatial order that privileges children is an important starting point because it demonstrates the need for the continued analysis of the social and spatial organization of everyday spaces of childhood and adulthood (Holloway and Valentine 2000). Moreover, as Aitken (2001: 23) further stresses, Bunge's radical geography "advocated . . . a 'dictatorship of children'" whereby "responsibility would still reside with adults" but that "responsibility . . . [would mean] simply letting children 'be all they can be'" (citing Bunge 1977: 65). In "letting children 'be all they can be'," social geographers therefore have to critically assess their own methodological practices, asking how they might let children "speak" in their research (Holloway and Valentine 2000).

In this broader spirit, social geographers have established an agenda on what Matthews and Limb (1999) call the "geographies of children" (this move is similar to other moves that have challenged social geography's other "blind spots" – see Chapter 6). In calling for geographers to make children more visible in their work, they ask how children actually see, use, and perceive the world around them. Children's experiences, visions, and imaginations of the spatial organization of that world are, after all, different from adults' (see Box 7.2). The development of this agenda is part of an attempt to examine the agency of children as well as the constraints that are placed on them in a world that is more often than not regulated and controlled by adults. Other social geographers have gone further, asking how the experiences of children and young people intersect with other important axes of difference related to ability (Holt 2004; Ryan 2005), sexuality (Thomas 2004; Hoy 2007), and sex/gender (Costello and Duncan 2006; Newman et al. 2006). Social geographers are also asking how the experiences of children and young people emerge through the spaces of education (Collins and Coleman 2008), play (Harker 2005), and homelessness (Beazley 2002). They are also complicating the relationships between neighborhood violence and mobility (Spilsbury 2005) and sexual practice and migration (Hoy 2007), as well as the politics of identity (Aitken 2001). Social geographers studying the experiences of children and young people are thus reflecting on the broader differences and inequalities operating across global space, suggesting how the social geographies of children and young people must account for the differences (and similarities) that appear in their experiences of place.

Across the north/south divide in children's geographies

One of the signal effects of "development" in Howa [Sudan] was the "deskilling" of young people who, it seemed to me, were unlikely to have the knowledge and skills necessary to make it in the futures that seemed possible. Something quite similar seemed to be going on in New York City. . . . As New York was reconfigured by the flight of manufacturing starting in the 1960s and the turn to a service and financial economy by the 1980s, young people, particularly working-class children, no longer seemed prepared for the employment futures that awaited them (Katz 2004: xii–xiii).

Box 7.2   Methodological Note: Differentiating Children's and Adults' Spatial Experiences

In 1999, Matthews and Limb set out a methodological agenda for studying how children see, use, and perceive the world around them. They lay out seven postulates to "frame" a geography of children:

1   Children and childhood are social constructions. Assumptions are made by adults about what it means to be a child and therefore what environments they need. In so doing they fail to recognize that children differ from adults in terms of their "ways of seeing." What goes on during the day of an average young person is different in rhythm, scale and content from that of adults. Understanding of these differences needs to be rooted in the lifeworlds of children.

2   The land uses and facilities which involve children are frequently different from those of adults and, even when shared, are largely used for different purposes. Collisions resulting from different patterns of usage are almost inevitable.

3   The free-range of children and the types of environmental setting which they enter are often more restricted than that of adults. In some respects, young people have much in common with other "outsider" groups in society, such as the disabled and the elderly, in that their behaviour is often constrained by caretaking conventions, physical ineptitude, limited access to transportation, lack of money and roles which separate them from a larger and more diverse daily round. A complex negotiated geography is also apparent through varying parental caretaking practices.

4   In the course of their environmental transactions, children commonly encounter threats which often go unnoticed by adults. Many childhood hazards are not dangers in later life.

5   Even when the same environment affects children and adults, their interpretation and evaluation of these places are not likely to be the same. Young people and adults often differ in how they see, feel about and react to a landscape and their views on environmental planning are unlikely to coincide.

6   Children are unable to influence decision-making and management which typically determine the structure of environments in general and land uses in particular. Thus the environments which have the greatest significance for young people are decided for them by adults and reflect values which pay scant regard to their needs, aspirations and behaviour.

7   Democratic responsibility is acquired only through practice and involvement. It does not arise suddenly in adulthood through maturation. Involving children in the design and management of their environments

is a valued end in itself, as well as an important step to developing competent, participating citizens. (Matthews and Limb 1999: 66)

Taking the seven postulates forward, Matthews and Limb set out an agenda for "the geographies of children" that consider how children construct, imagine, and organize their spatial world. Their work points to the agency of children as well as the constraints that are placed on them in a world that is more often than not regulated and controlled by adults.

Quick Exercise

In a group of three or four students, take one of the above postulates and brainstorm how you might go about framing questions related to and collecting data on children's spatial experiences. What are some of the ethical issues you have to consider when studying with children?

In *Growing Up Global*, Katz employs an ethnographic approach to examine how the processes of global capitalism are structuring and restructuring the social and spatial relationships, knowledges, and skills of children and young people in what, on the surface, appear to be two unique places. New York City, on the one hand, is one of *the* centers of capitalism and finance in the global north. It is a highly urbanized space in the midst of a predominantly service-centered economy. Howa, Sudan, on the other hand, is situated in the rapidly changing spaces of under-development in the global south. It is largely a rural space dominated by a large agricultural economy. Children in these two places have different sets of skills, experiences, and understandings of the spaces in which they are embedded. At the same time, in comparing children's spatial knowledges of their lifeworlds in these two disparate places, Katz offers insight into the interrelationships between the social practices associated with "work" and "play" and "childhood" and "adulthood" in the context of a rapidly expanding capitalist economy in the global north and global south.

Turning her attention to Howa, Katz examines how declines in the economic practices historically associated with this rural space – "herding, providing fuelwood, and gathering foods and other resources from the local environs" (ibid.: 148) – are declining in the wake of environmental changes and pressures on the land. These changes have a number of important effects on the social and spatial organization of everyday life for children in Howa. The changing economy places pressure on children to expand their formalized education through attendance at state-run schools. In an ever-changing globalizing economy education is a vital marker of social advancement and status, even if education provides little direct material benefit. This pressure to attend school, however, is impacted by the ongoing need to participate in the rural economy, leaving children torn between dueling and sometimes oppositional social and familial obligations. The changing economies of Howa also affect the meanings, tasks, and job assigned to boys and girls, men and women in the region. As boys and men are spatially extended – traveling to work further from home and for longer periods of time – girls and women are occupying the agricultural spaces that men had historically dominated. Moreover, whereas in the past children in Howa learned about the environment around them and its resources through play, the "changing valence of formal schooling and the grow-ing separation of work and play," coupled with "the increased time children spent in tasks related to income generation and capital accumulation," often leaves them with "little time for play in general and removed them from the company of their friends" (ibid.). In this context, the expanding space economy of capitalist accumula-tion and work in Howa has severed the spaces of play from the spaces of work. Where children once co-mingled in both spaces throughout the day, they now find themselves participating in spaces of work and school with increasing intensity. And, the spaces of play are being devalued as "goofing off" (ibid.). This is problematic because, as Katz suggests, it is through the co-mingling of work and play that children and young people in Howa learn about their world and the resources, social activ-ities, and daily work routines related to the rural economy around them.

Shifting her attention to Harlem, New York, Katz shows how children's lives and spaces are also being devalued in the wake of the massive restructuring of the urban economy. "By the 1990s," Katz argues, "poor and working-class children in New York, particularly those who were black or Latino, increasingly survived a present that *had* abandoned them. . . . These experiences were not played out as metaphor, but were played out on their bodies, on their homes, on their neighborhoods. Poor and working-class children could see their declining 'value' in the dilapidated conditions of the city's public schools, in the city's litter, which was strewn in poorly maintained neighborhood parks and playgrounds, and in the unsafe and decaying spaces of the residential city" (ibid.: 159, original emphasis). Interrogating the historical geographies of schooling and open space, Katz suggests that expanding "public–private" partnerships between corporations and the local government in New York has placed questions of "efficiency," "profit," and "accumulation" on top of ques-tions of "possibility," "after school programs," and "diverse educational experiences." What this means is that educational standards continue to drop as programs to meet the needs of the changing economy also dry up. Upward social mobility is thwarted further by the fact that the changing economies of cities, such as New York, mean that entry level working-class jobs are scarce. Paralleling these concerns for the education of young people is the lack of investment in the spaces of play in the city. Local play spaces have grown scarce in the wake of public fiscal problems, with larger signature parks, such as Central Park, receiving the bulk of the funding. But, in the structural context of violence and poverty, "children under twelve [in most US cities] spend almost all of their time within a few kilometers of where they live" (ibid.: 163). As open space has been consciously decreased, children in New York have suffered both mentally and physically: the mental and physical stimulation that comes from "free play" is lacking. Children must remain close to home and in poor and working-class neighborhoods where there is little in the way of open space to accommodate them. "At stake are both gross-motor and cognitive skills, cooperative and adjudicative skills, the development of self-regulation and mutual respect among peers, and all manner of serendipitous discovery from other kids, their joint activities, or the city itself" (ibid.: 178).

Katz's Marxist-feminist political economy research on the changing dynamics of childhood and the place of children offers important insights into the so-called north/south divide. First, her work suggests that children are being "deskilled" and "devalued" in the spaces of both the global north (New York) and the global south (Howa). Second, these processes are changing the relationship children have with the spaces of play and work, childhood and adulthood. Third, children's bodies and spaces are co-constitutive of their mental and physical health. Finally, Katz points out that "learning, development, and socialization are not restricted to children nor are they terminated upon arrival at the plateau of adulthood" (Katz 2006: 1020). The processes of education and socialization are ongoing, as people continually face changes – bodily, economically, socially – providing cause for constantly rethinking notions of social identities and subjectivities in any social geography.

Young people, identity, body spaces, and "child development"

Aitken's (2001) work is not a departure from Katz's research on children as much as it is a slightly different theoretical intervention into the concerns related to children's geographies. Aitken, like Katz, relies on feminist theory and has concerns related to the changing global economy's effects on children. Unlike Katz, however, Aitken draws more extensively from poststructuralism and psychoanalytic theory to "think through" how children develop their spatial identities and social bodies. His review of children's geographies and the geographies of young people traces the history of the debates about children and child development in and beyond geography to ask how children "become" children. On one side are those scholars who believe children "develop" through a universal *biological* process, acquiring knowledge and skills at predetermined points in time and space (e.g. a five-year-old can do X). On the other side are those scholars who believe children and childhood are *socially constructed* processes; their development is historically and spatially contextualized through local sociocultural and political-economic processes (i.e. children are assigned the characteristics that adults want them to have). Paralleling social geographies of health and ability, Aitken suggests that bodies are both biological *and* social, in that bodies are both materially experienced *and* socially interpreted and constructed. People fart because their bodies need to release gases built up in their digestive track. And, that fart is interpreted as appropriate or inappropriate depending on context, as "funny," "rude," or "unpleasant." This does not deny that the gas might hurt, or that the fart might be necessary to relieve real pain. It does suggest, though, that people can have both a physiological and social awareness of their body. Indeed, as Aitken, and others such as Valentine (1996a), note, the impulses of children at a young age are often constructed in western discourse as "wild" and "natural." It is through a process of socialization that such wild tendencies – the spasms of their bodies – are regulated and controlled. As such, "Through their bodies, children are seemingly exempted (or, rather, located differently) from the moral order until they can be marked as other or, with appropriate maturation, embraced" (Aitken 2001: 67). And, it is through their bodies that children are made to enter an adult-centric world that regulates the social repertoire of meanings from which children can choose to construct their identities and bodies.

The child's body as a natural and developmental project is embedded, today, in the culture of biomedicine. This is materially manifest in the real growth of a pediatric medicine on the one hand, and an adult medicine on the other. Growth charts mark the walls of pediatric offices and clinics, and are transmitted globally to measure, categorize, and determine how a child is "doing" relative to a gobalized "normal child." The measurement of the child is also represented in cognitive and developmental psychology, which suggests that children are "supposed to develop" in a certain way. Speech happens at age Y, while walking begins in month Q. Adolescence is marked by a number of pubescent cues – growth of hair around the genitalia, menstruation, deepening or changing of the voice. What emerges out of these benchmarks is a socially produced and linear progression from infant to child to adolescent to adult, which can then be legally reinforced through conventions around "age of sexual consent" or "age of alcoholic consumption," or "age of eligibility for military draft." These normative discussions of how children's bodies should function biologically, physiologically, or psychologically also have social meanings, which affect how children understand their subjectivities in relation to other people and spaces. Working from the ethnographic literature on "children's bodily awareness," then, Aitken notes that children focus on "normal development: height, shape, appearance, gender and performance" that, when not realized, can "produce extreme anxiety" among children (Aitken 2001: 76, referencing James 1993). Through these anxiety-producing (and adult) understandings of their bodies, children constitute their social identities around "fat" and "skinny" bodies, as well as abled, raced, classed, and sexed identities and subjectivities. Aitken thus draws from feminist and poststructuralist psychoanalytic theory to further conceptualize how children and young people emerge "through the influence of cultural, social, and political environments" as well as through the enactment of their own agency as individual subjects (ibid.: 113). Children use play, for example, to draw on objects found "out in the world" in constructing their identity and subjectivity.

For Aitken, the intimate relationship that exists between the "external" and "internal" worlds of children emerges in the form of a "transitional space" that affords them the opportunity for "flexible manipulation of meanings and relationships" (ibid.: 114). As children pull objects "which [are] neither self or mother" (ibid.) – blankets, toys, or books – into their transitional spaces, they manipulate and sometimes destroy them. The destruction, however, is never complete, and children begin to realize that objects can survive their efforts; they also begin to realize that there is "a world of shared meaningful reality" (ibid.). In the rapidly expanding global economies of capitalism, children are being asked to "grow up" more quickly. As such, their transitional spaces are shrinking or disappearing altogether. Their "shared meaningful reality" is, as a result, organized through an adult-centered worldview where social norms are inscribed externally onto their bodies through the organization of the spaces of play, classroom, and neighborhood. In short, in constructing "proper" children's bodies, adults have to actively produce them through the spatial structuring of appropriate behavior and relation, constructing what belongs "inside" and "outside" the normal child.

So, what does this have to say for the social geographies of children and young people? First, feminism, poststructuralism, and psychoanalytic theory draw attention to how biological bodies are socialized through various spatial relationships. Second, children's social identities are intimately related to their social bodies. It is through children's constructions of their self as social beings that they also "take on" and transform the social, cultural, and political models of "the normal" in their everyday lives. Third, as adults destroy the transitional spaces of play where children work out their understandings about their own agency and self, they risk eliminating the spaces and places that "enable an important form of corporeality through which sex, race and culture are experienced rather than imposed" (ibid.: 116). Put more directly, if adults eliminate the spaces of free play and negotiation that are so critical to children, they move children into a space where an adult-centered morality and ethics operates. Children, in this way, are denied their right "to be all they can be."

The Space(s) of Child Development(s)

Holloway and Valentine's edited collection *Children's Geographies* suggests that the spaces of play, learning, and living are geographically *and* historically situated, organized, and structured through the constructions of children and childhood. Moreover, they argue that playing, learning, and living are not separate social and spatial spheres. Instead, children's sociobiological development emerges through a plethora of community and organizational spaces, from playgrounds to schools to homes. And, while these spaces may appear materially distinct, they are always interconnected through the spaces and practices of childhood and adulthood. As such, the spaces of play, as Bunge, Katz, and Aitken discuss, are not materially or conceptually separate from spaces of living or work. As Gagen (2000b) points out in *Children's Geographies*, playgrounds built in early twentieth-century Cambridge, Massachusetts served an important educational function, teaching children how to be proper gendered subjects as boys and girls. With this caveat in mind – that the spaces of play, living, and learning are overlapping and complexly intertwined – it is still possible to tease out the broader spatial organization of play, on the one hand, and education, broadly speaking, on the other. These divisions are not meant to be absolute but are representative of the current social economies of childhood, which has constructed the spaces of the "school" and education as central to the development of children. Play has emerged as a space of difference, unique from the spaces of school and education. More generally, however, spatial and temporal access to the spaces of play and education is unequal across space, reinforcing the social and spatial divides that mark out the lives of different children in different places. With all this in mind, let's turn to a discussion of "the spaces of play" and the ways they are practiced by children (and adults).

Regulating and contesting the spaces of play

Play, like most concepts, appears to be a rather simple act. Children "play" with toys, in recreational spaces, with their friends. But play is not an isolated event, nor is it autonomous from other social activities, such as work, learning, or living more generally. This is perhaps why the concept of "play" is one of the more theorized in children's geography today (Harker 2005). On the one hand, play can open up new social networks and spaces where children can enact their own imaginations and possibilities (Aitken 2001), as well as construct their own understandings of social difference (Tucker 2003). On the other hand, play can be regulated and organized in favor of adult-centric discourses and practices of what is "appropriate" and "proper" behavior (Thomson 2005). The process of opening up or closing off play as *either* emancipatory *or* regulatory is difficult, however. Play is better theorized as *both* authoritative *and* resistant. In fact, play, like other social and spatial practices of identity formation, is what the social theorist Judith Butler (1988, 1990, 1993) called a performance. Butler's theory of performance suggests that social identities, subjectivities, and spaces are not natural. Focusing particularly on the performance of gender, Butler demonstrates how "male" and "female" identities are socially inscribed onto the body and then reinforced as an individual performs his or her gender as masculine or feminine. It is the reiterative (repetitive) act of performing certain acts over and over again in our everyday spaces that makes gendered identities and bodies appear natural and real – children become boys and girls because certain bodily practices (e.g. playing with toys that are socially gendered) are inscribed as either male or female. Obviously, then, when norms of gender are transgressed, these practices may be inscribed as "abnormal." A young boy dressing in his mother's clothing can be socially constructed as a performance that does not match the social identity of the male gender. These performances, more generally, occur across the life course and begin with children (Karsten 2003).

Gagen (2000a, 2000b) draws on Butler's performative theory to examine how "the playground" in turn of the twentieth-century Cambridge, Massachusetts provided the social cues for how boys or girls should perform their genders. She does this by arguing that the playground is not a neutral space of free play. City leaders, she suggests, "offered supervised play for all children who would otherwise play on the street" (Gagen 2000b: 216), addressing a general fear of children by the city's elite in several ways. First, the playgrounds were located in immigrant neighborhoods, as concerns with "wild" immigrant children were linked to a broader risk to community and city safety. Second, the city imposed strict age and gendered divisions in the park space to enforce the "proper" actions associated with the gendered identities of each child. In particular, boys over twelve were cordoned off from other children. What emerged was a gendered set of spaces in the playground where children were taught how to be boys and girls as well as proper citizens. In this context, "Playgrounds for older boys were devoted solely to sports, most commonly baseball," which "instructors considered . . . [an] ideal sport to correct wayward boys who were starved of a conventional American upbringing" (ibid.: 219). In the spaces of the girls' playgrounds they "were taught quiet, non-competitive activities like sewing, craft work, and knitting, or they learned song and dance routines" (ibid.).

In analyzing playground spaces, social geographers may critically investigate the roles of adults in the regulation of children's play. In the modern-day suburbs of the US, for example, "playgrounds have more ideological and symbolic, communal power to adults than actual play value to children" (Blackford 2004: 232). This is because these spaces are designed to enforce the disciplinary gaze of adults over children. Drawing on Foucault's theorization of the Panoptican – an idealized prison where everyone can be seen from every angle at all times – Blackford argues that playgrounds provide the idealized prison space. The playground functions just like the prison as the "idea of being watched is internalized" (ibid.: 236) by children and incorporated into their play. In short, children learn to self-regulate their behaviors in the playground. The playground, however, does not only enforce and govern the behavior of children. It also governs the gendered practices of mothers as "proper" and "appropriate" caretakers: the playground becomes a space for conversation and social regulation for women who engage with other mothers. In her ethnographic study of parenting on the suburban playground, Blackford concludes that "Maternal performances reveal a sense of competition in mothering, signifying the fact that mothers struggle to authenticate the performance of their role for the suburban community" (ibid.: 239). The playground regulates both childhood and parenting as idealized performances by scripting what are proper gendered and community subjects.[3]

Play also happens beyond the playground (and schoolground), and in less adult-regulated spaces, such as on the street, in the abandoned lot, in the woods, in the basement, or in the empty house. Children can create new spaces – or playscapes (Punch 2000) – in a number of provocative ways.[4] In rural Bolivia children create playscapes in their village and its wider environs (ibid.). They do this by transgressing the rules and regulations of both parents and teachers – stopping and playing on the way to school or during work and household chore-related activities. In fact, children use the rules and regulations of the spaces of "home/work" and "school" to extend their playtime. Punch notes that the playscapes of children in rural Bolivia are both spontaneous and calculated. In stopping to play football (soccer) along the side of the road before school, which makes them late, children might use the excuse of extended chores at home as the reason for why they were late. Reciprocally, travel back and forth to school provides them with excuses for why they might be late arriving home for chores and other activities. Harker (2005) echoes Punch in his discussion of play, arguing that what Punch finds in rural Bolivia is not isolated to rural spaces in the global south. In his study of the Hilltop Primary School in Bristol, England, Harker finds that "playing performances erupted everywhere" (ibid.: 58). Play appears in the "subtlety of gesture" (ibid.: 56) or a glance between friends standing in line waiting for the next moment of their education. It happens in the classroom as children joke and play, tease and cajole. Importantly, such acts of play are not exclusive to the spaces of children, as adults can and do participate in the possibilities that play offers as they also live in and through the same spaces that children occupy. In this way, play can (and does) happen everywhere, from the playground to the spaces of home to the spaces of education or work. It also offers up the possibilities for resistance in and across the lived spaces of children and young people, more generally.

Organizing the social body of children through education

On the primary schoolyard of northern Thailand, children speak in the northern Thai language (*kam muang*) as they play with each other before class. As they communicate with each other through the regulated spaces of play on the schoolyard, they also construct their own sense of identity as northern Thai (*khon muang*). When the school bell rings and teachers call them into the classroom, their language changes from northern to central Thai (*phasaa klang*). This shift in linguistic register spatially marks the informal spaces of play outside the school from the regulated spaces of the Thai nation in the classroom. Central Thai represents the colonizing effects of the Thai state, which uses the spaces of education to produce Thai citizens who are fluent in the language of Thailand (Smalley 1994). Although some may think of Thailand as a unitary space of "the Thai," it is actually a multilingual and multiethnic state with over eighty known languages. Education is the vehicle through which homogeneity and an imagined community of the Thai nation is partially constructed. In this way, the spaces of education are *the* site through which children are incorporated into "the modern and civilized Thai nation" (see Thongchai 2000), which positions the language, culture, and religion of central Thailand as *the* proper way of being Thai (Thongchai 1994). "[S]chools [therefore] have much in common with other institutional [organizational] geographies – such as those associated with the prison, the hospital, or the asylum – in which isolation from mainstream social life is a central organizing concept" (Collins and Coleman 2008: 283). Thought of this way, schools are organizational spaces that are a "bounded portion of geographical space within which certain rules apply and particular activities occur" while also having "a place within broader social landscapes" (ibid.) of the town, neighborhood, and nation.

Figure 7.2 "Say no to child labour yes to school" sign in Calcutta, India. Such narratives about schooling and education are ubiquitous across the global north and south today, raising questions about what such campaigns enable and what impacts they have on the marketable skills of young people. Such signage makes it is clear that the tension between "work" and "school" are being played out in today's urban landscapes. (Photo by author, 2008.)

While schools are by no means uniform in their use and construction of the spaces of education, there is an expectation of what is supposed to happen in these spaces – children are meant to learn. This learning is tied not only to the materialities of subject and content matter – mathematics, writing, science, history, or geography – but also to citizenship and the sexualized, racialized, gendered, and abled norms of children's identities and subjectivities. For children with "mind–body difference," Holt (2004: 226) argues that the "hidden curricul[um] is to teach children to adopt appropriate behaviour, in order to be useful, conforming citizens. Ideas of appropriate behaviour [are] underpinned by sociocultural constructions of a 'normally developing child' . . . as children are expected to increasingly self-regulate behaviour as they age." The spaces of education are deeply engrained with certain norms and prejudices. It is not surprising that Holt found that "Children with 'learning disabilities' . . . experienced a greater level of punishment and lower level of praise than their non-disabled peers in many school contexts" (ibid.: 227; also see Holt 2003).

Social geographers, in studying the spaces of education and schooling, focus on the geographies inside the classroom as well as the broader sociospatial context in which education is embedded. Often investigating the spatial practices of the classroom through qualitative methodological approaches, social geographers have illustrated that while classrooms may regulate children into certain routines and practices of proper bodily comportment (or behavior), these practices vary across classroom and teacher. In one year five classroom in Britain, Fielding (2000), for example, shows how the pedagogical – teaching – strategies of different teachers allow for alternative ways of learning, knowing, and interacting. Contrasting the teaching of two faculty, Wendy and David, Fielding demonstrates that one student, Rebecca, moves across the classroom during lessons with Wendy as she learns history, while with David her interactions are limited to the teacher and her own desk. In one classroom, then, with two different teachers, "it can be seen that the moral codes of this primary school classroom and their interpretation by different class teachers into a set of pedagogic practices, combined with the individual agency of children, operate over one particular classroom space" (Fielding 2000: 241). In the case of Wendy's classroom, "orderly disorder" (ibid.: 237) provides some autonomy for students to co-construct their education with peers and the teacher. While not without rules and norms – Wendy carefully crafts the seating chart to minimize disruption – this classroom does provide some agency to children to be part of their education.

Social geographers are also interested in the ways in which children transgress the norms, rules, and regulations of schooling and education in both mundane and direct ways. This includes challenging the often hidden geographies of heternormativity that structure school spaces as well as the power relations that take place between students (Blackman 1998). In studies of these resistant practices in the geographies of education, Collins and Coleman (2008) suggest that social geographers should examine much more than the spaces of the classroom. As an example, "the school hallway is more than a space in which students simply pass one another en route to classes and activities. Rather, it is a social site in which status is contested and hierarchies established. . . . These meanings may [in fact] complicate adult-imposed order of school environments" (ibid.: 291). In moving from the classroom to the broader spaces of education and schooling – the halls and playgrounds – as well as the expanding sites of schooling – after-school programs – social geographers can interrogate the broader spatial processes of education and resistance as they are performed in the educational environments in which children live (Smith and Barker 2000). Much of this work thus follows on the theories of Michel Foucault (see Chapter 5) and Judith Butler (see discussion above), which suggest that schools as organizational spaces are structured to inscribe certain normative notions of what is appropriate bodily practice for children and young people. As a hegemonic site of identity formation, the school overlaps with the spaces of other organizations – school boards, parent–teacher associations, police departments – and broader spaces of community, neighborhood, and nation from where educators draw on their understanding of "appropriate" practices.

Teen/Youth Spaces and Places

Thus far this chapter has focused on children's geographies. This section shifts the focus, examining the geographies of teen/youth spaces and places more specifically. This is an awkward shift, as the meanings ascribed to the categories of children and youth are ambiguous at best (see Box 7.1). Indeed, the category "youth" is often constructed as a middle ground between childhood and adulthood. With this in mind, Valentine (2003) argues that the social category "youth" is a transitional space between, for example, "home" and "education" and "dependence" and "independence." For Valentine, the social geographies of being a youth are intimately interwoven with the politics of identity and subjectivity. "For example," Valentine argues, "'the family' is often assumed to be the main source of continuity and support during the process of transition from dependent childhood to independent citizen yet many disabled young people have able-bodied parents, likewise most lesbian and gay young people have heterosexual parents. For both groups then the family often does not synthesise the experience of the generations or serve necessarily as a guiding 'norm'" (ibid.: 46–7). This is why Hopkins and Pain (2007: 290) write that "Young people's ability to move through transitions is likely to be influenced by their class position as well as their gender, race, sexuality (dis)ability, and locality." This period of transitioning to adulthood through the years of youth constitutes a distinct set of spaces and experiences deserving of extended social geographic attention. This section, therefore, focuses on teen/youth spatialities linked to the constructions of teen sex and sexualities as well as teen spaces as spaces of danger. As teens/youth construct their bodies and identities through the adult-centered spaces and discourses of appropriate and inappropriate practice, they develop new senses of self and subjectivity. In this way, teens/youth emerge as "young adults" creating new spaces where they work out their identities as sexual beings, community and national citizens, and autonomous subjects. As we will see, these identities intersect – not unproblematically – with their ethnic, race, sexual, class, abled, and homed identities.

Sex, sexualities, and the body politics of teen life

At this point it is not a stretch to argue that social identities and subjectivities are intimately tied to the spaces through which people practice and perform them. They are also complexly related to the systems of authority and regulation that mark out what is "appropriate" and "inappropriate." Teenagers and youth more generally have to "work out" their identities and subjectivities in spaces that are power-laden and structured through discourses of sex, sexuality, race, gender, ethnicity, and ability. For gay teenagers the spaces of education and play, life and work are often structured through what Adrienne Rich (1980) calls "compulsory heterosexuality." This process makes space appear as ubiquitously heterosexual; heterosexuality is the norm through which all other sexual identities must be understood. In this context, Clarke

(2004) argues that English school spaces, particularly those tied up in physical educational activities, reinforce compulsory heterosexuality by coding all bodies and spaces as "straight." The heteronormativity of the school is reinforced through both psychological and physical violence – queer subjects are meant to feel marginal and are, sometimes, at risk of direct physical attack. Working across the experiences of gay youth life, Brown (2006a) also interrogates the complexity of "coming out" in his reading of *Geography Club*, a teen novel "set during a few weeks around a contemporary high school in a small, generic American city" (ibid.: 313). The title suggests the important spatial metaphors of gay teen life, particularly as they reflect the experience of "the closet" as both a metaphor and a material condition of having to hide one's identity and desires within a wider heteronormative social space. Analyzing the spatialities embedded in the text's characters, Brown offers a reading of the material spatialities of gay life for teens in this context:

> Russell Middlebrook's [the text's gay protagonist] name suggests he's in the middle of a flowing stream. He can move with it or against it, but he is unlikely to stay where he is. By contrast, Jack Land [Russell's love interest] is coded as almost inert, fixed and immovable. As a popular jock, Kevin is unwilling to expose himself by standing up for Russell. Indeed, he ignores him and even joins in on some of the teasing of his own boyfriends in the cafeteria, lest he be exposed as queer and thus lose status as popular (ibid.: 320).

As this excerpt suggests, teens in this particular school operate in and through multiple spaces and identities as they negotiate their sexuality as queer in relation to the broader straight spaces of everyday life. In some cases, such as during their intimate relations with each other in the Geography Club, they are queer, while in other spaces – the larger social milieu – they may perform a straight identity. These performances of queer and straight complicate any straightforward reading of teen identity, suggesting that the spaces of youth are not defined by one set of social meanings and practices (also see Halberstam 2005).

    These social geographies of queer life also suggest that sexuality is not tied to any particular set of sexual practices. Instead, sexuality is performed through everyday sexualized spaces and identities. What this means, more simply, is that sexual practice does not necessarily determine sexual identity, although it can reinforce it. In this regard, Thomas (2004) investigates the complex sexualized identity politics and practices associated with teen life. In a study of the performance of heterosexuality by girls in South Carolina, Thomas argues that the practice of sex is "more than" an act; it is productive of and produced by heterosexuality and heterosexualized space. In discussing her interview with Monique, a fourteen-year-old pregnant black girl, Thomas examines the meanings ascribed to sex as a performance of heterosexuality:

> Monique is clear that sexual, erotic pleasure did not drive her sexual decisionmaking, and she told me that her boyfriend did not forcefully coerce her into sex. Instead, Monique sought out her boyfriend for sex, despite her lack of articulated desire and

her occasional weariness with sex . . . the pleasures that drove Monique's sexual practices were spatial. The teenager's party-like bantering and joking [Monique often had sex at the same time as friends in the same proximate space] produced the home space for sex as much as the sex acts themselves. . . . I am also arguing that one reason Monique had sex is because it is fun to make space for sex (ibid.: 779).

Although teen sex and pregnancy are socially problematic, Thomas argues that even though teen pregnancy is something often "hidden from adults as long as possible . . . heterosexuality is [ultimately] rewarded by a homophobic society (especially as girls become adult sexual subjects), and the taking on of heterosexuality by the youth is a function of this normativity" (ibid.: 781). Contrasting the experiences of Monique with those of Susan, another fourteen-year-old black girl, Thomas highlights how heterosexuality is spatially organized and reinforced even when penetrative sex does not take place. Susan codes spaces as "appropriate" and "inappropriate" sexual spaces: church parking lots and church youth retreats are inappropriate, while bedrooms and hotels are appropriate, although not for her at the time. As Thomas explains, "In order to be a proper heterosexual girl, Susan must choose the proper path and avoid the types of sex that endanger her cohesion as a feminine, middle-class, educated, and self-respecting and respected Christian girl. . . . Space and sexual-propriety combine the norms through which Susan enacts her rules for maintaining proper social positions and identities; following these spatial rules allows a proper sexual and social subjecthood and neglecting them would indicate a slip or social propriety – and may provoke a crisis of subjectivity" (ibid.: 784). Reinforcing certain Christianized heterosexual norms, Susan thus maintains a spatial division between "appropriate" and "inappropriate" uses of sexual space. In so doing, she reproduces a hetero-sexualized norm associated with her gendered identity as a middle-class and educated young women, although in ways that are very different from Monique, who reinforces heterosexuality through the acts of penetrative vaginal sex and pregnancy. As Monique demonstrates her heterosexuality through her new pregnant body, her juxtaposition to Susan also reinforces certain class-based norms that complicate any straightforward reading of teen performances of heterosexuality (see also Bettie 2003). In-depth interviewing can help to tease apart the space–sex–sexuality relationships that serve to normalize heterosexualized identities among teens. Moreover, this work also demonstrates that simple "abstinence only" programs will do little to alter the performances of heterosexuality among teens; sex is more than a desire, as it is a way to prop up and reinforce heterosexualized bodies and spaces as "normal."

Constituting the spaces of youth as spaces of danger

I was downtown, disgusted to park in the parking lot at Cathcart and Cedar and if there aren't 50 young people there from the ages of 10 up to 22 just hanging out, doing drugs with their dead-head clothes on, the entire hippie with the hippie wagons what the heck is going on? They're hanging out there all day, they're not from Santa Cruz [California] (Lucas 1998, citing a talk radio host in Santa Cruz).

Developmentalists would say that children and youth need structure, control, and regulation as they move from childhood to teenage years to adulthood. When these structures and regulations are not in place, children's and teen's "natural tendencies" to go "wild" will emerge and may go unchecked. The representations of youth life and social practice are, through such narratives, often constructed as outside the norm and out-of-place (see Chapters 2 and 5). In the context of a place like Santa Cruz, California, then, these narratives are central to the disciplinary practices of adults whose fear of teenagers and young adults is tied to their fear of "outsiders" or "others" entering their communities. In short, in many places of the global north, at least, there is a "moral panic" emerging, which suggests that the social practices and spaces of teenagers are dangerous if they go unregulated. Collins and Kearns (2001) document how the emergence of this "teenphobia" operates to regulate and control the mobility of youth and youth-centered spaces through the imposition of legal mechanisms, such as curfews in the US. As they argue, the curfew is a geographic as well as temporal mechanism of control. Such laws produce the times when and spaces where youth may gather, "hang out," and interact. As such, "[a] common feature of these initiatives has been an attempt to remove young people from public space . . . by containing them within the home or incarcerating them in prisons and juvenile detention facilities. This alerts us to the fact that moral panics may facilitate an erosion of spatial freedoms" (ibid.: 391). The emergence of the home and prison as sites of containment for children comes from the "fear" that public space is dangerous and unsafe for children and young people (Valentine 1996a) and that children are also dangerous to others in public spaces (Collins and Kearns 2001). Children and teenagers are to be feared, while at the same time adults are to fear for them. Valentine (1996a) defines this contradiction through the analysis of young people as both "angels" and "devils." Within this growing fear of teenagers, the "proliferation of curfews in the US can be connected to a near-universal desire among politicians to appear 'tough on youth crime' in an era during which it is widely believed that young people are increasingly lawless and disrespectful toward adults" (Collins and Kearns 2001: 393). This is ironic, particularly considering the fact that recently violent crime among youth has been decreasing (Aitken and Marchant 2003). The fear of youth, then, is based not in a real criminality but in a wider social field that projects youth life as dangerous.

The "culture of fear" around youth violence is also highly gendered, classed, and raced (Aitken and Marchant 2003; E. Brown 2007). In the US, Aitken and Marchant (2003) show through an analysis of scientific and popular literatures how certain acts of youth violence raise particularly high alarms socially, whereas others are largely unnoticed in public discourse.

> A random public shooting occurs in the United States every 10 days, but few warrant the media attention created by Loukaitis in Moses Lake or Williams in Santee [both in California]. Asian, Latino, and African-American youth violence is usually gang-related or caused by personal disputes, but these inner city minority crimes do not make front-page news and the larger social and economic issues that undergird

Box 7.3   Studying Youth on the Street

Susan Ruddick's (1996) groundbreaking book *Young and Homeless in Hollywood* investigates the complicated representational and material politics of homelessness among young people in Los Angeles. Ruddick notes that representations of youth homelessness, the street, and the city have changed over time, with new services emerging to meet the needs of homeless youth subjects. In discussing "punk squatters" in the 1970s and 1980s, for example, Ruddick shows how homeless youth created new spaces for themselves in "marginal" spaces of the city. She also examines the outreach models of service providers and how these changed over time to reflect the social relations found on "the street." "[M]any homeless youths in squats organize themselves into 'families,' sometimes designating 'mom' and 'dad,' sometimes referring to each other as sister and brother. Within the services, a family structure provides a model for daily routine" (ibid.: 151). These reconstructed service models informed a new type of outreach that afforded street youth both access to services and the flexibility to be "out there" in the world.

While Ruddick's analysis of policy and practice in Los Angeles provides insight into the complicated sociospatial relations of youth homelessness, other social geographers have turned their attention to the politics of mobility and identity of street children and youth in the global south. Lorraine van Blerk (2005) draws on a biographical approach to study the longer-term experiences of the street for children in Kampala, Uganda. In her study, van Blerk examines the mobile nature of street children's lifeworlds, tracing how children move back and forth between the public spaces (the street) of the city and non-street spaces (service organizations and familial homes). In tracing the importance of mobility – and in challenging the notion that being "on the street" demands a sedentary place-centered lifestyle – van Blerk suggests that for street children "mobility affords them a number of opportunities that enhance their survival strategies on the street. They are able to tap into a range of resources in street and off-street locations at different times" (ibid.: 18). This work parallels, to a certain degree, Ruddick's work. In both cases, images of street children and youth are complicated by their everyday practices, demonstrating the complex relationship between their identities and experiences of the city and the street.

Quick Exercise

All children spend time on the street – sometimes playing, sometimes living – and in "the home." Children also spend time in various organizational spaces, including schools, hospitals, and daycare facilities. Find one person in your class and develop a brief biography of their childhood. In the process of the interview, try to "tease out" the various spaces of their experience, tracing how their mobility varied at different points over their life course.

change in low-income neighborhoods (deindustrialization, disinvestment, flexible capital and globalization) are rarely articulated as root causes. Stabbings, shootings, suicides and drug-related violence amongst upper-class youth usually witness a flurry of media activity that drops precipitously as parents, school officials and local authorities seek a quick return to the private, sequestered life of privilege. Rather, moral panics engorge a larger swathe of society when the killings are of white lower-middle-class students, by white lower-middle-class boys who are ostensibly contextualized by the American small town or suburban dream. This is a process of racialization whereby "white" people are differentiated and valued above those of color and it is a process of class distinction whereby the actions of those of privilege are not scrutinized. And there is a coldly sexist demonization of young men. It is a sexist and classist process that denies the larger processes behind an exploitative geography of difference (ibid.: 162).

Elizabeth Brown (2007) also illustrates that there is a lack of broader societal attention paid to youth violence in inner city spaces, even though these same spaces, which are often dominated by people of color, are coming under increasing scrutiny, surveillance, and attention. While, as Brown notes, this is often justified by politicians, parents' groups, or community organizations as being "in the best interest of the child" (ibid.: 227), the criminalization of youth spaces and their surveillance also serves to place youth into the status of second-class citizens, where adults are able to control their mobility and daily practices. The intensified surveillance of youths has also led to an increase of youths being charged and imprisoned as adults, blurring further the transitional spaces between youthhood and adulthood (ibid.: 232). More and more, then, societies are employing a specific moral register that suggests that they must both protect youth and be protected from them. This protection serves to further disenfranchise youth, removing them from the decision-making processes of how to construct their homes, bodies, and subjectivities. In many parts of the world youth are an essential part of the family and community economy, working in industries that are both enabling of their autonomy and abusive of their rights. In this case, the home may not be "safe" at all, as violence extends into the home through varied forms of domestic violence and, in some cases, sexual abuse. These issues should not be taken lightly as social geographers attempt to construct "just" social geographies. Moreover, researchers should remain focused on the violence and inequalities that are part of the everyday geographies of millions of children and young people (Spilsbury 2005).

Ethical Geographies/Children's Geographies

There is an insidious irony in how we deal with children's play and their rights to justice. For the most part, young people as key sites of subversion and resistance are foreclosed upon while at the same time international conventions and scholars consider them as key sites in which politics and "the political" are centered. The irony highlights a disturbingly adultist project. What is missing is a consideration of children as playful, active, interpretive subjects, which at the same time understands that they are not autonomous subjects who are always dealt with justly. Keeping in mind that there is no universal form of play any more than there is a single, monolithic children's literature, it is worthwhile considering a space of justice that elaborates play and takes it seriously (Aitken 2001: 176).

Not without its controversy, Aitken's call for creating space for children's play suggests that social geographers may have to rethink the broader moral project of social geography and pay attention to areas and spaces that have been heretofore marginal in the discipline. That children need the space to "discover a morality that is not derived from adult moral panics" (ibid.: 180) suggests that we may need to reinvent our understandings of the morality–space relationship (see Chapter 6). At the same time, we have to be cautious not to idealize play as an oppositional moment to work (Katz 2004). As Nieuwenhuys (2007) suggests, the narratives against children's work, which are transmitted from the global north to the global south, fail to take into account the complex dynamics of familial social relations and labor in the household. This is often represented in the image of a "global childhood" (ibid.: 150), which universalizes children's experiences and also suggests what all children must and should be. Problematically, however, such narratives of ubiquitous "children's human rights" fail to understand the global relationship between changing children's rights in the US and Europe and those in the global south. As Nieuwenhuys argues, the "patchy evidence suggests . . . that child labour elimination in Europe and the USA went hand in hand with new forms of child exploitation unfolding in the colonial dominions. In other words, the success of the transformation of childhood into perceived period of innocent play and study, owed much to its territorialisation" (ibid.: 152). But the universal application of anti-child labor laws has actually created new spaces where children are exploited in more insidious and hidden ways – through attaching "schooling" directly to "factory work," for example. And child labor politics marginalize the significant role that children and youth play in the household economy and its systems of extended care. All of this suggests that the ethical geographies of children and youth experiences need to be considerate of the complex social geographies in which their lives are situated. If children are allowed to "to play" and "discover" their own moral and ethical registers, then researchers ought to begin by dissecting the complicated social geographies that operate through global and local narratives and practices to mediate the lives of children and young people. This demands, then, that social geographers rethink the binary logics of work and play, as Katz has suggested, and also provide a wider historical and geographical contextualization of how and why children are considered "safe" or "unsafe," "exploited" or "nurtured," "angels" or "devils." Moreover, we have to think about the "transitions" from childhood to adolescent and adult life as socially and spatially contingent, while also remaining sensitive to the complex intergenerational complexities that structure the lives of both children and adults (Hopkins and Pain 2007).

Notes

1 I would include myself in with other social geographers who have largely ignored the geographies of the life course in their work. While I have thought about it, and even alluded to the geographies of age and ageing in a few places, I have generally focused on a limited reading of experience within a much broader life course (e.g. Del Casino 2001, 2007a, 2007b).

2 See Aitken's (2001) *Geographies of Young People* for a further discussion of the work of Blaut and Stea as well as the longer tradition of studying children's mapping abilities. Aitken also discusses Denis Wood, who was one of the first geographers to examine how "built environments" impact childhood (ibid.: 12–18).

3 Aitken (2000) analyzes "fathering," highlighting the complex construction of this particular subject position.

4 Also see an interesting discussion of "hut building" in Norway by Kjørholt (2003).

Chapter 8

Social Geographies of the "Mid-Life"?

- Social Geography's Mid-Life Crisis?
- Production *and* Reproduction, Home *and* Work
- (Re)Producing Home and Work, Public and Private Space
  - Care at home and as work
  - When work takes us away from home
  - Bodies out of place and the home as public space
- Consumption *as* Social (Re)Production
  - Mundane geographies and consumptive practices
  - Reproducing the social identities and spaces of tourism
- Smashing the Binaries, Rethinking the "Crisis"

Social Geography's Mid-Life Crisis?

At the start of Chapter 7, I suggested that social geography has been a largely adult-centered discipline, focusing mostly on the lives and practices of those who might be considered "in the middle" between young people and older people. In Chapter 9, I will argue that social geographers have largely marginalized the study of age and ageing, particularly as it relates to populations defined by the social categories "elderly" and "older people." So, how does one think about this rather nebulous "space in the middle" between the geographies of children and the geographies of ageing? How is it best to operationalize the sociospatial processes associated with so-called adult life? Do mid-life adults not age? Do they not play? Are they not "responsible" for others who may be either young or old? Can social geographers carve out, at least for analytic and heuristic purposes, a space-in-between so that they might examine the processes of the "mid-life" of adults, wherever and whatever that may be? This is tricky. As I have already discussed in Chapter 7, and as I will return to in Chapter 9, the activities often assigned to so-called adult mid-life – work, home care, play (leisure) – occur throughout the life course. They are not exclusive to people over eighteen and under sixty-five. So, is social geography having a mid-life crisis? Is there no way to untangle and analyze the hegemonic elephant in the room – that is, the mid-adult life?

I think there is. To begin, it is necessary to understand that the mid-life adult-centrism of social geography is not unique to this discipline or the social sciences more broadly. Indeed, adult life, particularly those practices associated with people in their mid-life period, is *the* naturalized norm around which others, such as children and the elderly, are often constructed. What this means is that the lives of those in the "middle" of the life course are called upon in children's geographies and geographies of ageing when social geographers want to understand how their hegemony constructs, for example, the spaces of play or retirement. Like whiteness or hetero-sexuality, however, mid-adult life is rarely analyzed or interrogated on its "own terms." But it can be because mid-adult life is socially and spatially organized and structured through everyday norms and practices. Laws and social regulations construct what an adult is – at eighteen years of age in the US parents no longer have access to a child's school records – and set out the boundaries of what "retirement" means – at sixty-five many walk away from their job. The life of an adult is also complicated by the fact that "adulthood" is not a clean process but an emergent one where certain rights are "opened up" to you over time. So you can join the military in the US at eighteen but you cannot purchase alcohol until you are twenty-one or be president until you reach thirty-five. While certain rights are granted, new laws are imposed on the bodies of mid-life adults. An eighteen-year-old may enter the military but he or she may not legally have consensual sex with a partner who may not be eighteen, even if he or she was doing so before reaching the age of eighteen. And, while retirement ages might be pegged at certain levels – sixty-five, for example – the floor to garner retirement benefits is based on other arbitrary age limits – e.g. some can receive a pension at fifty-five. Of course, pensions do not apply everywhere, or even in most places, and work transcends the boundaries of the eighteen to sixty-five year old range, which are largely age limit constructs (and luxuries) found in the global north. So, understanding the "mid-life" as a process of making and remaking age and the spaces of the mid-life, we can start to ask how "the mid-life" is the naturalized norm around which so much social geography is developed.

There is a further way to escape the trap of mid-life adultcentrism and that is to understand adult life as a set of social and spatial practices as opposed to a set of age-specific conditions. As Monk and Katz (1993: 5) argue, "Chronological age by itself does not define the roles and statuses a woman may have, that she may do, or the timing of marriage, childbearing or attainment of various degrees of power in the family and society. Nevertheless, some understanding of the demography of women, country by country, does help us to identify how certain of their activities, such as caring for children or the elderly, will vary in salience across geographic contexts." Thought this way, adult life is structured like children's lives through the social and spatial practices of inclusion and exclusion, body politics, community identities, and organizational practices. Those in their adult life are productive of and thus produced by the spaces they create through the construction of "the home" or "the workplace." That adults also have to carve out spaces for play – through the expansion of mass tourism – is thus an important aspect of their everyday lives at both work and home and needs further social geographic investigation. This is not to say that "the home," "the workplace," or even "the resort" are spaces exclusive to adults in their mid-life. Obviously they are not. But they are organized around powerful practices of production and reproduction that often occupy the attention of those in their mid-life, even as adults co-construct these spaces through the inter-generational relationships (Hopkins and Pain 2007). How, then, adults produce and reproduce (as well as consume) the spaces of home and work, leisure and labor will be the focus of this chapter. As Bunge (1971) has rightly pointed out, there is a spatial preoccupation with producing spaces for adult consumption. And, as this text has already examined, the spatial re/production and consumption of many spaces is "given over" to adults, particularly those in the middle of the life course. While this chapter is treading on slightly new territory – analytically investigating the social geographies of mid-life adults – it does so by calling upon the research of social geographers who critically investigate the production and reproduction of the everyday spaces of life more generally.

The chapter starts with an analysis of production and reproduction, particularly as these concepts relate to the practices of mid-life adults. In many social theoretical frameworks, production and reproduction are conceptualized as distinct and separate spaces. Production is the space of "the economy," of the production of goods and services. Reproduction is the sphere of the "the social" – schooling and education systems, home and day care, hospitals and health care – sites through which bodies and societies are materially reproduced. As feminists such as Katz (2004) maintain, however, the distinction between production (e.g. paid work) and reproduction (e.g. unpaid work) is not real; production and reproduction are interdependent and interwoven. This is because the social and spatial relations of gender, race, class, ethnicity, ability, age, and sexuality are "worked out" in both the spaces of production and reproduction. Thus, while production and reproduction are commonly mapped onto the spaces of work (as production) and home (as reproduction), social geographic research demonstrates that this is a far too simple reading of these two concepts.

In complicating the relationship between production and reproduction, the second half of this chapter calls into question the arbitrary distinctions made between production/reproduction and consumption. Following Marston (2000), I argue that consumption is both a productive and a reproductive process. Through the everyday practice of consumption, people reproduce themselves and the places in which they live and work. Put simply, buying furniture, clothing, or a car reproduces

Box 8.1   On the Geographies of Intergenerational Studies

In a 2007 article, Peter Hopkins and Rachel Pain call for a sustained and critical assessment of how geographers study and think about age. They note that "there are no geographies of adults in sight" (p. 287), while further arguing that the explosion in children's geographies and the geographies of ageing ironically reinforces these subjects at the social and spatial margins of geographic inquiry. In engaging this particular concern, Hopkins and Pain urge social geographers to think relationally about age and ageing through three core concepts: "intergenerationality, intersectionality and lifecourse" (ibid.: 288). A relational framework, they argue, allows social geographers to "think about and work with age as being produced in the interactions between different people" (ibid.). As such, it becomes difficult to talk about geographies of children, "older people or anyone else in isolation" (ibid.). Let's take each of these three concepts in turn:

Intergenerationality. "[This] refers to the relations between generational groups. Viewing intergenerationality as an aspect of social identity suggests that individuals' and groups' sense of themselves and others is partly on the basis of generational difference and sameness. These identities are not fixed but dynamic, affected by the relations between different age groups or generations which may vary" (ibid.: 288).

Intersectionality. "[T]he ways in which age is lived out and encountered are likely to vary according to different markers of social differences [race, sexuality, ability, ethnicity, gender]; the everyday experiences of people belonging to age groups are diverse and heterogeneous. A primary question is *who else* older, middle-aged or young people are" (ibid.: 290, original emphasis).

Life course. "A lifecourse approach involves recognition that, rather than following fixed and predictable life stages, we live dynamic and varied lifecourses which have, themselves, different situated meanings. . . . There is much to be done from a geographical perspective in excavating pathways and experiences over the lifecourse. . . . This more relational work has begun with recent work on transitions [from child to youth or youth to adult]" (ibid.: 290, also see Box 7.1).

Quick Exercise

When Hopkins and Pain argue that age is "produced in the interactions between different people," what do they mean? In a group, or in independent work, list the different ways in which "age" is constructed through (a) intergenerationalities, (b) intersectionalities, and (c) the lifecourse. Can you find examples of these concepts in different chapters of this text?

the consumer as a particular social subject, while eating at a restaurant or traveling to a tourist destination reproduces these sites as spaces of consumption. At the same time, a space of consumption is a space of work for millions of people, who reproduce the restaurant, its toilet, and its food for others to consume. Again, these processes are not exclusive to the lives of mid-life adults. But the notion of "the vacation" and mass tourism more generally is a function of the artificial break that has been articulated between production and reproduction, work and leisure for mid-life adults of particular class backgrounds globally. And, it is through the practices of consumption that mid-life adults reproduce themselves and others (children, friends, colleagues) as particular types of aged subjects. The practice of consumption, therefore, is a complex process, one through which mid-life adults "work out" their social identities and subjectivities. In framing the spaces of "the mid-life" in relation to production, reproduction, and consumption, this chapter thus offers a conceptual framework for investigating the often taken-for-granted space-in-the-middle of the life course.

Production *and* Reproduction, Home *and* Work

Social geographers have long been interested in understanding how various social relations of class, gender, ethnicity, race, and sexuality operate to sustain broader systems of domination, particularly the hegemonic position of capitalism. As Marxist and feminist social geographies emerged in the field, social geographers turned their attention to Karl Marx and his theories of how social relations reproduce inequalities across classes. It was Marx who identified how capitalism's sustainability is dependent on more than the practices of economic and commodity production; it is also dependent on the social reproduction of class relations between capitalists and workers. Without people who identify and understand themselves as workers, capitalism cannot be maintained. Class relations are thus both economic *and* social; economic in the sense that labor is paid and social in the sense that being a worker is a social (class) relation produced through the categories of capitalist and worker. As Mitchell et al. (2004) point out in the introduction to *Life's Work: Geographies of Social Reproduction*, Marx was focused, in particular, on the social reproduction of capitalism through "waged" work. He largely ignored other forms of production and reproduction. As such,

> Marxist theory generally elides the great numbers of unwaged workers, including homemakers and people on public assistance, subsistence farmers, students, and the vast numbers involved in underground economies all around the world. Explanations of the reproduction of the social relations of production often neglect the many forms of labor that are not contracted or paid for in a monetary exchange. As feminists, antiracists, and others have noted, much of this work is done by women, racialized minorities, and those whose legal status is precarious (ibid.: 6).

The need to reproduce oneself as a laborer, which under capitalism demands the sale of one's labor in the market in exchange for money, is presumed by Marx to be *the* key to understanding the social reproduction of capitalism's workers. Capitalism and capitalist social relations are not necessarily ubiquitous (see Chapter 6). The social reproduction of "the economy" or class, gender, race, and sexual relations is based in "forms of economic activity [that] can be waged and non-waged" (ibid.: 8). Mitchell et al. further stress that, "the 'ethnic enclaves' existing in many cities, the 'informal sectors' of others, and the hybrid economies of countries as different as China and the UK are composed of a mix of capitalist and noncapitalist activities existing in relation to each other" (ibid.). Why and how people "work" and what they mean by work, then, operates spatially; work is constructed through a host of "obligations and ties" (ibid.) between husbands and wives, sexual and social partners, employers and employees, and parents and children.

This critical reinterpretation of social reproduction as something that is "more than" waged work is vitally important for the study of the life course for several reasons. First, social reproduction happens through all forms of social relations and institutions – "the religious, the educational, the family, the legal, and the political" (ibid.: 11) – as well as through everyday material practices, such as "shopping, cooking and cleaning, daily paperwork, social networking, minding the family store during or after hours, participating in religious or civic organizations, caring for children and the elderly" (ibid.). Second, the inequalities found in the economy are dependent on the differences between and across "gender, race, and colonial status" (ibid.: 13) as well as age, sexuality, and ability. Across these differences are assigned the categories of work and nonwork that reinforce the "values" – economic and social – ascribed to certain activities. In this way, the work of child or elder care is constituted as nonproductive and the appropriation of child labor by parents on the family farm is thought of as social obligation and not as economic production. Third, these divisions are deeply spatial, reflected in the ways in which we assign certain tasks of work and nonwork to particular spaces/places. The home has been constructed over time as a place of nonwork (or domestic labor) and as nonproductive, although the labor found in the home is absolutely essential socially and spatially (Hayden 2002). Reciprocally, the spaces of work are seen as the productive sphere where laborers produce real "things" that can be exchanged through market relations. As feminist, antiracist, and postcolonial scholars have pointed out, these spaces are often gendered, classed, raced, and sexed in real material ways – the work of women and ethnic minorities in the domestic (private) sphere is socially devalued in favor of "white collar" men's work in the public sphere. It is highly problematic to think of home and work as sociospatially distinct. Work happens in the home all the time and people "make homes" in the context of their work (see the discussion of transnational communities in Chapter 5, for example). Various forms of economic production and social reproduction are converting homes into 24-hour sites of work, thereby blurring the distinctions between the "economic" sphere of production and the "social" sphere of reproduction (Mitchell et al. 2004: 15).

Box 8.2   Methodological Note:
The Social Geographies of Housing

In "Performing (Housing) Markets," Susan Smith, Moira Munro, and Hazel Chrsitie (2006: 82) argue that housing studies could benefit from utilizing "socially inflected qualitative inquiry" to study housing as both an economic and a social process. Through an analysis of "housing bubbles" (or localized housing price increases) in Edinburgh, Scotland, Smith et al. demonstrate that "trade in private homes hinges critically on the work of key market managers" (ibid.: 83). Studying this "work" – and how housing is socially valued – is central, they suggest, to understanding how and why housing prices spike. Methodologically, they turn their attention to "three types of market intermediaries: those who lubricate the flow of information between buyers and sellers, especially concerning price (solicitors [lawyers], estate agents and property developers), those who attach an 'official' value to property (surveyors [appraisers]) and those who deal with the legalities of property exchange (solicitors)" (ibid.).

Housing studies remain a central part of social geography because of the importance that houses have for everyday experience. Changes in social theoretical approaches have turned social geographers' attention to new methodological questions, data, and analytical tools in the study of housing, however. In studying the social geographies of housing markets, Smith et al. offer a corrective to economic-based models of housing by showing how the "market" is made to work through social interactions. "Lay perspectives and behaviours," after all, "contain a rich store of ideas, experiences, hopes, aspirations and impulses which are as relevant to markets as to any set of institutional arrangements. Taking those on-board may provide a fuller account of what markets are and inspire a normative debate with what they might, one day, become" (ibid.: 95). Housing, like "the home," is a relational concept that is dependent on social networks for its meaning. In studying the managers of the "market," these authors show how a qualitative analysis of housing markets adds another layer to an important story of housing accessibility and availability.

Quick Exercise

Using an archival newspaper approach, briefly trace the recent history (for the past five years) of a local housing market. What type of language is used to describe that market? Who is interviewed and what role do they play in the market? Have the language and the players changed over time?

More generally, this discussion of social reproduction and its value to the so-called productive (economic) spaces of capitalism suggests that social geographers need to think carefully about "home" and "work" as social spaces. Let's begin by thinking a bit more about the home. As Blunt and Dowling (2006) point out, the home is a social construction: the meanings attached to it are spatially diverse and historically situated. In much of the global north, the home's idealized form is manifest in the image of the suburban neighborhood and the single-family structure (see Chapter 5). Emerging in mass production in the post-Second World War period throughout North America, the suburban home has been idealized as a heterosexualized familial space where workers are socially reproduced through domestic activities, such as food preparation or laundry services. This idealized home is also nuclear, encompassing mainly parents and children. As Marston (2000) points out, this idealized home draws on a longer history of feminizing home space as the site of "domestic social reproduction." "Increasingly," Marston (2000: 236) argues, "women came to regard the home as a sort of small-scale manufacturing site with directly delivered utilities and new technologies and products reducing the need for live-in servants." Through the active production of the domestic sphere as a site of social reproduction, manuals and handbooks constructed "scientific principles of domestic management" (ibid.). In the process, the home became a professionalized space of domesticity, albeit without a "wage" and without value as productive (economic) real work. Marston's study of the home, though, goes beyond a critique of home as a feminized space by reading home space as distinct and separate from wider sets of social relations. Marston points out, for example, that the workings of the home at the turn of the nineteenth century in the US became a site through which social relations of community and citizenship were also reproduced. Through the home and homemaking, then, women demonstrated their support for the community and the nation, socially reproducing the necessary conditions of production (e.g. for men's civic duty as labor in the workforce). And, today, these narratives of the idealized home and its stark distinctions between production and reproduction are continually being globalized.

The work of the home, while devalued in the sphere of capitalist production, is an essential component of the social reproduction of our everyday economies. So, it is necessary to rethink the concept of work as a social relation solely based in the production of "things" or services. Work is an ongoing and complex process that operates in and through the home, while also stretching the home across space through migratory and transnational networks. The boundaries of work as *the* site of production and home as *the* site of reproduction thus collapse under the weight of social geographic scrutiny. In fact, the activities associated with social reproduction – child rearing, house cleaning – are being incorporated into systems of the wage economy as the dismantling of the social safety net of the welfare state forces people into the workforce. Middle-class workers must expend their own resources, paying others to do the work of social reproduction through child care, house cleaning, or cooking. Although still a minority in North America, men are also staying home to engage the tasks of social reproduction as women stay in the work-force, often because they earn more than husbands. The expanding economies of so-called housework are taken up unevenly across gender, class, race, and ethnic categories of difference. This works across international boundaries in the example of the "maid trade" and the massive movement of women from poorer regions in some countries to the wealthy cities and suburbs of others. Even as people are stretched across space and through transnational networks, linkages to home and the pro-cesses of social reproduction are woven through work lives. For mid-life adults, the lines between "home" and "work" are thus complicated by their own responsibilities, sociospatial locations and subjectivities as parents, partners, children, laborers, or migrants, to name a few. In this context, home *and* work are constantly being recast and rethought by social geographers as material, symbolic, and ideological sites of production *and* reproduction.

(Re)Producing Home and Work, Public and Private Space

In common practice, home is idealized as a space associated with notions of "safety," "comfort," and "security." The home is also most commonly thought of as a material space where people live, eat, and sleep. Home, of course, is much more (Domosh 1998). Materially, home is constructed across other scales, from the body to the community to the nation. Humanistic geographer Yi Fu Tuan (1975) even called geography the study of how humans make the earth into a home; in humanistic terms people construct spaces of comfort through the practices of home (or place) making. In this theoretical articulation, home is conceptualized as "private, familial, or feminine" (Blunt and Dowling 2006: 16). While the home can be socially constructed as a space of retreat from work (often for men) and as a private space, it is actually intimately tied to the social reproduction of human subjects as public, social beings. Laws and social sanctions structure homes as adult-centered spaces, for example. In many parts of the world, children under a certain age are not allowed to have their own homes, and parents and grand-parents are given "rights" over others in their home. The home can also be a place of violence, both emotional and physical. Those who "act out" in the spaces of the home may find themselves socially and physically sanctioned (e.g. LGBTQI teens might be pressured to conform to heterosexualized ideals in the home). The home is thus a key space through which the subjectivities of children and adults, young and old, male and female, straight and gay, white and black are made "real." In tracing some of these subject making processes, this section interrogates the home as a site of caring, as an extended social relation that is made more com-plex through migration, and as a public space where bodies are constructed and regulated.

Care at home and as work

> When I first gave birth to my child at the hospital there was a note at the head of my bed that read "No mother's milk." People would come and visit and see the sign. . . . They would ask why I was using a milk substitute and not "caring" (*liang*) for my child. I was upset and felt a lot of agony. Before I left the hospital they gave me a shot so that I could not give milk. When I got home my father saw that I did not have any milk. So, he went to look for an herbal medicine that would help me give milk because my parents didn't know that I was HIV positive. . . . I almost thought about killing myself (Siriporn,[1] HIV+ woman, Chiang Mai, Thailand, Interview, 1998).

When Siriporn told me this story, we were sitting in her home. Her parents were there and so was her young son. She told the story in a rather matter-of-fact way, although you could also hear the emotions that underpinned her narrative. The home for Siriporn is a complicated space where familial and gendered obligations and responsibilities collide with the identity and body politics of being a woman, mother, and caregiver to both child and parent. Like millions of other women, Siriporn is "in the middle," responsible for young and old, and her home is *the* site through which that care must take place. At the time of her son's birth, however, Siriporn's image of her home was one of dread; it reminded her of the fact that she could not meet her obligations as a "good" Thai woman. Her body had been medically altered so that she could not breastfeed her child and because she was not "out" (as HIV positive) she could not receive services to help her pay for the milk substitute so essential for her son's early growth. Home was neither safe nor comfortable; its symbolic power reinforced the fact that she was a social "failure." She could not perform her socially reproductive role essential to her home. There was only one escape, or so she thought at the time, and that was suicide. Fortunately, Siriporn did not take that route and she "came out" to family and friends; she eventually became a volunteer for a local organization that helped other parents in similar situations (Del Casino 2006).

This story raises a number of important questions for how to think about the home. First, the home is a symbolic space where the subjectivities of men and women, mothers and fathers, are "worked out." For Siriporn, the home has been a symbolic reminder of what she was not – a good mother. Now that she is "out" as HIV positive, the home also reinforces the fact that she will not be able to care for her elderly parents, which is a responsibility often socially assigned to women in northern Thailand. In fact, it may be her parents who eventually have the full-time responsibility to care for her son. This parallels social problems in other contexts, such as sub-Saharan Africa, where younger children must take on the role of caregiver in the wake of death from epidemic diseases such as HIV. In this way, children are entering the realm of social reproduction currently associated with adult "mid-life," forsaking their participation in school or youth-centered social activities with friends (Robson and Ansell 2000; Ansell et al. 2006). This process complicates any straightforward reading of the transition between childhood and adulthood, and reminds us that the life course cannot be divided into a straight-forward set of age-based categories and practices.

Second, it is clear that the home is an essential component of a broader geography of care and caring. Throughout the world, the home is the space through which adults care for both children and the elderly. The home serves an essential function within the larger system of social welfare, particularly when governments refuse to support the care of children or the elderly. In the context of HIV in Thailand, there have never been enough hospital beds to care for people living with HIV, so the home is the place where that care is taking place. In this way, the home serves as an extension of other spaces of care, such as the hospital, clinic, family, and community. Moreover, as Brown (2003) and others (Wiles 2003; Dyck et al. 2005) note in their discussion of care in the global north, the practices of care in the home break down the notion that home is a space of nonwork: caregiving can often take place through the paid work of others who come into the home to provide care. More generally, the opening up of the home to other spaces of care destabilizes the notion of home as a private space because the practices of caregiving in the home, particularly by "others," expose the home to public scrutiny. In similar ways, Siriporn's home is a public space of care and scrutiny where neighbors, extended family, health care workers, NGO activists, and wayward social geographers discuss her needs and caregiving arrangement in the home.

Third, as an essential site of social reproduction, the home is the place through which gendered, raced, ethnic, and sexed identities are worked out, and the site in which the responsibilities of adults are reinforced. More and more, when children and the elderly are left to be the "caregivers" in the home it is constructed as a "tragedy." In this narrative, the entire responsibility of the home, home care, and home-making should be in the hands of those in their mid-life, particularly (although not exclusively) women. This is because "education" and preparation for pro-ductive economic work is often seen as an essential part of being a child and age-ing and post-productive life is seen as a space of leisure and post-work. The home as the "space of mid-life responsibility" informs the reading of "the family" itself. Single-parent homes are constructed as "abnormal" and incapable of providing the appropriate care for others. This is more than an issue of familial care; this speaks to the powerfully gendered and sexualized politics of the state, which, in many places, idealizes the home as a two-parent hetoersexual space where mid-life adults "raise" the future generation of active and productive citizens. Wong et al. (2004: 44) argue that in Singapore, "Single-parent families, widowed parents and unmarried mothers are seen as configurations that are 'less than ideal' for bringing up children and, ultimately, as potentially undermining a social reproduction that conforms to government goals for the population." In this context, the heterosexual nuclear home is good for both the immediate family *and* the nation. Care is seen to socially reproduce not just the physical bodies of workers but active state citizens. The single parent, particularly the single mother, thus represents a tragic and victimized figure with little or no agency (Patton 1994). In the Thai context, programs to assist single mothers who were HIV positive dominated the broader landscapes of care throughout the 1990s to the almost absolute exclusion of single fathers or single men in similar positions. Siriporn's story thus suggests that new forms of family and home are produced through both demographic change and social narratives of what constitutes an "ideal" home space. As a single mother, Siriporn does not have the dual earner potential that comes with marriage, which is common for families in northern Thailand.[2] As a site of "work" and social reproduction, her home is intricately tied into the broader relations of power that construct appropriate gendered and sexed practices of family, community, and citizenship. The home is thus a productive space not only because it can be and is used to produce commodities for the market but also because it is a space through which social difference and inequalities are actively produced. The work of care reinforces certain gendered notions of home that have real material effects that locate care and the social reproduction of the household, ideally, with mid-life adults. This home is thus much more than a space where people live, eat, and sleep. It is a space through which their subjectivities are constructed and where the boundaries between their understandings of production and reproduction, as well as public and private, are blurred or, better yet, erased completely.

Moving away from and toward home

It is already clear that home is a complex concept that is always changing in relation to the broader social and spatial networks in which it is situated (Lawson 1998: 48). At the same time, the social geographies of global population distributions are changing rapidly as people migrate and move, either by force or voluntarily, to enter a new workforce, to avoid conflict and tension, to engage in new social networks or communities, or to connect with extended familial networks that have been stretched across space (Knodel and Saengtienchai 2007). In the process, people move away from home and their "roots" and create new homes as transnational and mobile "routes" (Blunt and Dowling 2006: 199). In comparing home as roots with home as routes, Blunt and Dowling argue that "Rather than view home as rooted, located and bounded, and often closely tied to a remembered or imagined homeland, an emphasis on 'routes' invokes more mobile, and often deterritorialized, geographies of home that reflect transnational connections and networks" (ibid.). For some, home is both root and route: migrants connect to their "rooted" home through remittances back to family and create new "routed" homes within new transnational social networks (see Chapter 5). For many, mobility is an essential aspect of the social reproduction of their conceptually "rooted" home as remittances afford opportunities for children to remain in school or for partners or elderly parents to remove themselves from the paid workforce so that they can care for children, siblings, or grandchildren. In Vancouver, Canada, Pratt notes that Filipina women working in the nation's Live-in Caregiver Program (LCP) can transfer the wealth earned in Canada back to the Philippines, investing in properties and homes that would otherwise be out of their reach (Pratt and Philippine Women's Centre 2005).

This support goes not only to immediate family members but to the extended familial networks, which utilize the physical homes purchased by overseas relatives to care for children and parents. For those who have managed to purchase property in the Philippines, the "rooted" home is idealized and envisioned as a space of leisure and relaxation, a place to which they hope to retire when they are done working as transnational migrants. At the same time, the extension of the home across transnational networks can impose high personal costs on migrants in their "routed" homes as women working in LCP struggle with issues of self-esteem. As one respondent suggested, "in our community [Filipinas in Vancouver, Canada], people looked down on nannies because you are working as a waitress, they think you are no good" (ibid.: 133). Moreover, women have to deal with "the cost of family dislocation" (ibid.: 134) and their inability to maintain existing marriages, find new partners in their transnational networks, remain connected to family across long distances, or find a partner in Canada itself.[3]

Blunt's (2005) analysis of home, migration, and mobility further complicates a straightforward reading of home as rooted. Through her analysis of the diasporic communities of Anglo-Indians – peoples of "mixed-decent" Indian and British – in post-independence India, Blunt illustrates how the politics of race, gender, and citizenship highlight the inequalities associated with the transnational home experience. This community traces its history back to the earliest period of British colonial life – the eighteenth century – when British men were encouraged to intermarry with Indian women. Although this policy was later struck down, the policy rested on the notion that an intermarried (and British-dominated) home space would increase loyalty to the British homeland through the material reproduction of an "in-between" group that could transcend the British–Indian cultural divide. For those of mixed Indian/British decent, who spent the majority of their lives as children and adults in India, movement within and across the spaces of the former British empire as adult migrants forced them to confront the politics of difference that marked their bodies as neither British nor Indian. The hybridized identity of the Anglo-Indian reinforced a feeling of being "out-of-place" in the social context of the imperial home (Britain), the post-imperial spaces of the British (Australia), and the post-independence spaces of their birthplace (India). Even though "a 'homing desire' for Britain often invoked ideas of imperial masculinity . . . the difficulties of tracing British paternal ancestry" (ibid.: 106) presented challenges to the identities of Anglo-Indians as British citizens. As a result, attempts to migrate to the "fatherland" of Britain or other parts of the British Empire meant that Anglo-Indians had to directly face the racism of British migration policy, which impeded the movement of Anglo-Indians. When they did move, the establishment of "home space" in Britain was dramatically different than it was in India. In India, many Anglo-Indian families had domestic servants and much larger houses. Once in Britain, Anglo-Indian women were confronted by the fact that the care of home and family was now in their personal hands. Even as some Anglo-Indians rejected British identity, they did not believe themselves to be "Indian" either and felt out-of-place in an independent postcolonial India as well. Anglo-Indians have thus struggled with their identities in India, while having tried to maintain their hybridized homes and families. This has become an even greater challenge in recent years because Anglo-Indian women – many of whom have excelled professionally – are intermarrying outside the Anglo-Indian community. As such, "Current debates about the status and existence of the community are embodied by Anglo-Indian women, and revolve around their marriage to men from other Indian communities and their ability to raise their children as Anglo-Indian" (ibid.: 201). Anglo-Indian identity in India is thus embodied in the home and family, and in the bodies of women, whose spatial mobilities are challenging the "intergrity" of the Anglo-Indian home and community.

For other international migrants, such as asylum seekers or refugees, the space of home is also a critical site for the social reproduction of their identities as either displaced or relocated. "While some refugees will devote their exile to recreating the home they left behind, others will commit themselves to constructing a niche in their new country of asylum" (Shoeb et al. 2007: 443). For Iraqi refugees living in Dearborn, Michigan, maintaining their relationship with their home in exile and their homeland abroad is often tied to their own social reproduction as Muslims. Men and women draw on Islam differently in reconstructing themselves as "at home" in their status as exiles, but do so in ways that help them restructure their routed home as connected to a larger social sense of self as Iraqi and as Muslim. Men, on the one hand, "describe themselves as *Muahjirin* ('those who leave their home in the cause of Allah' . . .), conferring a noble aura to the Iraqi plight" (ibid.: 449), while women "found that forced migration led to the breakdown of cultural expectations by threatening the notion that marriage is associated with settling down and establishing a family" (ibid.: 450). This suggests that mobile subjectivities draw on visions of a rooted home while their experience of home is really routed; this also shows that the process of exile affects men and women differently. It is thus clear that mobility has a profound impact on home as a site for constructing identity and subjectivity. The transnational homes of domestic workers, mixed-descent migrants, or refugees illustrate how understandings of home are remade by everyday experience. Through various migratory practices, the home is being stretched, extended, and rethought, shifting how people perform their roles as productive and reproductive citizens, community members, and adults more generally.

Bodies out of place and the home as public space

As I have already discussed, the notion of the "home" as a private space is difficult to sustain when taking into consideration the complex relationships between reproduction and production. This is because the home is neither contained by nor sheltered from the broader sociospatial contexts in which it is embedded. It is one of the most important spaces through which the tensions around the public and private are individually and collectively negotiated. The powerful discourses around the appropriateness of certain bodies in public spaces can recreate the home, for example, as a site of confinement and retreat – this is how "the closet" works for some queer subjects (Brown 2000). The home might also be a site for the containment and regulation of reproduction – this is why the home may be a space of retreat from a public gaze for pregnant women in western societies (Longhurst 2001). Homes may also be sites of confinement because of the limited resources in other public spaces for those who have bodies that do not conform – such as those whose abilities limit access to space beyond their home (Kitchin 1998a). People with disabilities who cannot conform to ableist notions of productivity in the public realm are "being in effect told to 'go home' (being sacked [fired], not having a contract renewed, failing exams and not being allowed to retake)" (Hansen and Philo 2007: 498). Home, then, may be neither safe nor comfortable; instead, it can become isolating and disabling. The home can be *the* site through which certain "unproductive" and "unwanted" social practices and identities are reproduced through homophobia, sexism, or ableism. Reciprocally, homes may serve as an ideal space to express one's sexuality, flaunt the pregnant body, or normalize bodily comportments that are constructed as abnormal in public space. Home, in this case, is still complicated by its relationship to its public self – as the performances found in the home draw on an array of social and spatial discourses and practices that exist "outside" it. Either way, the notion that the home is a purely private space is hard to sustain either in day-to-day practice or intellectually; it is too caught up in the broader processes of social reproduction that enable and disable certain subjective experiences of home and work.

In the interest of destabilizing the private/public binary that often accompanies discussions of home in social geography, Valentine (1993, 1996b) offered one of the first extended discussions of lesbian experiences of heterosexualized public spaces, illustrating how "the public sphere" is extended into the everyday "private" spaces of lesbian women's lives (see also Bell 1995b). In her analysis, she examines how lesbian women have to negotiate "a number of statutory and common laws . . . [that can] be used to criminalize public displays of same sex desire on the streets [of the United Kingdom]" (Valentine 1996b: 148). These overt politics are coupled by "heterosexual looks of disapproval, [and] whispers and stares are used to spread discomfort and make lesbians feel 'out of place' in everyday spaces" (ibid.: 149). As Valentine goes on to suggest, the heternormativity of the street may be challenged overtly through public events, such as gay pride parades, and through the use of home spaces to create and sustain lesbian communities. In a similar vein, Elwood (2000) demonstrates how lesbian women in Minneapolis, Minnesota can use their home to contest heterosexualized norms. This is done through the creation of non-heteronormative families, outward material expressions of lesbian and gay identity, and the use of their homes to maintain extended social networks and support. In Australia, "gay men [also] use their homes as sites of non-heteronormative socialization and sexual activities" (Gorman-Murray 2006: 57), expanding the spaces of their home through "a great deal of functional interchange – and consequent movement of bodies – between gay men's homes and the public gay world of bars and beats" (ibid.). Gorman-Murray's analysis suggests that the "home is stretched" as gay men expand their sociospatial networks in and across so-called public and private space. In this way, the processes of social reproduction of queer space take place in home and other "home*like*" spaces, such as familiar "bars" (ibid.: 58, original emphasis; also see the discussion of queer activism in Chapter 6).

The heteronormativities that blur public and private space operate in conjunction with masculinist practices that construct home as a domestic and private sphere of biological and social reproduction. In this case, pregnant women are also made to feel that their bodies and the biological changes associated with pregnancy are out of place in public space (Longhurst 2001). Through social norms and pressures, pregnant women in New Zealand, for example, have to "retreat" to their home spaces to maintain a distance between their changing bodies and the normative gaze of "the public." Longhurst (2001: 45) suggests that the "body that threatens to vomit is not a body that can be easily trusted to occupy the respectable realm, including the workplace." As women begin to "show" as pregnant, their bodies also become part of a larger public discourse, where people feel comfortable touching their stomachs and giving them personal and parental advice (Longhurst 1999). While this might not be a "problem" for some (ibid.), pregnancy for others has meant "withdrawing from sport, paid employment, restaurants, bars, and cafés" (ibid.: 37). The pregnant body becomes socially and spatially confined to "the home."

The powerful link between "home" and birthing is also being pushed out into the public spaces of health care. Fannin (2004) examines how birthing rooms for women in the United States are becoming more "homelike," representing the powerful links made between pregnancy and "the home." "The domestic is reiterated as the 'natural' site of women's agency, yet control of the body and of the process of birth in a hospital birthing room is often translated into control over the landscape of birth at its most superficial: lighting, the choice of music, and so on" (ibid.: 104). In different ways, Fannin argues, the home birthing movement in the United States (literally birth in one's home) believes it can challenge the hospital as a "homelike space" for birthing by bringing birth back to its "natural" origins in the home. Of course, the home birthing movement in the United States is embedded in a "historically specific . . . understanding of a white, middle class subject" (ibid.). And, the movement denies the fact that "rural woman who cannot afford to travel to a distant hospital and the teenager who is hiding her pregnancy," give birth at home without the social (and medical) safety net provided by midwives, family, and friends involved in home birthing. The home is thus a contradictory space for pregnant women. It serves to conceal their "out of control bodies" (Longhurst 2001: 45) from public sight, while also maintaining the historical link between home, maternity, and women's private role in social and biological reproduction.

Consumption as (Re)Production

In this section, we turn our attention to how social geographers have theorized consumption, focusing on the mundane practices of consumption as a form of social reproduction, particularly the reproduction of social spaces, identities, and subjectivities for and by mid-life adults. Social geographers are particularly interested in understanding how consumption productively creates spaces, identities, and subjectivities, such as "the café," "the consumer," or "the parent." Following this discussion of consumption as a set of social practices is a discussion of spaces of tourism as sites of consumption. These spaces are socially and materially constructed as oppositional to the performances of work and home, often idealized as spaces of "relaxation" where adults can "recharge" and socially reproduce themselves as productive workers. As a practice of conspicuous consumption, the activities of tourism are powerful markers of difference and inequality. The practices of tourism are also an intricate component of the social reproduction of home. By seeking out "other" non-homed spaces, tourists construct what home means by consuming experiences and spaces they believe are "different." In this historical context, where it appears that capitalism has severed work and play as well as production and consumption through the expanding diversification of social relations and identities, tourism sites are *the* new spaces of play, where adults may "act out" and do things they might not do otherwise in the spaces of home and work. In the process, the consumptive practices of tourism reproduce the social meanings, spaces, and identities of tourism and tourists, tourism work and tourism workers.

Mundane geographies and consumptive practices

In the earlier discussion of social reproduction, Marston (2000) argued that the home is a site through which many of the practices of social reproduction take place. Pushing this further, Marston also stresses that consumption is inextricably tied to the social reproduction of the home. Consumption is a productive act, in that the consumption of goods and services in/for the home also reproduces the social and spatial relations of class, race, ethnic, and sexed identities and practices. Consumption is thus more than an economic practice; it is a critical part of the reproduction of social relations and the politics of difference and inequality. As such, it is possible to analyze the powerful productive capacities of consumption (Mansvelt 2005). Social geographers can investigate, for example, how consumption links people and places together, as goods are produced, sold, and resold across disparate spaces, and then investigate how the spaces of consumption are produced for and by consumers through everyday social and spatial interactions. This has been famously applied to the study of the mall (Goss 1993), where the mall is seen as a space designed to satisfy consumer tastes and reinforce an idealized set of consumer identities and practices. Social performances in these spaces may reproduce certain aged, abled, classed, raced, sexed, and gendered identities, as well as consumers and consumptive practices more generally. The mall is thus an idealized space in which adults train children how to "shop" and participate in the reproduction of the household *and* leisured activities that are "not work." It is not surprising in this context that social geographers are interested in rethinking the binary logic of production and consumption, challenging

Figure 8.1   A tannery in Marrakech, Morocco. It is hard to overestimate the intense conditions of labor under which certain goods and products are produced. In this case, hides are produced through an intense process in which workers literally get into the pits with the hides as part of the process of "tanning" the materials. Viewing this process is a common part of a tour of Marrakech (Photo by author, 2005).

the assumption that goods are simply produced and then consumed through economic mechanisms associated with the market (Laurier 1993; Gregson 1995). Production and consumption are social processes, inextricably tied to the spatial practices, identities, and subjectivities of everyday life. As Jackson (2000: 10) points out, "there is mounting evidence of the continued significance of local contexts of consumption," suggesting that there is a need to examine consumption further to understand how spaces are produced through these practices.

   There are thus numerous ways to conceptualize consumption in social geography. One way would be to examine consumption through the diffusion of the spaces created to accommodate it – mapping these sites across an absolute space or across a series of commodity chains and relationships. Another way would be to investigate when and where consumption "happens," interrogating the meanings of and identities tied to the social practices of consuming specific places, such as produce markets, restaurants, or even historical sites. Or, we could examine the social relations of production and reproduction that are inextricably woven into the fabric of the spaces of consumption – teasing apart the "work" involved in consumption. Thought this way, consumption can be theorized as "Practices . . . [that might] be understood as routinized and socially embedded forms of behaviour that require skill and competence to enact" (Jackson 2004: 172). Consumption is not only part of a broader set of leisured practices, therefore. It is "embedded within the complex rhythms and everyday domestic routines of contemporary households" (ibid.: 173). These practices and rhythms are certainly not exclusive to mid-life adults, as children and older people also actively take part in the consumptive practices of spaces, such as "the home." Indeed, consumption is an important site through which social geographers can untangle the intergenerational relationships that work to reproduce the identities of young and old, child and adult. Privatized and corporate play spaces appeal to younger people (and parents), who use them to engage in "safe" play, while older people may purchase homes in "retirement communities," consuming space in a way that reinforces age-based differences. Children and adults might also engage in the same spaces of consumption but may use these in very different ways. So, a family may go to Disneyland and the children might have fun in certain spaces, while the adults may prefer to participate in nighttime dining activities with friends and other adults. The consumption of goods, such as clothing and electronic equipment, can also be utilized in ways that distinguish children and adults. And, the active nonuse of certain goods – such as cell phones – might serve to reinforce generational differences. In this way, the spaces and practices of consumption are intimately tied to age-based sets of practices, even as there are numerous sites through which intergenerational relationships also take place.

It is also important to recognize that the "cultures of consumption" and the concomitant social practice of consumer identities are globalizing at a rapid pace. The so-called north/south divide is often blurred by the geographies of consumption. For example, malls can be found across the spaces of the global south, and wealth differences mean that the consumption of goods and spaces distinguishes class, gender, and ethnic differences in both the global north and the global south. Indeed, it may be possible to argue that the consumer classes of Mumbai, Rio de Janeiro, Los Angeles, and Paris have more in common with each other than people living in, say, Harlem and midtown Manhattan in the city of New York. The wealthiest classes as well as the so-called middle classes of the world go to Starbucks, buy Gucci purses, purchase expensive sports cars, and eat at fine fusion restaurants. Indeed, drinking Starbucks signals one's class status while also reinforcing the practices of "fast food," which meets the needs of those whose work life minimizes time at home or in the kitchen. In this way, social geographers examine consumption as both a set of spaces and a set of social practices that construct social identities and subjectivities. These practices are, of course, tied to the spaces of consumption themselves, which are reinforced and reproduced through the social expectations of how someone is "supposed to be" in, say, the café (Laurier et al. 2001). It is the mundane social practices of how people "act" in the café that produce and reproduce both space and identity, creating diverse and dynamic consumptive experiences in and across local and global space. At the same time, Jackson (2004) argues that the "globalization" of various commodities and consumptive practices can never be a

complete and totalizing process. Tracing the complex social politics of consumption across a comparative analysis of India, China, and Russia, Jackson offers a nuanced
analysis of the social geographies of consumption in these places, suggesting that
consumer culture does not move in a singular trajectory from global north to global
south. In fact, consumer practices in Mumbai reinforce upper middle-class Indian
notions of their identities as modern and cutting edge consumers of global fashion
compared to what they see as conservative British-based Indian consumers. The
boundaries between so-called "western" and "eastern" clothing are blurred, however, in the daily practice of actually buying and wearing clothes, as genres of dress
are mixed and matched (Jackson et al. 2007). The global expansion of consumer
goods is therefore not an uncontested process, as national, class, sexual, gender,
race, and ethnic identities are intimately wrapped up in the production of the spaces
and goods of/for consumption.

Gregson et al. (2007: 188) take this further, suggesting that social geographers
should investigate not only the different ways consumption "works" across various
spaces, but also how consumption is complicated by the "transient . . . utilization of
particular objects." Turning our attention, therefore, to the practices of "divestment"
– or the nonuse or resuse of consumptive goods – Gregson et al. show how this
process is also subject to certain "normative" practices and is intimately tied
into the broader social networks and meanings we subscribe to ourselves and our
identities as consumers (ibid.). Put more directly, throwing out certain goods
while keeping others, or turning certain goods over to particular people (family,
neighbors, or charities), says something about how people "think about" and perform their own home space and identities. Grounding this in the lives of different
households in Nottingham, England, Gregson et al. investigate the practices of
divestment as part of a broader strategy of social and spatial identity formation. In
the case of two sisters, Daphne and Dorothy, we see that what "they do not do, and
indeed use the bin [trash] to avoid doing, is passing things on that might be seen
(by themselves and others) to reflect negatively on them" (ibid.: 196). Daphne and
Dorothy thus divest themselves in ways that help them avoid giving away objects
they see as socially inappropriate, dirty, or polluting. These practices of divestment
are also tied to their social identities through which they value "the new" (ibid.: 195).
In contrast, Karen and John use their social networks to reinforce a different set of
social identities. In particular, "Karen offers the material culture of her babies to
her sister, and that these gifts are accepted, works to reconstitute the sister relation
as a relation of sisters who are also mothers. In the manner of sharing clothing,
it uses things to signify the social bond or connection, materiality to symbolize
and indeed materialize their social relation . . . what Karen does with her children's
things constitutes a particular (middle class) practice of mothering" (ibid.: 192).
In conclusion, they argue that "consumption practices are not just founded on
the acquisition and utilization of particular objects in particular ways, but also
by their divestment in particular ways. To be a competent practitioner involves a
thoroughly reflexive engagement with the ways in which objects are used, even
not used, and to know what to do with those things that have fallen-out of use"

(ibid.: 197, original emphasis). Consumption is an ongoing process, which operates through numerous social networks and spaces as goods are moved from one place to another, between people and organizations, or tossed aside and into the world's landfills. More generally, consumption can be theorized as a complex *and* mundane social process of making and remaking space and identity. In comparison, the next section examines tourism as a form of consuming space, rethinking or reinforcing social identities, and as an important site for interrogating the mutual constitution of consumption and production.

Reproducing tourism through consumption

Studying the mundane acts of consumption demonstrates that the geographies of these acts are quite complex. Consumption is not a process that can simply be juxtaposed against production, nor is it a purely economic practice. Consumption is a productive and reproductive social practice caught up in the everyday politics of social identity. Consumption is also a practice that reinforces social and spatial difference and inequality. Some can "consume" certain goods, while others cannot. Some participate actively in social networks that reuse goods rather than toss them away, while others insist on reinforcing their social identities as consumers through the repeated purchase and consumption of the "latest and greatest." People consume more than just goods; they also consume spaces as well as the emotions and bodies of so-called "others" in the act of being consumers. This is particularly salient in the context of the world's largest industry, tourism. Tourism is a multibillion dollar industry that involves millions of tourists and nontourists every day. The spaces of tourism have expanded dramatically in the post-Second World War period, opening up to a "new leisure class" (MacCannell 1989) of middle- and upper middle-class people through the reduction of the costs of travel globally and the increased speed of that same travel. Tourism is also available to people from all parts of the world. This is demonstrated by the massive movement of people within so-called world regions, such as Asia-Pacific or South Asia, and across regions between, for example, North America and South America.

Social geographers have long been interested in tourism not only because it involves the massive movement of peoples but also because tourism spaces are sites through which different social identities and subjectivities come into "contact" and are mutually reproduced (Cuthill 2007). Tourists most often travel to engage with other peoples and places they see as "different." The study of tourism is interesting because as a consumptive practice it both reproduces social identities and constitutes differences and potential inequalities. It does so "by capitalizing on real and imagined differences between familiar and unfamiliar places" (Mansvelt 2005: 140). This might manifest itself in overt racist and colonialist ways, as "a thrust of tourism promotional literature often portrays indigenous peoples as members of primitive, static, unchanging societies, removed from relationships which characterize the 'modern' world" (ibid.). In seeking out an "other," tourists can reinforce their own racialized, gendered, classed, and sexed assumptions and norms about both themselves as "civilized" and others as "exotic." This happens in a variety of complex ways that serve to reproduce the uneven relations of power that are present in so many tourist encounters between those who have money to travel in the first place and those who do not. That said, tourism is also a multifaceted set of practices, and there is no one way of "doing" tourism or studying it (Crouch 1999), as tourism is tied to heritage sites, conspicuous consumption markets through shopping, or travel for the purposes of engaging in sex or drugs (see Box 8.3). There are certain broad processes of tourism, however, that might guide the study of how the consumption of tourism is a productive and reproductive act, particularly for mid-life adults.

> ### Box 8.3   Arun Saldanha's *Psychodelic White:*
> ### *Goa Trance and the Viscosity of Race*
>
> Arun Saldanha's *Psychodelic White* is both an argument for taking race more seriously in geography and tourism studies *and* against the typical ways in which scholars in these fields theorize race. This makes the book a rather bold endeavor and a challenging read. At its core, it provides social geographers with a set of questions for critically analyzing the landscapes of tourism where people of different races, ethnicities, abilities, sexualities, and genders meet and intermingle. Focusing, in particular, on the "rave scene" in Anjuna, Goa – a former Portuguese colony along the southern west coast of India – Saldanha examines how a space of tourism, which claims to be "free" and "open" to alterity, is also invested in a racist material practice of difference. Put rather simplistically, he interrogates how the rave scene maintains its whiteness while marginalizing local, Indian differences.
>
> Saldahna's book is also an argument against a social constructionist approach to race. In a social constructionist approach, race is seen as a process emerging out of language and discourse – it is not real nor is it biological. For Saldanha, however, this approach is incapable of analyzing racial formations in Goa's tourism rave scene or the segregation he witnessed between tourists and locals, whites and nonwhites. Race, he argues, is, instead, an embodied and material process constituted through how bodies come together, or in his words how bodies start "sticking together" (ibid.: 5). As he explains in his introduction:
>
>> At that Dolce Vita [rave] party . . . there was a viscosity of predominantly white ravers. They stuck together in time and space because they all saw each other regularly, smoked chillum together, and danced Goa trance, wore flashy clothing, and had money to spend on LSD and Ecstasy. Others, especially domestic tourists, weren't habituated to all this; they didn't have the cultural or economic resources to join in. When the sun came up, most Indians felt visible and out of place between so many white bodies (ibid.: 5–6).

Saldanha's ethnographic and qualitative approach suggests that geography and tourism studies turn their attention to such bodily interactions and how those interactions create spaces of segregation and difference. In the end, Saldanha does not argue against whiteness per se but against particular forms of whiteness designed to maintain exclusions even as people travel to engage the so-called other. He argues against the spatial formation of cliques, which exclude those who do not perform their bodies in the right way (e.g. the ability to speak right, to carry the body correctly, to take drugs appropriately, and to dance in a particular way). The material performances of "rave tourism" in Goa are thus complex and multifaceted, brought together through the body politics of race. Race, then, is more than a social construct, it is a material practice that is maintained through the mashing together of individuals into collective, albeit temporary, communities of tourists and nontourists, white and nonwhite, insider and outsider.

Quick Exercise

In a group of four or five students discuss the following two statements from Saldanha:

1   "Seemingly more than any racial formation . . . the white racial formation is defined by movement, by its urge to become different – especially during the period called modernity" (ibid.: 197).
2   "What I want to argue is, I hope, uncontroversial: that whites have been squarely in the business of producing and rearranging racial difference, whether it was through relatively benign exoticism and adventurous anthropology or state-sponsored genocide or apartheid laws" (ibid.).

Social theorists have often thought of tourism as a ritualized (and religious-like) performance, whereby people travel seeking out "other" places where they might experience something "different" or "unique" (MacCannell 1989; Urry 1990). Intimately tied into these consumptive practices are feelings of pleasure and, more broadly, the subjective desires of those engaging in tourism. As Kingsbury (2005: 123) points out, for example, Jamaica's "tourism product . . . depends on providing spaces for enjoyment, but not too much enjoyment, that is, arousal not anxiety." Tourism is, like other social practices, complicated by the spatial contexts in which it is embedded. In this case, tourism, which is a lucrative industry in Jamaica, is a social practice that involves the "desire" to both seek out the other and be "outside" one's self, but to do so in a relatively safe and comfortable context. As Kingsbury stresses, the desires and performances of enjoyment are not located solely in the spaces of the tourist. Tourism workers can also participate in the spaces of tourism, allowing them to "transgress" their own social norms and practices. It is not only tourists, after all, who consume the spaces of tourism. Consumption operates across social networks and spaces, with those working in tourism locations consuming the goods and products of tourism as well.

Tourism is also a consumptive practice through which tourists and nontourists reproduce their subjectivities. Imagine a nuclear family in the US, a heterosexual unit with a mother, father, and two children, one girl and one boy. They travel from the suburbs of Washington, DC to Fredericksburg, Virginia to tour the monuments and historical spaces of the colonial and civil war US. As they travel from one place to the next, the parents stop the car, get out, and point out historical monuments identified in the town's landscapes. From a monument of Mary Washington, the mother of George Washington, to the Hugh Mercer Apothecary Shop, tourists travel through the city of Fredericksburg, reproducing it through their consumption of these spaces (Hanna et al. 2004; Del Casino and Hanna 2005). The family

Figure 8.2   The "Night Bazaar" in Chiang Mai, Thailand. Tourist spaces, such as this one, are an essential part of the practices of tourism for both workers and consumers. These intense spaces are the sites through which tourists reinforce their difference – speeding motorcycles or advertisements in Thai – and recognize their own comfort – McDonald's signals the "safety" of this particular space. In these spaces, people construct themselves as "different" while also working through their own subjectivities as tourists and nontourists, travelers and workers in these sorts of spaces (Photo by author, 2008).

visiting Fredericksburg is doing more than simply reproducing the spaces of tourism, though, it is also reproducing its members as historic and political subjects: by consuming the Civil War and American Revolution they reproduce these historical moments and spaces for their identities as "American" citizens. What might be called a "family vacation" is also an educational, political, and cultural excursion for children and parents. The experience serves to reinforce a certain narrative of the history of the US and the tourists' identities as proper American citizens paying homage to these "sacred" spaces. By interrogating the practices of tourism by tourists, it is possible to see how they reproduce certain social identities through the practices of tourism. Pushing this further, it is possible to interrogate how tourism workers reproduce both the spaces of tourism and their own social identities through their work. Staying in Fredericksburg for a moment, Beatrice, who works in the Fredericksburg Visitor's Center, reproduces the city through her own spatial imagination: "I feel that just walking down the street [is a great thing to do] because the same drug store is there that I went in as a child. I just think it's charming, a charming city. It really hasn't changed all that much. The people are still friendly. It's a very friendly place" (Hanna et al. 2004: 472). Although Fredericksburg's tourism identity is politically tied to its place in the broader historical memory of the US, Beatrice ties her own imagining as a citizen and as a "small town" person into her narrative of the city. In this way, her consumption of Fredericksburg reproduces it (and her) as an idealized space where the small town ethos is sustained. In many ways, this parallels the narrative of the idealized rural community, whereby certain differences are marginalized in favor of a utopian vision of the small town as homogeneous (see Chapter 5).

The spaces of tourism are thus complicated by fluid and dynamic relationships with other spaces and networks (M. Crang 1999; P. Crang 1994, 1997). More generally, the production of the spaces of tourism depends on the connections between these spaces and other spaces, such as the factories and shops that produce the commodities sold by tourism workers or the homes of workers where their labor, social relations, and bodies are reproduced. Indeed, without the tourists there would be no tourism spaces; there would also be little need for the commodities of tourism (maps, postcards, souvenirs, and photographs) or the bodies and labor necessary to sustain tourism (store clerks, tour guides, janitorial staff, hotel managers, and so forth). As Ateljevic (2000: 382) rightly notes, "'consumption work' influences demands for particular 'types of employees'." Tourism is both a ritualized social practice for tourists and a site of work where people produce tourism spaces for the consumption of others. The social geographies of tourism are not only processes through which certain social relations are worked out – between tourists and nontourists for example. Tourism as a consumptive set of practices also reproduces places as tourism sites in the first place. For mid-life adults, tourism serves as a site through which they may reinforce their identities as adults. They do this by performing certain "adult roles," such as drinking and eating in particular ways (consuming alcohol, for example), going to specific sites for adults (such as adult only resorts), satisfying their own desires (traveling to places of particular interest to them), or through their own practices of parenting (and taking their children to idealized children's places). More importantly, the spaces of tourism may be thought of as sites through which social reproduction and consumption can be studied as interwoven processes. This is because, as Edensor (2007: 202) illustrates, "particular tourist contexts generate a shared set of conventions about what should be seen, what should be done, how to travel and which actions are appropriate. These embodied, shared assumptions about what constitutes appropriate behavior in particular contexts initiate tourists into the ways to be a backpacker, a package tourist or a member of a Club 18–30 [year old] holiday." In this way, then, the spaces of tourism are sites of social reproduction where people enact their identities and subjectivities as tourists in ways that can both reinforce and transgress certain norms of their gendered, raced, classed, and sexed identities.

Smashing the Binaries, Rethinking the "Crisis"

At the beginning of this chapter, I argued that social geography may be experiencing a "mid-life crisis." This is because social geographers, while often situating their work in the lives of adult subjects, rarely interrogate the geographies of mid-life adults on their own terms. The reason for this "lack" in social geography is twofold. First, social geography is relatively blind to the underlying normative adult-centeredness of its own practices. Second, social geography has failed to come to grips with what might be the "mid-life" either conceptually or empirically. To address this gap, I moved away from the notion that social geographers can easily quantify the mid-life as an age-specific category of difference, suggesting, instead, that the mid-life is a subjective and geographically relative concept that is complexly related to the processes of production, reproduction, and consumption. In particular, this chapter highlights how the social geographies of the mid-life might be examined as a broader set of processes whereby certain identities and subjectivities, particularly tied to what we might mean by the term "adult," are reproduced through everyday social practices of home and work, production and reproduction, and consumption as social reproduction. Under the weight of intense social geographic scrutiny, the divisions between these concepts break down. The naturalized links between home as *the* site of social reproduction and work as *the* site of production collapse when we examine how bodies are disciplined to reinforce the spatial distinctions between home and work. Following Hopkins and Pain (2007), this chapter also argues that it is impossible to study the geographies of the "mid-life" as independent from other aspects of the life course. This becomes abundantly clear when interrogating the home as a site of care. By examining production and reproduction as processes that involve more than "the economic" we have begun to chip away at the integrity of a binary logic that cleaves apart the experiences of mid-life adults. Although we know that intergenerational relationships are important, we can also see how certain spaces are organized to reinforce the differences that often define the terms parent and child, motherhood and fatherhood, and young and old. And, we can see how the boundaries between public and private, particularly in relation to production and reproduction, home and work, are blurred. In moving forward, then, it is important to consider how the social geographies that are realized through the life course are constructing a dynamic set of spaces, networks, and relationships that reinforce how social geographers think about the mid-life. We also want to ask how "the transitions" between child and adolescent, adolescent and adult, adult and elderly are being worked out through new geographic processes of work and home, as well as production, reproduction, and consumption.

Notes

1   In other publications, I refer to Siriporn by her nickname "Porn" (e.g. Del Casino 2006). The pronunciation of Porn is closer to Pawn (as in a chess pawn). But it is common practice to transliterate the "aw" sound as "or" when going from Thai to English.
2   It is important to note that Siriporn had a new *faen* (partner or boyfriend) when I last saw her in 2004. In fact, she had re-engaged in the streams of migrant labor with her *faen* when I went back to see her, so she was not at home. Instead, I found her son with his grandparents.
3   Jampaklay (2006) also offers an interesting discussion of the relationship between marriage and mobility/migration.

Chapter 9

Ageing and the "New" Social Geographies of Older People

Thinking Relationally about Age and Ageing in Social Geography

Studying the social geographies of the life course is not a simple and straightforward process. It is challenging to articulate when one life phase begins and another ends. Indeed, as suggested by Hopkins and Pain (2007), social geographers have to actively interrogate the "transitions" between one part of the life course and the next. The transitions from child to adult or from younger adult to older adult are contested and incomplete processes, dependent on myriad social processes and local contingencies. Put simply, time and space impact how people *think about* and *experience* age and ageing. This is not to deny the reality that bodies and minds change over the life course. Instead, it is to argue that it is important to think contextually when conceptualizing the different phases of the life course. In examining age and ageing as social and spatial processes, it is critical to remain open to the contradictions that occur as people transition from one life phase to the next. Everyone gets older but how they understand what that means will depend on where they are, what they do, and how they do it. It also depends on other people and social networks, as most do not grow old completely alone. In some places, extended family networks are an essential component of the ageing process. In other places, the ageing process is socialized through the government and is embedded in a wider network of caring-based organizations. In thinking relationally, then, about the social categories of age and the processes of ageing, social geographers should investigate these geographies as dynamic processes.

To that end, in the following section I begin by asking, "is there a geography to ageing?" Through a brief discussion of a global and national comparative of ageing, it is possible to discern some significant trends related to age and ageing geographically. Moving from a discussion of the social geographies of ageing, the next section of the chapter traces the field of geographical gerontology, focusing specifically on the geographies of ageing and older people. Social geographers have made contributions to gerontology – the biological, sociological, and geographical study of older adults and ageing – since the 1960s and 1970s when both spatial scientific and humanistic geographers began investigating the diverse geographies of ageing both across space and through places. As social geography has engaged other social theories, the geographies of age and ageing have also changed. This brief discussion sets the stage for the remainder of the chapter, which examines ageing across a number of spaces. I loosely follow the conceptual framework offered by Kearns and Andrews (2005), who suggest that social geographers investigate the geographies of ageing through several broadly conceived analytic categories, including the body, the home and the residential facility, and the landscape. Working across these analytic categories, this chapter suggests that the social geographies of growing older are complicated by the various spaces through which people experience the social processes associated with age and ageing. Moreover, the chapter signposts how the processes of age and ageing are interrelated to and complicated by other nodes of difference as well as experiences of inequality, access to services, and broader sociospatial processes of, for example, ageism. In so doing, it highlights themes and issues that are both unique to elderly populations and representative of the intergenerational connections between the so-called elderly and adult, older and younger peoples.

Is There a Geography to Ageing?

A recent study by a group of public health scholars points to a provocative and disturbing trend in the distributions of elderly populations in the US (Ezzati et al. 2008). The study suggests that in certain parts of the country average life expectancies actually decreased between 1983 and 1999. This is particularly true

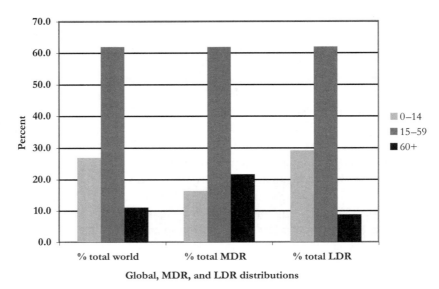

Figure 9.1   The world's population by age, 2010. MDR, "more developed" world; LDR, "less developed" world. (*Data source*: United Nations 2006.)

for women, and poor rural women specifically. The life expectancy among both men and women in the US south, which is home to the country's highest concentrations of African-American populations, is dramatically shorter than for men and women along the California coast, the upper Midwest and the northeast of the country (Kornblum 2008). More generally, this research suggests that "the higher disparity partly resulted from stagnation or increase in mortality among the worst-off segment of the population, with life expectancy for approximately 4% of the male population and 19% of the female population having had an either statistically significant decline or stagnation" (Ezzati et al. 2008). This study, which has entered the popular consciousness just as the world struggles with a global food crisis, a major economic recession, and the increasing diffusion of new (and old) epidemic diseases, suggests a need to remain vigilant and critical of the geographies of ageing: reaching an older age is not a given in many parts of the world, even though the world's population has been getting older – by 2010 it is estimated that 11 percent of the world's population will be aged 60 years or older (see Figure 9.1). As Figure 9.1 suggests, though, that 11 percent is unevenly distributed across the so-called "more developed"[1] and "less developed" regions of the world. On the one hand, the 60+ population will outstrip the 0–14 population in the world's "more developed" regions by 21.7 to 16.4 percent by 2010. In the world's "less developed" regions, on the other hand, the 0–14 population will be three times larger than the population over 60 years of age (29.2 versus 8.8 percent). Thus, while the 15–59-year-old population should be relatively consistent as a percentage of the population in 2010 across these two divergent spaces, the relative size of the younger and older populations is quite different. This raises important geographic questions, particularly because a larger 0–14 population and a large 60+ population raise different social geographic challenges and produce a unique set of questions related to the broader discussions of inequality and difference in social geography. Such a difference may also suggest why such a huge percentage of the work in geographical gerontology focuses more on the global north, where the ageing population as a percentage of the total population is so significant.

Despite the geographic differences across these two global regional spaces, population projections also suggest that an even larger percentage of the world will be over the age of 60 in both regions by 2050 (see Figure 9.2). It is estimated that 32.6 and 20.1 percent of the world's population in "more developed" and "less

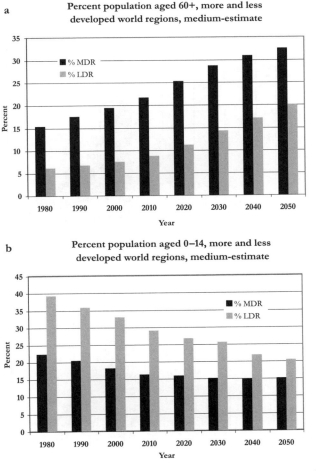

Figure 9.2   The world's ageing population. More developed regions (MDR) equate, roughly, to the global north, while less developed regions (LDR) equate, roughly, to the global south. In both cases, though, the populations have been getting older since 1980 and will continue to do so throughout the first half of the twenty-first century. (*Data source*: United Nations 2006.)

developed" regions will be over 60 years of age by 2050 respectively. This trend is coupled with a change in the percentage of people who will be between the ages of 0 and 14 in both regions as well, with that group declining between 1980 and 2050 from 22.4 to 15.2 percent in the "more developed" region and from 39.4 to 20.6 percent in the "less developed" region of the world. By 2050, the percentage of the population either under 14 or over 60 in the "more developed" region of the world will equal more than 50 percent of the total population in that region, while just over 40 percent of the population in the "less developed" world will be under 14 or over 60. Such trends raise some basic questions about the social practices associated with these different age-based categories. As McCracken and Phillips

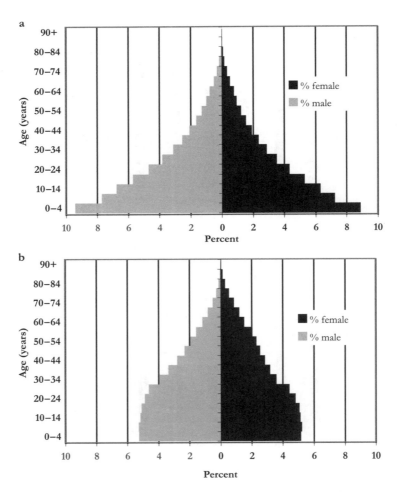

Figure 9.3 Population pyramids, 2010, for (a) a relatively young population (Afghanistan); (b) a growing population (South Africa); (c) a relatively stable population (the US); and (d) a hyper-ageing population (Italy). (*Data source*: United Nations 2006.)

(2005: 38) explain, "the major underlying cause of demographic ageing is falling fertility [birth rates]." This is coupled with "Rising life expectancy through combinations of social and medical advances [which] has led to greater numbers of people surviving into their 60s, 70s, 80s, and higher" (ibid.). More generally, what these trends demonstrate is that the world's social demographics are changing and will continue to change throughout the remainder of the first half of the twenty-first century. And, they suggest that new social geographies will likely emerge in relation to these demographic changes, begging the question of how societies will negotiate the new geographies of their ageing populations more generally.

Shifting from a global scale to a national one, Figure 9.3 shows four population pyramids that illustrate just how much *local* context affects population distributions. In Afghanistan, a country that has suffered an extended period of war and conflict over the past thirty years, a large percentage of its population is between 0 and 14, while very few people live into their fifties, sixties, and seventies. In this context, the study of age and ageing might take on a different character from that of

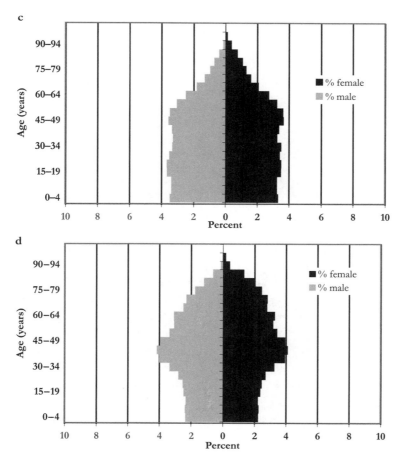

Figure 9.3   *(Cont'd)*

South Africa, which has a slightly older population and fewer people under 14 as a percentage of its total population. These two examples across the global south warn against oversimplifying analyses of ageing through macroregional comparisons across two world regions. In a similar way, it is possible to compare national demographic dynamics across the global north.[2] In this case, two population pyramids outline the projected population distributions for the US and Italy in 2010. While the US is fairly evenly distributed across its population between 0 and 64 years, Italy's distribution is dramatically skewed toward its growing older population. In fact, Italy's overall population growth is negative, meaning that it has more deaths than births. From a social geographic perspective, such a distribution begs the question of the extent to which Italy will be able to sustain itself socially or economically as its ageing population taxes social welfare services and extended familial networks. Without children and with a dwindling "mid-life" population, Italians may very well be forced to work well beyond the ages of others in the global north in order to maintain the support for their ageing population. Of course, Italy is not alone in its growing 60+ population and the problems that such a demographic outlook might create.[3] As McCracken and Phillips (2005: 47) argue, "The ageing of the aged population has huge implications for social, medical and economic policies in ageing, as levels of need and dependency tend to escalate in late old age. Even if future cohorts of the oldest old are more healthy than those of today, there will still be considerable increases in demand for services, pensions and personnel care assistance."

Box 9.1   Methodological Note: The Demographic Transition

The Demographic Transition Model (DTM) conceptualizes the relationships between births (fertility), deaths (mortality), and population change. This model is commonly used to explain population change at the national and world regional level. While the original model, first proposed by Warren Thompson in 1929, had four stages, recent demographic changes globally – particularly in countries with declining populations – now warrant a fifth category. In the first stage of the model, high birth and death rates are a result of limited access to needed resources, while the second stage is distinguished by increasing access to medical care or limited conflict (i.e. war), leading to declining death rates with stable birth rates. In the third stage, birth and death rates continue to decline, while the fourth stage is marked by a period of stability in population growth (similar to the first stage) but for very different reasons. The newly emerging "fifth category" has increasing death rates relative to birth rates, leading to negative population growth.

This model is not without its controversies, as it tends to oversimplify a much more complicated story of demographic change. First, it is sometimes theorized that all countries will go through these stages in this order. This

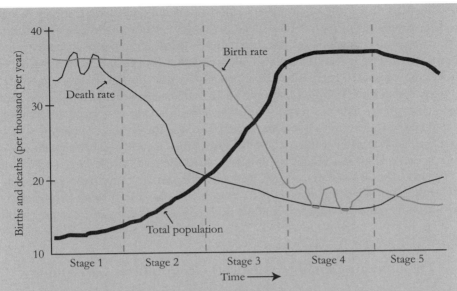

Figure 9.4   The Demographic Transition Model (DTM).

is because the model is invested within a colonial conceptual framework suggesting societies move through a set of discreet stages, which have sometimes been labeled as "premodern" to "urbanizing/industrial" to "mature industrial" to "postindustrial." In this vocabulary, all societies are striving for the postindustrial. Second, it is widely recognized that certain parts of the world are not witnessing the same declines in birth rates even as death rates also decrease. The model has been criticized for its Eurocentrism and limited vision of how fertility is socially and culturally constructed in different regional and national contexts. Nonetheless, the model, if divested from its colonial heritage, does show the trending of populations if certain social conditions of fertility and mortality are maintained. It also raises questions on how to conceptualize the relationships between fertility, mortality, and population growth and the social geographies of birth and death in different contexts.

Quick Exercise

Go to the Population Reference Bureau website (http://www.prb.org/) and download the free "World Population Data Sheet." In a group of three or four students have each person choose a different world region. For each region, trace births and deaths per thousand as well as the rate of natural increase. What can you say about the population dynamics of your region? Does your region fit into the DTM? If so, where? What is the problem with this regional approach?

This brief treatment of the diverse global and national demographics related to the world's ageing population suggests that it is important to pay attention to the complex and dynamic relationship between the geographies of age and ageing. Across the diverse spaces of the global north and global south, the meanings ascribed to certain age-based categories, the inequalities that continue to mark age-based differences, and the politics of age and ageing will become increasingly important. While we engage with the relationships between difference and inequality in more depth below, it is important to remind ourselves that the "failings of [ageing] policy [are] being felt more be women – both because of their greater numbers and life spans, and because of greater inequities inherited form the past" (Rosenberg and Everitt 2001: 164). This is often exacerbated by the experiences of, for example, race, ethnicity, ability, and sexuality. In this light, then, there is value in turning to a brief history of geographical gerontology and the study of age and ageing in social geography.

The Emerging Field of (Critical) Geographical Gerontology

At its most basic level, geographical gerontology is the spatial study of ageing and older age. This rather simple definition belies, however, the diversity and complexity of both the ageing process and social geographers' study of that process. Indeed, from its earliest inception, geographical gerontology, while often dominated by geographers interested in issues related to health, has engaged in studies that cross the epistemological and ontological approaches of social geography. Emerging in the 1970s, social geographers interested in ageing were strongly influenced by two major traditions in geography: spatial science and humanistic geography. On the side of spatial science were those scholars concerned with the spatial distributions and migration patterns of ageing populations (Golant 1972; Warnes 1982). Warne's (1982) edited collection, *Geographical Perspectives on the Elderly*,[4] travels ground familiar to spatial scientific social geographers, "with foci predominantly on the distributive features of older population and services for older population in space . . . [while] including [studies on] population movement, retirement migration, specialized housing, activity patterns, travel difficulties and the distribution and planning of service provision" (Andrews and Phillips 2005: 9). Applying a spatial scientific approach to the study of an ageing population in the UK, for example, Warnes and Law (1984) argue that diffusing elderly populations are not spread evenly across space. Mapping the 65+ population, they conclude that certain spaces are much more likely to receive elderly populations. Tying this analysis to policy, Warner and Laws also argue that the social changes related to the ageing of the UK population raise a number of important questions related to available housing for the elderly as they migrate to suburban and rural places for their retirement. Turning particularly to government policy, they further suggest that "national policies for accommodating and supporting the elderly would not normally state explicit distributional objectives. . . . They tend to encourage or discourage the segregation of the elderly into specific types of dwellings and areas. . . . From a macro-distributional perspective [however] there are grounds for attempting to minimizing the spatial disassociation of the elderly from the remainder of the population" (ibid.: 56). As a spatial scientific endeavor, then, geographical gerontology can contribute analyses of how age-based populations are becoming spatially isolated over time.

Humanistic social geographers, such as Rowles (1978a, 1986), however, employ qualitative methodologies to study older people's experience of place and their perceptions of the broader social spaces in which they live. Arguing the need to look beyond the typical studies of spatial scientists – who focus on the relationship between ageing and transportation networks, demographic changes, and housing issues – Rowles suggests that geographers could also engage in a more radical social geography by investigating questions such as: "To what extent does the spatial organization of the environment facilitate or prevent the elderly from enjoying the kind of lifestyle they deem appropriate? Are we forcing the elderly to adapt to a system that is designed exclusively for the active and the mobile? Even more serious, are we subtly and invidiously removing elderly from our society by creating an environment that reduces their flexibility and makes institutionalization almost inevitable?" (Peet and Rowles 1974: 288–9). Although Rowles focuses, like Warner and Laws, on the global north, his work suggests that a social geography of ageing concentrate on a variety of spaces often marginalized by a quantitative geographical gerontology, including home spaces and residential care facilities as well as the urban (and rural) environment more generally. Rowles's extensive work in the area of geographical gerontology utilizes detailed qualitative studies of older people's experiences of their homes and neighborhoods. In so doing, he has advocated humanistic geography's tradition of "revealing meanings, values, and intentionalities" (Rowles 1978b: 190), encouraging geographers to use "simple *description*, [and] the presentation of raw experiences in an account of the participant's lives and what had transpired among us" (ibid.: 181, original emphasis). As Rowles argues, this intensive research experience with older people is incredibly valuable for him personally because it has challenged his own assumptions about the lives of older people: he has learned that to understand how older people perceive the world around them we have to ask them what they think and do. While this might seem a rather simple and perhaps obvious conclusion today, Rowles's work remains innovative because of its critical stance toward knowledge production. More generally, his work also points out that we cannot simply apply our own generational assumptions to the lives of others.

Following the work of Rowles and the humanistic turn in geographical gerontology, other social geographers began to extend the study of ageing through an engagement with critical social and cultural theory. Harper and Laws (1995) encourage an extended conversation between geographic gerontology and social theory so that social geographers might further interrogate the "political economy of care, the role of the state in service provision, gender roles and stereotypes and peoples' life courses" (Andrews et al. 2007: 153). Following this call for more a thorough engagement between geographical gerontology and critical social theory, feminist geographers began to provide studies of the lifeworlds of elderly women in places such as Canada (Dyck et al. 2005), while other geographers turned their attention to the intergenerational dynamics between elderly parents and their adult children and the social politics of migration in developing countries such as Thailand (Knodel and Saengtienchai 2007). Out of this work, feminist social geographers, such as Sachs (1993: 170), argue that the social and spatial experiences of age and ageing are relational, tied to community and organizational identities and practices that develop between "elder residents . . . [and] their new, younger neighbors." In tracing the changing demographics of one town in West Virginia, Sachs demonstrates how the accumulation of knowledge tied to systems of informal economic (and social) exchange, which develops between women over time, does not always translate across generational boundaries. Over time, in fact, as younger women migrate into the area, "older people [may be] becoming disenfranchised within their own community as a result of changed economic conditions and diminishing numbers" (ibid.).

Importantly, such work suggests that geographical gerontology is much more than the study of "frailty or ill-health" (Hugman 1999: 194). Indeed, as Hugman argues, "Although ageing is a major factor in the incidence of disability and ill-health, the overall rates are less than 50 per cent below the age of 85 years and the incidence does not begin to increase rapidly until the age of 75 [in the UK]" (ibid.). Thus, ageing might be culturally identified as a debilitating process, yet, on a day-to-day basis, many people live healthy lives as they age. Put more directly, just because someone is 65 years old it does not mean they will be ill, feel sick or frail, or have to deal with extended managed care. In this way, geographical gerontology can (and should) work in conjunction with a broader "critical gerontology," which seeks to critically examine dominant research paradigms of ageing in the social sciences (Biggs et al. 2003). This interdisciplinary research is important because, as Katz (2003: 26) averred,

> The predominance of biomedically-driven funding policies, the privatization of health care resources, the priorities of corporate and pharmaceutical research, and the popularity of an alarmist demography that blames growing aging populations for the fiscal collapse of social programs, all contribute to the marginaliztion of critical thought. At the same time, much gerontological research is increasingly affiliated with government project to *responsibilize* a new senior citizenry to care for itself in the wake of neoliberal programs that divest Western welfare states of their health, educational, and domestic life course commitments and extend their political power to new areas of micro-scale management and community affairs (original emphasis).

Following Katz, and a broader critical gerontological approach, ageing should be conceptualized as a process complicated by the everyday social and spatial practices of categories, such as "old age" and "elderly." Even more than this, social geographers can investigate how ageing is worked out through any number of spaces, from the body to the home to the community and organization to produce both dominant and resistant possibilities to a unitary ageing subject, one that is increasingly envisioned as socially and spatially marginal as well as materially and socially "unproductive."

The Variegated Spaces of Ageing

Kearns and Andrews (2005) suggest that the study of the social geographies of ageing operates across a number of spaces from the body to the home to the organization to the landscape. As we have already traced throughout this volume, these spaces are fully interrelated. How can we think about the body without also considering how bodyspaces move through and are constructed within the social relations of home or work? That said, there are certain social geographies that are worked through each one of these spaces, and this provides us an opportunity to study how age and ageing are constructed and experienced both within and across a dynamic set of spaces. The remainder of this section loosely applies the conceptual framework provided by Kearns and Andrews to theorize the social geographies of ageing. Social geographers can and should investigate the uniqueness of these different spaces as well as the politics that operate through the body and the home, the organization and the landscape, thereby untangling how the ageing process is socially constructed and materially experienced through everyday practice.

Modifying and changing ageing bodies

> Bodies may not fit idealized representations on account of being considered ill, impaired, disabled, poor, dowdy, sexually "deviant," "ugly," or the "wrong" colour. Often, however, people do not fit idealized representations on account of not adhering to society's exacting standards of size, shape and weight. More often than not people's bodies (or "bits" of their bodies) are considered too large, too short, too chubby, too heavy or too flabby (Longhurst 2005: 248).

As people get older, their bodies change. Taken alone, this is not an extraordinarily provocative statement. As social geographers have argued, though, the body is both material and social, constructed through the everyday experiences of its physiological changes and constituted through the discourses of power that define, articulate, and regulate what is "appropriate" and "normal" about it. "Hence," Kearns and Andrews (2005: 15) argue, "the body is both a geography unto itself and is assigned meaning through the geographies in which it dwells. The nursing home, for instance, is a common institutional basis of everyday life for many older people. Here, the body becomes a surface of signs, monitored for evidence of varied concerns for stakeholders – from the resident's own maintenance of identity to family members' 'lingering sense of responsibility after placement'" (citing Gubrium and Holstein 1999: 520). As such, within and across different social and spatial contexts, older people experience their material and social bodies differently. As people age, they must contend with the physicalities that come along with the ageing process, including the extended lines, graying hair, or changing skin tones and textures. Also, they are confronted with the changing meanings ascribed to their bodies and the social constructions associated with the ageing body. As Mowl et al. (2000: 190) explain, "bodily characteristics are especially important in the definition of people as 'old' by others." A central question, then, is: how is age experienced relationally – i.e. in relation to so-called others – in and across the spaces of the everyday life-worlds of ageing? With this in mind, the body politics of ageing and how people negotiate these politics on a day-to-day basis are the focus of this section.

In moving forward, however, it is necessary to consider that ageing is not a universal category that can be applied similarly across nodes of difference. Women and men, for example, are clearly asked to age in different ways. Women's ageing bodies may be constructed as a sign of decline whereas men's bodies may become more "distinguished" as they grow older (Hugman 1999). Ageing is also interpreted and experienced differently across the categories of sexuality, as ageism – or the "culturally prescribed sets of norms and prejudices about people and behavior at various stages in the life course" (Mowl et al. 2000: 190) – is performed differently through hetero- and homonormative spaces. In this context, bodily differences and experiences across generations create distinct spaces for the performance of "older" and "younger" gay and lesbian identities (Rosenfeld 1999). This might marginalize ageing gay men from certain spaces of the city or neighborhood, either through self-choice – older gay men choose to remove themselves from certain spaces – or through a broader social stigma – older gay men may feel isolated in spaces catering to younger gay men (or vice versa). At the same time, while the ageing body may be constructed through a discourse of weakness and frailty in some societies (particularly the societies where ageing is tied to production and retirement), in others it denotes an important site of respect and wisdom (particularly in societies where extended familial and social networked relations are still an essential characteristic of everyday life). Thus, while it is true that in many spaces of the global north, "nursing and residential homes represent, both literally and in terms of image, concealment and disengagement of the body from society" (Kearns and Andrews 2005: 16), in other contexts, such as Ghana, Africa, "Traditionally, the parent–child bond does not weaken on the child's marriage, and it is this which provides security in old age" (Harper 2006: 243). The ageing body, therefore, is not an inherently "good" or "bad" thing; it is a biological process that is widely interpreted and contested.

Within the context of geographical gerontology and the social geographies of ageing more generally, the intellectual focus has centered predominantly on the relationship between bodily change and experiences of health. This work has been particularly interested in investigating how ageing people negotiate their changing bodies as they become more "frail" or enter a stage of "dementia" wherein they might begin to lose control of their bodies (Nair 2005; also see Chapter 4). This work points to how "in western societies, ageing bodies tend to be identified with physical and mental decline, closeness to death, economic and physical dependency, and social isolation" (Mowl et al. 2000: 189). Equally important, but of less concern in most geographical gerontology, is how people negotiate their bodily changes through a literal reworking and modification of the body. Virginia Blum, in her book

Flesh Wounds: The Culture of Cosmetic Surgery, critically interrogates the practices of ageing in relation to surgical changes to the physical body, suggesting that the ageing body is constantly working back and forth across its material and social definitions (Blum 2003). As she argues:

> As for the social experience of one's own identity, surgery is presented as a necessary corollary to the oddly relentless coercions of a youth-and-beauty-centered culture, despite the actual statistical aging of the United States. That we're desperate to be seen as fit and energetic and young and attractive makes sense when we are told on so many tacit and overt levels that we will find neither work nor sexual partners without these attributes; moreover, we are fated to lose both if we don't retain at least the superficial vestiges of the original assets. As a result of such extreme cultural imperatives, we cannot help but locate who we are on the surface of our bodies. The "culture of cosmetic surgery," paradoxically enough is a postbody culture inasmuch as the material body seems to lose all its pathetic vulnerability in the face of a host of medical/technological advances meant to keep you perfect from the beginning to the end, indefinitely. In this sense, the body itself is both more and less important (ibid.: 49).

In this context, the body becomes both a site for the material *and* social reconstruction of the self (Grosz 1994). As cosmetic surgery becomes more ubiquitous in the US, the body becomes "less important" because as it is modified people no longer have to simply "let it go." At the same time, the body emerges as "more important" because it is such an essential part of the tensions that exist between the differences of "youth" and "age." Indeed, as Blum goes on to trace, women (and men) are engaging in plastic surgery at a younger and younger age, hoping to maintain a youthful appearance throughout the mid *and* later stages of the life course. The practices of plastic surgery thus illustrate how the notion of an interior ageing self – the internal workings of the body – can be adjusted on the surface to make one "feel better" about one's age, health, and identity both personally and socially. Although quite different, this struggle to rework the body as it ages also manifests itself in the clothes that people choose to wear as they age; they may want to rework the surface body to remain "in style" and "youthful" as they get older (also see Twigg 2008). The clothes that people wrap around their bodies are thus tied to the contours of that body, which can also be made and remade through the addition of breast material or calf implants or the removal of fatty tissue and "unwanted" cartilage.[5] As the geographies of consumption suggest more broadly, then, how we practice our consumer identity is also intimately tied to how we conceptualize our own subjective experience as "men" and "women," "straight" and "gay," or "young" and "old" (see Chapter 8). Of course, the ability to modify the body is highly contingent on the social and material location of that body in the first place, as access to the biomedical "fixes" that can transform the external body to maintain its "youthfulness" is highly unequal.

Clearly, the ageing body is highly contested; age and ageing are much more than a linear progression marking out time. Also clear is that it is difficult, if not impossible, to discuss the material body outside of the social one. The ageing body is not an isolated space. Instead, it is worked and reworked in relation to a myriad number of other social and spatial relations. With this in mind, we shift our focus from the body to the home and organization. We do so, however, without losing the body as an important geographic space of experience because the body, after all, is often the place through which the processes of age and ageing are understood.

Box 9.2   "Trans Individuals": Ageing in Your Own Body

Social geographers have paid limited attention to trans individuals: "defined as people who live as members of the opposite sex to which they were born or as people who live *between* the categories male/female or man/woman" (Browne 2007b: 116). Yet, social geographers interested in the body and the politics of sexuality should be interested in the spatialities of trans individuals. After all, the category of "trans" challenges "the process whereby the dichotomy of gendered norms are read off from what is taken as a permanent and uniform sexed body" (ibid.). Moreover, trans individuals upset the spatial structures of heternormative gendered identities. In interviewing trans women and their experiences of public bathroom spaces in the UK, Browne (2004) notes, for example, that women who do not appear, on the surface, as gender normed women (i.e. they appear to look like men) may be socially and physically ostracized from women's bathrooms. Such violences are not isolated to public places, such as toilets, but manifest themselves in personal familial and other social relationships – as people who transgress the boundaries of the male/female dichotomy are ostracized and/or abused, both mentally and physically.

It is important to note, as well, that being "trans" is not a unitary category, as people choose to age differently in relation to their social and physical body. "Some trans individuals may seek to reinforce gender/sex categorizations such that gendered understandings result in surgical procedures that 'correct' gender dysphoria. . . . Others, for numerous reasons, exist between man/woman, for example taking hormones but not undergoing surgical procedures that (re)construct genitalia" (ibid.). Gallagher's (2008) study of transgendered sex tourism in Thailand illustrates just how complex the lives of those who transgress typical gendered norms might be. As he notes, is it difficult to find "older" transsexual women – pre- and postoperative – in Phuket, an active tourism resort. The economic options for trans individuals in Thailand are limited and the sex tourism industry is not only difficult but also dangerous. Moreover, the difficult transitions and the complex social relationships that are part of the everyday lives of trans individuals in Thailand mean that life may be cut short by health concerns such as HIV or mental health issues, which sometimes lead to suicide. Just the fact, though, that Gallagher was hard pressed to find an "older" trans individual in Phuket should raise questions for our social geographies and turn our attention to how we might begin to understand, think about, and study trans lives and spaces.

Quick Exercise

On your own, make a list of the "norms" associated with the gender categories "men" and "women." How do people talk about people who transgress those categorical boundaries? In a group, share your list and then begin a discussion about how spaces may be organized to reinforce a dualistic notion of gender and sexuality.

Ageing in and through the home and residential care

As people get older, they experience their changing bodies and the places in which they live differently. This is not confined to a brief period at the end of one's life; it is an ongoing process that occurs over the entire lifecourse. Within the broader confines of geographical gerontology and the social geographies of ageing, Kearns and Andrews (2005: 16) point out that "the majority of research on ageing, health and place has focused on the experience, meaning and construction of two locales: the home and supportive residential care facilities." Indeed, it is "the home" and "the residential care facility" that play a significant role in the lives of older people, as they may become confined over time to a different geography mediated by their physical and mental abilities (Dyck et al. 2005; Wiles 2005b; Andrews et al. 2007; Milligan et al. 2007). There is a distinctive set of social geographies related to the intersections between ageing and home as well as ageing and the broader spaces of care. While Chapter 8 already traced theories of "home," highlighting some of the important aspects of home as a site of care, this chapter further disentangles the ways in which home operates as a space of care *and* difference for ageing and older populations. Working within the health-place literature, scholars have long argued that the home is not simply a site of confinement for older people (e.g. Rowles 1978a). In fact, the home can be a site of progressive politics, self-affirmation, and autonomy. "[T]he home," as Mowl et al. (2000: 195) argue, may be "viewed as a site of resistance to ageing in that it is a place in which independence can be maintained in the face of ill health or disability." As people age they may be more reticent to move from their home and into another space of care, such as a residential care facility, and this complicates the relationship between home and ageing identities. After all, the material and emotional processes of ageing are intimately tied to broader understandings of the spaces in which individuals experience older age (Wiles 2005b). This, Wiles (2005b: 87) argues, is because "For many, the difference is a matter of 'living' at home as opposed to 'waiting to die' at an institution." The powerful contrast that marks out home and other institutional spaces of ageing, then, suggests the need to further interrogate the social constructions of these spaces as well as the material realities of growing older in the "home" and "the residential facility."

More broadly, Wiles (2003, 2005a, 2005b) traces the complicated relationships between home and care for ageing populations, arguing that while older people may have long-time and intimate connections to their homes, as home and care become intertwined the emotional geographies attached to that particular place become more complicated. Put more directly, Wiles (2005a: 101) stresses that "receiving care at home impacts on the daily rhythms of all members of the household. Many older persons grieve the loss of their home as a place in which they could socialize with family and friends, as well as changing their homes physically to meet their needs of care." Care in the home is further complicated by the fact that it is maintained often through both "formal" (e.g. state-sponsored) and "informal" (e.g. family and friends) social networks and relations (Wiles 2005b).

> Attitudes to the role of family relative to the state and the market in the provision of home-based care to frail elderly people vary widely between cultures, places and times. For example, in Sweden the assumption is that the state will provide most care for the elderly . . . whereas in Japan and Korea the assumption is that family will take primary responsibility. . . . Even this is subject to change: in Sweden, cutbacks to services in the 1980s and 1990s have led commentators to argue the state is placing responsibility on families to provide care; in Japan, a mandatory long-term care social insurance system with the goal of the "socialisation" or state assumption of care for the elderly introduced in 2000 now caters to around 10% of the population aged 65 and over. . . . In some countries, the state provides funding either to care recipients or to "informal" care-givers to provide care, thus blurring the commonly held perceptions of the distinction between formal and informal, paid and unpaid care. For example, in Britain, in Austria, in Denmark, in the United States and in the Netherlands, there are various forms of provision for the compensation of care work given by families or other informal providers (Wiles 2005b: 87–8).

Dyck (1995, 1999; Dyck et al. 2005) has also examined the diversity of spaces that women living with chronic illnesses must negotiate as they manage their day-to-day lives, including their homes. Her research suggests that any space of care, from the home to the workplace to the clinic, does not exist in isolation of broader relationships between health and care, space and identity. Instead, all spaces of care are managed through socially produced knowledges regarding ageing bodies as well as healthy and ill identities. Dyck et al.'s (2005) study demonstrates that home care for elderly, low-income women is complicated by the fact that their care is being managed by others in and through a number of spaces of health and care, for example.

How the ill or disabled body is lived is shaped by its interpretation and management at various scales: through diagnostic practices in a physician's office; the encoding of definitions of disability (and therefore of "need"), eligible levels of care and delimitation of care-worker tasks in policy documentation at the provincial level [in Canada]; the allocation of health care funding at federal and provincial levels; and the wider machinations of capital accumulation and global economic and political processes that construct conditions within which labour marker characteristics – and even health itself – are constructed (Dyck et al. 2005: 182).

The home spaces of these women are part of a much broader landscape of care, which includes the public health and social welfare sectors. Their homes and the management of their health are thus neither fully private nor fully public. As these women lose certain control over their physical bodies they find themselves subject to new regimes of control over their social bodies as their self-presentation – as "groomed," for example – is taken up by others. Importantly, then, in the wake of a massive restructuring of health care across the globe, the home is a vital site of care as disinvestment in broader social services increases.[6] In certain spaces this divestment in social services is linked to naive assumptions about how home-based care operates within certain social groups. The Canadian government makes certain "assumptions that care of older native people" within Aboriginal or First Nations communities is already provided by relatives. As such, the government assumes that ageing populations in these communities are "not in need of support." This has been "leading to a lack of support for their care-givers, most of whom are women" (Wiles 2005b: 93). As Wiles rightly points out, and other geographers also note (e.g. Milligan 2000), the gendering of care in the home cuts across social spaces and identities, placing an additional burden on women who may have to quit their jobs to care for elderly family members.

Box 9.3 Welfare Geographies and the Spatial Politics of Care

In a recent editorial in *Environment and Planning A*, Lynn Staeheli and Michael Brown ask: "Where has welfare gone?" This rather simple question suggests that the geographies of welfare have been submerged under broader discussions of political economy with less attention paid to the mundane but no less important "work" of care and caring. Staeheli and Brown want to broaden how geographers analyze and conceptualize care, focusing attention, in particular, on a feminist geography of welfare, care, and justice. They do so in order to ask how it might be possible to create "concepts of justice [that] are . . . *inclusive*" (ibid.: 773, original emphasis). Importantly, "because marginalization is sustained through relationships in a range of social, political, economic, and geographical settings," they further argue, "a norm of inclusion also requires that we look beyond legal standing in the public sphere to consider the ways that actions and relationships in the private sphere constitute political subjects" (ibid.). Working from a feminist theoretical position, therefore, Staeheli and Brown suggest that welfare and care are "more than" public endeavors, they are "located . . . in the market, the home, and the community – in short, everywhere" (ibid.).

As Brown (2003: 833) stresses in his study of hospice (end of life) care, the relationships between welfare, care, and justice are of growing importance because "There has been a clear spatial shift in death away from hospital and towards the home" in the US. The move of care from hospital to home, particularly for those who are in the last stages of their life, creates a number of spatial paradoxes, Brown argues, as professional hospice workers are invited into the home to help family, friends, and partners with the process of dying. First, home hospice is paradoxical because it is both a "public" and a "private" practice: the home becomes public as people come in to perform "hospice." Second, home hospice is a space of paradox because the "public care of dying" is increasingly being taken care of by "private health care organizations." Home hospice, therefore, is not simply about caring for someone during the last stages of their life. It is also a site through which social geographers might examine the very complicated relationships among the deinstitutionalization of death and dying, the intersections between death and dying as both a private and a public practice, and the politics of care, welfare, and justice. Who has access to the practices of home hospice, and the personalized, yet public, care provided by this service, varies dramatically across space.

Quick Exercise

Design a brief semi-structured interview instrument that focuses on issues of terminal and end-of-life care. Next, locate someone – a friend, acquaintance, or family member – you can interview about his or her experience as a caregiver. Tape the interview if possible, then transcribe it. Finally, code the interview, allowing themes and codes to emerge as you read through the transcript.

In some cases, as frailty or certain physical and mental disabilities affect ageing people, and familial and other social networks are unable to provide assistance (or in-home care becomes too expensive), older people may need to move into "residential care facilities" or RCFs (Kearns and Andrews 2005: 18). Cutchin (2003: 1081) traces this "move" from home into other institutionalized spaces of care, suggesting that the geographies of care facilities are complicated by a number of nodes of social difference, including "class status." Furthermore, Cutchin's work suggests that lifecourse transitions are conceptually important when examining ageing and eldercare. This is particularly true because not all people need to move immediately from their home into a nursing facility. Instead, older people, and this is particularly true in the US, may manage their health through a variety of transitional institutional spaces from "adult day centers (ADCs)" to "assisted living residences (ALRs)" (ibid.: 1077). While both spaces serve as transitional sites in the lifecourse for "those who need some assistance in the continuation of a somewhat independent life in their places and do not want to move into, or are not ready for, a nursing home" (ibid.), many older people may chose an ADC over an ALR simply because of cost. Importantly, though, in both contexts, Cutchin argues that "When participants arrive at the center, they enter into their community to belong, see, do, help, and be cared for. A larger part of belonging is the way staff treat older adults in their care" (ibid.: 1084). These organizations thus serve as transitional spaces, not only at the individual and bodily level, but at the level of the social as well – creating new social nodes through which networks of ageing can be constructed and developed. This does not assume, however, that these spaces are free of the broader socialities in which they are embedded; it is easy to identify, for example, intergenerational and intragenerational tensions and conflicts within these spaces of care. In reality, the "power and right to make important decisions about place are contested among older adults, family, staff, and management [of facilities] in intricate ways . . . it appears that management . . . has the upper hand in making decisions about moving a resident to another level of care. This is not to suggest a great deal of solidarity or militancy by residents . . . but there was a frustration among some residents who did not feel they can make their ALR a place they want to be" (ibid.: 1086). There is a danger, and a problem, that with eldercare comes the subjectification of older people as "children," whose rights to make decisions about their own lives may be slowly removed as they are "managed" through the institutional spaces of residential care. There is a need to eschew an essentialist identity position for "the elderly," which constructs this social group as a unitary whole with an identical (and natural) physiological and social developmental trajectory (i.e. all older people are elderly and all elderly people need X type of care). Just consider, for example, that within the confines of residential facilities tensions emerge within and among residents. "A common concern of more mentally and physically fit older adults," Cutchin argues, "centered on the frail population in their midst. Some research participants voiced that spending time and sharing space with the more vulnerable was bothersome and troubling" (ibid.: 1086). As people age, therefore, new nodes of difference emerge, which might be deployed to construct unequal access to new communal social networks and spaces, creating sites of difference within sites of difference.

In a different context, Bartlett and Phillips (1997) show how China's changing urban economies – in which it was typical for families to care for their ageing parents – have shifted the care of elderly people out of the family home and into "residential care homes." The response has been the diversification of health care spaces operating across the urban landscape in Chinese cities.

In residential care for elderly people, a range of types of homes is evolving at the national level. These include small, local street based homes in which conditions and care are meager. Next come rather larger hostels and, at the apex of the provision, a number of "first grade" and some particularly high quality homes which enjoy both public and private income (ibid.: 154).

Cross-cutting these new spaces of care are the social politics of class that continue to evolve as China rethinks its own relationship to socialism, given that China is de-emphasizing state-based welfare for privately organized health care and social welfare options. The changing nature of eldercare in China is also linked to the longstanding one-child policy, which has resulted in single children needing to be responsible for two ageing parents. These realities are forcing ageing adults in China, particularly in urban areas, to make "their own non-traditional and independent plans for their futures" (Zhang and Goza 2006: 161). In this context, then, the social politics of fertility and the realities of the broader demographics of China are impacting the longstanding cultural practices of filial piety – respect (and care) for one's parents.

As new spaces of eldercare emerge in and across the so-called developed and developing worlds, we have to consider the broader discourses of identity and subjectivity that undergird the social values assigned to those who are both "responsible" and "productive" citizens. The reorganization of care from the home in the context of China to the residential facility may indeed suggest that elderly bodies be placed "out-of-the-way" as families see the elderly as a burden rather than as an essential part of the larger social fabric of the family and the community. While this may be driven, in large part, by economic realities, and the changing nature of work for caregivers, those economic changes are intimately interwoven into the social narratives and spaces of home, work, and care. These narratives are changing as new social realities, identities, and subjectivities are being enacted in relation to changing local and global economic conditions and systems.

Making space for ageing

With the broader literature in geographical gerontology there remains a debate between the notion that ageing adults are marginalized in society through the construction of spaces of isolation, such as RCFs, and that ageing adults enjoy and choose to be part of spaces of difference that exclude them from other mid-life-adult and children-centered spaces. Underpinning this debate are the social geographies of mobility, migration, and retirement, which suggest that older adults, particularly those who may no longer work, are seeking out new community spaces that serve their own generational and leisured interests. Indeed, as Laws (1995, 1997) and Mansvelt (1997) have both pointed out, the production of new spaces, such as retirement communities, and activities, such as leisure, is intimately tied to the consumptive identities of ageing populations, particularly those of middle- and upper-class backgrounds. The notion that one can retire from work, of course, is already a class-based reality. At the same time, the notion that retiring or leisure are post-productive is highly contested among ageing populations, who see their new community spaces as enabling an "active adult" identity (McHugh and Larson-Keagy 2005). As McHugh and Larson-Keagy suggest in their discussion of "Sunbelt retirement" in the southwest of the US, "Retirees who flocked to Sunbelt retirement communities [in the 1960s and 1970s] thought themselves to be pioneers forging a new way of life, disproving stereotypes of older age as decline and decrepitude" (ibid.: 247). Mansvelt (1997: 291–2) describes a similar narrative among "Pekaha" (New Zealanders of European ethnic background), who see " 'Real' leisure, leisure activity constructed as non-work . . . [as] idleness, inactivity, laziness, ageing and retirement." As such, "Constructions of leisure as work appeared to be prominent in resisting what individuals felt were stereotypical representations of being old. 'Real' leisure was seen as the antithesis of value and usefulness" (ibid.). That ageing populations are not necessarily "economic drains" but may actually be "economic boosts" to local places because of their powerful consumer identities means that, particularly in countries with large ageing populations, "communities across the nation [of the US, for example], are developing strategies to attract retirees with the intent of capturing the multiplier effects of the retiree dollar" (Laws 1996: 172). Rural, urban, and suburban landscapes are being reworked as new spaces of ageing are constructed – in both material and social terms – to serve later life adults.

The spaces of "the retirement community" – neighborhoods either exclusive to or dominated by certain age-based cohorts – are relatively new social constructs that allow ageing populations to reconstitute their identities as oppositional to those older adults who live in RCFs or who are confined to their home and home-based care (Hugman 1999). Retirement spaces, that is, challenge broader representations of older peoples as frail and dependent (Laws 1996). "The material form of the 'retirement community' becomes, to some extent, a site of resistance: a place in which elderly people resist ageist stereotypes by asserting a new identity" (Laws 1996: 183). At the same time, "When these communities brush up against a non-retiree population they can develop into very real sites of struggles; places in which young and old (supposedly) argue over school and property taxes" (ibid.), for example, because older populations may be less interested in supporting the social services of younger generations (also see McHugh 2007). These intergenerational tensions are, in part, a result of the social and spatial forces of ageism that have marginalized ageing populations in the first place. In thinking through the spaces of retirement, however, we must also be conscious of the fact that these spaces serve to maintain other nodes of difference based on, for example, class and race. This is dramatically clear if one looks at retirement communities throughout Phoenix, Arizona (McHugh and Larson-Keagy 2005). As shown in Table 9.1, McHugh and Larson-Keagy (2005) illustrate the "whiteness" of three large retirement communities in the Phoenix area, suggesting that "This narrow banding, while it breeds camaraderie and collective identity, has been subject to criticism . . . [as] a 'plasticized' place, a dreary world devoid of youth and spontaneity, an excessively planned and

Table 9.1 Selected demographic and housing characteristics: three retirement communities and the Phoenix Metro Area overall, 2000

	Sun City	Sun City West	Sun Lakes	Phoenix Metro Area
Race (%)				
White	98.1	98.5	98.1	76.9
African-American	0.7	0.5	0.8	3.6
American Indian	0.1	0.1	0.2	2.1
Asian and Pacific Islander	0.4	0.3	0.4	2.3
Other race	0.1	0.1	0.3	12.1
Two or more races	0.6	0.5	0.2	3.1
Hispanic or Latino (%)				
No	99.3	99.6	99.2	74.9
Yes	0.7	0.4	0.8	25.1
Income (1999)				
Median household ($)	32,508	43,347	43,634	44,752
Per capita ($)	25,935	32,049	33,394	21,907
Percent below poverty line	4.6	1.8	2.8	12.0
Housing				
Percent owner-occupied	88.9	95.4	96.0	68.0
Median value ($)	92,300	141,900	144,200	119,600
Percent without a mortgage	66.9	71.3	53.5	20.8

Source: McHugh and Larson-Keagy (2007: 245), based on data drawn from the US Bureau of the Census 2000 Summary File 3 (SF 3), reprinted with permission.

immaculate community where inhabitants are 'free to follow the rules'" (ibid.: 246, citing Laws 1995). Of course, these communities are home to both permanent residents and "snowbirds," people who winter in warmer climates and summer back in their home communities. These migratory patterns of temporary movement between two homes are striking, as they signal the importance that social networks, beyond the spaces of retirement, play in the lives of ageing adults. "The vast of majority of snowbirds with children at home," McHugh (2007: 300) argues, "expressed a desire to continue circulating, echoing the adage of family is a tie that binds." On the other hand, "Those without children in their state of origin were more likely to entertain permanent residence in Arizona" (ibid.). The issue of extended familial networks is complicated by the fact that many Sun City, Arizona retirement communities restrict entry based on age, including children and grandchildren. This demands, then, that such retirees must travel if they are to maintain intergenerational connections between themselves and their families.

Ageing also cuts across other nodes of difference, including sexuality. As critical social gerontologists have long noted, the spaces of ageing are often informed by broader heteronormative assumptions about who is living in ageing spaces (Tolley

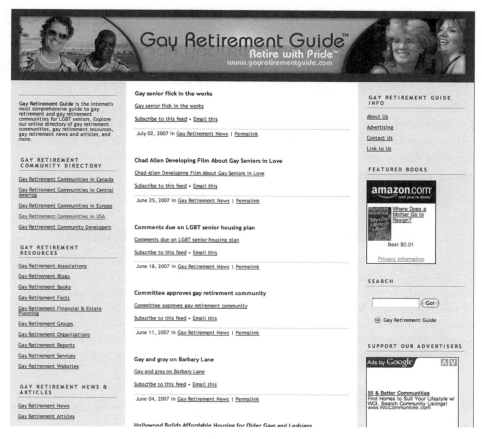

Figure 9.5 Gay Retirement Guide, Retire with Pride website. (Downloaded May 1, 2008 from http://www.gayretirementguide.com/, reprinted with permission.)

and Ranzijn 2006). Older LGBT peoples are thus also carving out spaces of ageing and retirement in ways that parallel the practices of straight, white couples in Sun City, Arizona, in places such as Florida, with developments emerging in "Boston, San Francisco, Santa Fe, and Palm Springs" (McHugh and Larson-Keagy 2005: 254). The "gay retirement community" is also expanding further, taking on a global flavor, as a snapshot from the "Gay Retirement Guide" website can attest (Figure 9.5). With links to retirement possibilities in Canada, Central America (Mexico), Europe, and the US, this site highlights the growing and dynamic possibilities of retirement for "LGBT seniors." The links across this site also suggest, however, that issues of ageing among LGBT retirement communities parallel many of the issues that non-LGBT communities also face – to include intergenerational conflicts, the plasticity of the retirement experience, and its social exclusionary practices.

The complex activism associated with the fight against ageism may create tensions and spaces of exclusion for later life adults who cannot maintain an "active" lifestyle.

Moreover, the social geographies of exclusion that are so powerful in some retirement community spaces are producing, on the one hand, new landscapes of health and vitality for older adults, and landscapes devoid of intergenerational possibilities and connections, on the other. In its extreme, then, the new landscapes of retirement may serve to cleave apart extended familial relationships and minimize the possibilities of a politics of inclusion that works across and against ageism and ageist practices. If they are actively engaged, however, McHugh (2007) has shown how these new spaces of retirement might be brought into dialogue with surrounding community spaces to work across so-called generational divides. This requires an active set of practices that would work against the calcification of the social and spatial boundaries that are becoming more common across generations.

Older Geographies and the Politics of Anti-Ageism

[T]he civic engagement narrative extends into old age rewards for public activity and not private acts of sustenance and nurture, including self-nurturing, without which life could not continue. Its emphasis on the fit and healthy further divides the "third" and the "fourth" ages and deepens the social devaluation of those no longer able to make recognizable contributions. It speaks to some lives – the relatively prosperous and healthy – while eliding the most vulnerable. It reflects an uneasy mix of obligation, expectation, and choice (Minkler and Holstein 2008: 197).

Within the broader literature in critical gerontology and geographical gerontology more specifically, there remains a tension around what action – political or social, economic or cultural – social geographers should be engaged with when it comes to our ageing populations. In Minkler and Holstein's reading of the current movement to increase the "civic engagement" of older peoples in everyday political practice, they suggest that underlying this participatory call to arms is an unintended consequence that reinforces the so-called public productive over the private nonproductive. This echoes the debates and concerns traced in Chapter 8 around the politics of production and reproduction for mid-life adults. Returning, then, to the discussion of social justice and social movements in Chapter 6, it is important to ask: what does a politics of ageing look like? How do we create a new spatiality that not only respects people's contributions across the lifecourse but also allows for participation in and across age-based communal identities? This is not an easily resolvable concern. Ageing people are no less subject to the broader social and spatial politics of race, class, gender, sexuality, and ability than someone in their so-called early or mid-life. Indeed, it is these "intersectionalities" (Hopkins and Pain 2007: 290) with which we want to concern ourselves as social geographers. Age and ageing, after all, are not unitary and singular categories, and the experiences of ageing in and across the spaces of care or retirement, family, and community are complex and multifaceted. A politics of ageing should first and foremost identify the intersectional possibilities – across nodes of difference – as well as the relational construction of age and ageing. Further, cross-comparative examinations of ageing can and should tease apart and break down the arbitrary boundaries of young and old, productive and post-productive that currently distinguish the everyday social geographies of ageing. In this way, we can move away from demands that a new "civically engaged" later life adult meet the expectations of a narrowly and mid-lifecentric productive political and economic citizen. Instead, we can begin to revel in the possibilities, knowledges, and experiences that come out of and emerge through the life course.

Notes

1   I use these terms because this is how the United Nations identifies a broadly conceived global north and global south. This conceptual language – of developed and developing – is highly problematic and has been criticized by numerous scholars, particularly scholars critical of typical development discourse (for a classic critique of this language see Escobar 1995). I leave these concepts in quotation marks, then, to highlight their contested nature (see extended discussion in Box 1.2).
2   Rosenberg and Everitt (2001) offer a sophisticated discussion of the social geographies of ageing in Canada, investigating ageing across a variety of nodes of difference (gender, race, class). Their extended research utilizes a spatial analytic approach to argue that planners and social geographers need to examine how they envision the spatial organization of ageing.
3   For an extended discussion of these issues more generally, see Harper (2006), and for specifics on Italy, see p. 149.
4   It is common practice to describe ageing populations as "elderly" in the broader geronotogical literature. This term, however, has been deprivileged recently because of its cultural equation with frailty and disability.
5   Holliday and Cairnie (2007) argue that for both men and women such surgeries are investment in "bodily capital."
6   Institutionalized care is not only limited, it is expensive, leaving it out of reach as an option for many ageing people and their families (Harper 2006).

Part IV

Conclusions

This final part traces out two sets of "moments" in social geography. The first revisits the epilogue in Chapter 2, where questions were raised regarding a "post-human" social geography. In revisiting this discussion, Chapter 10 highlights how this text has touched on post-human possibilities and how social geographers continue to call into question the arbitrary boundaries between human and nonhuman (inhuman) geographies. Chapter 11 retraces the questions raised throughout the book, asking how we might work toward a social geography invested in the politics of resistance, hope, and care. Focusing on the twin concerns of difference and inequality, this final chapter asks how social geography and social geographers can challenge the processes that maintain inequalities and reinforce stigmatizing differences while opening up the possibility for alternative and progressive spaces, identities, and subjectivities.

Chapter 10

Epilogue v. 2.0

- Post-Human *and* Post-Social Possibilities?
- Let's Not Burn the House Down to Spite Our Face . . .
- Post-Social Natures and Hybrid Subjectivities

Post-Human *and* Post-Social Possibilities?

There is no doubt that social geography is a subdiscipline deeply invested in a human-centered narrative. Within this narrative, social geographers have historically focused on the differences and inequalities between human beings, among human social groups and communities, and across human social relations. Indeed, much of this book has examined these explicitly *human* social relations and practices. As I discussed briefly in Chapter 2, in recent years there has been greater attention paid to the complex relations between the so-called "human" and "nonhuman", or as Urry (2000: 14) has put it, the "inhuman." In many ways, this volume has already traced some of these human–nonhuman relations. Reclus's early anarchist work points to the arbitrary boundaries between society and nature, suggesting that humans are part of, not separate from, the physical environment around them. Indeed, Reclus's anarchy posits "humanity as emerging *within* nature rather than *out of* it" (Clark and Martin 2004: 24, original emphasis). Social geographers of health also work across the boundaries of the human–nonhuman through the study of disease as well as body politics. Because the body is both social and biological, it is impossible to mark where the social body ends and the biological one begins. Moreover, the "healthy" body is maintained through all sorts of human–nonhuman relations, from the drugs that people take to the instruments used to measure and mark out the body to the structures through which people live and survive. Organizations are also "made up of" nonhuman actors that regulate, contain, and enable the practices of certain bodies. Children play in schools and parks that help define how that play happens. Children also rethink the nonhuman objects in their lives, as they seek out creative alternatives through their transitions across childhood, youthhood, and adulthood. As humans age, they also "take on" new possibilities by rethinking the relationship between their social and material bodies and other nonhuman objects, like their automobiles, homes, implants, or even their clothing.

This means that, at a basic level, social geographers cannot simply theorize that the nonhuman exists "out there" *beyond* the human. Instead, it might be better to conceptualize the material world of objects and technologies or the spaces of "the natural" world of animals, insects, and plants as co-creating human subjects. In short, human life and human social interactions, organizations, and mobilities are intimately interwoven with and constitutively related to nonhuman actors and processes. Social theorists such as Donna Haraway (1991) suggest that the human–nonhuman binary collapses when we examine the hybridity of the human and nonhuman in everyday life. Turning her attention to a socio-techno-biological body, Haraway argues that people are neither completely human nor nonhuman, nor are they entirely social or natural. Instead, humans are "cyborgs" because their bodies are made up of the social, technological, and biological characteristics of both the human and nonhuman. This is not simply a matter of adding the nonhuman to the human. It is about transgressing the arbitrary boundaries distinguished in everyday language between the human and nonhuman, human and animal, and the natural and the social.

Haraway's "manifesto" suggests a posthuman world in which "cyborgs . . . offer an escape from the maze of dualisms through which our bodies have been explained" (Coyle 2006: 507).[1] This is not an easy concept to wrap one's head around, though, and some social geographers have engaged such notions of hybridity with some reluctance or outright rejection. That said, there is no doubt that the perfunctory bounding of the human from the nonhuman is being called into question more regularly within the realms of social geographic analysis (Castree and Nash 2006). And these challenges are coming from within the subdisciplinary spaces of social (and cultural) geography (Wolch and Emel 1998; Philo and Wlibert 2000), as well as more broadly from the area of nature–society studies (Whatmore 1999, 2002, 2005; Braun and Castree 2001; Braun 2004a, 2007; Robbins 2007). This work suggests that it is time to rethink the ways in which social geographers *do* social geography; they may have to reconsider what are appropriate subjects of their research, activism, and practice. It is necessary, then, that social geographers think about a broader array of objects/subjects in their research, including, for example, the technological and the biological, particularly as these two subjects are co-constructed through advancements in biotechnology – e.g. the development of nanotechnology that can alter life at the molecular level (N. Rose 2007).

Revisiting, even briefly, a "more-than-human"[2] social geography seems a valuable endeavor because it provides an opportunity to further expand notions of "the social" and "society" in the study of difference and inequality. After all, how people engage the nonhuman varies spatially. The access that individuals and social groups have to the possibilities offered by new cyborg bodies varies dramatically depending on one's subject position (Braun 2007). The ability of the wealthy to have heart surgery and biomedical fixes for a clogged artery is but one possibility among many. How people engage the "nonhuman" in and across space, therefore, is an issue for any study of inequality. Moreover, social differences are articulated through these unique engagements, as the interrelationships between the human and nonhuman take place differently depending on where someone is and how they view their relationship to plants, animals, or technology. More than this, though, it is possible to discern traces of how the nonhuman is part of everyday life and has "agency" in constructing that world. After all, computers interpret signs just as humans do (Jöns 2006), animals embody their own subjectivities (Philo and Wlibert 2000), and plants and grasses are not only socially produced but help to create new human subjects (Robbins 2007). It is impossible, of course, in this rather short chapter to discuss all these possibilities. So, as a way of further expanding social geography's own critical gaze, I want to offer a brief discussion of how social geographers might think about the post-human or post-social possibilities that confront social geography today. I begin by turning to some of the "nonhuman" agents that constitute the social world. I conclude with a further discussion of a post-social future in which the hybrid subject offers a way out of the duality that continues to maintain distinctions between "social" and "natural" geographies.

Let's Not Burn the House Down to Spite Our Face . . .

In a 2004 editorial in the journal *Urban Geography*, Susan Smith argues that geographers have lost touch with the materiality of the everyday and the importance of the "nonhuman" in studies of urban life and experience (Smith 2004). She points out that studies of housing remain rather static, with geographers treating housing as a "backdrop to other (seemingly more engaging) urban affairs" (ibid.: 89). Yet, she argues,

> there are certainly some powerful reasons for rethinking the geography of housing. Not least among these is *the "postsocial" turn* that entangles human relations in new ways into the forms and forces of the material world. From this perspective, it is conceivable that some people are more engaged by or enmeshed within their relationships with domestic spaces – with the fabric, layout and contents of their home – than they are with their human relations. . . . Other entanglements between human and nonhuman actants might be teased out of the changing articulations of bodies with structures, across human life courses, set within aging if periodically renewed stocks of housing. Various bodily characteristics, capabilities, and impairments, for example, may be differently enabled and disabled by the (changing) design, technologies, and infrastructures built into homes. . . . I am not suggesting that attention to the

interplay of objects, embodiments and subjectivities that shape living room(s) is entirely absent from a wide ranging literature in housing studies. My point is that processes animating such engagement are rarely explicitly addressed. For example, the area of housing and health . . . has been doggedly preoccupied with the impact of environment on wellbeing. . . . [This perspective] seems resistant to a relational framework weaving mice, mites and moulds in woods and wools, through airways and organs, between bodies, onto scientific instruments, and into political imaginations (ibid.: 89–90, original emphasis).

Smith's criticism of housing studies, and the social geographies of housing more broadly, is an important one because it signposts that social geographers should place conceptual weight on the world beyond human bodies, communities, and organizations. Indeed, the animals with which humans share their living space, the insects that swirl around their heads, and the wiring, beams, and nails that hold together their living spaces are a significant part of their social worlds. On a conceptual level, Smith's call also suggests that, particularly within Anglophone geographic thought, there is a compulsion to conceptualize human and nonhuman spaces as distinct and separate. Indeed, humans, as Philo (2005b: 825) argues, have an "impulse to cleave apart the world conceptually into neat boxes (delimiting objects, categories, classes): human/non-human, culture/nature, and a myriad more fine-grained distinctions (i.e. different facets of nature recorded in taxonomies, registers and the like, as often linked to worldly spaces such as identifiable regions, nation-states, field of corporate endeavour, etc)." In actor-network theory (ANT), from which Philo draws inspiration, nonhuman subjects are implicated in the networks of social and spatial relations that constitute everyday life. Put simply, nonhuman aspects of the social world are actants, performing roles in the co-construction of everyday social worlds. To put it another way, the city is a "zoöpolis" in which multiple species interact through social networks and relationships that cross the human–nonhuman divide (Wolch 1998). Within and across these networks and relationships, "Animals [for example] have their own realities, their own worldviews; in short, they are *subjects*, not objects" (Wolch 1998: 121, original emphasis). In enacting their own worldviews and realities animals come into contact and conflict with humans in ways that shape the city itself, as well as human subjectivities as "human." Humans are constantly "reacting" to the "natural world in the midst" of the so-called cultured and socialized spaces of the city.

Of course, the zoöpolis consists of much more than humans and animals; it is also made up of vegetation, physical structures, fluvial (water) processes, and technologies, for example. In *Lawn People*, Robbins (2007: 14–15) traces some of the other "actants" that constitute the social world of homeowners in the US, arguing that "the lawn is a political and economic network . . . because the lawn, among myriad other objects of daily life, constitutes who we are. In daily life, this means that personal identity, the way people imagine themselves as members of their families and communities, might be as much a product as a driver of lawn care." Drawing from the work of Bruno Latour[3] and ANT more generally, Robbins

Box 10.1 Social Geography and Actor-Network Theory (ANT)

Fernando Bosco (2006) provides an overview of ANT in human geography, arguing that this particular social theory is important because of its commitment to a "relational" understanding of social actors and agency. As a relational theory, ANT posits that "agency" is not an autonomous act. Agency, instead, is "given to actants" – "something that acts or to which activity is granted by others" (ibid.: 137, citing Latour 1996: 373) – through relationships with human and nonhuman subjects. Simplifying this complex theory with an example, Bosco argues that "I would no longer be a geographer with the ability to write papers and produce knowledge if my computer, my colleagues, my books, my job, my professional network, and everything else in my life that allows me to act as what I am were taken away from me" (ibid.). ANT is also a social theoretical approach that focuses attention on relations of power: "once we conceptualize agency as a network [of relations], uncovering the heterogeneous 'actor-networks' of associations allows us to explain the mechanics of power and organization in society, and to understand how different things (from knowledge to institutions to material artifacts and technologies) come to be, how they endure over time, or how they fail and exit from our lives and our world" (ibid.).

As Bosco notes, ANT is not the first social theory in geography to engage in a relational approach to space. Doreen Massey, he suggests, developed a view of "place as open and porous and as the product of the spatiality of networked relations" (ibid.: 142). Massey's relational theory also provides an important "pause" when considering an ANT approach. "Some have argued," Bosco explains, "that when it comes to recognizing different people and different voices and the politics associated with them (i.e. 'the other' or 'otherness'), ANT can almost be seen as a colonial framework" (ibid.: 143). For some social theorists, ANT does not leave any space for an "outside," a space that is different from or not inclusive of a particular actor network. This, they argue, may limit the political efficacy and explanatory power of ANT when it comes to understanding resistance (and domination). That said, "Many see ANT as a poststructural approach to power relations that can be adapted, transformed, and modified to fit their research . . . [because] it is an approach that encourages fluidity of the social, the natural, and very importantly, of space, place and scale" (ibid.: 144).

Quick Exercise

Keep a diary in which you identify all the actants with which you network in a 24-hour period. Remember to include both human and nonhuman actants. Next, take your log and outline what role each actant plays in enabling your own agency as another actant in a wider actor network.

suggests that both human and nonhuman subjects intersect, creating "networks of associations" whereby "each of the separate pieces is not independent, but is instead made to be the way it is by virtue of its relationship to all the other parts. . . . In such a network, individuals or organisms do not have free 'agency' (will and capacity of their own), but are instead given the capacity or incapacity to act only by virtue of their position in a complex of different elements" (ibid.: 14). While this is certainly not the first challenge to a sense of human autonomy in social geography – Marxists among many other social theorists have long argued that capitalism creates structures that blind us to the truth about our social world – the notion that nonhuman subjects are part of human social networks and limit their capacities "to be" as humans complicates any straightforward reading of social geography as the study of human societies.

The blurring of the boundaries between the human and nonhuman raises social anxieties, as the integrity of the so-called human world of evolutionary and cultural superiority is broken down. In the context of xenotransplantation, where organs or cells are transferred across species, there is a growing concern that this practice disrupts the "natural rhythms" and integrity of the human subject (Coyle 2006). Humans are faced with the possibility that xenotransplantation might allow for more than the movement of cells and parts across species, it might also promote "the spread of disease from animals to humans" (ibid.: 519) or it might break down the stability of crops needed to sustain basic agricultural production. These anxieties are premised, in part, on the notion that the human subject has, at one time, been an autonomous subject, distinct from other species and objects in the world. This, of course, is a difficult premise to sustain in the wake of extended scrutiny. Indeed, as scholars have long pointed out, it is only in recent history that the social world has somehow been so radically torn apart from the so-called natural one, which humans believe they can "tame" and "control" (cf. Wolch 1998).

Post-Social Natures and Hybrid Subjectivities

A place without *us* populated by creatures (including, surreptitiously, a variety of human "kinds") at once monstrous and wonderful, whose very strangeness gives shape to whatever *we* are claimed to be. The enduring coincidence between the species and spaces of wildlife as the antipodes of human society means that to ask what is wild is always simultaneously a question of its whereabouts. This framing of the wild renders the creatures that live "there" inanimate figures in unpeopled landscapes, removing humans to the "here" of a society from which all trace of animality has been expunged (Whatmore 2002: 12, original emphasis).

In *Hybrid Geographies*, Sarah Whatmore rethinks the arbitrary and capricious bounding of the "natural" and "social" worlds, society and nature. In its place, she offers a theoretical position wherein all "agents" are given space to be "impure" (Braun 2005: 836). This notion of "impurity" is an interesting one because it calls into question the idea that people are somehow only human or that the social world is only invested in and by human beings. In this context, "the possibility is raised . . . of thinking about animals [among other subjects] as a social group with at least some potential for what might be termed 'transgression' or even 'resistance' when wriggling out of cages, fields, and wildernesses allotted to them by their human neighbors" (Philo 1998: 52). In theorizing "the social" from a position of impurity, the integrity of "the natural" is also called into question in Whatmore's hybrid politics, for the confines of nature are also social, cultural, and political. In the nascent twenty-first century, the boundaries of the social and the natural are further being eroded by the fact that "we have new bodies, a new world, and a new universe" as Braun (2004b: 269) suggests. In this "new world," "Genetic engineering, nanotechnologies, and pharmaceuticals have made projects of organisms. Ecology and cybernetics have given us bodies understood in terms of exchange and circulation. New information technologies have articulated mind, body and machine in ever-new ways" (ibid.). The "hybrid subject" is thus a subject fraught with tensions that emanate from the networked relations among the bodies of animal, human, and machine.

The bounding of the human and the social is thus a problematic political position that allows humans to treat other "nonhuman" objects as "things" ready for consumption. Challenging these boundaries emboldens a radically different ethical position in which "humans are not the only actors" (Braun 2005: 836) and subjectivities are woven together networks of human and nonhuman, social and natural. This is not an easy position to sustain, as humans are often socially driven to maintain their hegemony as *the* subject among a world of objects (cf. Whatmore 2002: 158). What this broader body of literature does, however, is break down the artificial boundaries erected between a social (human) world and a natural (nonhuman) world of animals, plants, water, land, and machines. It conceives of a "social" world that includes both human and nonhuman subjects. It suggests the possibility that both "nature" and "society" are partial, incomplete processes that cannot be contained by a social geographic compulsion to carve up and bound the everyday lifeworld between "the human" and "the nonhuman."

Ignoring the fluid and hybrid subjectivities that have occurred historically and are now enabled by new technological modifications of both the human and nonhuman may paralyze social geographers' abilities to fully understand how the social world is differentiated between those who "have" and those who "do not have." This includes the possibility that some subjects can engage a cyborg life that extends their existence while others cannot – new biotechnologies and the choices these enable are intimately tied to the political economies of access. In this context, then, social geographers may need a new ethical (and methodological) framework that takes seriously the multiplicity of "cyborg" and "hybrid" subjectivities present in our everyday. This demands shifting the conceptual register, thinking about new positions, and engaging in questions that have heretofore been marginal to social geography. At the same time, this should not diminish a commitment to engaging with a positive notion of difference. Instead, a transgressive politics that operates across the human–nonhuman "divide" can enable new social geographies that sup-port even more variegated forms of difference, further engaging with the problematics of everyday inequalities.

Notes

1   It is important to note that the use of the term posthuman here is not meant to signal a temporal shift from a human to a posthuman epoch. Instead, it represents an onto-logical possibility whereby the body is always becoming through the intervweaving of its human and nonhuman components (see Braun 2004b).
2   This issue of a "more-than-human" geography has occupied the time of cultural geo-graphers more than social geographers in recent years. This is the case for several reasons. First, culture and nature are often juxtaposed as oppositions in "western" thought. Second, cultural geography has cast a large shadow over social geography, thus marginalizing a discussion of the relationship between "the social" and "the natural" at least among social geographers. Third, the debates and discussions of a "social nature" have been dominated by those scholars who consider themselves "nature–society" geographers or Marxist geographers, the latter of which examine nature as socially produced.
3   See, for example, Bruno Latour's *We Have Never Been Modern* (1993).

Chapter 11

Rethinking the Social Geographies of Difference and Inequality

- Grounding Inequalities, Rethinking Differences
- Power, Politics, and the Spontaneous Geographies of Resistance
- Social Geographies of Hope and Care

Grounding Inequalities, Rethinking Differences

The challenge for social geographers . . . is how we can address broader social concerns about oppression and exclusion in ways which allow the sub-discipline to have a greater critical voice beyond the academy, and how we can become more politically engaged, without losing sight of the specificities of the everyday experiences of different social groupings. One possible way forward is offered by Anne Snitow (1990). She argues that academics need to retain a constantly shifting scale of focus, in which sometimes it is appropriate to focus on difference and minimise claims to a shared identity or goal, whereas at other times it is politically expedient to "maximise" a shared identity or position to proclaim common needs and political aims (Valentine 2001: 171).

Social geography is a subdiscipline that has long been committed to learning from and rethinking broader social theoretical approaches and practices. From positivism and critical rationalism to anarchy, Marxism, feminism, and queer theory to postmodernism, psychoanalysis, and poststructuralism, social geographers engage the world around them in an attempt to understand how differences are spatially realized and inequalities maintained through the sociospatial organization of our everyday worlds. After all, "Rather than drawing on one theoretical perspective, contemporary social geographies are eclectic in their approach" (Valentine 2001: 170). Social geographers are therefore interested in learning from the past by incorporating theoretical suppositions and methodological approaches that help them explain and conceptualize how and why inequalities exist and are maintained, while also recognizing that the world is a complicated and variegated place in which multiple sets of different identities and subjectivities are practiced and realized all the time. Social geographers are thus always already activists because they are not simply interested in explanation; they are also interested in affecting change through their use of social theories and methodologies that are politically and intellectually appropriate. As such, social geographers are well placed to work across constituencies to "minimize" and "maximize" social differences in ways that enable a politics of difference to flourish and a politics of inequality to be marginalized.

This means recognizing that social geography's theoretical plurality is an essential aspect of its own criticality: a spatial scientific methodology realized through a PPGIS has as much value as a poststructuralist one that focuses on the study of the body as a object of a biomedical gaze. In both cases, social geography is informed by its own interest in the "weighty materiality" that keeps social geographers' research grounded in social experience, practice, and performance. This "materiality" is realized through the study of the body, the city, the rural community, the hospital, school, and prison, or, even, the nation. Returning to the example of the prison discussed in Chapter 5, we can see how a spatial scientific perspective can be used to analyze the prison as a system spatially disenfranchising individuals from "inner city" communities of color. Coming from a different conceptual angle, it is possible to investigate "the prison" as a method of social control, whereby individuals self-regulate their bodily practices to maintain their place in a particular social order. Mapping public education resources, a social geographer might also be able to explain how the ability to advance one's education is tied directly to the resources available in one's neighborhood. Or, a social geographer might ethnographically investigate how public education can be used as a vehicle to reinforce certain subjectivities as citizens by constituting "others" as exceptional (i.e. different) and therefore "dangerous." In both these cases, social geographers can draw from a wide array of tools available to them, from computer cartography and GIS programs to qualitative techniques and analytic approaches.

There is an embedded complexity in social geography because social geographers examine both the extraordinary and the mundane, broader spatial patterns and distributions as well as everyday social practices and interactions. While the quantitative revolution ushered in a socially relevant spatial science through the study of racial and class inequalities, feminist, Marxist, and humanist geographers called into question the efficacy of a purely spatial scientific social geography. The differences that social geographers "take on" in their research were thus expanded, as capitalism, patriarchy, and racism were further interrogated. Over time, critical race theorists and queer scholars exemplified social geography's insistence that social geographers expand on what they consider to be important nodes of difference.

Queer social geographies, for example, provide space for the study of sexual differences in and out of academic geography. The recent turn toward the study of age in social geography has also brought forth an array of important research in children's geographies as well as in the geographies of ageing. The wide breadth of conceptual possibilities offered to the nascent social geographer is significant and can be, at times, quite intimidating. That said, social geography's recognition of the world's complexity provides all social geographers with the opportunity to transgress the historical boundaries between a spatial scientific social geography on the one hand and a feminist one on the other, or a Marxist social analytic framework and a psychoanalytic one, and so on. This complexity does provide a real conceptual and methodological challenge for social geographers because the "social category" – of say, men and women, black and white, or global north and global south – is no longer conceptualized as having an essential character. A positive space of difference is only possible when social geographers allow individuals, communities, and groups to inhabit subject positions that afford them the most epistemological flexibility, while also understanding that any subject position can become sedimented in the sociospatial practices of authority and power (and resistance and alterity) that are part of everyday life. Put more simply, while social geographers may think of the world as a partial and incomplete process people do experience the spaces of class, race, ethnicity, gender, sexuality, and ability in real and sometimes painful ways.

Power, Politics, and the Spontaneous Geographies of Resistance

Opening up social geography to the possibilities of alternative identities and subjectivities – to new and exciting practical and conceptual ways of thinking about and knowing the world – does not allow social geographers to deny the effects of power that continue to socially and spatially construct and regulate a world of difference and inequality. In fact, critical social geographers remain firmly situated against the practices of capitalism, sexism, heterosexism, ableism, ethnocentrism, and racism in their research (and often in their own everyday politics): it is absurd, after all, to deny the relations of power – as social, cultural, political, or economic – that are part of the practices of "the social" and "society" today. We can see power in the organization of the city, which remains highly segregated across race, class, or ethnic lines in many parts of the world – one need only travel to the shanty towns of Buenos Aries or into the temporary tent cities for the homeless in Long Beach, California to get a sense of this process. We can see power in the practices of "gay bashing" that take place in both rural and urban spaces, reinforcing with physical violence the boundaries of a normative heterosexuality. We can also see power in the subtle practices of the spaces of home and care, where women, more than men, suffer the "double" burden of home and work.

Power is also subtle in a number of other ways, as the mechanisms of authority and domination are "sewn into" individual practices through systems of self-regulation. Individuals perform their identities and subjectivities in relation to others to "fit in" so they can be seen as "normal." This is true not only for adults but also for children who want to feel like they belong to a certain social group (the "in crowd") and in a particular space (the "schoolyard"). Power also operates through the very real materiality of the street, where people with certain physical and mental abilities are meant to feel excluded or marginalized. This happens both overtly through a general set of exclusionary practices – denying people in wheelchairs access to the sidewalk – or more covertly through a denial of access to services or inclusion in various social activities – in spaces of interaction, such as the coffee house, so-called abled people may present themselves as "put out" if they have to make space for someone whose body extends out into the world because of a pair of crutches. Power also operates through multiple nodes of difference, co-constructing the marginalization of certain bodies through the twin practices of, for example, classism and racism. The current economic crisis in the US demonstrates how predatory loan corporations have targeted certain class- and race-based groups for high interest mortgages to purchase new homes and then disenfranchised those same groups when the bottom fell out of the loan market. The "American Dream" of home ownership – a cultural and social goal for millions – remains regulated through the very real economic and social power of corporate banks, which received massive bailouts from the Federal Reserve Bank in the US in 2008, while homeowners have been largely left to fend for themselves.

Reciprocally, resistances are enacted every day to combat any number of inequalities and systems of domination. This includes the active and outward sets of resistances that come from direct action protests or civil disobedience. The continued and sustained anti-globalization movement is one such example, producing all sorts of resistances to the assertion of a corporate global vision of unequal capitalist development. The global women's movement, represented in the World Women's Forums, also demonstrates the power that comes from the "maximization" of a temporary coalescence around an identity position. This is not to deny that important differences were present at the recent Forum in Beijing – across the global north and south, for example. Instead, it is to suggest that resistances might take place in ways that try to maximize difference in positive ways. Yet, what social geographers continue to learn is that resistance often happens in much more subtle and mundane ways. This could include the gay couple holding hands in a museum, challenging the heteronormative assumptions of that space. Feminist geographers have long called on social geographers to embrace a politics of the everyday, suggesting that it is necessary to challenge patriarchal power and authority, as it is present in everyday communities and organizations. Such challenges are reminiscent of Gramsci's call to create space for spontaneous resistances and possibilities. Resistance can be scripted but it also happens spontaneously all the time in all kinds of spaces. Resistances, particularly those spontaneous possibilities, serve a valuable function in any social geography – they provide for new arrangements and configurations of "the social" and "the spatial" by fostering a politics of partiality. Recognizing that no space can be assigned to any one dominant or resistant subject position, it is possible to rethink the geographies of power that regulate and normalize how we (as social beings) should be. Making space for spontaneity extends the politics of resistance by challenging the power and authority of the shop floor or the city street or the central government in small but significant ways. When resistances come together not to deny difference but to embrace it, politics can be effective and affective.

In all of this, it is important to remember that power and resistance are creative (and destructive) processes. Power creates identities – the elite and the non-elite – and produces organizations that reinforce subject positions – biomedical authority creates the patient. Power creates dominant social positions as well through the deployment of authority and knowledge. And social geographers can (and do) participate in these systems of authority and knowledge. At the same time, resistances also create new identities and spaces, alternative subject positions and sites of alerity. And, social geographers can (and do) participate in these resistant practices and spaces as well. Indeed, part of the history of social geography has been to participate in the creation of a new sociospatial order that mitigates inequity and opens up the possibility for more just societies. This work is always incomplete, though. It remains imperative, therefore, that social geographers continue to employ their skills to critically interrogate how power and resistance rework identities, subjectivities, and spaces in new and hopeful ways.

Social Geographies of Hope and Care

We *are* a caring discipline (Lawson 2007: 2, emphasis added).

As members of a "caring discipline," social geographers have to think about the hopes that can be derived by research that favors spontaneous forms of resistance and sustains extended networks of support and care. This is a monumental responsibility, but an essential one for any academic or activist moving forward in today's age, especially because we live in a world in which growing global interconnections make categories such as "near" and "far" largely moot. After all, the problems of everyday life – famine, poverty, ill health – and extraordinary crises – tied to earthquakes, tsunamis, war, and conflict – are not as far away as we might imagine them to be. Class- and ethnic-based exploitation taking place in a factory in Indonesia is intimately connected to the systems of production and consumption that are part of the everyday lives of millions in the US, while the rapidly changing global climate, a result of massive emissions from the global north and rising economic powers such as the People's Republic of China, is affecting fisheries and people who fish for a living across the world. That is why Victoria Lawson, in her 2006 Presidential Address to the Association of American

Geographers, suggests that geographers focus more specifically on questions related to an ethics of care:

> Analyzing relationships that produce the need for care opens up important questions all across our discipline. Caring for person-to-person relations involves understanding how difference is socially constructed, and so a critical ethic of care must be coupled with analysis of the structures and institutions that reproduce exclusion, oppression, environmental degradation, and the like. I argue for bringing a critical ethics of care into conversation with feminist political-economy, with political-ecology, with geospatial analysis, with physical geography in order to build theoretical and empirical analyses of the structural and historical relationships producing disease, hunger, poverty, environmental decline, and disasters – or more broadly – the need for care (Lawson 2007: 7).

First and foremost, then, Lawson argues that the analytic work of geography can provide a valuable contribution to broader societal debates and discussions. Social geographic research can (and should) affect social policy, impact political discussions, and open up dialogue in places where conversations regarding difference and inequality are largely silent. This means, as was suggested in Chapter 3, that social geographers think about both their audience and their output: producing texts purely for academic consumption is valuable, as it is part of the training of future educators and activists, but equally important are texts that speak to a wider activist audience. There is no need to denigrate one form of writing for another. Both serve a valuable purpose and both produce scholarship that would be of value to those both "near" and "far." Social geographers must also not be afraid to point their critical gaze inward, interrogating how differences are considered and inequalities manifest inside their own disciplinary boundaries.

The notion that geography is a "caring discipline" should also give us hope, hope that we can co-create social networks that transgress the normative marginalization of difference(s) and undermine the structures of inequality that distinguish the so-called "haves" and "have nots." This might involve not only working across historical definitions of what it means to "have"; it might also involve rethinking the terms of social geographic analysis, such as "standard of living," which is socially and culturally tied to a rather narrow (northern-based) vision of a consumer society. A broader vision of "having" might mean to control one's own surplus (Gibson-Graham 2006), to live in communities that not only tolerate but also offer space for the experiences of hybridity and "impurity" (Whatmore 2002), and to let children be children (Katz 2004). Being hopeful, of course, is not always easy. We live in a world where both human and nonhuman subjects are marginalized from the discussion, placed in a position of second, third, or fourth class status, and isolated from the decisions that regulate daily experience. But a geography of hope recognizes that social geographers are part of the world they study, live in, and experience. This is why Jennifer Wolch (2007: 381) remains somewhat hopeful that geographers, in general, "can together help craft greener, more helpful urban worlds." To do so, however, as Wolch stresses, social geographers must be involved in the discussion about how to recreate the urban world so that urban renewal projects, such as greening the city, are inclusive of difference across the categories of class, ethnicity, race, gender, sexuality, and ability. Don Mitchell (2004: 768) is even more direct in an evocation of a "just geography": "I say we don't collaborate. I say we resist. I say we turn the age of extremes into the age of emancipation, that we turn the geography of violence and oppression into the geography of justice. We – as scholars and as people in this world – have only limited power: but we have important power. That power is to develop and promote a liberal and liberating education (for all); and that power include the skills, resources, and knowledge base necessary to intervene – intellectually and politically, for those are never, ever separate – in the world to help fashion a basis, in knowledge, for action."

Throughout this text, I have argued that social geographers should, can, and do have an impact on the worlds in which they live, work, and research. To form a basis for action, social geographers must engage with the world around them and ask how and why inequality exists, what inequality means, and how they might go about changing the structures and institutions that maintain such inequalities. Social geographers are also well placed to offer an alternative vision of spatial differences, providing the empirical groundwork that illustrates how identities and subjectivities are complexly related to everyday social practices and performances. As such, social geographers can further implode the notion that the individual is somehow distinct from society and that those far away are somehow less significant than those close by. In creating a more caring, hopeful, and just social geography, therefore, social geographers must continue to question how social differences are spatially enacted and maintained through systems of power and authority, resistance and alterity. This is not easy work, and this text has barely scratched the surface of the questions that social geographers might ask or the possibilities that social geographers might help to bring forward in the future. To ignore injustice, to bracket off inequality, and to marginalize differences, however, is to remain part of an "ivory tower" of the academy that believes itself to be "beyond" the social and spatial politics of the everyday world in which it is situated. This is not the view of critical social geography today. Social geography is active. Social geography is creative. Social geography is engaged. And social geography is hopeful and caring.

References

Adams, P. (2005) *The Boundless Self: Communication in Physical and Virtual Spaces.* Syracuse, NY: Syracuse University Press.

Agamben, G. (2005) *State of Exception.* Chicago: University of Chicago Press.

Agger, B. (2006) *Critical Social Theories: An Introduction.* Boulder, CO: Paradigm.

Aitken, S. (2000) Fathering and faltering: "sorry, but you don't have the necessary accoutrements." *Environment and Planning A* 32.4: 581–98.

Aitken, S. (2001) *Geographies of Young People: The Morally Contested Spaces of Identity.* London: Routledge.

Aitken, S. and Marchant, R. C. (2003) Memories and miscreants: teenage tales of terror. *Children's Geographies* 1.1: 151–64.

Akinleye, S. R. (2006) Against the odds: does geography make a difference? *Gender, Place and Culture,* 13.1: 27–31.

Altman, D. (2001) *Global Sex.* Crows Nest, NSW: Allen and Unwin.

Anderson, B. (1991) *Imagined Communities.* London: Verso.

Anderson, P. and Kitchin, R. (2000) Disability, space and sexuality: access to family planning services. *Social Science and Medicine* 51: 1163–73.

Andrews, G. (2003) Placing the consumption of private complementary medicine: everyday geographies of older people's use. *Health and Place* 9: 337–49.

Andrews, G., Cutchin, M., McCracken, K., Phillips, D., and Wiles, J. (2007) Geographical gerontology: the constitution of a discipline. *Social Science and Medicine* 65: 151–68.

Andrews, G. and Phillips, D. R. (2005) Geographical studies in ageing: progress and connection to social gerontology. In: G. Andrews and D. R. Phillips (eds), *Ageing and Place: Perspectives, Policy, and Practice.* London: Routledge.

Andrews, G., Wiles, J., and Miller, K.-L. (2004) The geography of complementary medicine: perspectives and prospects. *Complementary Therapies in Nursing and Midwifery* 10: 175–85.

Ansell, R., Huber, U., Gould, W., and van Blerk, L. (2006) Young caregivers in the context of the HIV/AIDS pandemic in sub-Saharan Africa. *Population, Space and Place* 12: 93–111.

Ateljevic, I. (2000) Circuits of tourism: stepping beyond the "production/consumption" dichotomy. *Tourism Geographies* 2.4: 369–88.

Barnes, D. (1995) *The Making of a Social Disease: Tuberculosis in Nineteenth-Century France*. Berkeley: University of California Press.

Bartlett, H. and Phillips, D. (1997) Ageing and aged care in the People's Republic of China: national and local issues and perspectives. *Health and Place* 3.3: 149–59.

Baxter, J. and Eyles, J. (1997) Evaluating qualitative research in social geography: establishing "rigour" in interview analysis. *Transactions of the Institute of British Geographers* 22.4: 505–25.

Beazley, H. (2002) "Vagrants wearing make-up": negotiating space on the streets of Yogyakarta, Indonesia. *Urban Studies* 39.9: 1665–83.

Bell, D. (1995a) Guest editorial: [Screw]ing geography: censor's version. *Environment and Planning D: Society and Space* 13: 127–31.

Bell, D. (1995b) Perverse dynamics, sexual citizenship and the transformation of intimacy. In: D. Bell and G. Valentine (eds), *Mapping Desire*. London: Routledge.

Bell, D. (2007) Fucking geography, again. In: K. Browne, J. Lim and G. Brown (eds), *Geographies of Sexualities: Theory, Practices, and Politics*. London: Ashgate.

Bell, D. and Binnie, J. (2000) *The Sexual Citizen*. Cambridge: Polity Press.

Bell, D. and Valentine, G. (1995) *Mapping Desire*. London: Routledge.

Belton, B. (2005) *Questioning Gypsy Identity: Ethnic Narratives in Britain and America*. Walnut Creek and Oxford: Altamira.

Berry, B. (1964) Approaches to regional analysis: a synthesis. In: B. Berry and D. Marble (eds), *Spatial Analysis*. Englewood Cliffs, NJ: Prentice Hall.

Berry, B. (1971) Introduction: the logic and limitations of comparative factorial ecology. *Economic Geography* 47: 209–19.

Bettie, J. (2003) *Women without Class: Girls, Race, and Identity*. Berkeley: University of California Press.

Biggs, S., Lowenstein, A., and Hendricks, J. (2003) *The Need for Theory: Critical Approaches to Social Gerontology*. Amityville, NY: Baywood.

Binnie, J. (2004) *The Globalization of Sexuality*. London: Sage.

Blackford, H. (2004) Playground panopticism: ring-around-the-children, a pocketful of women. *Childhood* 11.2: 227–49.

Blackman, S. (1998) The school: "poxy cupid!" An ethnographic and feminist account of a resistant female youth culture: the new wave girls. In: T. Skelton and G. Valentine (eds), *Cool Places: Geographies of Youth Culture*. London: Routledge.

Blaut, J. (1983) Assimilation versus ghethoization. *Antipode* 15.1: 35–41.

Blaut, J. (1997a) Piagetian pessimism and the mapping abilities of young children: a rejoinder to Liben and Downs. *Annals of the Association of American Geographers* 87.1: 168–77.

Blaut, J. (1997b) The mapping abilities of young children. *Annals of the Association of American Geographers* 87.1: 152–8.

Blaut, J. and Stea, D. (1971) Studies of geographic learning. *Annals of the Association of American Geographers* 61.2: 387–93.

Blaut, J. and Stea, D. (1974) Mapping at the age of three. *Journal of Geography* 73.7: 5–9.

Blum, V. (2003) *Flesh Wounds: The Culture of Cosmetic Surgery*. Berkeley: University of California Press.

Blunt, A. (2005) *Domicile and Diaspora: Anglo-Indian Women and the Spatial Politics of Home*. Malden, MA: Blackwell.

Blunt, A. and Dowling, R. (2006) *Home*. London: Routledge.

Blunt, A., Gruffurd, P., May, J., Ogborn, M., and Pinder, D. (2003) *Cultural Geography in Practice*. New York: Arnold.

Blunt, A. and McEwan, C. (2002) *Postcolonial Geographies*. New York: Continuum.

Blunt, A. and Wills, J. (2000) *Dissident Geographies: An Introduction to Radical Ideas and Practice*. Engelwood Cliffs, NJ: Prentice Hall.

Bondi, L. and Davidson, J. (2005) Situating gender. In: L. Nelson and J. Seager (eds), *A Companion to Feminist Geography*. Malden, MA: Blackwell.

Bonnett, A. (1997) Geography, race, and whiteness: invisible traditions and current challenges. *Area* 29: 193–9.

Bosco, F. (2006) Actor-network theory, networks, and relational approaches in human geography. In: S. Aitken and G. Valentine (eds), *Approaches to Human Geography*. Thousand Oaks, CA: Sage.

Boyle, P. (2002) Population geography: transnational women on the move. *Progress in Human Geography* 26.4: 531–43.

Braun, B. (2004a) Nature and culture: on the career of a false problem. In: J. Duncan, N. Johnson and R. Schein (eds), *A Companion to Cultural Geography*. Malden, MA: Blackwell.

Braun, B. (2004b) Querying posthumanisms. *Geoforum* 35: 269–73.

Braun, B. (2005) Writing geographies of hope. *Antipode* 37.4: 834–41.

Braun, B. (2007) Biopolitics and the molecularization of life. *Cultural Geographies* 14: 6–28.

Braun, B. and Castree, N. (2001) *Social Nature: Theory, Practice, Politics*. Oxford: Blackwell.

Brenner, N. (2001) The limits to scale? methodological reflections on scalar structuration. *Progress in Human Geography* 15: 525–48.

Brown, E. (2007) "It's urban living, not ethnicity itself": race, crime and the urban geography of high-risk youth. *Geography Compass* 1/2: 222–45.

Brown, G. (2007) Autonomy, affinity and play in the spaces of radical queer activism. In: K. Browne, J. Lim, and G. Brown (eds), *Geographies of Sexualities: Theory, Practices, and Politics*. Aldershot: Ashgate.

Brown, L., Golledge, R., and Williamson, F. (1972) Behavioural approaches in geography: an overview. *Australian Geographer* 12.1: 59–79.

Brown, M. (1995) Ironies of distance: an ongoing critique of the geographies of AIDS. *Environment and Planning D: Society and Space* 13: 159–83.

Brown, M. (1997) *Replacing Citizenship: AIDS Activism and Radical Democracy*. New York: Guilford.

Brown, M. (2000) *Closet Space*. London: Routledge.

Brown, M. (2003) Hospice and the spatial paradoxes of terminal care. *Environment and Planning A* 35: 833–51.

Brown, M. (2006a) A geographer reads *Geography Club*: spatial metaphor and metonym in textual/sexual space. *Cultural Geographies* 13: 313–39.

Brown, M. (2006b) Sexual citizenship, political obligation and disease ecology in gay Seattle. *Political Geography*, 25.8: 874–98.

Brown, M. (2007) Counting on queer geography. In: K. Browne, J. Lim, and G. Brown (eds), *Geographies of Sexualities: Theory, Practice and Politics*. Aldershot: Ashgate.

Brown, M. and L. Knopp (2003) Queer cultural geographies – we're here! we're queer! we're over there, too! In: K. Anderson, M. Domosh, S. Pile, and N. Thrift (eds), *Handbook of Cultural Geography*. Thousand Oaks, CA: Sage.

Brown, M., Knopp, L., and Morrill, R. (2005) The culture wars and urban electoral politics: sexuality, race, and class in Tacoma, Washington. *Political Geography* 24.3: 267–91.

Browne, K. (2004) Genderism and the bathroom problem: (re)materialising sex sites, (re)creating sexed bodies. *Gender, Place and Culture* 11.3: 331–46.

Browne, K. (2007a) A party with politics? (Re)making LGBTQ Pride space in Dublin and Brighton. *Social and Cultural Geography* 8.1: 63–88.

Browne, K. (2007b) Drag queens and drag dykes: deploying and deploring femininities. In: K. Browne, J. Lim, and G. Brown (eds), *Geographies of Sexualities: Theory, Practices, and Politics*. Aldershot: Ashgate.

Browne, K., Lim, J., and Brown, G. (2007) *Geographies of Sexualities: Theory, Practice, and Politics*, Aldershot: Ashgate.

Bunge, W. (1962) *Theoretical Geography*. Lund, Sweden: Royal University of Lund Department of Geography.

Bunge, W. (1971) *Fitzgerald: Geography of a Revolution*. Cambridge, MA: Schlenkman.

Bunge, W. (1973a) Ethics and logic in geography. In: R. J. Chorley (ed.), *Directions in Geography*. London: Methuen.

Bunge, W. (1973b) The geography of human survival. *Annals of the Association of American Geographers* 63.3: 275–95.

Bunge, W. (1977) The point of reproduction: a second front. *Antipode* 9.1: 60–76.

Burawoy, M., Burton, A., Ferguson, A., Fox, K., Gamson, J., Gartrell, N., Hurst, L., Kurzman, C., Salzinger, L., Schiffman, J., and Ui, S. (1991) *Ethnography Unbound: Power and Resistance in the Modern Metropolis*. Berkeley: University of California Press.

Burgess, E. (2005) The growth of the city: an introduction to a research project. In: N. R. Fyfe and J. T. Kenny (eds), *The Urban Geography Reader*. London: Routledge.

Butler, J. (1988) Performative acts and gender constitution: an essay in phenomenology and feminist theory. *Theatre Journal* 40: 519–31.

Butler, J. (1990) *Gender Trouble: Feminism and the Subversion of Identity*. New York: Routledge.

Butler, J. (1993) *Bodies that Matter: On the Discursive Limits of "Sex."* New York: Routledge.

Butler, R. (1999) Double the trouble or twice the fun? disabled bodies in the gay community. In: R. Butler and H. Parr (eds) *Mind and Body Spaces: Geographies of Illness, Impairment, and Disability*. London: Routledge.

Buttimer, A. (1969) Social space in interdisciplinary perspective. *Geographical Review* 49: 417–26.

Buttimer, A. (1971) *Society and Milieu in the French Geographic Tradition*. Chicago: The Association of American Geographers.

Buttimer, A. (1976) Grasping the dynamism of lifeworld. *Annals of the Association of American Geographers* 66.2: 277–92.

Campbell, J. and Livingstone, D. (1983) Neo-Lamarckism and the development of geography in the United States and Great Britain. *Transactions of the Institute of British Geographers* 8.3: 267–94.

Carter, G. (1977) A geographical society should be a geographical society. *Professional Geographer* 29.1: 101–2.

Castells, M. (2000) *The Rise of the Network Society*. Malden: Blackwell.

Castree, N. and Nash, C. (2006) Posthuman geographies. *Social and Cultural Geography* 7.4: 501–4.

Chiotti, Q. and Joseph, A. (1995) Casey House: interpreting the location of a Toronto AIDS hospice. *Social Science and Medicine* 41.1: 131–40.

Clark, J. and Martin, C. (2004) *Anarchy, Geography, Modernity*. Lanham, MD: Lexington Books.

Clarke, D., Doel, M., and Segrott, J. (2004) No alternative? The regulation and professionalization of complementary and alternative medicine in the United Kingdom. *Health and Place* 10: 329–38.

Clarke, G. (2004) Threatening space: (physical) education and homophobic body work. In: J. Evans, B. Davies, and J. Wright (eds), *Body Knowledge and Control: Studies in the Sociology of Physical Education and Health*. London: Routledge.

Cloke, P. (ed.) (2003a) *Country Visions*. Harlow: Pearson.

Cloke, P. (2003b) Knowing ruralities? In: P. Cloke (ed.), *Country Visions*. Harlow: Pearson.

Cloke, P., Cook, I., Crang, P., Goodwin, M., Painter, J., and Philo, C. (2004) *Practicing Human Geography*. Thousand Oaks, CA: Sage.

Cloke, P., Milbourne, P., and Widdowfield, R. (2003) The complex mobilities of homeless people in rural England. *Geoforum* 34: 21–35.

Cloke, P., Philo, C., and Sadler, D. (1991) *Approaching Human Geography: An Introduction to Contemporary Theoretical Debates*. New York: Guilford Press.

Coleman, M. (2007) Immigration geopolitics beyond the Mexico–US border. *Antipode* 39.1: 54–76.

Collins, D. and Coleman, T. (2008) Social geographies of education: looking within, and beyond, school boundaries. *Geography Compass* 2.1: 281–99.

Collins, D. and Kearns, R. (2001) Under curfew and under seige? legal geographies of young people. *Geoforum* 32: 389–403.

Connell, J. (2006) Medical tourism: sea, sun, sand and . . . surgery. *Tourism Management* 27: 1093–100.

Corburn, J., Osleeb, J., and Porter, M. (2006) Urban asthma and the neighborhood environment in New York City. *Health and Place* 12: 167–79.

Costa-Font, J. (2008) Housing assets and the socio-economic determinants of health and disability in old age. *Health and Place* 14.3: 478–91.

Costello, L. and Duncan, D. (2006) The "evidence" of sex, the "truth" of gender: shaping children's bodies. *Children's Geographies* 4.2: 157–72.

Cowen, D. (2005) Suburban citizenship? the rise of targeting and the eclipse of social rights in Toronto. *Social and Cultural Geography* 6.3: 335–56.

Cox, K. and Mair, A. (1988) Locality and community in the politics of local economic development. *Annals of the Assocation of American Geographers* 78.2: 307–25.

Coyle, F. (2006) Posthuman geographies? biotechnology, nature and the demise of the autonomous human subject. *Social and Cultural Geography* 7.4: 505–23.

Craddock, S. (2000a) *City of Plagues: Disease, Poverty, and Deviance in San Francisco*. Minneapolis: University of Minnesota Press.

Craddock, S. (2000b) Disease, social identity, and risk: rethinking the geography of AIDS. *Transactions of the Institute of British Geographers* 25.2: 153–69.

Craddock, S. (2004) AIDS and ethics: clinical trials, pharmaceuticals, and global scientific practice. In: E. Kalipeni, S. Craddock, J. Oppong, and J. Ghosh (eds), *HIV and AIDS in Africa: Beyond Epidemiology*. Malden, MA: Blackwell.

Crampton, J. (2003) *The Political Mapping of Cyberspace*. Chicago: University of Chicago Press.

Crampton, J. and Elden, S. (2007) *Space, Knowledge and Power: Foucault and Geography*. Aldershot: Ashgate.

Crang, M. (1999) Knowing, tourism and practices of vision. In: D. Crouch (ed.), *Leisure/Tourism Geographies*. London: Routledge.

Crang, M. (2002) Qualitative methods: the new orthodoxy? *Progress in Human Geography* 26.5: 647–55.

Crang, M. (2003) Qualitative methods: touchy, feely, look-see? *Progress in Human Geography* 27.4: 494–504.

Crang, P. (1994) It's showtime: on the workplace geographies of display in a restaurant in southeast England. *Environment and Planning D: Society and Space* 12: 675–704.

Crang, P. (1997) Performing the tourist product. In: C. Rojek and J. Urry (eds), *Touring Cultures: Transformations of Travel and Theory*. London: Routledge.

Cresswell, T. (1996) *In Place, Out of Place: Geography, Ideology, and Transgression*. Minneapolis: Minnesota.

Cresswell, T. (2001) *Tramp in America*. London: Reaktion Books.

Cresswell, T. (2004) *Place: A Short Introduction*. Oxford: Blackwell.

Cromley, E. and McLafferty, S. (2002) *GIS and Public Health*. New York: Guilford.

Crooks, V. (2006) "I go on the Internet; I always, you know, check to see what's new": chronically ill women's use of online health information to shape and inform doctor–patient interactions in the space of care provision. *ACME: An International E-Journal for Critical Geographies* 5.1: 50–69.

Crooks, V. and Chouinard, V. (2006) An embodied geography of disablement: chronically ill women's struggles for enabling places in spaces of health care and daily life. *Health and Place* 12: 345–52.

Crouch, D. (1999) *Leisure/Tourism Geographies: Practices of Geographical Knowledge*. London: Routledge.

Cutchin, M. (2003) The process of mediated aging-in-place: a theoretically and empirically based model. *Social Science and Medicine* 57: 1077–90.

Cuthill, V. (2007) Consuming Harrogate. *Space and Culture* 10.1: 64–76.

Dear, M. and Gleeson, B. (1991) Community attitudes toward the homeless. *Urban Geography* 12.2: 155–76.

Dear, M. and Taylor, S. (1982) *Not on Our Street: Community Attitudes to Mental Health Care*. London: Pion.

Dear, M., Wilton, R., Gaber, S., and Takahashi, L. (1997) Seeing people differently: the socio-spatial construction of disability. *Environment and Planning D: Society and Space* 15: 455–80.

Dear, M. and Wolch, J. (1987) *Landscapes of Despair: From Deinstitutionalization to Homelessness*. Princeton, NJ: Princeton University Press.

Del Casino, V., Jr (2001) Healthier geographies: mediating the gaps between HIV/AIDS and health care in Chiang Mai, Thailand. *Professional Geographer* 53.3: 407–21.

Del Casino, V., Jr (2004) (Re)placing health and health care: mapping the competing discourses and practices of "traditional" and "modern" Thai medicine. *Health and Place* 10.1: 59–73.

Del Casino, V., Jr (2006) NGOs and the reorganization of "community development": mediating the flows of people living with HIV and AIDS. In: B. Yeoh (ed.), *Population Dynamics and Infectious Diseases in Asia*. London: World Scientific Publishers.

Del Casino, V., Jr (2007a) Flaccid theory and the geographies of sexual health in the Age of Viagra. *Health and Place* 13.4: 904–11.

Del Casino, V., Jr (2007b) Health/Sexuality/Geography. In: K. Browne, G. Brown, and J. Lim (eds), *Geographies of Sexualities: Theory, Practice, and Politics*. Aldershot: Ashgate.

Del Casino, V., Jr (2009) Living with and experiencing (dis)ease. In: T. Brown, S. L. McLafferty, and G. Moon (eds), *A Companion to Medical Geography*. Malden, MA: Blackwell.

Del Casino, V., Jr, Dorn, M., and Gallaher, C. (1997) Cindi Katz: creating safe space and the materiality of the margins. *disClosure: A Journal of Social Theory* 6: 37–56.

Del Casino, V., Jr, Grimes, A., Hanna, S., and Jones, J. P. III (2000) Methodological frameworks for the geography of organizations. *Geoforum* 31: 523–38.

Del Casino, V., Jr and Hanna, S. (2000) Representations and identities in tourism map spaces. *Progress in Human Geography* 24.1: 23–46.

Del Casino, V., Jr and Hanna, S. (2005) Beyond the "binaries": a methodological intervention for interrogating maps as representational practices. *ACME: An International E-Journal for Critical Geographies* 4.1: 34–56.

Del Casino, V., Jr and Jocoy, C. (2008) Neoliberal subjectivities, the "new" homelessness, and struggles over spaces of/in the city. *Antipode*, 40.2: 192–9.

Del Casino, V., Jr and Jones, J. P. III (2007) Space for social inequality researchers: a view from geography. In: L. Lobao, G. Hooks, and A. Tickmayer (eds), *Who Gets What Where: The Sociology of Spatial Inequality*. Albany, NY: SUNY Press.

Del Casino, V., Jr and Marston, S. (2006) Social geography in the United States: everywhere and nowhere. *Social and Cultural Geography* 7.6: 995–1010.

Deleuze, G. and Guattari, F. (1987) *A Thousand Plateaus: Capitalism and Schizophrenia*. Minneapolis: University of Minnesota.

Desmarais, A. (2008) The power of peasants: reflections on the meaning of La Vía Campesina. *Journal of Rural Studies* 24: 138–49.

DeVerteuil, G. (2000) Reconsidering the legacy of urban public facility location theory in human geography. *Progress in Human Geography* 24.1: 47–69.

DeVerteuil, G. (2003a) Homeless mobility, institutional settings, and the new poverty management. *Environment and Planning A* 35.2: 361–79.

DeVerteuil, G. (2003b) Welfare reform, institutional practices, and service-delivery settings. *Urban Geography* 24.6: 529–50.

Dixon, D. (2003) Working with crabs. In: P. Cloke (ed.), *Country Visions*. Harlow: Pearson.

Dodge, M. and Kitchin, R. (2001) *Mapping Cyberspace*. London: Routledge.

Doel, M. (1999) *Poststructuralist Geographies: The Diabolical Art of Spatial Science*. Lanham, MD: Rowman and Littlefield.

Dolhinow, R. (2005) Caught in the middle: the state, NGOs, and the limits of grassroots organizing along the US–Mexico border. *Antipode* 37: 566–78.

Domosh, M. (1998) Geography and gender: home, again? *Progress in Human Geography* 22.2: 276–82.

Domosh, M. (2005) An uneasy alliance? Tracing the relationships between cultural and feminist geographies. *Social Geography* 1: 37–41.

Dorn, M. (1997) Beyond nomadism: the travel narrative of a "cripple." In: H. Nast and S. Pile (eds), *Places through the Body*. London: Routledge.

Dorn, M. and Laws, G. (1994) Social theory, body politics, and medical geography: extending Kearn's invitation. *Professional Geographer* 46.1: 106–10.

Downey, L. (2003) Spatial measurement, geography, and urban racial inequality. *Social Forces* 81.3: 937–52.

Doyle, L. (1999) The big issue: empowering homeless women through academic research? *Area* 31.3: 239–46.

Drew, C. (2005) Transparency – considerations for PPGIS research and development. *URISA Journal* 15: 73–8.

DuBois, W. E. B. (1967 [1899]) *The Philadelphia Negro: A Social Study*. New York: Benjamin Blom.

Dunbar, G. (1978) *Elisée Reclus: Historian of Nature*. Hamden, CT: Archon Books.

Dunbar, G. (1979) Elisée Reclus, geographer and anarchist. *Antipode* 10.3: 16–21.

Dunbar, G. (1981) Elisée Reclus, an anarchist in geography. In: D. R. Stoddart (ed.), *Geography, Ideology and Social Concern*. Totowa, NJ: Barnes and Noble Books.

Duncan, J. (1980) The superorganic in American cultural geography. *Annals of the Association of American Geographers* 70.2: 181–98.

Dunning, H., Williams, H., Abonyi, S., and Crooks, V. (2007) A mixed method approach to quality of life research: a case study approach. *Social Indicators Research* 85.1: 145–58.

Dwyer, O. (1997) Geographical research about African Americans: a survey of journals, 1911–1995. *Professional Geographer* 49.4: 441–55.

Dwyer, O. and Jones, J. P. III (2000) White socio-spatial epistemology. *Social and Cultural Geography* 1.2: 209–22.

Dyck, I. (1995) Hidden geographies: the changing lifeworlds of women with multiple sclerosis. *Social Science and Medicine* 40.3: 307–20.

Dyck, I. (1999) Body troubles: women, the workplace and negotiations of a disabled identity. In: R. Butler and H. Parr (eds), *Mind and Body Spaces: Geographies of Illness, Impairment, and Disability*. London: Routledge.

Dyck, I. and Kearns, R. (1995) Transforming the relations of research: towards culturally safe geographies of health and healing. *Health and Place* 1.3: 137–47.

Dyck, I., Kontos, P., Angus, J., and McKeever, P. (2005) The home as site for long-term care: meanings and management of bodies and spaces. *Health and Place* 11: 173–85.

Earikson, R. (1970) *The Spatial Behavior of Hospital Patients: A Behavioral Approach to Spatial Interaction In Metropolitan Chicago*. Chicago: University of Chicago Department of Geography.

Edensor, T. (2007) Mundane mobilities, performances and spaces of tourism. *Social and Cultural Geography* 8.2: 199–215.

Elden, S. and J. Crampton (2007) Space, knowledge and power: Foucault and geography. In: J. Crampton and S. Elden (eds), *Space, Knowledge and Power: Foucault and Geography*. Aldershot: Ashgate.

Elder, G. (1995) Of Moffies, Kaffirs, and perverts: male homosexuality and the discourse of moral order in the Apartheid state. In: D. Bell and G. Valentine (eds), *Mapping Desire*. London: Routledge.

Elder, G., Knopp, L., and Nast, H. (2004) Sexuality and space. In: G. Gaile and C. Willmont (eds), *Geography in America at the Dawn of the 21st Century*. Oxford: Oxford University Press.

Elmhirst, R. (2007) Tigers and gangsters: masculinities and feminised migration in Indonesia. *Population Space and Place* 13: 225–38.

Elwood, S. (2000) Lesbian living spaces: multiple meanings of home. In: G. Valentine (ed.), *From Nowhere to Everywhere: Lesbian Geographies*. Binghamton, NY: Harrington Park Press.

Elwood, S. and Leitner, H. (2003) Community-based planning and GIS: aligning neighborhood organizations with state priorities? *Journal of Urban Affairs* 25.2: 139–57.

Emch, M. (1999) Diarrheal disease risk in Matlab, Bangladesh. *Social Science and Medicine* 49: 519–30.

England, K. (1993) Suburban pink collar ghettos: the spatial entrapment of women? *Annals of the Association of American Geographers* 83.2: 225–42.

England, K. (1994) Getting personal: reflexivity, positionality, and feminist research. *Professional Geographer* 46.1: 80–9.

Entrikin, J. (1976) Contemporary humanism in geography. *Annals of the Association of American Geographers* 66.4: 615–32.

Entrikin, J. (1980) Robert Park's human ecology and human geography. *Annals of the Association of American Geographers* 70.1: 43–58.

Environmental Perspectives Inc. (2001) http://www.epi.freedom.org (no longer accessible).

Escobar, A. (1995) *Encountering Development: The Making and Unmaking of the Third World*. Princeton, NJ: Princeton University Press.

Eyles, J. (1986) Introduction: diffusion or convergence? In: J. Eyles (ed.), *Social Geography: An International Perspective*. London: Croom Helm.

Eyles, J. and A. Litva (1996) Theory calming: you can only get there from here. *Health and Place*, 2.1: 41–3.

Eyles, J. and Woods, K. (1983) *The Social Geography of Medicine and Health*. New York: St Martin's Press.

Ezzati, M., Friedman, A., Kulkarni, S., and Murray, C. (2008) The reversal of fortunes: trends in county mortality and cross-county mortality disparities in the United States. *PLoS Medicine* 5.4: e66 (http://medicine.plosjournals.org/perlserv/?request=get-document&doi=10.1371/journal.pmed.0050066).

Fannin, M. (2004) Domesticating birth in the hospital: "family-centered" birth and the emergence of "homelike" birthing rooms. In: K. Mitchell, S. Marston, and C. Katz (eds), *Life's Work: Geographies of Social Reproduction*. Malden: Blackwell.

Fannin, M., Fort, S., Marley, J., Miller, J., and Wright, S. (2000) The battle in Seattle: a response from local geographers in the midst of the WTO Ministerial Meetings. *Antipode* 32.3: 215–21.

Farmer, P. (1992) *AIDS and Accusation: Haiti and the Geography of Blame*. Berkeley: University of California Press.

Fielding, S. (2000) Walk on the left! Children's geographies and the primary school. In: S. L. Holloway and G. Valentine (eds), *Children's Geographies: Playing, Living, Learning*. London: Routledge.

Fine, M., Weis, L., Weseen, S., and Wong, L. (2000) For whom? Qualitative research, representations, and social responsibilities. In: N. Denzin and Y. Lincoln (eds), *Handbook of Qualitative Research*, 2nd edn. Thousand Oaks, CA: Sage.

Finney, N. and Simpson, L. (2008) Internal migration and ethnic groups: evidence for Britain from the 2001 census. *Population, Space and Place*: DOI: 10.1002/psp.481.

Fleming, M. (1988) *The Odyssey of Elisée Reclus: The Geography of Freedom*. Montréal: Black Rose Books.

Flint, C. (ed.) (2004) *Spaces of Hate: Geographies of Discrimination and Intolerance in the USA*. New York: Routledge.

Forrest, J., Poulsen, M., and Johnston, R. (2006) A "multicultural model" of the spatial assimilation of ethnic minority groups in Australia's major immigrant-receiving cities. *Urban Geography* 27.5: 441–63.

Foucault, M. (1973) *The Birth of the Clinic: An Archaeology of Medical Perception*. New York: Vintage Books.

Foucault, M. (1995) *Discipline and Punish: The Birth of the Prison*. New York: Vintage Books.

Foucault, M. (1999) Space, power and knowledge. In: S. During (ed.), *The Cultural Studies Reader*. New York: Routledge.

Froehling, O. (1997) The cyberspace "war of ink and Internet" in Chiapas, Mexico. *Geographical Review* 87.2: 291–307.

Fuller, D. (1999) Part of the action, or "going native"? Learning to cope with the "politics of integration." *Area*, 31.3: 221–7.

Fyfe, N. R. and Kenny, J. T. (2005) *The Urban Geography Reader*. London: Routledge.

Gage, A. (2007) Barriers to the utilization of maternal health care in rural Mali. *Social Science and Medicine* 65: 1666–82.

Gagen, L. (2000a) An example to us all: child development and identity construction in early 20th-century playgrounds. *Environment and Planning A* 32: 599–616.

Gagen, L. (2000b) Playing the part: performing gender in America's playgrounds. In: S. L. Holloway and G. Valentine (eds), *Children's Geographies: Play, Living, and Learning.* London: Routledge.

Gallagher, R. (2008) Queering sex tourism: the geographies of gay, transgender, and female sex tourism in South-East Asia in the time of HIV. Unpublished PhD, Department of Geography, Cambridge University.

Gallaher, C. (2003) *On the Fault Line: Race, Class, and the American Patriot Movement.* Lanham, MD: Rowman and Littlefield.

Geertz, C. (1973) *The Interpretation of Cultures: Selected Essays.* New York: Basic Books.

Geores, M. (1998) Surviving on metaphor: how "health – hot springs" created and sustained a town. In: R. Kearns and W. Gesler (eds), *Putting Health into Place: Landscape, Identity, and Well-Being.* Syracuse, NY: Syracuse University Press.

Gesler, W. (1991) *The Cultural Geography of Health Care.* Pittsburgh: University of Pittsburgh Press.

Gesler, W. (1992) Therapeutic landscapes: medical issues in light of the new cultural geography. *Social Science and Medicine* 34.7: 735–46.

Gesler, W. (1998) Bath's reputation as a healing place. In: R. Kearns and W. Gesler (eds), *Putting Health into Place: Landscape, Identity, and Well-Being.* Syracuse, NY: Syracuse University Press.

Gesler, W. and Kearns, R. (2002) *Culture/Place/Health.* London: Routledge.

Ghose, R. and Elwood, S. (2003) Public participation GIS and local political context: propositions and research directions. *URISA Journal* 15 (APA II): 17–24.

Gibbs, G. (2000) Rural revolt over asylum seekers hostel. *Guardian Online* June 17 (http://www.guardian.co.uk/uk/2000/jun/17/immigration.immigrationandpublicservices1), accessed August 2008.

Gibson-Graham, J. K. (1996) *The End of Capitalism (As We Knew It): A Feminist Critique of Political Economy.* New York: Blackwell.

Gibson-Graham, J. K. (2006) *A Postcapitalist Politics.* Minneapolis: University of Minnesota Press.

Giggs, J. (1973) The distribution of schizophrenics in Nottingham. *Transactions of the Institute of British Geographers* 59: 55–76.

Gilbert, E. (2007) Leaky borders and solid citizens: governing security, prosperity and quality of life in the North American partnership. *Antipode* 39.1: 77–98.

Gilbert, E. and Steel, R. (1945) Social geography and its place in colonial studies. *Geographical Journal,* 106.3/4: 118–31.

Gilbert, M. (1997) Feminism and difference in urban geography. *Urban Geography,* 18.2: 166–79.

Gilmartin, M. and Berg, L. (2007) Locating postcolonialism. *Area* 39.1: 120–4.

Gleeson, B. (1999) *Geographies of Disability.* London: Routledge.

Godlewska, A. and Smith, N. (1994) *Geography and Empire.* Oxford: Blackwell.

Golant, S. (1972) *The Residential Location and Spatial Behavior of the Elderly.* Chicago: University of Chicago Press.

Goldhaber, R. (2007) A spatio-perceptual segregation model: a case study of Jewish and Arab experiences in Jaffa, Israel. *Urban Geography* 28.6: 578–603.

Golledge, R. (1993) Geography and the disabled: a survey with special reference to vision impaired and blind populations. *Transactions of the Institute of British Geographers* 18.1: 63–85.

Golledge, R. and Stimson, R. (1997) *Spatial Behavior: A Geographic Perspective.* New York: Guilford Press.

Goodchild, M. and Janelle, D. (2004) *Spatially Integrated Social Science.* Oxford: Oxford University Press.

Goodrich, J. (1993) Socialist Cuba: a study of health tourism. *Journal of Travel Research* 32.1: 35–41.

Gorman-Murray, A. (2006) Homeboys: uses of home by gay Australian men. *Social and Cultural Geography* 7.1: 53–69.

Goss, J. (1993) The "magic of the mall": an analysis of form, function, and meaning in the contemporary retail built environment. *Annals of the Association of American Geographers* 83.1: 18–47.

Gould, P. and White, G. (1974) *Mental Maps.* London: Penguin.

Gramsci, A. (1971) *Selections from the Prison Notebooks.* New York: International Publishers.

Gramsci, A. (1996) *Antonio Gramsci: Prison Notebooks, Volume II.* New York: Columbia University Press.

Gregory, D. (1994) Social theory and human geography. In: D. Gregory, R. Martin, and G. Smith (eds), *Human Geography: Society, Space, and Social Science.* Minneapolis: University of Minnesota.

Gregory, D. (2000) Spatiality. In: R. J. Johnston, D. Gregory, G. Pratt, and M. Watts (eds), *The Dictionary of Human Geography*, 4th edn. Oxford: Blackwell.

Gregory, D. (2004) *The Colonial Present.* Malden: Blackwell.

Gregson, N. (1993) "The initiative": delimiting or deconstructing social geography? *Progress in Human Geography* 17.4: 525–30.

Gregson, N. (1995) And now it's all consumption? *Progress in Human Geography* 19: 135–41.

Gregson, N. (2003) Reclaiming "the social" in social and cultural geography. In: K. Anderson, M. Domosh, S. Pile, and N. Thrift (eds), *Handbook of Cultural Geography.* London: Sage.

Gregson, N., Metcalfe, A., and Crewe, L. (2007) Moving things along: the conduits and practices of divestment in consumption. *Transactions of the Institute of British Geographers* 35: 187–200.

Grineski, S., Bolin, B., and Agadjanian, V. (2006) Tuberculosis and urban growth: class, race and disease in early Phoenix, Arizona, USA. *Health and Place* 12: 603–16.

Grosz, E. (1994) *Volatile Bodies.* Bloomington: Indiana University Press.

Grundfest Schoepf, B. (2004) AIDS, history, and struggles over meaning. In: E. Kalipeni, S. Craddock, J. Oppong, and J. Ghosh (eds), *HIV/AIDs in Africa: Beyond Epidemiology.* Malden, MA: Blackwell.

Gubrium, J. and Holstein, J. (1999) The nursing home as a discursive anchor for the aging body. *Ageing and Society* 29.5: 519–38.

Gwanzura-ottemöller, F. and Kesby, M. (2005) "Let's talk about sex, baby . . .": conversing with Zimbabwean children about HIV/AIDS. *Children's Geographies* 3.2: 201–18.

Hague, E. (2002) Intervention roundtable Antipode, Inc? *Antipode* 34.4: 655–61.

Halberstam, J. (2005) *In a Queer Time and Place: Transgendered Bodies, Subcultural Lives.* New York: New York University.

Hall, S. (1996) Gramsci's relevance for the study of race and ethnicity. In: D. Morley and K.-H. Chen (eds), *Stuart Hall: Critical Dialogues in Cultural Studies.* London: Routledge.

Halseth, G. and Rosenberg, M. (1988) The Kingston regional ambulance service. In: M. Anderson, M. Rosenberg, and R. Tinline (eds), *Proceedings of the Third International Symposium in Medical Geography.* Kingston, Ontario: Queens University.

Hamnett, C. (1996) Editor's introduction. In: C. Hamnett (ed.), *Social Geography: A Reader*. London: Arnold.

Hanna, S., Del Casino, V., Jr, Selden, C., and Hite, B. (2004) Representation as work in "America's most historic city." *Social and Cultural Geography* 5.3: 459–82.

Hannah, M. (2000) *Governmentality and the Mastery of Territory in Nineteenth-Century America*. Cambridge: Cambridge University Press.

Hansen, N. and Philo, C. (2007) The normality of doing things differently: bodies, spaces, and disability geography. *Tjidschrift voor Economische en Sociale Geografie* 98.4: 493–506.

Haraway, D. (1991) *Simians, Cyborgs, and Women*. New York: Routledge.

Haraway, D. (2004) Situated knowledges: the science question in feminism and the privilege of partial perspective. In: S. Harding (ed.), *The Feminist Standpoint Theory Reader: Intellectual and Political Controversies*. New York: Routledge.

Harding, S. (1987) *Feminism and Methodology*. Bloomington: Indiana University Press.

Harker, C. (2005) Playing and affective time-spaces. *Children's Geographies* 3.1: 47–62.

Harper, S. (2006) *Ageing Societies*. London: Hodder Arnold.

Harper, S. and Laws, G. (1995) Rethinking the geography of ageing. *Progress in Human Geography* 19: 199–221.

Harvey, D. (1969) *Explanation in Geography*. London: Edward Arnold.

Harvey, D. (1972) Social justice and spatial systems. *Antipode* 4.1: 87–106.

Harvey, D. (1973) *Social Justice and the City*. London: Edward Arnold.

Harvey, F. (2001) Constructing GIS: actor networks of collaboration. *URISA Journal* 13.1: 29–37.

Hay, I. (2000) *Qualitative Research Methods in Human Geography*. Oxford: Oxford University Press.

Hayden, D. (2002) *Redesigning the American Dream: Gender, Housing, and Family Life*. New York: W. W. Norton & Company.

Herbert, S. (1997a) Territoriality and the police. *Professional Geographer* 49.1: 86–94.

Herbert, S. (1997b) The normative ordering of police territoriality: making and marking space with the Los Angeles Police Department. *Annals of the Association of American Geographers* 86.3: 567–82.

Herbert, S. (2007) The "Battle of Seattle" revisited: or, seven views of a protest-zoning state. *Political Geography* 26: 601–19.

Herman, R. (2007) Playing with restraints: space, citizenship and BDSM. In: K. Browne, J. Lim, and G. Brown (eds), *Geographies of Sexualities: Theory, Practices, and Politics*. Aldershot: Ashgate.

Herod, A., Ó Tuathail, G., and Roberts, S. (1998) *An Unruly World? Globalization, Governance, and Geography*. London: Routledge.

Herod, A. and Wright, M. (2002) Placing scale: an introduction. In: A. Herod and M. Wright (eds), *Geographies of Power: Placing Scale*. Oxford: Blackwell.

Hickey, M. and Lawson, V. (2005) Beyond science? human geography, interpretation and critique. In: N. Castree, A. Rogers, and D. Sherman (eds), *Questioning Geography*. Malden, MA: Blackwell.

Hirsch, M. and Keller, E. F. (1990) Conclusion: practicing conflict in feminist theory. In: M. Hirsch and E. F. Keller (eds), *Conflicts in Feminism*. London: Routledge.

Hoke, G. (1907) The study of social geography. *Geographical Journal* 29.1: 64–7.

Holliday, R. and Cairnie, A. (2007) Man made plastic: investigating men's consumption of aesthetic surgery. *Journal of Consumer Culture* 7.1: 57–78.

Holloway, S. and Valentine, G. (2000) Children's geographies and the new social studies of childhood. In: S. Holloway and G. Valentine (eds), *Children's Geographies: Playing, Living, Learning*. London: Routledge.

Holt, L. (2003) (Dis)abling children in primary school micro-spaces: geographies of inclusion and exclusion. *Health and Place* 9: 119–28.

Holt, L. (2004) Children with mind–body differences: performing disability in primary school classrooms. *Children's Geographies* 2.2: 219–36.

Hopkins, P. and Pain, R. (2007) Geographies of age: thinking relationally. *Area* 39.3: 287–94.

Howard, A. and Omlin, F. (2008) Abandoning small-scale fish farming in western Kenya leads to higher malaria vector abundance. *Acta Tropica* 105.1: 67–73.

Howitt, R. (1998) Scale as relation: musical metaphors of geographical scale. *Area* 30: 49–58.

Howitt, R. (2003) Scale. In: J. Agnew, K. Mitchell, and G. Ó Tuathail (eds), *A Companion to Political Geography*. Oxford: Blackwell.

Hoy, C. (2007) Migration as sexual liberation? Examining the experience of young female migrants in China. *Children's Geographies* 5.1/2: 183–7.

Hubbard, P. (2000) Desire/disgust: mapping the moral contours of heterosexuality. *Progress in Human Geography* 24.2: 191–217.

Hubbard, P., Kitchin, R., and Valentine, G. (2004) *Key Thinkers on Space and Place*. Thousand Oaks, CA: Sage.

Huberman, L. and Sweezy, P. (1969) *Socialism in Cuba*. New York: Monthly Review Press.

Hugman, R. (1999) Embodying old age. In: E. Teanor (ed.), *Embodied Geographies: Spaces, Bodies and Rites of Passage*. London: Routledge.

Hunter, J. (2003) Inherited burden of disease: agricultural dams and the persistence of bloody urine (*Schistosomiasis hematobium*) in the Upper East Region of Ghana, 1959–1997. *Social Science and Medicine* 56: 219–34.

Huntington, E. (1915) *Civilization and Climate*. New Haven, CT: Yale University Press.

Huxley, M. (2007) Geographies of governmentality. In: J. W. Crampton and S. Elden (eds), *Space, Knowledge and Power: Foucault and Geography*. Aldershot: Ashgate.

Imrie, R. (1999) The body, disability and Le Corbusier's conception of radiant environment. In: R. Butler and H. Parr (eds), *Mind and Body Spaces: Geographies of Illness, Impairment and Disability*. London: Routledge.

Inkpen, R. (2004) *Science, Philosophy, and Physical Geography*. London: Routledge.

Jackson, P. (1983) Principles and problems of participant observation. *Geografiska Annaler* 65.1: 39–46.

Jackson, P. (1989) *Maps of Meaning*. London: Unwin Hyman.

Jackson, P. (2000) Rematerializing social and cultural geography. *Social and Cultural Geography* 1.1: 9–14.

Jackson, P. (2003) Introduction: the social question. In: K. Anderson, M. Domosh, S. Pile, and N. J. Thrift (eds), *Handbook of Cultural Geography*. London: Sage.

Jackson, P. (2004) Local consumption cultures in a globalizing world. *Transactions of the Institute of British Geographers* 29: 165–78.

Jackson, P., Thomas, N., and Dwyer, C. (2007) Consuming transnational fashion in London and Mumbai. *Geoforum* 38: 908–24.

Jackson, S. and Sleigh, A. (2000) Resettlement for China's Three Gorges Dam: socio-economic impact and institutional tensions. *Communist and Post-Communist Studies* 33: 223–41.

James, A. (1993) *Childhood Identities: Self and Social Relationships in the Experience of the Child*. Edinburgh: Edinburgh University Press.

James, S. (1990) Is there a place for children in geography? *Area* 22: 278–83.

Jampaklay, A. (2006) How does leaving home affect marital timing? An event-history analysis of migration and marriage in Nang Rong, Thailand. *Demography* 43.4: 711–25.

Johnsen, S., Cloke, P., and May, J. (2005) Transitory spaces of care: serving homeless people on the street. *Health and Place* 11: 323–36.

Johnson, D. and Mitchell, D. (2004) Syracuse Hunger Project: Executive Report Presentation to the Community (http://www.maxwell.syr.edu/geo/redesigned_site/syr_hp/Executive%20Report%20ver4-22.pdf), accessed January 13, 2008.

Johnston, L. (2005) *Queering Tourism: Paradoxical Performances at Gay Pride Parades.* London: Routledge.

Johnston, L. (2007) Mobilizing pride/shame: lesbians, tourism and parades. *Social and Cultural Geography* 8.1: 29–46.

Johnston, R., Poulsen, M., and Forrest, J. (2003) And did the walls come tumbling down? Ethnic residential segregation in four US metropolitan areas 1980–2000. *Urban Geography* 24.7: 560–81.

Johnston, R. (1976) Areal studies, ecological studies, and social patterns in cities. *Transactions of the Institute of British Geographers* 1.1: 118–22.

Johnston, R. (1986) North America. In: J. Eyles (ed.), *Social Geography in International Perspective.* Totowa, NJ: Barnes and Noble Books.

Johnston, R. (2000) Social area analysis. In: R. J. Johnston, D. Gregory, G. Pratt, and M. Watts (eds), *The Dictionary of Human Geography.* Malden, MA: Blackwell.

Johnston, R. and Sidaway, J. (2004) *Geography and Geographers: Anglo-American Human Geography since 1945.* London: Arnold.

Jones, J. P. III and Kodras, J. (1990) Restructured regions and families: the feminization of poverty in the US. *Annals of the Association of American Geographers* 80.2: 163–83.

Jones, J. P. III, Nast, H., and Roberts, S. (1997) Thresholds in feminist geography: difference, methodology, representation. In: J. P. Jones III, H. Nast, and S. Roberts (eds), *Thresholds in Feminist Geography: Difference, Methodology, Representation.* Lanham, MD: Rowman & Littlefield.

Jones, K. (1998) Scale as epistemology. *Political Geography* 17.1: 25–8.

Jöns, H. (2006) Dynamic hybrids and the geographies of technoscience: discussing conceptual resoures beyond the human/non-human binary. *Social and Cultural Geography* 7.4: 557–80.

Joseph, A. and Bantock, P. (1982) Measuring potential physical accessibility to general practitioners in rural areas. *Social Science and Medicine* 16: 85–90.

Karsten, L. (2003) Children's use of public space: the gendered world of the playground. *Childhood* 10.4: 457–73.

Katz, C. (1991) Sow what you know: the struggle for social reproduction in rural Sudan. *Annals of the Association of American Geographers* 81.3: 488–514.

Katz, C. (1994) Playing the field: questions of fieldwork in geography. *Professional Geographer* 46.1: 67–72.

Katz, C. (2004) *Growing Up Global: Economic Restructuring and Children's Everyday Lives.* Minneapolis: Minnesota.

Katz, C. (2006) Reworking, replaying. *Social and Cultural Geography* 7.6: 1019–22.

Katz, S. (2003) Critical gerontological theory: intellectual fieldwork and the nomadic life of ideas. In: S. Biggs, A. Lowenstein, and J. Hendricks (eds), *The Need for Theory: Critical Approaches to Social Gerontology.* Amityville, NY: Baywood.

Kearns, R. (1993) Place and health: towards a reformed medical geography. *Professional Geographer* 45.2: 139–47.

Kearns, R. and Andrews, G. (2005) Placing ageing: positionings in the study of older people. In: G. Andrews and D. Phillips (eds), *Ageing and Place: Perspectives, Policy and Practice*. London: Routledge.

Kearns, R. and Gesler, W. (1998a) *Putting Health Into Place: Landscape, Identity and Well-Being*. Syracuse, NY: Syracuse University Press.

Kearns, R. and Gesler, W. (1998b) Introduction. In: R. Kearns and W. Gelser (eds), *Putting Health into Place: Landscape, Identity, and Well-Being*. Syracuse, NY: Syracuse University Press.

Kearns, R. and Joseph, A. (1997) Restructuring health and rural communities in New Zealand. *Progress in Human Geography* 21.1: 18–32.

Kesby, M. (2004) Participatory diagramming and the ethical and practical challenges of helping Africans themselves to move HIV work "beyond epidemiology." In: E. Kalipeni, S. Craddock, J. Oppong, and J. Ghosh (eds), *HIV and AIDS in Africa: Beyond Epidemiology*. Malden, MA: Blackwell.

Khan, F. and Pieterse, E. (2004) *The Homeless People's Alliance: Purposive Creation and Ambiguated Realities*. Durban: University of Kwazulu-Natal, School of Development Studies.

King, L. and Golledge, R. (1978) *Cities, Spaces, and Behavior: The Elements of Urban Geography*. Englewood Cliffs, NJ: Prentice Hall.

Kingsbury, P. (2005) Jamaican tourism and the politics of enjoyment. *Geoforum* 36: 113–32.

Kitchin, R. (1998a) "Out of place," "knowing one's place": space, power and the exclusion of disabled people. *Disability and Society* 13.3: 343–56.

Kitchin, R. (1998b) Towards geographies of cyberspace. *Progress in Human Geography* 22.3: 385–406.

Kitchin, R. (2007) *Mapping Worlds: International Perspectives on Social and Cultural Geographies*. London: Routledge.

Kitchin, R. and Hubbard, P. (1999) Research, action, and "critical" geographies. *Area* 31.3: 195–8.

Kitchin, R. and Tate, N. (2000) *Conducting Research in Human Geography: Theory, Methodology, and Practice*. Harlow: Prentice Hall.

Kitchin, R. and Wilton, R. (2000) Disability, geography and ethics. *Ethics, Place and Environment* 3.1: 61–102.

Kjørholt, A. (2003) "Creating a place to belong": girls' and boys' hut-building as a site for understanding discourses on childhood and generational relations in a Norwegian community. *Children's Geographies* 1.1: 261–79.

Klinkenberg, E., van der Hoek, W., and Amerasighe, F. (2004) A malaria risk analysis in an irrigated area in Sri Lanka. *Acta Tropica* 89: 215–25.

Knodel, J. and Saengtienchai, C. (2007) Rural parents with urban children: social and economic implications of migration for the rural elderly in Thailand. *Population, Space and Place* 13: 193–210.

Knopp, L. (1990a) Exploring the rent-gap: the theoretical significance of using illegal appraisal schemes to encourage gentrification in New Orleans. *Urban Geography* 11.1: 46–64.

Knopp, L. (1990b) Some theoretical implications of gay involvement in an urban land market. *Political Geography Quarterly* 9.4: 337–52.

Kobayashi, A. (2006) Why women of colour in geography? *Gender, Place and Culture*, 13.1: 33–8.

Kobayashi, A. and Peake, L. (2000) Racism out of place: thoughts on whiteness and an antiracist geography in the new millennium. *Annals of the Association of American Geographers* 90.2: 392–403.

Kochems, L. and Del Casino, V., Jr (2004) *Manipulating Multiple Life Identity-Shifts: Points of HIV Risk in Overlapping Drug Cultures and Gay Cultures in Long Beach, CA*. Washington, DC: Oral Presentation at the American Public Health Association Meetings.

Kodras, J. (1984) Regional variation in the determinants of food stamp participation program. *Environment and Planning C: Government and Policy* 2: 67–78.

Kodras, J. (1986) Labor market and policy constraints on the work disincentive effect of welfare. *Annals of the Association of American Geographers* 76.2: 228–46.

Kodras, J. (1997) The changing map of American poverty in an era of economic restructuring and political realignment. *Economic Geography* 73.1: 67–93.

Kodras, J., Jones, J. P. III, and Falconer, K. (1994) Contextualizing welfare's work disincentive: the case of female-headed families. *Geographical Analysis* 26.4: 285–99.

Kornblum, J. (2008) Life expectancy worsening or stagnating for large segment of the US population. *USA Today* (http://www.usatoday.com/news/health/2008-04-21-life-span-study_N.htm).

Kropotkin, P. (1905) Obituary: Elisée Reclus. *Geographical Journal* 26.3: 337–43.

Kropotkin, P. (1971) What geography ought to be. *Antipode* 10.3: 6–15.

Kuhkle, O. (2006) Epistemology. In: B. Warf (ed.), *Encyclopedia of Human Geography*. Thousand Oaks, CA: Sage.

Laclau, E. and Mouffe, C. (2001) *Hegemony and Socialist Strategy: Towards a Radical Democratic Politics*, 2nd edn. London: Verso.

Ladusingh, L. and Singh, C. (2006) Place, community education, gender and child morality in North-East India. *Population, Space and Place* 12: 65–76.

Latour, B. (1993) *We Have Never Been Modern*. Cambridge, MA: Harvard University Press.

Latour, B. (1996) On actor network theory: a few clarifications. *Soziale Welt* 47: 360–81.

Lauria, M. and Knopp, L. (1985) Toward an analysis of the role of gay communities in the urban renaissance. *Urban Geography* 6.2: 152–69.

Laurier, E. (1993) "Tackintosh": Glasgow's supplementary gloss. In: G. Kearns and C. Philo (eds), *Selling Places: The City as Cultural Capital, Past and Present*. Oxford: Pergamon Press.

Laurier, E., Whyte, A., and Buckner, K. (2001) An ethnography of a neighbourhood café: informality, table arrangements and background noise. *Journal of Mundane Behavior* 2.2: 195–232.

Lawrence, M. (1995) Rural homelessness: a geography without a geography. *Journal of Rural Studies* 11.3: 297–307.

Laws, G. (1995) Embodiment and emplacement: identities, representation and landscape in Sun City retirement communities. *International Journal of Aging and Human Development* 40.4: 253–80.

Laws, G. (1996) "A shot of economic adrenalin": reconstructing "the elderly" in the retiree-based economic development literature. *Journal of Aging Studies* 10.3: 171–88.

Laws, G. (1997) Spatiality and age relations. In: A. Jamieson, S. Harper, and C. Victor (eds), *Critical Approaches to Ageing and Later Life*. Buckingham: Open University Press.

Lawson, V. (1998) Hierarchical households and gendered migration in Latin America: feminist extensions to migration research. *Progress in Human Geography* 22.1: 39–53.

Lawson, V. (2007) Geographies of care and responsibility. *Annals of the Association of American Geographers* 97.1: 1–11.

LeCompte, M. and Schensul, J. (1999a) *Analyzing and Interpreting Ethnographic Data*. New York: Rowman and Littlefield.

LeCompte, M. and Schensul, J. (1999b) *Designing and Conducting Ethnographic Research*. New York: Rowman and Littlefield.

Ley, D. (1977) Social geography and the taken-for-granted world. *Transactions of the Institute of British Geographers* 2.4: 498–512.

Ley, D. and Mountz, A. (2001) Interpretation, representation, positionality: issues in field research in human geography. In: M. Limb and C. Dwyer (eds), *Qualitative Methodologies for Geographers: Issues and Debates*. London: Arnold.

Ley, D. and Samuels, M. (1978) *Humanistic Geography: Problems and Perspectives*. London: Croom Helm.

Li, Y., Sleigh, A., Ross, A., Williams, G., Tanner, M., and McManus, D. (2000) Epidemiology of Schistosoma jaonicum in China: morbidity and strategies for control in the Donting Lake region. *International Journal for Parasitology* 30: 273–81.

Li, Y., Qian, H., Tak Sun Yu, T., and Wong, T. (2006) Probably roles of bio-aerosol dispersion in the SARS outbreak in Amoy Gardens, Hong Kong. In: A. Sleigh, C. Heng Leng, B. Yeoh, P. Kai Hong, and R. Safman (eds), *Population Dynamics and Infectious Diseases in Asia*. London: World Scientific.

Lim, J., Brown, G., and Browne, K. (2007) Conclusions and future directions, or our hopes for geographies of sexualities (and queer geographies). In: K. Browne, J. Lim, and G. Brown (eds), *Geographies of Sexualities: Theory, Practices, Politics*. Aldershot: Ashgate.

Limb, M. and Dwyer, C. (2001) *Qualitative Methodologies for Geographers: Issues and Debates*. London, Arnold.

Lincoln, Y. and Guba, E. (2000) Paradigmatic controversies, contradictions, and emerging confluences. In: N. K. Denzin and Y. S. Lincoln (eds), *Handbook of Qualitative Research*. Thousand Oaks, CA: Sage.

Little, J. (2003) "Riding the rural love train": heterosexuality and the rural community. *Sociologia Ruralis* 43.4: 401–17.

Livingstone, D. (1992) *The Geographical Tradition*. Oxford: Blackwell.

Lobao, L., J. Rulli, and L. Brown (1999) Macrolevel theory and local-level inequality: industrial structure, institutional arrangements, and the political economy of redistribution, 1970 and 1990. *Annals of the Association of American Geographers* 4: 571–601.

Loe, M. (2004) Sex and the senior women: pleasure and danger in the Viagra age. *Sexualities* 7.3: 303–26.

Longhurst, R. (1999) Pregnant bodies, public scrutiny: "giving" advice to pregnant women. In: N. Duncan (ed.), *BodySpace*. London: Routledge.

Longhurst, R. (2001) *Bodies: Exploring Fluid Boundaries*. London: Routledge.

Longhurst, R. (2005) Fat bodies: developing geographical research agendas. *Progress in Human Geography* 29.3: 247–59.

Lucas, T. (1998) Youth gangs and moral panic in Santa Cruz, California. In: T. Skelton and G. Valentine (eds), *Cool Places: Geographies of Youth Culture*. London: Routledge.

MacCannell, D. (1989) *The Tourist: A New Theory of the Leisure Class*. New York: Schocken Books.

McCracken, K. and Phillips, D. (2005) International demographic transitions. In: G. Andrews and D. Phillips (eds), *Ageing and Place: Perspectives, Policy, and Practice*. London: Routledge.

McDowell, L. (1997) Women/gender/feminisms: doing feminist geography. *Journal of Geography in Higher Education* 21.3: 381–400.

MacEachren, A. (2000) Cartography and GIS: facilitating collaboration. *Progress in Human Geography* 24.3: 445–56.

MacEachren, A. (2004) *How Maps Work*. New York: Guilford.

McHugh, K. (2007) Generational consciousness and retirement communities. *Population, Space and Place* 14: 293–306.

McHugh, K. and Larson-Keagy, E. (2005) These white walls: the dialectic of retirement communities. *Journal of Aging Studies* 19: 241–56.

McKenrick, J. (1999) Multi-method research: an introduction to its application in population geography. *Professional Geographer* 51.1: 40–50.

McKinnon, K. (2007) Postdevelopment, professionalism, and the politics of participation. *Annals of the Association of American Geographers* 97.4: 772–85.

McLafferty, S. (2002) Mapping women's worlds: knowledge, power, and the bounds of GIS. *Gender, Place and Culture* 9.3: 263–9.

MacLeod, G. (1998) In what sense a region? Place, hybridity, symbolic shape, and institutional formation in (post-) modern Scotland. *Political Geography* 17.7: 833–63.

McNee, B. (1984) If you are squeamish . . . *East Lakes Geographer* 19: 16–27.

McNee, B. (1985) It takes one to know one. *Transition* 14: 2–15.

Mahler, S. (1999) Engendering transnational migration: a case study of Salvadorans. *American Behavioral Scientist* 42: 690–719.

Mahtani, M. (2006) Challenging the ivory tower: proposing anti-racist geographies within the academy. *Gender, Place and Culture* 13.1: 21–5.

Mains, S. (2006) Discourse. In: B. Warf (ed.), *The Encyclopedia of Human Geography*. Thousand Oaks, CA: Sage.

Maintz, J. (2008) Synthesizing the face-to-face experience: e-learning practices and the constitution of place online. *Social Geography* 3: 1–10.

Mansfield, B. (2005) Beyond rescaling: reintegrating the "national" as a dimension of scalar relations. *Progress in Human Geography* 29.4: 458–73.

Mansvelt, J. (1997) Working at leisure: critical geographies of ageing. *Area* 29.4: 289–98.

Mansvelt, J. (2005) *Geographies of Consumption*. Thousand Oaks, CA: Sage.

Marston, S. (2000) The social construction of scale. *Progress in Human Geography* 24.2: 219–42.

Marston, S., Jones, J. P. III, and Woodward, K. (2005) Human geography without scale. *Transactions of the Institute of British Geographers* 30.4: 416–32.

Matthews, H. and Limb, M. (1999) Defining an agenda for the geography of children: review and prospect. *Progress in Human Geography* 23.1: 61–90.

May, J. (2000) Of nomads and vagrants: single homelessness and narratives of home as place. *Environment and Planning D: Society and Space* 18: 737–59.

Mayer, J. (1982) Medical geography: some unsolved problems. *Professional Geographer* 34.3: 261–9.

Mayer, J. (2000) Geography, ecology and emerging infectious diseases. *Social Science and Medicine* 50: 937–52.

Mayo, P. (1999) *Gramsci, Freire, and Adult Education: Possibilities for Transformative Action*. London: Zed Books.

References

Meade, M. and Earickson, R. (2000) *Medical Geography*. New York: Guilford Press.

Merrill, H. (2006) *An Alliance of Women: Immigration and the Politics of Race*. Minneapolis: University of Minnesota.

Miller, B. (2000) *Geography and Social Movements: Comparing Antinuclear Activism in the Boston Area*. Minneapolis: University of Minnesota Press.

Milligan, C. (2000) "Bearing the burden": towards a restructured geography of caring. *Area* 32.1: 49–58.

Milligan, C., Atkinson, S., Skinner, M., and Wiles, J. (2007) Geographies of care: a commentary. *New Zealand Geographer* 63: 135–40.

Minkler, M. and Holstein, M. (2008) From civil rights to . . . civic engagement? Concerns of two older critical gerontologists about a "new social movement" and what it portends. *Journal of Aging Studies* 22: 196–204.

Misra, R. (1970) *Medical Geography of India*. New Delhi: National Book Trust.

Mitchell, D. (1995) There's no such thing as culture: towards a reconceptualization of the idea of culture in cultural geography. *Transactions of the Institute of British Geographers* 20: 102–16.

Mitchell, D. (1997) The annihilation of space by law: the roots and implications of anti-homeless laws in the United States. *Antipode* 29.3: 303–35.

Mitchell, D. (2000) *Cultural Geography: A Critical Introduction*. Oxford: Blackwell.

Mitchell, D. (2004) Geography in an age of extremes: a blueprint for a geography of justice. *Annals of the Association of American Geographers* 94.4: 764–70.

Mitchell, K. (2003) Cultural geographies of transnationalism. In: K. Anderson, M. Domosh, S. Pile, and N. Thrift (eds), *Handbook of Cultural Geography*. London: Sage.

Mitchell, K., Marston, S., and Katz, C. (2004) Life's work: an introduction, review, and critique. In: K. Mitchell, S. Marston, and C. Katz (eds), *Life's Work: Geographies of Social Reproduction*. New York: Blackwell.

Mohanty, C. T. (2006) US empire and the project of women's studies: stories of citizenship, complicity and dissent. *Gender, Place and Culture*, 13.1: 7–20.

Monk, J. and Hanson, S. (1982) On not excluding half of the human in human geography. *Professional Geography* 34.1: 11–23.

Monk, J. and Katz, C. (1993) When in the world are women? In: C. Katz and J. Monk (eds), *Full Circles: Geographies of Women over the Life Course*. London: Routledge.

Morrill, R. (1965) The Negro ghetto: problems and alternatives. *Geographical Review* 55: 339–61.

Morrill, R. (1970) *The Spatial Organization of Society*, 2nd edn. Belmont, CA: Wadsworth.

Morrill, R. (1973) Socialism, private property, the ghetto and geographic theory. *Antipode* 5.2: 84–5.

Mosher, W., Chandra, A., and Jones, J. (2005) *Sexual Behavior and Selected Health Measures: Men and Women 15–44 Years of Age, United States, 2002*. Atlanta, GA: Centers for Disease Control and Prevention.

Moss, P. and Dyck, I. (1999) Body, corporeal space, and legitimating chronic illness: women diagnosed with ME. *Antipode* 31.4: 372–97.

Moss, P. and Dyck, I. (2002) *Women, Body, Illness: Space and Identity in the Everyday Lives of Women with Chronic Illness*. Lanham, MD: Rowman and Littlefield.

Moss, P. and Falconer Al-Hindi, K. (2007) *Feminisms in Geography: Rethinking Space, Place, and Knowledges*. Lanham, MD: Rowman and Littleflied.

Mowl, G., Pain, R., and Talbot, C. (2000) The ageing body and the homespace. *Area* 32.2: 189–97.

Murdie, R. (1969) *Factorial Ecology of Metropolitan Toronto, 1951–1961*. University of Chicago Department of Geography, Research Paper 116.

Nair, K. (2005) The physically ageing body and the use of space. In: G. Andrews and D. Phillips (eds), *Ageing and Place: Perspectives, Policy, and Practice*. London: Routledge.

Nash, C. (2003) Cultural geography: anti-racist geographies. *Progress in Human Geography* 27.5: 637–48.

Nast, H. (2002) Queer patriarchies, queer racisms, international. *Antipode* 24.4: 864–909.

Natter, W. and Jones, J. P. III (1997) Identity, space, and other uncertainties. In: G. Benko and U. Strohmayer (eds) *Space and Social Theory: Interpreting Modernity and Postmodernity*. Oxford: Blackwell.

Nelson, L. (2006) Geographies of state power, protest, and women's political identity formation in Michoacan, Mexico. *Annals of the Association of American Geographers* 96.2: 366–89.

Nelson, L. and Seager, J. (2005) Introduction. In: L. Nelson and J. Seager (eds), *A Companion to Feminist Geography*. Malden, MA: Blackwell.

Newman, M., Woodcock, A., and Dunhamn, P. (2006) "Playtime in the borderlands": children's representations of school, gender and bullying through photographs and interviews. *Children's Geographies* 4.3: 289–302.

Nieuwenhuys, O. (2007) Embedding the global womb: global child labour and the new policy agenda. *Children's Geographies*, 5.1/2: 149–63.

Nystuen, J. (1968) Identification of some fundemental spatial concepts. In: B. Berry and D. Marble (eds), *Spatial Analysis*. Englewood Cliffs, NJ: Prentice-Hall.

Onsrud, H. and Graglia, M. (2003) Access and participatory approaches in using geographic information. *URISA Journal* 15.1: 5–7.

Oswin, N. (2004) Toward radical geographies of complicit queer futures. *ACME: An International E-Journal for Critical Geographies* 3.2: 79–86.

Pahl, R. (1970) Trends in social geography. In: R. Chorley and P. Haggett (eds), *Frontiers in Geographical Teaching*. London: Methuen and Company.

Pain, R. (2003) Social geography: on action-orientated research. *Progress in Human Geography* 27.5: 649–57.

Pain, R. (2004) Social geography: participatory research. *Progress in Human Geography* 28.5: 652–63.

Pain, R. (2006) Social geography: seven deadly myths in policy research. *Progress in Human Geography* 30.2: 250–9.

Panelli, R. and Welch, R. (2005) Why community? Reading difference and singularity with community. *Environment and Planning A* 37: 1589–611.

Park, D. C., Radford, J., and Vickers, M. (1998) Disability studies in human geography. *Progress in Human Geography* 22.2: 208–33.

Park, R., Burgess, E., and McKenzie, R. (1967 [1925]) *The City*. Chicago: University of Chicago Press.

Parr, H. (2000) Interpreting the "hidden social geographies" of mental health: of inclusion and exclusion in semi-institutional places. *Health and Place* 6.3: 225–37.

Parr, H. (2002) Medical geography: diagnosing the body in medical and health geography, 1999–2000. *Progress in Human Geography* 26.2: 240–51.

Parr, H. (2004) Medical geography: critical medical and health geography? *Progress in Human Geography* 28.2: 246–57.

Parr, H. (2008) *Mental Health and Social Space: Toward Inclusionary Geographies?* Malden, MA: Blackwell.

Parr, H. and Boyd, C. (2008) Social geography and rural mental health research. *Rural and Remote Health* 8 (http://www.rrh.org.au).

Parr, H. and Butler, R. (1999) New geographies of illness, impairment and disability. In: R. Butler and H. Parr (eds), *Mind and Body Spaces: Geographies of Illness, Impairment, and Disability*. London: Routledge.

Patton, C. (1990) *Inventing AIDS*. New York: Routledge.

Patton, C. (1994) *Last Served? Gendering the HIV Pandemic*. London: Taylor and Francis.

Peach, C. (1999) Social geography. *Progress in Human Geography* 23.2: 282–8.

Peach, C. (2000) Discovering white ethnicity and parachuted plurality. *Progress in Human Geography*, 24.4: 620–6.

Peach, C. (2002) Social geography: new religions and ethnoburbs – contrasts with cultural geography. *Progress in Human Geography* 26.2: 252–60.

Peake, L. and Schein, R. (2000) Racing geography into the new millenium: studies of "race" and North American geographies. *Social and Cultural Geography* 1.2: 133–42.

Peck, J. (2003) Geography and public policy: mapping the penal state. *Progress in Behavior Modification* 27.2: 222–32.

Peet, R. (1977) *Radical Geography: Alternative Viewpoints on Contemporary Social Issues*. Chicago: Maaroufa.

Peet, R. (1998) *Modern Geographical Thought*. Malden, MA: Blackwell.

Peet, R. and G. Rowles (1974) Social geography. *Geographical Review* 64.2: 287–9.

Pew Center of the States (2008) *One in 100: Behind Bars in America 2008*. Washington, DC: The Pew Charitable Trusts.

Phillips, D. (1981) *Contemporary Issues in the Geography of Health Care*. Norwich: Geo Books.

Phillips, M. (1998) The restructuring of social imaginations in rural geography. *Journal of Rural Studies* 14.2: 121–53.

Philo, C. (1991) Introduction, acknowledgements and brief thoughts on older words and older worlds. In: C. Philo (ed.), *New Words, New Worlds: Reconceptualising Social and Cultural Geography*. Lampeter: St David's University College.

Philo, C. (1992) Foucault's geography. *Environment and Planning D: Society and Space* 10: 137–61.

Philo, C. (1996) Staying in? Invited comments on "coming out: exposing social theory in medical geography." *Health and Place* 2.1: 35–40.

Philo, C. (1998) Animals, geography, and the city: notes on inclusions and exclusions. In: J. Wolch and J. Emel (eds), *Animal Geographies: Place, Politics, and Identity in the Nature-Culture Borderlands*. London: Verso.

Philo, C. (2000) The Birth of the Clinic: an unknown work of medical geography. *Area* 32.1: 11–19.

Philo, C. (2004) Michel Foucault. In: P. Hubbard, R. Kitchin and G. Valentine (eds), *Key Thinkers on Space and Place*. Thousand Oaks, CA: Sage.

Philo, C. (2005a) Sex, life, death, geography: fragmentary remarks inspired by "Foucault's population geographies." *Population, Space, and Place* 11: 325–33.

Philo, C. (2005b) Spacing lives and lively spaces: partial remarks on Sarah Whatmore's hybrid geographies. *Antipode* 37.4: 824–33.

Philo, C. and Wlibert, C. (2000) *New Geographies of Human–Animal Relations*. London: Arnold.

Pickerill, J. and Chatterton, P. (2006) Notes toward autonomous geographies: creation, resistance and self-management survival tactics. *Progress in Human Geography* 30: 730–46.

Pickles, J. (1995) *Ground Truth: The Social Implications of Geographic Information Systems.* New York: Guilford Press.

Pickles, J. (2004) *A History of Spaces: Cartographic Reason, Mapping, and the Geo-Coded World.* London: Routledge.

Pile, S. (1997) Introduction. In: S. Pile and M. Keith (eds), *Geographies of Resistance.* London: Routledge.

Pile, S. and Thrift, N. (1997) Introduction. In: S. Pile and N. Thrift (eds), *Mapping the Subject: Geographies of Cultural Transformation.* London: Routledge.

Pink, S. (2001) *Doing Visual Ethnography.* Thousand Oaks, CA: Sage.

Plath, D. (1990) Fieldnotes, filed notes, and the conferring of note. In: R. Sanjek (ed.), *Fieldnotes: The Making of Anthropology.* Ithaca, NY: Cornell University Press.

Popke, J. (2003) Poststructuralist ethics: subjectivity, responsibility and the space of community. *Progress in Human Geography* 27: 298–316.

Popke, J. (2006) Geography and ethics: everyday mediations through care and consumption. *Progress in Human Geography* 30.4: 504–12.

Popke, J. (2007) Geography and ethics: spaces of cosmpolitan responsibility. *Progress in Human Geography* 31.4: 509–18.

Popke, J. (2009) The spaces of being-in-common: ethics and social geography. In: S. Smith, S. Marston, R. Pain, and J. P. Jones III (eds), *Handbook of Social Geography.* London: Sage.

Potts, A., Gavey, N., Grace, V., and Vares, T. (2003) The downside of Viagra: women's experiences and concerns. *Sociology of Health and Illness* 25.7: 697–719.

Pratt, G. and Philippine Women's Centre (2005) From migration to immigrant: domestic workers settle in Vancouver, Canada. In: L. Nelson and J. Seager (eds), *A Companion to Feminist Geography.* Malden, MA: Blackwell.

Pratt, G. and Yeoh, B. (2003) Transnational (counter) topographies. *Gender, Place and Culture* 10.2: 159–66.

Pratt, M. (1992) *Imperial Eyes: Travel Writing and Transculturation.* London: Routledge.

Probyn, E. (2003) The spatial imperative of subjectivity. In: K. Anderson, M. Domosh, S. Pile, and N. Thrift (eds), *Handbook of Cultural Geography.* Thousand Oaks, CA: Sage.

Proctor, J. and Smith, D. (1999) *Geography and Ethics: Journeys in a Moral Terrain.* London: Routledge.

Puar, J. (2005) Queer times, queer assemblages. *Social Text* 23.3/4: 121–39.

Puar, J. (2006) Mapping US homonormativities. *Gender, Place and Culture* 13: 67–88.

Pugh, J. (2005) The disciplinary effects of communicative planning in Soufriere, St Lucia: governmentality, hegemony, and space-time politics. *Transactions of the Institute of British Geographers* 30.3: 307–21.

Pulido, L. (2002) Reflections on a white discipline. *Professional Geographer* 54.1: 42–9.

Pulido, L. (2006) *Black, Brown, Yellow and Left: Radical Activism in Los Angeles.* Berkeley: University of California Press.

Punch, S. (2000) Children's strategies for creating playscapes: negotiating independence in rural Bolivia. In: S. L. Holloway and G. Valentine (eds), *Children's Geographies: Playing, Living, Learning.* London: Routledge.

Pyle, G. (1977) International communication and medical geography. *Social Science and Medicine* 11: 679–82.

Pyle, G. (1983) Three decades of medical geography in the United States. In: N. McGlashen and J. Blunden (eds), *Geographical Aspects of Health.* London: Academic Press.

Radcliffe, S. (2000) Entangling resistance, ethnicity, gender, and nation in Ecuador. In: J. Sharp, P. Routledge, C. Philo, and R. Paddison (eds), *Entanglements of Power: Geographies of Domination/Resistance*. London: Routledge.

Raimondo, M. (2003) "Corralling the virus": migratory sexualities and the "spread of AIDS" in the US media. *Environment and Planning D: Society and Space* 21: 389–407.

Reclus, E. (1864) L'homme et la nature. De l'action humain sur la géographie physique. *Revue des Deux Mondes* 46 (December 15): 762–71.

Reid-Henry, S. (2007) Exceptional sovereignty? Guantánamo Bay and the re-colonial present. *Antipode* 39.4: 627–48.

Relph, E. (1970) An inquiry into the relations between phenomenology and geography. *Canadian Geographer* 14.3: 193–201.

Relph, E. (1976) *Place and Placelessness*. London: Pion Publishers.

Rich, A. (1980) Compulsory heterosexuality and lesbian experience. *Signs* 5 (Summer): 631–61.

Robbins, P. (2006) Research is theft: environmental inquiry in a postcolonial world. In: S. Aitken and G. Valentine (eds), *Approaches to Human Geography*. London: Sage.

Robbins, P. (2007) *Lawn People: How Grasses, Weeds, and Chemicals Make Us Who We Are*. Philadelphia: Temple University.

Roberts, S. (2000) Realizing critical geographies of the university. *Antipode* 32.3: 230–44.

Robinson, J. (2003) Postcolonialising geography: tactics and pitfalls. *Singapore Journal of Tropical Geography* 24: 273–89.

Robson, B. (1969) *Urban Analysis: A Study of City Structure*. Cambridge: Cambridge University Press.

Robson, E. and Ansell, N. (2000) Young carers in Southern Africa: exploring stories from Zimbabwean secondary school students. In: S. Holloway and G. Valentine (eds), *Children's Geographies: Playing, Living, Learning*. London: Routledge.

Rose, G. (1993) *Feminism and Geography: The Limits of Geographical Knowledge*. Minneapolis: University of Minnesota Press.

Rose, G. (1997) Situated knowledges: positionalities, reflexivities, and other tactics. *Progress in Human Geography* 21: 305–20.

Rose, G. (2007) *Visual Methodologies*. Thousand Oaks, CA: Sage.

Rose, N. (2007) *The Politics of Life: Biomedicine, Power, and Subjectivity in the Twenty-First Century*. Princeton, NJ: Princeton University Press.

Rosenberg, M. (1988) Linking the geographical, the medical and the political in analyzing health care delivery systems. *Social Science and Medicine* 26.1: 179–86.

Rosenberg, M. and Everitt, J. (2001) Planning for aging populations: inside or outside the walls. *Progress in Planning* 56: 119–68.

Rosenfeld, D. (1999) Identity work among lesbian and gay elderly. *Journal of Aging Studies* 13.2: 121–44.

Rothenberg, T. (1995) "And she told two friends": lesbians creating urban social space. In: D. Bell and G. Valentine (eds), *Mapping Desire: Geographies of Sexuality*. London: Routledge.

Rowles, G. (1978a) *Prisoners of Space? Exploring Geographical Experiences of Older People*. Boulder, CO: Westview.

Rowles, G. (1978b) Reflections of experiential field work. In: D. Ley and M. Samuels (eds), *Humanistic Geography: Prospects and Problems*. Chicago: Maaroufa Press.

Rowles, G. (1986) The geography of ageing and the aged: towards an integrated perspective. *Progress in Human Geography* 10: 511–39.

Ruddick, S. (1996) *Young and Homeless in Hollywood: Mapping Social Identities.* New York: Routledge.

Rudwick, E. (1974) W. E. B. Dubois as socioligist. In: J. Blackwell and M. Janowitz (eds), *Black Sociologists: Historical and Contemporary Perspectives.* Chicago: Chicago University Press.

Ryan, S. (2005) "People don't do odd, do they?" Mothers making sense of the reactions of people towards their learning disabled children in public places. *Children's Geographies* 3.1: 291–306.

Sachs, P. (1993) Old ties: women, work and ageing in a coal-mining community in West Virginia. In: C. Katz and J. Monk (eds), *Full Circles: Geographies of Women over the Life Course.* London: Routledge.

Saldanha, A. (2007) *Psychodelic White: Goa Trance and the Viscosity of Race.* Minneapolis: University of Minnesota Press.

Sanders, R. (2006) Social justice and women of color in geography: philosophical musings, trying again. *Gender, Place and Culture* 13.1: 49–55.

Sangtin Writers (2006) *Playing with Fire.* Minneapolis: University of Minnesota Press.

Sauer, C. (1925) The morphology of landscape. *University of California Publications in Geography* 2: 19–54.

Schaefer, F. (1953) Exceptionalism in geography: a methodological examination. *Annals of the Association of American Geographers* 43.3: 226–49.

Schatzki, T. and Natter, W. (1996) Sociocultural bodies, bodies sociopolitical. In: T. Schatzki and W. Natter (eds), *The Social and Political Body.* New York: Guilford Press.

Schuurman, N. (2004) *GIS: A Short Introduction.* Malden, MA: Blackwell.

Scott, D., Curtis, B. and Twumasi, F. O. (2002) Towards the creation of a health information system for cancer in KwaZulu-Natal, South Africa. *Health and Place* 8: 237–49.

Seager, J. (2003) *The Penguin Atlas of Women in the World,* 3rd edn. New York: Penguin.

Semple, E. (1910) The Anglo-Saxons of the Kentucky mountains: a study in anthropogeography. *Bulletin of the American Geographical Society* 42.8: 561–94.

Semple, E. (1911) *Influences on the Geographic Environment: On the Basis of Ratzel's System of Anthropo-Geography.* London: Constable.

Shannon, G. and Dever, G. (1974) *Health Care Delivery: Spatial Perspectives.* New York: McGraw-Hill.

Shannon, G. and Spurlock, C. (1976) Urban ecological containers, environmental risk cells, and the use of medical services. *Economic Geography* 52.2: 171–80.

Sharp, J., Routledge, P., Philo, C., and Paddison, R. (2000) Entanglements of power: geographies of domination/resistance. In: J. Sharp, P. Routledge, C. Philo, and R. Paddison (eds), *Entanglements of Power: Geographies of Domination/Resistance.* New York: Routledge.

Sheppard, E. and McMaster, R. (2004) *Scale and Geographic Inquiry.* Oxford: Blackwell.

Shields, R. (2003) Political tourism: mapping memory and the future of Québec City. In: S. Hanna and V. Del Casino, Jr (eds), *Mapping Tourism.* Minneapolis: University of Minnesota Press.

Shoeb, M., Weinstein, H., and Halpern, J. (2007) Living in refugee time and space: Iraqi refugees in Dearborn, Michigan. *Journal of Rural Studies* 20.3: 441–60.

Sibley, D. (1995) *Geographies of Exclusion.* London: Routledge.

Sibley, D. (2003) Psychogeographies of rural space and practices of exclusion. In: P. Cloke (ed.), *Country Visions.* Harlow: Pearson.

Simon, S. (2006) Hundreds of teenagers plan to make Valentine's a "day of purity." *Los Angeles Times* February 13: A9.

Sleigh, A. (2006) Water, dams and infection: Asian challenges. In: A. Sleigh, C. Heng Leng, B. Yeoh, P. Kai Hong, and R. Safman (eds), *Population Dynamics and Infectious Diseases in Asia*. London: World Scientific.

Smalley, W. (1994) *Linguistic Diversity and National Unity: Language Ecology in Thailand*. Chicago: University of Chicago Press.

Smith, D. (1974) Who gets what, where, and how: a welfare focus for human geography. *Geography* 59.4: 289–97.

Smith, D. (1994) *Geography and Social Justice*. Malden, MA: Blackwell.

Smith, F. and Barker, J. (2000) "Out of school," in school: a social geography of out of school care. In: S. Holloway and G. Valentine (eds), *Children's Geographies: Playing, Living, Learning*. London: Routledge.

Smith, M. (1986) Physician's specialties and medical trade areas: an application of central place theory. Paper presented to the Applied Geography Conference, Kansas State University.

Smith, N. (1984) *Uneven Development: Nature, Capital, and the Production of Space*. Oxford: Blackwell.

Smith, N. (1992) Contours of a spatialized politics: homeless vehicles and the production of geographical space. *Social Text* 33: 54–81.

Smith, N. (2000a) Scale. In: R. J. Johsnston, D. Gregory, G. Pratt, and M. Watts (eds), *The Dictionary of Human Geography*. Oxford: Blackwell.

Smith, N. (2000b) Socializing culture, radicalizing the social. *Social and Cultural Geography* 1.1: 25–8.

Smith, S. (1981) Humanistic method in contemporary social geography. *Area* 13: 193–8.

Smith, S. (1984) Practicing humanistic geography. *Annals of the Association of American Geographers* 74: 353–74.

Smith, S. (2004) Living room? *Urban Geography* 25.2: 89–91.

Smith, S., Munro, M., and Christie, H. (2006) Performing (housing) markets. *Urban Studies* 43.1: 81–98.

Smyth, F. (2005) Medical geography: therapeutic places, spaces, and networks. *Progress in Human Geography* 29.4: 488–95.

Snitow, A. (1990) A gender diary. In: M. Hirsch and E. Fox Keller (eds), *Conflicts in Feminism*. London: Routledge.

Social and Cultural Geography Study Group Committee (1991) De-limiting human geography: new social and cultural perspectives. In: C. Philo (ed.), *New Words, New Worlds: Reconceptualising Social and Cultural Geography*. Lampeter: Cambrian Printers.

Soja, E. (1980) The socio-spatial dialectic. *Annals of the Association of American Geographers* 70.2: 207–25.

Soja, E. (1989) *Postmodern Geographies: The Reassertion of Space in Critical Social Theory*. London: Verso.

Sothern, M. (2004) (Un)queer patriarchies: or, "what we think when we fuck." *Antipode* 36: 183–90.

Sparke, M. (1995) Between demythologizing and deconstructing the map: Shawnadithit's New-Found-Land and the alienation of Canada. *Cartographica* 32: 1–21.

Sparke, M. (1998) A map that roared and an original atlas: Canada, cartography, and the narration of nation. *Annals of the Association of American Geographers* 88.3: 463–95.

Sparke, M. (2007) Geopolitical fear, geoeconomic hopes, and the responsibilities of Geography. *Annals of the Association of American Geographers* 97.2: 338–49.

Spilsbury, J. (2005) "We don't really get to go out in the front yard" – children's home range and neighborhood violence. *Children's Geographies* 3.1: 79–100.

Staeheli, L. and Brown, M. (2003) Where has the welfare gone? Introductory remarks on the geographies of care and welfare. *Environment and Planning A* 35.5: 771–7.

Stea, D. (1969) Positions, purposes, pragmatics: a journal of radical geography. *Antipode* 1.1: 1–2.

Stenning, A. (2008) For working class geographies. *2008* 40.1: 9–14.

Stoddart, D. (1975) Kropotkin, Reclus, and "relevant" geography. *Area* 7: 188–90.

Sumartojo, R. (2004) Contesting place: antigay and -lesbian hate crime in Columbus, Ohio. In: C. Flint (ed.), *Spaces of Hate: Geographies of Discrimination and Intelorance in the USA*. London: Routledge.

Swearigen, S. and Klausner, J. (2005) Sildenafil use, sexual risk behavior and risk for sexually transmitted disease, including HIV infection. *American Journal of Medicine* 118: 571–7.

Swyngedouw, E. (1997) Neither global nor local: "glocalization" and the politics of scale. In: K. Cox (ed.), *Spaces of Globalization: Reasserting the Power of the Local*. New York: Guilford Press.

Swyngedouw, E. (2004) Scaled geographies: nature, place and the politics of scale. In: E. Sheppard and R. McMaster (eds), *Scale and Geographic Inquiry*. Oxford: Blackwell.

Takahashi, L. (1998a) Concepts of difference in community health. In: R. Kearns and W. Gesler (eds), *Putting Health Into Place: Landscape, Identity, and Well-Being*. Syracuse, NY: Syracuse University Press.

Takahashi, L. (1998b) *Homelessness, AIDS, and Stigmatization: The NIMBY Syndrome in the United States at the End of the Twentieth Century*. Oxford: Oxford University Press.

Takahashi, L., McElroy, J., and Rowe, S. (2002) The sociospatial stigmatization of homeless women with children. *Urban Geography* 23.4: 301–22.

Taylor, P. (1982) A materialist framework for political geography. *Transactions of the Institute of British Geographers* 7: 15–34.

Thien, D. (2005) After or beyond feeling? A consideration of affect and emotion in geography. *Area* 37.4: 450–4.

Thomas, M. (2004) Pleasure and propriety: teen girls and the practice of straight space. *Environment and Planning D, Society and Space* 22.5: 773–89.

Thomas, M. (2008) Resisting mothers, making gender: teenage girls in the United States and the articulation of femininity. *Gender, Place and Culture* 15.1: 61–74.

Thomson, S. (2005) "Territorialising" the primary school playground: deconstructing the geography of playtime. *Children's Geographies* 3.1: 63–78.

Thongchai, W. (1994) *Siam Mapped: A History of the Geo-Body of a Nation*. Honolulu: University of Hawaii Press.

Thongchai, W. (2000) The quest for "siwilai": a geographical discourse of civilizational thinking in late nineteenth and early twentieth-century Siam. *Journal of Asian Studies* 59.3: 528–49.

Thrift, N. (1996) *Spatial Formations*. Thousand Oaks, CA: Sage.

Thurlow, C., Lengel, L., and Tomic, A. (2004) *Computer Mediated Communication: Social Interaction and the Internet*. Thousand Oaks, CA: Sage.

Till, K. (2001) "Returning to the field": time, social relations, and follow-up research. *Geographical Review*.

Timms, D. (1970) Quantitative techniques in urban social geography. In: R. J. Chorley and P. Haggett (eds), *Frontiers in Geographical Teaching*. London: Methuen.

Timms, D. (1971) *The Urban Mosaic: Toward a Theory of Residential Differentiation*. Cambridge: Cambridge University Press.

Tolley, C. and Ranzijn, R. (2006) Heteronormativity amongst staff of residential aged care facilities. *Gay and Lesbian Issues and Psychology Review* 2.2: 78–86.

Trotz, D. (2006) Rethinking Caribbean transnational connections: conceptual itineraries. *Global Networks* 6.1: 41–59.

Tuan, Y. F. (1974) *Topophilia: A Study of Environmental Perception, Attitudes, and Values*. Englewood Cliffs, NJ: Prentice Hall.

Tuan, Y. F. (1975) Place: an experiential perspective. *Geographical Review* 65.2: 151–65.

Tuan, Y. F. (1976) Humanistic geography. *Annals of the Association of American Geographers* 66.2: 266–76.

Tucker, F. (2003) Sameness or difference? Exploring girls' use of recreational spaces. *Children's Geographies* 1.1: 111–24.

Turkle, S. (1995) *Life on the Screen: Identity in the Age of the Internet*. New York: Simon and Schuster.

Twigg, J. (2008) Clothing, aging and me – routes to research. *Journal of Aging Studies* 22: 158–62.

United Nations (1981) *Global Strategy for Health for All by the Year 2000*. Resolution 36/43, 64th Plenary Meeting.

United Nations (2006) *World Population Prospects*. New York: Population Division of the Department of Economic and Social Affairs of the United Nations Secretariat (http://esa.un.org/unpp).

Urry, J. (1990) *The Tourist Gaze: Leisure and Travel in Contemporary Society*. London: Sage.

Urry, J. (2000) *Sociology Beyond Societies: Mobilities for the Twenty-First Century*. London: Routledge.

Valentine, G. (1993) (Hetero)sexing space. *Environment and Planning D: Society and Space* 11: 395–413.

Valentine, G. (1996a) Angels and devils: moral landscapes of childhood. *Environment and Planning D: Society and Space* 14: 581–99.

Valentine, G. (1996b) (Re)negotiating the "heterosexual street": lesbians' productions of space. In: N. Duncan (ed.), *BodySpace*. New York: Routledge.

Valentine, G. (1998) "Sticks and stones may break my bones": a personal geography of harassment. *Antipode* 30.4: 305–32.

Valentine, G. (1999) What it means to be man: the body, masculinities, disability. In: R. Butler and H. Parr (eds), *Mind and Body Spaces: Geographies of Illness, Impairment, and Disability*. London: Routledge.

Valentine, G. (2000) *From Nowhere to Everywhere: Lesbian Geographies*. Binghamton, NY: Harrington Park Press.

Valentine, G. (2001) Whatever happened to the social? Reflections on the "cultural turn" in British human geography. *Norsk Geografisk Tidsskrift* 55.3: 166–72.

Valentine, G. (2003) Boundary crossings: transitions from childhood to adulthood. *Children's Geographies* 1.1: 37–52.

Valentine, G. (2007) Theorizing and researching intersectionality: a challenge for feminist geography. *Professional Geographer* 59.1: 10–21.

van Blerk, L. (2005) Negotiating spatial identities: mobile perspectives on street life in Uganda. *Children's Geographies* 3.1: 5–21.

Vidal del la Blache, P. (1903) *Tableau de la Geographie de la France*. Paris: Librarie Jules Tallandier.

Voigt-Graf, C. (2004) Towards a geography of transnational spaces: Indian transnational communities in Australia. *Global Networks* 4.1: 25–49.

Walker, D., Jones, J. P. III, Roberts, S., and Fröhling, O. (2007) When participation meets empowerment: the WWF and the politics of invitation in the Chimalapas, Mexico. *Annals of the Association of American Geographers* 97.2: 423–44.

Walmsley, D. (2000) Community, place, cyberspace. *Australian Geographer* 31.1: 5–19.

Walton-Roberts, M. (2004) Transnational migration theory in population geography: gendered practices in networks linking Canada and India. *Population, Space and Place* 10: 361–73.

Warf, B. and Grimes, J. (1997) Counterhegemonic discourses and the Internet. *Geographical Review* 87.2: 259–74.

Warnes, A. (1982) *Geographical Perspectives on the Elderly*. Chichester: Wiley.

Warnes, A. and Law, C. (1984) The elderly population of Great Britain: locational trends and policy implications. *Transactions of the Institute of British Geographers* 9.1: 37–59.

Whatmore, S. (1999) Hybrid geographies: rethinking the human in human geography. In: D. Massey, J. Allen, and P. Sarre (eds), *Human Geography Today*. Cambridge: Polity Press.

Whatmore, S. (2002) *Hybrid Geographies: Natures, Cultures, Spaces*. Thousand Oaks, CA: Sage.

Whatmore, S. (2005) Hybrid geographies: author's response and reflections. *Antipode* 37.4: 842–5.

Wiles, J. (2003) Daily geographies of caregivers: mobility, routine, scale. *Social Science and Medicine* 57: 1307–25.

Wiles, J. (2005a) Conceptualizing place in the care of older people: the contributions of geographical gerontology. *Journal of Clinical Nursing* 14.8: 100–8.

Wiles, J. (2005b) Home as a new site of care provision and consumption. In: G. Andrews and D. R. Phillips (eds), *Ageing and Place: Perspectives, Policy and Pratice*. London: Routledge.

Wills, J. (2002) Political economy III: neoliberal chickens, Seattle and geography. *Progress in Human Geography* 26.1: 90–100.

Wilson, B. (2000) *Race and Place in Birmingham: The Civil Rights and Neighborhood Movements*. Lanham, MD: Rowman and Littlefield Publishers.

Wilson, D. (2005) *Inventing Black-on-Black Violence: Discourse, Space, and Representation*. Syracuse, NY: Syracuse University Press.

Wilton, R. and DeVerteuil, G. (2006) Spaces of sobriety/sites of power: examining social model alcohol recovery programs as therapeutic landscapes. *Health and Place* 63: 649–61.

Winchester, H. (1996) Ethical issues in interviewing as a research method in human geography. *Australian Geographer* 27.1: 117–31.

Winders, J. (2006) "New Americans" in a "new south" city? Immigrant and refugee politics in the music city. *Social and Cultural Geography* 7.3: 421–36.

Winders, J. (2007) Bringing back the (b)order: post-9/11politics of immigration, borders, and belonging in the contemporary US South. *Antipode* 39.5: 920–42.

Winders, J. (2008) An "incomplete" picture? Race, Latino migration, and urban politics in Nashville, Tennessee. *Urban Geography* 29.3: 246–63.

Wolch, J. (1998) Zoöpolis. In: J. Wolch and J. Emel (eds), *Animal Geographies: Place, Politics, and Identity in the Nature–Culture Borderland*. London: Verso.

Wolch, J. (1990) *The Shadow State: Government and the Voluntary Sector in Transition*. New York: The Foundation Center.

Wolch, J. (2007) Green urban worlds. *Annals of the Association of American Geographers* 97.2: 373–84.

Wolch, J. and Emel, J. (eds) (1998) *Animal Geographies: Place, Politics, and Identity in the Nature–Culture Borderland*. London: Verso.

Wolch, J., Emel, J., and Wilbert, C. (2003) Reanimating cultural geography. In: K. Anderson, M. Domosh, S. Pile, and N. Thrift (eds), *Handbook of Cultural Geography*. Thousand Oaks, CA: Sage.

Wolch, J. and Philo, C. (2000) From distributions of deviance to definitions of difference: past and future mental health geographies. *Health and Place* 6.3: 137–57.

Wolpert, J., Dear, M., and Crawford, R. (1975) Satellite mental health facilities. *Annals of the Association of American Geographers* 65.1: 24–35.

Wong, T., Yeoh, B., Graham, E., and Teo, P. (2004) Space for silence: single parenthood and the "normal family" in Singapore. *Population, Space and Place* 10: 43–58.

Wood, A. and Roberts, S. (2008) *Economic Geography: Places, Networks, and Flows*. London: Routledge.

Wood, M. (2005) *Rural Geography: Processes, Responses and Experiences*. Thousand Oaks, CA: Sage.

Woods, M. (2003) Deconstructing rural protest: the emergence of a new social movement. *Journal of Rural Studies* 19: 309–25.

Woods, M. (2008) Social movements and rural politics. *Journal of Rural Studies* 24: 129–37.

Zhang, Y. and Goza, F. (2006) Who will care for the elderly in China? A review of the problems caused by China's one-child policy and their potential solutions. *Journal of Aging Studies* 20: 151–64.

Index

Note: "n" after a page reference refers to a note on that page.